PATRICK SARSFIELD AND THE WILLIAMITE WAR

Patrick Sarsfield, earl of Lucan; the Franciscan Portrait.

PATRICK SARSFIELD
AND THE
WILLIAMITE WAR

Piers Wauchope

IRISH ACADEMIC PRESS

This book is set in
10½ on 12 pt Times by
Seton Music Graphics, Gurtycloona,
Bantry, Co. Cork, for
Irish Academic Press,
Kill Lane, Blackrock, Co. Dublin.

A catalogue record for this title
is available from the British Library.

ISBN 0-7165-2476-7
ISBN 0-7165-2496-1 pbk

Printed in Ireland by
Colour Books Ltd, Baldoyle, Dublin

Contents

List of Illustrations

Preface

I am deeply grateful to many people for their generous assistance to me while I was writing this book.

I especially owe thanks to Harry Treherne and Susan Law who read the first proofs and made many corrections and useful suggestions. I have also been most fortunate in being able to call upon both the patience and the typing skills of Fiona MacPherson, Jayne Perry and Jenny Moroney without whose help I would have been faced with a daunting task.

I have also been greatly helped over the years by the staff of the British Library, The Public Records Office, The Bodleian Library, The National Library of Ireland and The National Gallery of Ireland. I am also indebted to the Earl of Rosse who allowed me to inspect the manuscripts held in the muniment room at Birr Castle, and to Lady Rosse for her kind assistance and hospitality on my visit to Birr.

I am grateful to the following for permission to reproduce illustrations: The Franciscan Fathers in Killiney for the frontispiece (photograph by Tony Hurst Associates Ltd); The National Gallery of Ireland, Dublin for plates 1, 2, 16 and 20a, b and c; The National Maritime Museum, London for plates 3 and 9; The National Portrait Gallery, London for plate 4; The National Library of Ireland, Dublin for plates 5 and 11; The British Library, London for plates 14, 17, 18 and 19; the National Army Museum, London for plates 6, 8, 10, 12 and 15; and the Office of Public Works, Kilkenny Castle for plate 7 (photograph by Gerry Deegan).

The index was prepared by David Wilson.

CHAPTER I

Introduction

*Of the early particulars of this great warrior's life
we are wholly unacquainted.*
Richard Ryan, *Biographica Hibernica,* 1821

IT IS NOT KNOWN when Patrick Sarsfield was born, but the best estimate would be about the year 1655. This would date him as having been some five years younger than his great English contemporary, the duke of Marlborough. Marlborough lived to be the greatest soldier of his time. His most celebrated victories took place after his fiftieth birthday and he died peacefully in bed in his seventy-third year. Sarsfield died of his wounds whilst still in his thirties, but in his short life his military achievements and his fame were greater than Marlborough's had been at the same age. Although this comparison is of little value in itself, it does at least beg the question as to what Sarsfield might have achieved had he also lived to see the eighteenth century.

In a continental context Sarsfield's military achievements were not great, but they threatened to change the history of his country at a time when the balance of Europe could well have been altered by events in Ireland. Although he never commanded the Irish army in battle he had a profound effect on his countrymen. By the time of his death Sarsfield was by far the best known and most loved of all Irishmen. With the exception of the early saints, none of his predecessors or his contemporaries have been written about as much as he has been, and no Irish leader until the times of Wolfe Tone a century later.

The English held him in awe. To them he was the most dangerous and gallant of the Irish; he was the one gentleman amongst a race of savages, the one heroic figure amongst a nation of cowards. To the Irish he was the 'Father of the Nation'. Men were even prepared to swear allegiance to him over and above the king or the viceroy. There is great significance not only in his widespread popularity but also in the fact that Sarsfield's followers were to be found in all classes of Irishmen. He was not a man owed any tribal allegiance, and unlike the loyalty that had been commanded by the Irish leaders of his father's generation and before, his was not generally confined to either the English or the Gaelic speaker. He was neither Anglo-Norman nor Gaelic. He was both, and as such he was the seventeenth century representative of the new Ireland.

Sarsfield is not a Gaelic name. The first of the Sarsfields to come to Ireland did so as the standard bearer to Henry II in 1172. Down the next five centuries the Sarsfields established themselves in the Pale and in the English dominated commercial centres of Cork and Limerick. For services to the English crown they were given grants of land, and by the sixteenth century some members of the family thrived as merchants. With wealth came authority, and they served as mayors of the city of Dublin, and as sheriffs of the counties of Dublin and Kildare. Patrick Sarsfield's great-great-grandfather, Sir William, was knighted in 1566 for his part in the suppression of Shane O'Neill's rebellion against Queen Elizabeth. In that year he bought the lands of Lucan in Co. Dublin and of Tully in Co. Kildare. On his death his eldest son inherited Lucan Manor, and his second son inherited Tully Castle.[1]

By the coming of the Stuarts, the Sarsfields as 'gentlemen of the Pale' were part of a powerful interest. The Dublin government needed their support. Like most of the old Anglo-Norman families they were Roman Catholics, but belonged to a class of Roman Catholics willing to show loyalty to a Protestant crown. They were perhaps the only group of Catholics in the British Isles that the crown would suffer gladly, for beyond the Pale lurked something far worse then mere Catholicism. The Gaels were seen to be disloyal, violent and unpredictable and Protestant Dublin was forced into an uneasy alliance with the Catholic Pale.

Although the Sarsfields lived in an English-speaking society with English traditions, they did not live in isolation from their Irish neighbours. Sir William's grandson, Peter Sarsfield of Tully Castle, married Lady Eleanor O'Dempsey, a daughter of Lord Clanmalier, and their son, Patrick Sarsfield (senior), married Anne O'Moore, a daughter of the notorious rebel Colonel Rory (Roger) O'Moore. Patrick senior fathered five children—William, Frances, Anne, Mary and Patrick, the last-named being the subject of this biography.

The Sarsfields were not untypical of the old Anglo-Irish gentry in the seventeenth century. As the new Protestant settlers from England, the 'upstart gentry' of the Cromwellian settlement, noted: 'What by meetings, intermarriages* and gossipings, they grow as arrant Irish.'[2] By the mid seventeenth century the Sarsfields were quite distinct from their English contemporaries, but culturally they were still much closer to the English than to the Gaelic Irish. They were members of a ruling caste with lands and possessions to maintain, and the Irish who wanted to join that society and share in its wealth and influence did so by adopting the manners and the customs of the English world, not by exaggerating their own.

It is perhaps this that led nineteenth-century Irish historians, whose imaginations and passions were fired with romantic notions of their Gaelic origins, to scorn Sarsfield as not being one of them; one even described him as 'a puffed Palesman'.[3] But Sarsfield was no foreigner in his own country. His family embodied both the traditions that have united in the Irish of today. He was neither a pure Gael nor an Englishman untainted by his family's five centuries in Ireland.

---

* 'What death, what punishment is equal to
  this sin, this crime, this worse than bestiality?'
        The Royal Voyage, II. i., 1690

His mother, Anne O'Moore, came from a family who owned lands adjacent to his father's property at Tully outside Kildare. Tradition, and indeed earlier biographers, have it that at his mother's knee Sarsfield learnt of his Gaelic ancestry, of wild tales of distant and unlikely deeds, and of generations of Gaels each one confidently named. Back stretched the O'Moores through the fog of mythology to the dawn of time itself, through legendary warrior chieftains to Ir, after whom the country took its name, and to his father, King Milesius the Spaniard.*4 But to attribute to Sarsfield a passion for his country's Gaelic past would be to misunderstand the nature of the Ireland in which he grew up. Even his grandfather, Rory O'Moore, the descendant of the O'Moores of Leix who had risen in rebellion nineteen times during the reign of Elizabeth, had been brought up in Kildare amongst Anglo-Irish relations, friends and neighbours.5 Rory O'Moore, just as his father and grandfather had done, married into an Anglo-Irish family. There was no obvious cultural difference between the O'Moores and the Sarsfields, as although most of the population of Ireland in the seventeenth century spoke Gaelic, the Pale was predominantly English speaking. The Sarsfields undoubtedly spoke Gaelic (to what degree of proficiency we can only speculate), but it was to them a secondary language.

However, in the prime of his life, when Patrick Sarsfield was to find himself in a position as great as that ever occupied by any of his barbarian forebears, he was to show particular favour to the Gaels around him. This, perhaps, is the best indication that his loyalties were not only those of a Palesman. But whatever feelings Sarsfield developed in his later years, it was certainly not the suffering of the wild Gaels that had the greatest effect on his emotions as a youth. It was a sense of loss and injustice at his family's treatment by the English Republic. Events were to force the Palesmen and the Gaels, substantially for the first time, to stand together against a foe that had deprived the Sarsfields of their lands and cast them out into the wilderness of Connaught.

At the end of 1641 the Gaels, and most particularly the Ulster Gaels, rose up in rebellion. Their aim was to drive out the English once and for all, without alienating the Scottish settlers in the north. The leaders of the rebellion at first may have had set plans, but soon the rising degenerated into a general massacre. The violence was so unexpected that it took the government forces by surprise. They held what they could from the rebels and waited for reinforcements. But reinforcements were not quick in coming. Whilst the fiercest of the massacres were being committed in Ireland, King Charles I was forced to leave London and his queen fled to Holland. Parliament and monarchy, and consequently England herself, were divided by questions of religion and liberty. Within months the king had raised his standard over Nottingham and signalled the start of the English civil war.

*   According to the genealogies set out in O'Hart's *Irish Pedigrees*, Sarsfield could claim to be the great (x 80) grandson of Milesius, the great (x 106) grandson of Noah and the great (x 116) grandson of Adam and Eve.

In Ireland the massacres of 1641 and early 1642 became engrained in the Protestant consciousness.* It became widely (and absurdly) believed that a hundred thousand Protestants—men, women and children—had been butchered in the most terrible circumstances. The reaction, when it came, was fearful. Massacres were followed by counter-massacres of such violence that modern scholarship is of the opinion that 'it is far from clear on which side the balance of cruelty rests.'6 But to those Protestants who grew up with Sarsfield it was not to be questioned that the blame for the greatest horror of their century rested with the Irish nation as a whole. They were determined to crush any future attempt by the Irish with the utmost severity. To the Protestants, civil war included the threat of genocide.

In November 1641 Colonel Rory O'Moore, one of the chief conspirators in the rebellion and yet to be Sarsfield's grandfather, marched on Dublin at the head of an army of Gaels. Their marching song was said to be 'For God, and our Lady and Rory O'Moore'.7 They scattered a small detachment of government troops in a skirmish at Julianstown Bridge, and the capital found itself threatened by a victorious rebel army. The gentlemen of the Pale, the Sarsfields included, found themselves without protection. They had been loyal to the crown and had no intention of rebelling, but the crown could no longer help them.

O'Moore, or Roger Moore as he was known to the English, was no wild chieftain fresh from the mountains; he was then one of the most educated of the Gaelic leaders. 'He had judgement, penetration, and a refinement of manners unknown to his predecessors. He was allied by intermarriages to several of the old English, and lived in intimacy with the most civilised and noblest of their race. Some parts of his youth had been spent on the continent, where his manners were still further polished and his hatred of the English power confirmed by an intercourse with his exiled countrymen.'8 His resentment grew from the knowledge that 'his ancestors, in the reign of Mary had been expelled from

---

* 'Sometimes they enclosed them in some house or castle, which they set on fire, with a brutal indifference to their cries, and a hellish triumph over their expiring agonies. Sometimes the captive English were plunged into the first river, to which they had been driven by their tormentors. One hundred and ninety were, at once, precipitated from the bridge of Portadown. Irish ecclesiastics were seen encouraging the carnage. The women forgot the tenderness of their sex; pursued the English with execrations, and embrued their hands in blood: even children, in their feeble malice, lifted the dagger against the helpless prisoners.

'They, who escaped the utmost fury of the rebels, languished in miseries horrible to be described. Their imaginations were overpowered and disordered by the recollection of tortures and butchery. In their distraction, every tale of horror was eagerly received, and every suggestion of frenzy and melancholy believed implicitly. Miraculous escapes from death, miraculous judgments on murderers, lakes and rivers of blood, marks of slaughter indelible by every human effort, visions of spirits chanting hymns, ghosts rising from rivers and shrieking out REVENGE, these and such like fancies were propagated and received as incontestable.

'An enthusiastic hatred of the Irish was the natural and necessary consequence' Leland (iii, pp. 127-8).

1 Old Lucan Manor, painted by Thomas Roberts *c*.1770.

their princely possessions by violence and fraud; and their sept harassed and almost extirpated by military execution.'[9] But O'Moore was able to address all the Palesmen as neighbours and some as kinsmen. 'A few of us have made an attempt to rescue the nation from the mischiefs of such a nature as are not heard of by any other people', he announced. He did not want them to rebel, but to join him in serving the king against 'the malignant party of the Parliament of England' who were planning to land a Scottish army in Ireland to massacre the Catholics.[10] Professing loyalty to the crown, but with little love for either the Dublin government or the Gaelic rebels, the Palesmen passively gave way to O'Moore. Although they had never raised a sword against the King's men, in the eyes of the Dublin government they too became rebels.

Amongst the leaders of the Palesmen was Patrick Sarsfield senior who was not only a substantial landowner but was also one of the two members of parliament for Kildare. On 22 June 1642 he was indicted for high treason and expelled from the Irish House of Commons as being one of those 'adjudged to be rotten and unprofitable members, fit to be cut off and not worthy any longer to be esteemed as members of this honourable house'. There were to be difficult times ahead. The insurgents were not powerful enough to attack Dublin, but they put a garrison into Tully Castle and used Lucan Manor for their conferences.[11]

For the next ten years civil war raged in Ireland. It was a complex and bloody struggle. The civil war in England spilled across the Irish sea. Both Protestant and Catholic royalists fought against the Protestant republicans, and both royalists and republicans fought the Catholic confederates. Caught in the middle the Palesmen had little stomach to fight anyone. They shifted their position from the confederates to the royalists as the Gaelic tide ebbed. When the republicans held Dublin, the Sarsfields were happy to help the royalists in their attack on the capital, if only to redeem themselves for their earlier alliance with O'Moore. Charles II later noted in a decree that Patrick Sarsfield senior 'was very diligent and active in providing all necessaries for the advancement of our service in the siege of Dublin'.[12]

By then Patrick senior had married Anne, the daughter of Rory O'Moore, but if he was looking for protection he was to be disappointed. O'Moore lived to see little of the war that he had started. Although he had been the victor at Julianstown and although it was his influence and character that had won the Palesmen over, his was a falling star. The fear generated by the Gaelic army soon began to wane. Within a few months O'Moore was defeated in battle by the royalist marquis of Ormonde at Kilrush, Co. Kildare. He, one of the rebellion's founders, fell from favour shortly afterwards when his comrades set up a provisional government in Kilkenny, 'The Supreme Council of the Confederates of Ireland', and the war continued without him.*

Over the next few years the warring parties made and broke alliances and Ireland was devastated. In England the civil war came to an end; the royalists were defeated and the king was captured and later beheaded. In 1649, having pacified his own country, Oliver Cromwell arrived in Dublin to finish the Irish war. His party triumphed and the Sarsfields were among those to suffer as a result. The war had been won by the one side with whom they had never been in alliance. They were both Catholics and royalists, and were now allied by marriage to the family of the man who had been one of those firstly responsible for a decade of carnage.

Patrick Sarsfield senior emerged from the war with more land than he had had at the beginning. Following the death of his father's cousin he had inherited the Lucan estate. He left Tully Castle and moved to the manor outside Dublin, but his religion and his behaviour during the preceding few years ensured that his stay there was to be a short one. With Ireland subdued the English Parliament set about preventing an Irish resurgence. Loyal parliamentarians, those

---

* 'The most moderate of them affected to abhor the cruelty of the original insurrection. They wished to obliterate the memory of all transactions previous to their convention, and to consider the civil war as but now commenced. Hence in the disposal of their offices, several of the first conspirators were purposely neglected. Sir Phelim O'Neill was disappointed and provoked: even Roger Moore, whose temper was more generous, and more abhorrent of barbarity, found his zealous services unnoticed and unrewarded. He had spirit, abilities and activity to render him a formidable malcontent, but for the present he was soothed and flattered: his death which happened soon after this convention, at Kilkenny, was an incident possibly not displeasing to the Confederates' Leland (iii, p. 185).

who had fought for the English Republic, were rewarded with grants of land in Ireland. The Catholic landowners, who had opposed the just wishes of Parliament, were offered the choice of going to 'Hell or Connaught'. They were transplanted to the west. On 20 June 1657, Patrick Sarsfield senior, with his wife and five children, was ordered to leave Lucan and go to a new estate of a hundred and five acres of wilderness in Connaught, a province 'so bare of corn and other food that the present inhabitants perish daily'.[13] The new lands were to compensate him for the loss of Tully and Lucan, which had been held by his family for ninety-one years.

The whereabouts of Patrick Sarsfield's birth is not known. It has already been stated that he was most probably born in 1655, but the date of his birth could have been as late as 1658. It is most probable that he was born either in Lucan Manor, which his father had recently taken possession of, or in Tully Castle where both his father and grandfather had been born before him.* But then the Sarsfields also held property in Dublin, and if he was born after 1657 it is not wholly improbable that he was born in the west, perhaps in Mayo where his brother was later said to have come from.

In 1660 the monarchy was restored and Charles II, titular king since 1649, became at last the *de facto* king of England, Scotland and Ireland. With the Restoration came the hope that the land confiscated by the Cromwellians would be returned. It was not to be so. The Restoration had only taken place on the initiative of those who had been leading Cromwellians. Others had acquiesced on assurances that they would come to no harm, and to take back the land from those who had now settled themselves in Ireland would cause an immediate uprising, especially if that land was to be given back to those Roman Catholics who in the minds of the new Protestant owners were the very people responsible for ten years of bloody civil war. Many of the Irish were clearly guilty of treason against the King. The 1641 rebellion had been against the crown, not against the Republic. Only after the execution of Charles I had Cromwell and his generals come to Ireland to finish the war. Now that both the war and the Cromwellians had run their course, the fighting that was to come was to be in Parliament and the courts. Only those Irishmen who had shown unswerving loyalty to the crown since 1641 could expect any relief from the new government.

As soon as it was clear that the Republic had fallen, the Sarsfields took steps to get their lands restored to them.[14] Lucan Manor had been granted to Sir Theophilus Jones and Tully had been granted to a Dublin alderman, David Hutchinson. Patrick Sarsfield senior petitioned the king in November 1660 for the return of all his land. His petition stated that he had been granted 'a small piece of land in Connaught which in value is not worth one-twentieth of his said estate', and he begged that his claim would not be prejudiced by his

---

* Lucan Manor was demolished in the eighteenth century and the existing Lucan House was built in its place. Only the remains of a few outhouses and the chapel are still to be seen. Tully Castle has also long since been demolished to make way for new buildings.

acceptance of that grant. A second petition was backed by a report signed by Lord Ormonde and Lord Chancellor Eustace advising that the Sarsfields be restored to their land. Certificates were signed by the Lords Dillon, Ormonde, Donegal, Loftus and others attesting to old Patrick Sarsfield's loyalty. In the summer of 1661 the king issued an order granting him possession of all his land except that which was still in the hands of the Cromwellian 'Adventurers'. This enabled him to gain possession of Tully Castle from Alderman Hutchinson, and it is there that young Patrick Sarsfield grew up.*

But at Lucan Manor, Sir Theophilus Jones was to prove himself to be a difficult man to oust. He was the youngest of the two sons of the bishop of Killaloe who had enjoyed high military rank and success in the commonwealth forces during the Irish war. His brother, Michael Jones, had been Cromwell's second in command in Ireland. Sir Theophilus had been the governor of Dublin for the first ten years of the interregnum, but after his dismissal in 1659 he had been one of those who had plotted the King's return. To encourage such men Charles had issued a declaration from the Dutch town of Breda in April 1660 to the effect that those who acted for the king would be permitted to keep the estates that they then held. In Ireland, Jones had paved the way for the Restoration by seizing three leading republicans. The King's duty to Jones under the Breda declaration clearly conflicted with the duty he owed to the Sarsfields if, that is, they could show themselves to have been loyal subjects.

Patrick Sarsfield senior kept up what pressure he could on Sir Theophilus. His influence was such that his case was made known to government officials both in Dublin and London, and it is not unlikely that sums of money changed hands to ensure that the government would not forget the Sarsfields' case. The king even mentioned their plaint in a personal letter to the Lord Lieutenant, the duke of Ormonde. The best way around the problem seemed to be to have Lucan valued so that Sir Theophilus Jones could be moved to another estate that would provide him with the same income. But the rule of law was such that all claims had to pass under the scrutiny of the Court of Claims for the Trial of Innocents. Those claimants found to have been loyal to the crown since the rebellion of 1641 could expect their estates back. Those found 'nocent' of rebellion could expect nothing.

On 17 June 1663 Patrick Sarsfield senior's claim was brought before the Court. The Commissioners of Claims had adjudged him innocent of rebellion 'because of the king's letter'. The court was unimpressed. It refused to take cognisance of any such recommendation and set a new date when fresh evidence could be heard.

*   It was stated in the *Irish Magazine* of May 1814 that as an adolescent Sarsfield 'often offered his devotions in this (i.e. Lucan) chapel, and was remarkable for being the tallest person in the congregation', but as will be shown this is most unlikely. Nothing is known of Sarsfield's childhood or adolescence although it has been confidently asserted by Dr Todhunter that 'he was educated in a French military college.' This error flows from the correct assertion that Sarsfield received a military education in France. That is to say that he served in the French army as a young man; not that he attended a French boarding school.

In the meanwhile, Sir Theophilus Jones, who had no intention of leaving Lucan Manor, strengthened his case. Having recently been appointed scoutmaster general of Ireland he remained one of the most respected and influential men in the country. He had good reason to be confident that the Sarsfields' claim would fail. Although he knew that they would be able to show that they had assisted the royal army as it conducted its ill-fated march on Dublin during the civil war, he also knew several facts that the Sarsfields would have liked to have kept quiet. Old Peter Sarsfield had aided the rebels in 1641. He and his son had allied themselves to the traitor O'Moore and had given succour to a bloody rebellion against the Crown twenty two years before. Let Mr Sarsfield explain why he had been expelled from the Irish House of Commons in 1642, and how he had come to be indicted for high treason.

On 1 August 1663 the Court of Claims found Patrick Sarsfield senior 'nocent' of rebellion. Any claim that he might have to Lucan was forfeit. Only one thing saved the family: his father's cousin, William Sarsfield, from who he had hoped to inherit the Lucan estate, was declared innocent as indeed was Mrs Anne (O'Moore) Sarsfield and her son, William Sarsfield. This ruling had the effect of debarring Patrick senior from holding the lands. But his son was still entitled to inherit Lucan after his death. It gave Sir Theophilus Jones an interest in Lucan only during Patrick Sarsfield senior's lifetime. After that, Sarsfield's heirs had an absolute claim to the lands.

Sir Theophilus rejoiced and stayed at Lucan. The years passed and little changed. Young Patrick was brought up on the Tully estate in Kildare as his father and grandfather had been before him. But the Sarsfields did not give up the fight for Lucan, and they were to find a powerful ally.

In 1671, when Patrick was perhaps sixteen years old, his brother William married a girl named Mary Walter, who was the charge of the earl of Carling-ford. She was the second child of Lucy Walter who had once been the king's mistress. Mary Walter's brother was James, duke of Monmouth, the king's bastard. There can be little doubt that Patrick Sarsfield's sister-in-law was the King's daughter. William Sarsfield and his new wife moved to London where they had two children, who they named Charlotte and Charles to identify them as being the king's grandchildren. Although Mary Sarsfield was never openly recognised by King Charles as his daughter, he did grant her husband an annual pension of £200.[15]

From the time of this marriage, William Sarsfield was able to enlist some influential support in his claim for the Lucan estate. The duke of Monmouth made efforts to help his young sister and her new husband, and the king wrote to the lord lieutenant of Ireland on the subject. Pressure was put on Sir Theophilus to sell his life interest in the estate and in 1674 William Sarsfield entered into an agreement with him whereby the old colonel would receive some other lands in exchange for which he was to allow the Sarsfields immediate possession of Lucan. These alternative lands were to be granted to 'our right trusty and well beloved counsellor Sir Theophilus Jones'[16] by the king, and on taking possession of the estate William Sarsfield was to settle a jointure of £800 on his wife should he predecease her. This he failed to do.

William Sarsfield died of smallpox on 13 April 1675. His will, suspiciously dated 12 April, left his wife £200 a year but nothing else. His widow suspected that there had been some underhand dealing. She had been all but squeezed out of the will by the Sarsfield family.

> Owing to the nature of the illness (smallpox), both the physician and priest persuaded Mrs Sarsfield to keep away from the sick bed, but when at length she saw her husband, he was both 'blind and lightheaded', and by her account the will, which sent the property in the wrong channel, was signed only the day before.[17]

William Sarsfield's will provided that the rents from Lucan should be used to provide annuities of £100 to his mother, £350 to each of his unmarried sisters and £105 to his only brother, Patrick. His other lands were to be divided so that Patrick would receive a further £750, and his sisters a further £4,000. Provision was also made for his daughter Charlotte on her reaching the age of twenty-one, and as his wife was four months pregnant at his death provision was also made for his child as yet unborn. His father, Patrick Sarsfield senior, was made guardian of William's heir, Charles Sarsfield, who was then only six months old.[18] The widow Sarsfield challenged the will immediately. Even if it was not a forgery, it was invalid as the king had arranged the possession of the estate not for the benefit of the Sarsfield family but for her benefit as she was his daughter. William Sarsfield had contracted with the King's agent to make certain provisions for her in return for which the king had granted him a pension. In any event, she claimed that her husband had been in no fit state to make a will on the day before his death. She appealed to the courts for their intervention and in the meanwhile Sir Theophilus Jones quite predictably refused to leave Lucan until the matter had been settled.

Worse still, it was found that William Sarsfield had run up large debts and much of his estate was claimed by his creditors. A further complication was that his two sisters, Frances and Anne, claimed part of the estate on the ground that they had lent William money during his lifetime. Mary Sarsfield was desperate and King Charles provided her with a further annuity of £600 to bring her jointure up to the £800 that William was supposed to have settled on her. In September 1675 she gave birth to a second son, and named him after her late husband. The king arranged for more pressure to be put on Jones to give her the estate, but Jones would not move. The legal dispute that followed was to outlast Patrick Sarsfield's life.*

In 1676 Mary Sarsfield married William Fanshawe who, as Patrick Sarsfield senior was disqualified by his religion, became Charles Sarsfield's guardian. The Fanshawes were very poor. Charles II's 'secret service' payments that were to provide Mary with her annuity were slow and irregular and soon fell into

---

* The case was finally resolved in the reign of King William when Charlotte Sarsfield was adjudged to be the lawful beneficiary.

arrears. Necessity forced them to apply increasing pressure to gain the Lucan estate. At the end of 1676 little William Sarsfield died and his uncle Patrick was again second in line to inherit the land.

In the meantime, probably in early 1675, Patrick Sarsfield left Ireland. He had no reason to expect that he would ever be the master of Lucan or that he would live the life of a landed gentleman. Now twenty years old, he had grown into a strikingly powerful and tall young man, a man of 'prodigious stature',[19] and had decided to become a soldier. Perhaps using his late brother's wife as an introduction, he joined the Duke of Monmouth's regiment of foot, the 'Royal Anglais', which served as a battalion in the French army.

It would have been almost impossible for Sarsfield to pursue a military career in the British Isles. In England, Roman Catholics were generally debarred from public office and especially from the officer corps after the first Test Act was passed in 1673. All office holders were to produce a certificate that they had received communion in accordance with the rites of the Church of England, they were to take the three hundred and fifty word oaths of supremacy and allegiance, and they were to make the following declaration:

> I, A.B., do declare That I do believe there is not any Transubstantiation in the Sacrament of the Lord's Supper, or in the Elements of Bread and Wine, at or after the Consecration thereof by any Person whatsoever.

Very few Catholics could agree to make such a declaration. Those who did remain in office usually did so only by virtue of the Test Act not being enforced. (The fact that this Act was not wholly effective is evidenced by the passing of the second Test Act in 1678 which amongst other things extended the declaration to deny the mass and the adoration of the Virgin and the saints as being 'superstitious and idolatrous'.)

The Test Act did not apply to Ireland, but there similar steps were taken. As the officer corps of the Irish army was so much smaller and had at the beginning of the reign been dominated by the Cromwellians, it was completely free from Catholics. Those Catholic officers who sought to become professional soldiers did so by serving foreign masters.

It has been asserted elsewhere (although on what authority is unknown) that Sarsfield served Charles II as a 'gentleman of the guard'.[20] It is quite possible that he did so as the life guards served as a school 'for young gentlemen of very considerable families, who are there made fit for military commands'.[21] Certainly for most of the 1670s the Test Act applied only to officers, so Catholic troopers were not affected. There was at the same time a regiment of Irish life guards organised along the same lines but based in Dublin. Although the overwhelming majority of the soldiers on the Irish establishment had to provide certificates that they had taken Protestant communion, the life guards were subject to different rules as they were appointed by and took orders only from the lord lieutenant. Sarsfield's association with the life guards at this stage of his life is mere speculation, but what is certain is that he did join a regiment that formed part of the French army.

Sarsfield's name does not appear in any of the commission registers until 1678, and then it is as a lieutenant, and as is clear from subsequent events, a senior lieutenant at that. Where or when he was first commissioned as an ensign in not known, but it must have been either in Monmouth's regiment of foot or else in Sir George Hamilton's Irish regiment,[22] and the best guess would be that this took place in 1675.

In 1670 Charles II had entered into a secret treaty with Louis XIV. It was secret because if the terms of the agreement had become known in England they could well have precipitated a rebellion as great as that which had destroyed his father. The treaty of Dover provided for payments to be made to Charles in return for which England would aid the French in their planned invasion of the Netherlands. More shocking still, 'the King of Great Britain, being convinced of the truth of the Catholic Faith, is determined to declare himself a Catholic . . . as soon as the welfare of his realm shall permit.' Part of the support that Charles was to give the French was to be in the form of six thousand troops who would serve under a French commander in chief.

In pursuance of the treaty, both Monmouth's and Hamilton's regiments were raised to serve on the continent. As they formed part of the French rather than the English establishment, and as the commissions were granted by the colonel (or in reality, the lieutenant-colonel) rather than by the king, there was no necessity for the provisions of the Test Act to be applied. Consequently both these regiments had a disproportionate number of Roman Catholic officers, many of whom were Irishmen.

There was no better or more dangerous way in which to gain military experience than to join one of King Charles's regiments in the French service. England was not at war and so opportunities for active service in the regular army were limited. Furthermore, the French had no intention of keeping these loaned regiments in reserve. The 'English' regiments suffered very high losses in battle. In the summer of 1674 they fought at the battle of Sinzheim under the great Marshal Turenne. The defeat of the imperialist forces had enabled the French to ravage the palatinate and desolate five towns and twenty five villages. The worse excesses of this campaign were attributed to the Anglo-Irish troops. When the Imperialists chased the French back across the Rhine, Monmouth's and Hamilton's regiments were again at the centre of the fighting, this time at Entzheim where the two battalions 'lost a great many officers killed and wounded'.[23] They accompanied Turenne on his winter campaign and fought in the victories at Mulhouse and Turckheim. In the summer of 1675 they were with Turenne's army when he was shot in Alsace and they played a most important part in the French victory at Altenheim when they were said to have worked wonders in halting a German advance. In 1676 the two regiments were in Marshal Luxembourg's rearguard when Sir George Hamilton was killed in the duke of Lorraine's attack. They wintered in Vitry and Saint-Dizier and spent the next year incorporated in Crequy's eastern army in which they fought in the successful siege of Freiburg in November 1677.

The names of these battles and campaigns may mean little to the reader, but they were greater battles than were ever to be fought in the British Isles. The French army successfully beat the Dutch and the imperialists at every turn, and the borders of Louis XIV's empire were shifted to the east. There was no one who could stand against the might of France. The Franche-Comté along the Swiss border; twelve new towns along what is now the Belgian border including St-Omer, Cambrai, Valenciennes and Maubeuge, and the towns of Breisach and Freiburg east of the Rhine: were all ceded to the French by the treaty of the Nymwegen. 'In 1661, France did not have any allies; in 1678, she did not have any enemies left.'[24] It was the most glorious period of Louis's reign. No longer Louis XIV, he was henceforth Louis le Grand.

Life in the regiments sent to France was hard and brutal. The men were ill-equipped and irregularly paid. When Monmouth's regiment had first arrived in France, half the men died from starvation and exposure without ever seeing an enemy. There was great difficulty in getting recruits and those that the regiment did manage to attract were often of the worst type. The regiment provided an asylum for the most terrible of rogues who, rather than face justice at home, were more than willing to practise on foreigners that which they had lately practised on their own countrymen. Others were taken straight from prison to the troop ships, and many of the men, especially those from Scotland and Ireland, were simply press-ganged and taken to France in chains.[25]

Once they were in France the officers and men came under the direct control of the commanding officer. Monmouth had returned to England in 1673 and left his regiment in the hands of Lieutenant-Colonel Robert Scott. While the regiment remained on the continent, Scott's word was law. He had the power of life and death over his officers and men. He held courts martial, appointed and commissioned his own officers, and even produced his own articles of war.

Such was the nature of Patrick Sarsfield's military apprenticeship. When he did eventually return it was as a man who had experienced all the terrors of war. Had he been allowed to join the regular Irish army, he would have learnt of nothing but garrison life.

By early 1678 England's relationship with France was much altered. It was greatly feared that England would enter the war alongside King Louis's enemies. The British regiments were recalled. Louis at first refused to allow them to return but, eventually, rather than release them in northern France, he ordered them to march down to the Savoy border to be disbanded. The French treatment of these men was shameful. It was noted that they were given '4 livres 10 sols a man to bring them home, and they pass here (Paris) in great want'.[26] Some of them spent months making their way home, arriving in late 1678 dressed in rags and living on alms.

CHAPTER II

A Misspent Youth

Oh! To have lived brave Sarsfield's life—to live for a solemn end,
To strive for the ruling strength and skill God's saints to the chosen send.
                                        D.P. Conyngham, *Sarsfield*, 1871

LIEUTENANT PATRICK SARSFIELD left France and travelled to London in the early summer of 1678. Fortunately for him he continued to receive his pay as King Charles had no intention of wasting his talents. The king's plan was to collect together those officers who had served in Monmouth's regiment, especially those whose religion made them unsuitable for service in an English battalion, and to form them into a new regiment to be commanded by Sir Thomas Dongan. As soon as normal relations with France were restored, this new regiment was to be sent into King Louis's service in exchange for French gold. As Secretary Williamson had noted in the previous year: 'We must have a great care of employing papists except in service abroad, not in service at home.'

Plans for Dongan's regiment of foot had been under way long before Sarsfield had left France. The new commissions had even been signed by the king and countersigned by Secretary Williamson as long ago as February. In the intervening months the preparations for raising the new regiment were discussed, but little was done. At some stage the officers were to be given their commissions and sent to Dublin to raise men.

For over four months Sarsfield lodged at the king's saddler's house at Charing Cross where he received his pay. His position was typical of the officers in his regiment. They had nothing useful to occupy themselves with and no appointments to keep except the periodic visits by Captain Dominic Trant, the regimental paymaster.[1]

All this changed in October 1678. Captain Trant and Lieutenant Colonel Lawrence Dempsey, both veterans of Monmouth's Regiment, set about contacting those officers whose names were on the new commissions. They summoned Lieutenant Sarsfield to the Crown and Sceptre Tavern in Piccadilly. When he walked out clutching a piece of paper it was as Captain Sarsfield. But his pleasure was not to last. The commission that he held in his hand was to be worthless within a month.

Sarsfield little knew when he received his promotion that one of the most bizarre episodes in England's history was unfolding. Titus Oates ('a most consummate cheat, blasphemer, vicious, perjured, impudent and saucy, foul mouthed wretch')[2] and Israel Tonge ('a mental casualty of the civil wars')[3] claimed to have uncovered the 'Popish Plot', a Jesuit conspiracy to murder the king and all leading Protestants and replace them with the duke of York and a new Catholic order. According to Oates, the Jesuits were to achieve this by means of an uprising and massacre in London which was to be followed by a series of invasions from France, Scotland and Ireland.

There was nothing very new in these allegations and people were unwilling to believe Oates. There was something very doubtful about his evidence, and his astonishing revelations would have been ignored altogether had it not been for two unrelated events. Edward Coleman, the queen's secretary, was found to have once been engaged in a treasonable French correspondence, and a London magistrate was murdered.

The magistrate was Sir Edmund Berry Godfrey, a coal merchant, who had taken the affidavits of Oates and Tonge. On 12 October 1678 Godfrey went missing. The alarm was raised and the suspicion was formed that he had been kidnapped or murdered by the Papists to ensure his silence. Within a week his body, beaten and strangled, was found in a ditch on Primrose Hill. His own sword had been rammed through his chest. Four days later Parliament was in session. The members were outraged. On 30 October the king issued a proclamation banishing all Catholics from within a radius of twenty miles of London.

As soon as it became known that Godfrey had disappeared it was clear that there was going to be trouble. That is why Williamson had instructed Dempsey to issue all the commissions and at the same time to tell the officers to go with all possible speed to Dublin. Sarsfield rode northwards to Chester with a group of Irish officers in a similar plight. But news of the Popish Plot raced ahead of them. They were arrested in Chester and locked up.

Sarsfield was brought before two justices of the peace—the mayor of Chester, William Harvey, and Alderman William Streete. He made a statement to them outlining his movements over the last few months and was then returned to the cells. The justices acted with caution. After all, as the justices' clerk had noted of Sarsfield, 'This said Captain doth declare himself to be a Roman Catholic'.[4] Godfrey's murderers were still at large and as it was not possible to verify Sarsfield's version of events his signed deposition was sent back to London while the magistrates awaited further instructions.

On 8 November, while Sarsfield was in Chester gaol, the new colonel of his regiment, Justin MacCarthy, was arrested while strolling about outside the House of Commons.* He was questioned and told to get out of London. MacCarthy did so but was then promptly re-arrested in Barnet and locked up. He was eventually only released by an order from the Privy Council. There were angry scenes in the House of Commons when it was learnt that an Irish Catholic was holding

---

* What he was doing there is not known, perhaps not even by MacCarthy himself as he was notoriously short-sighted. As John Michelburne was to unkindly remark: 'My colonel, old Justin Maccartie, looks damn'd squinting upon me with his blind eyes'.[5]

a colonel's commission. On the next day the news that a whole group of Irish officers were being held under lock and key in Chester was greeted by uproar. These men held the king's commission and had been excused both the test and the oath of allegiance. And all this while the country was in imminent danger of being overwhelmed by Papist violence. Although Parliament could not lock the king up, Secretary Williamson was sent straight to the Tower 'for countersigning such commissions and warrants contrary to the late Act'.[6]

It was not the best of times to be an Irishman in England. As news of the Popish Plot spread, a search was made for two Irishmen who were supposed to have assisted in Godfrey's murder. Many Catholics were arrested, and in time some were convicted on false evidence and were executed. It was a great relief to Sarsfield and his fellow officers when the mayor received a letter from Secretary Williamson written a few days before his own imprisonment:

> His Majesty greatly approves of his [the mayor's] care in staying certain persons passing towards Ireland who had no passes, but the writer is commanded to let the mayor know that these particular persons... are such as have his Majesty's leave to return to their own country, being Irishmen and dismissed from his Majesty's service. His Majesty has lately caused to be dismissed out of his service a considerable number more of that contingent, with leave to return to Ireland, a list of whose names he encloses.[7]

So it was that Sarsfield heard of his dismissal from the army from the mayor of Chester. He was given no explanation. As they sailed for Dublin, he and the other officers could only guess at the cause of their change in fortune.

Sarsfield's return to Dublin was not a happy one. He was in debt in England, and without income he was soon in debt in Ireland. The country was still in the grip of the Popish Plot and there was unlikely to be a change of policy in Whitehall in the near future. Sarsfield petitioned the lord lieutenant of Ireland, the Duke of Ormonde, who in turn wrote to the king's paymaster, Sir Stephen Fox, to find out if MacCarthy's officers could expect anything for their service. The duke noted that 'several of them are in prison for their lodging and diet' and that 'their religion brings them into suspicion.' He mentioned Sarsfield as being one of those 'of my acquaintance and for whom I am particularly concerned', and demanded an early reply as he could not bear this 'sight of men that deserve some consideration and relief which is not in my power to give them'.[8]

Despite the pleas of the lord lieutenant, the Treasury was slow to act. Back pay for Irish officers was hardly a priority and it was not until October 1680 that the Treasury lords agreed to make an interim payment to MacCarthy's officers. Even then the payment was made on the condition that the recipients left London and Westminster and did not 'presume to return again upon any pretence whatsoever without due licence according to law'. Sarsfield was allotted ten pounds. Three years later he would still be petitioning for the £108 due to him for the money that he had spent on his company in MacCarthy's regiment.[9]

Of greater concern to Sarsfield at that time was the dispute over Lucan Manor. A month after he had written to Fox, the duke of Ormonde received instructions from Whitehall to settle the Fanshawe-Jones affair. Sir Theophilus Jones still lived in Lucan Manor and was entitled to all the rents from the estate while Patrick Sarsfield senior was still alive. After pressure had been applied at the king's request by the lord lieutenant some of the Lucan land had been transferred to the two Sarsfield sisters. This had helped neither the Fanshawes nor little Charles Sarsfield, and certainly would not have pleased King Charles who in 1680 was petitioned by the five year old child. The lord lieutenant had a report prepared on the increasingly complex dispute and had a copy delivered to Patrick Sarsfield.[10]

Sarsfield delayed for months before doing anything about it, but in March 1681 he entered the dispute for the first time. He petitioned for a grant of the rest of the Lucan estate as he was now 'heir in remainder' after Charles. He waited, but to no avail. It was clearly a dispute that was going to last for a long time. Eventually, with the lawyer still deliberating, he returned to London, still unemployed and still with no idea of what the future would bring.

The year 1681 was a one of great uncertainty for Sarsfield. Although the violence of the Popish Plot was all but spent, the political situation in London was still dangerous. On the last day of 1680 the sixty-nine year old Viscount Stafford was beheaded for high treason. He was the last of Oates's victims. The new Parliament called for March 1681 had revived the Exclusion Bill to prevent a Catholic acceding to the English throne. On 1 July, Oliver Plunket, the archbishop of Armagh, was executed for supposedly having planned a French invasion of Ireland.

In London Sarsfield was as idle as he had been since he left France three years before. Although he now received sufficient income from the Tully estate to support himself, he was unemployed and frustrated by the legislation that denied him employment. It was going to be several years before he would be able to put his skills to any worthwhile purpose, and on Monday, 5 September 1681 he was involved in the first of a series of incidents that was to give him something of a reputation in certain London circles.

In those days Bartholomew Fair was still held in West Smithfield near to St Bartholomew's Hospital. On that Monday Lord Grey of Warke was walking through the fair with some friends. Grey was a very able young man, still not yet twenty-six years old but already an accomplished politician. Although he had entered the world of politics only three years before, he had gained the confidence of the earl of Shaftesbury who had done so much to whip up anti-Catholic feeling during the Popish Plot. Grey was deeply involved in furthering the interests of the 'Protestant duke', and was known as 'Monmouth's elector-general'. He was quick-witted, clever, humourous and dedicated to a cause that was everything that endangered Sarsfield. But that cause was declining and Shaftesbury was now in the Tower awaiting his trial for treason. The substance of the prosecution case against him was the very dubious evidence of a one time Catholic priest and a series of rough Irishmen.

Amongst the stalls and the fairground crowds, there was a sideshow that had as its principal attraction a giant. This giant was an Irishman. Grey took one look at the size of the man and turning to his companions quipped that 'He would make a swingeing evidence'.* This was a reference to those unscrupulous Irishmen who had that year given false prosecution evidence not only against Whigs, but even against their fellow countryman, Oliver Plunket, who had been executed only two months before. Without giving a further thought to what had been said, Grey and his party strolled off to Grey's house a short walk away in Charterhouse Yard.[11]

But that was not the end of the matter. The remark was repeated to another tall Irishman, and he was less than amused. Sarsfield sent Lord Grey a note challenging him to a duel. The remark was an affront to his countrymen, he wrote, and reflected on the Irish nation in general. This was not a wise move on Sarsfield's part. Although they were the same age, Grey was an influential young man. He not only had friends in very high places, but he also had some very violent friends. It is a mystery as to what Sarsfield hoped to achieve by sending the challenge. Grey would hardly have agreed to meet him, and certainly could not have been expected to apologise. Indeed the episode is so strange that one confidently suspects that Sarsfield was encouraged to send the note by his drinking companions, and that he felt far less inclined to meet Grey when he woke up the next morning, alone and sober.

Grey was amazed. He had not even heard of Sarsfield, let alone met him. He sent a message back that 'If he should answer every such pretence he might be obliged to fight all his countrymen.' His reply ended with the warning that he intended to go about his lawful business and that should Sarsfield be thinking of attacking him, he should remember that he wore a sword and would defend himself.

As Sarsfield was to find out, Grey was not a man to tangle with. He did not stop at sending a reply; he had to be more careful than that. Sarsfield was both an Irishman and a Papist, and for all he knew was mad as well. Grey sent a report of the incident straight to the secretary of the Privy Council, the Welshman Sir Leoline (Llewellyn) Jenkins. Duelling had been proscribed two years before, and the government showed no hesitation in locking up those who broke this law. Jenkins had a good idea as to how the Privy Councillors would react. They were not going to give any encouragement to Irishmen who threatened peers of the realm, even if the peer concerned was Grey. He did something usually reserved for those suspected of high treason. He issued a warrant to the sergeant at arms for Sarsfield's arrest. The sergeant at arms, Joseph Harvey, wasted little time in seeking out Sarsfield and took him into custody to await the next meeting of the council.

*   An evidence is an archaic term for a witness.

2 Patrick Sarsfield by John Riley. It may be supposed that
the building in the background is Tully Castle.

Sarsfield escaped. How long Harvey managed to hold him is not clear, but it was not more than five days before he had disappeared. The Privy Council, presided over by the now ageing Prince Rupert, next met in the court at White-hall on 14 September, nine days after Grey's remark in Bartholomew Fair. After they discussed the weighty matter of allowing foreign Protestants to become free English citizens, they turned to the Sarsfield case. They ordered that the unfortunate Joseph Harvey be suspended from duty and they issued a further warrant to Henry Derham, another sergeant at arms, to arrest Sarsfield and to bring him 'before this board to be examined concerning a challenge he is accused to have sent to the Lord Grey of Warke'.[12]

The warrant was signed by the archbishop of Canterbury, the lord chancellor, the earl of Oxford, Viscount Fauconberg, the bishop of London and Secretary Jenkins.[13] But whereas Harvey had been able to get his man, if not hold him, Derham could not even find him, although it was not without trying. A fort-night later there was still 'a great enquiry' made after Sarsfield, but to no effect.[14] It is not recorded whether Grey suffered any sleepless nights.

1681 was certainly not a year in which to get too upset about what was said about the Irish. When the annual 'pope burning' took place in Smithfield on 17 November the Whigs decided to use it as a show of their strength in a procession that wound its way from Whitechapel across the city to the Temple, up Chancery Lane to Gray's Inn and on to Smithfield. Whereas in the previous year the effigies had only been those of the pope along with cardinals and Catholic bishops, and the theme had been 'Remember Justice Godfrey', in 1681 the usual figure of Godfrey was followed not only by the pope but a mock pillory in which were pinioned the effigies of three Irishmen, one labelled 'Suborner' and the other two 'Suborned'. A great crowd roared with approval as the effigies were pitched in the flames and toasts were drunk to the king and the duke of Monmouth.

Although he had avoided a duel with Sarsfield, it was not long before Grey's observations earned him another challenge. And this time Grey was obliged to reply in less dismissive terms. He had entered a gunsmith's shop and while inspecting the firearms on display his eye fell upon a particularly ornate weapon. 'What coxcomb's fancy is this?' he sneered. 'This is some fool's gun on which there is more cost than worth.' The gunsmith, clearly less than pleased at this assessment of his work, told him that the gun had been ordered by the duke of Albemarle. Grey said no more on the subject. Albemarle was one of the king's favourites and was known to be greatly disliked by Monmouth.

Gossip travels quickly, and it was not long before Grey's remark was repeated to Albemarle. The duke was furious. Despite his recent appointment as recorder of the borough of Colchester, being 'someone learned in the law', he resolved upon an illegal act. He challenged Grey to a duel. Grey accepted.

Duelling was then conducted in the old style, whereby each principal was backed by a second. In those days the seconds did not merely stand back and ensure fair play. They also joined in. There would be two fights at once in which the principals fought each other and the seconds did likewise. Albemarle chose his cousin Sir Walter Clarges, Bt, the Colchester member of Parliament to act as his second. Grey intended to take no such chance on amateur assistance and managed to secure the services of Captain Charles Godfrey. Godfrey was an extraordinary man. He had left Monmouth's regiment before Sarsfield had joined, and had transferred to the foot guards, but being like Grey a committed Whig he had recently been cashiered. He was a very able swordsman and had already proved himself willing to stand by a fellow Whig in a duel.

They met at Tottenham Court. The duel did not last long, for although Godfrey was initially cut he wasted little time in disarming Clarges. He then ran at Albemarle like a wounded bull 'swearing to the duke unless he delivered his sword he'd run him through the guts'. Albemarle surrendered his weapon, and Grey and Godfrey walked away smirking.

Although it was the end of the duel, it was not the end of the affair. Albemarle and Grey were hauled before the king who remarked balefully that 'he was sorry to see those that should be patterns for keeping laws, break'em under his nose'. But he accepted that Grey had not deliberately insulted Albemarle and pardoned them. Considering that Grey was able to call upon such a proficient swordsman as a second, Sarsfield was perhaps fortunate in that his challenge was not accepted. As will be seen, swordsmanship was not to be his most obvious talent.

Life still held little for Sarsfield. As he could not be a soldier in England, he attempted to join the only part of the English army that was willing to enlist Irish Catholics. He made arrangements to join the garrison of Tangier which had then been occupied by the English for twenty years. Of all England's overseas possessions, this was arguably the most unpleasant and beleaguered outpost. To volunteer for garrison duty there was an exhibition of desperation. Sarsfield's desperation stemmed from his financial situation. Whatever small allowance he had from home was soon eaten up by his high living, and while Jones still occupied Lucan, he had very little income from the family estates. His debts were such that he found living in London difficult. He resorted to petitioning the king for the money still owed to him for the company of foot he had commanded in MacCarthy's regiment. Although the outstanding debt was now only £58, it was money that he needed badly as 'being bound for the Straits (he) desires the balance to furnish him with necessaries for the voyage'.[15]

If Sarsfield had fled from London after the Grey affair, he was not away for long. He returned to wait for his petition to be presented to the King, and having failed to fight Grey in September, he managed to get involved in a duel that was fought on 6 December 1681.[16] The two principals were both teenagers, Lords Newburgh and Kingsale. Newburgh, who came from 'a most bigoted popish family',[17] was only fifteen or sixteen years old at the time. He chose as his second a Mr Kirk, probably a Scot like himself. Kingsale was sixteen and a half. He came from the oldest Norman family in Ireland and like Newburgh he was a Roman Catholic. He had been in the process of completing his education at Oxford University, but he had proved himself to be so unsuccessful and troublesome that he had been withdrawn. The old Duke of Ormonde, still the leading figure in the Irish establishment, had taken a particular interest in his wellbeing and suggested that the youth be sent back to Ireland. The Privy Council disagreed and wanted him to be educated at 'the house of Monsieur Fobart in Westminster' and so Ormonde was instructed to send money to London to support him. It is probably through Ormonde that Sarsfield became involved in looking after the little devil. Sarsfield was his second.

There can be few more foolish and unprofitable ways to risk one's life than to do so for the sake of a schoolboy scrap, but that is just what Sarsfield did. While the two adolescents lashed wildly at each other's swords, Kirk and Sarsfield got down to the more serious business. Sarsfield was very lucky to survive. Kirk ran him straight 'through the body, near the shoulder, very dangerously', and then doubtlessly approached Kingsale in the same manner that Godfrey had Albemarle. Kingsale was obliged to surrender.

It is not known how long Sarsfield took to recover from his wound, but he remained in London. While convalescing, his petition was presented in his absence to the king at Whitehall. It was not granted. It was no secret that he was no longer going to Tangier. Mr Kirk had put paid to that.

Although the political climate in England was slowly changing against the Whigs, the anti-Catholic sentiment that had been generated by the Popish Plot remained. On 4 May 1682 Sarsfield's name appeared on a warrant along with many others said to be 'popish recusants convicted or indicted for recusancy who have of late repaired to London and Westminster and the places adjacent'.[18] It is not recorded whether Sarsfield was arrested but, if he was, it was a minor matter as before the month was out he was engaged in an unusual adventure that was to become the subject of diplomatic exchanges between England and France.

Sarsfield's circle of friends in London was far from being exclusively Irish, but he did keep in close touch with other Irish officers, or rather, one-time officers, who were living there. Amongst them were Captain Robert Clifford, who like Sarsfield had been commissioned in Monmouth's regiment, and Captain James Purcell who had been commissioned in the shortlived Dongan's regiment.

Robert Clifford, who will be of some importance in the narrative to come, had by May 1682 become very interested in a young widow, Ann Siderfin.[19] He wanted to marry her. However, there were certain obstacles in his way. Her husband, Robert Siderfin, a Middle Temple barrister, had only recently died. She was young, English and rich and she had her own circle of friends. It had not even crossed her mind that she should consider Clifford as a suitor. Clifford thought otherwise. He imagined that the looks she gave him betrayed her true feelings and he intended to force her hand. He resolved upon a desperate course of action, which apart from being highly illegal could only have ended in success if Mrs Siderfin really did feel a great measure of affection towards him. Clifford decided to abduct her.

He could not do this alone so he turned to his friends and asked them to help. They were amused by the idea, and having nothing better to do at least two of them agreed. They were James Purcell and Patrick Sarsfield. Between them they were able to gather together some others (probably private soldiers who had served with them on the continent) so that they soon had some seven or eight men prepared to carry out the enterprise.

Clifford found out something of the lady's movements, and discovered that on Saturday 27 May 1682 she was going to take her coach to Windsor with a few other London ladies. As they made their way slowly across Hounslow Heath this female excursion was surprised by Clifford's gang. Mrs Siderfin was 'in a most barbarous manner dragged out of her coach'. The coachmen who intervened were beaten up or wounded and the horsemen galloped off with their captive.

The Privy Council was alerted and the messengers searched all the Irishmen's lodgings. The culprits had gone. Their servants, who were identified as being part of the highway gang, were thrown into Newgate Prison. The government, and indeed all London, was outraged at this disgraceful incident. This appalling crime, that could never have been acceptable even if it had taken place in wildest Connemara, had been committed in broad daylight within a few miles of the capital of England. King Charles sent an urgent message to his secretary of state to use all his 'endeavours to rescue this lady, Mrs Siderfin, from the violence which is upon her'. This was not going to be easy, as although the guilty parties still in England were under lock and key, the others, including Clifford and Sarsfield, had left the country. They had ridden to the coast, bundled their captive into an open boat and had crossed the Channel to Calais.

The English authorities moved quickly. There was clearly no time to be lost as 'if the ravisher have not his will there (in Calais) he will go to further extremities and in all probability carry her to Paris.' Not that that would have done Clifford much good. 'Marriage', it was noted, 'cannot be solemnised between strangers in that country'. Messages were sent to the president of Calais directly from the secretary of state, Sir Leoline Jenkins, outlining the situation to him.

Clifford had by now realised that his plan had gone seriously wrong. Mrs Siderfin had succumbed neither to his charm nor to his pleas. If he had expected her to be moved by the lengths to which he would go to win her, he was to be disappointed. She was beside herself with rage. Clifford, Sarsfield, a man named Dorneson and one other, perhaps Purcell, had bundled her into a Calais inn and kept her there, still much against her will, in the hope that she would cool down. There was to be no such luck.

The president of Calais, de Tasse, received the urgent note from Leoline Jenkins in the early hours of the morning. He called the town guards. They felt that they knew where Mrs Siderfin was and so at four in the morning they marched up to the inn and the president banged on the door. The Irish gentlemen were to come out. The Irish gentlemen, after much shouting and sword waving, did come out, but promptly disappeared into the darkness.

It was with some relief that Ann Siderfin wrote of her liberation to the English ambassador in Paris, Lord Preston, but:

> Three of the men that were at Monsieur de Ruvigny's house; Clifford, Sarsfield and Dorneson, have made their escape. It was reported that Clifford and Dorneson were gone for England. Sarsfield, they say, is at Gravlines.

She begged Preston to have them arrested as soon as possible as she could not feel secure while they were at large as they had 'been so bold as to threaten even the president himself'. Preston promptly obliged and wrote to the king of France requesting that the Calais magistrates be empowered to arrest Clifford and Sarsfield, and that the only one that they had been able to detain, Mrs Siderfin, be released. The French obliged and she was allowed to return home on one of King Charles's yachts that had been sent to Calais to take her back.

Things settled down for a while. For the next few months Sarsfield sensibly kept away both from London and Calais, but Clifford grew bored on the continent and decided to take a chance before his money ran out. He returned to London at the end of July 1682 and was promptly arrested. After three months in prison he was charged with 'taking away' Mrs Siderfin. He pleaded not guilty and a date was set down for him and his co-conspirators to be tried at the King's Bench bar on 21 November.

As Preston was soon to hear: 'On Tuesday the widow Siderfin pleaded her case singularly well against Captain Clifford, who also made a speech like an Irishman, as he is.' Clifford was quite candid. Although he had previously pleaded not guilty, he confessed that he had 'taken away' the complainant, but said that he had done so because he felt so passionately for her and knew that there was no other way to get her. What clearly hurt him was the suggestion that he was a penurious Irish adventurer who had kidnapped 'a young lady of a very considerable fortune both in money and in land' to make his own fortune. Clifford hotly told the court that 'he was a gentleman of a good family, and has the prospect of a better estate than hers.'

Lord Chief Justice Pemberton directed the jury that as they had heard Mrs Siderfin's unchallenged evidence, and as they had heard Clifford's confession they had no option but to find all the accused guilty. The jury gave their verdict without leaving the court room. The Lord Chief Justice reserved sentence and Clifford was returned to his cell.

Over six months after his arrest, Clifford was brought back to court to hear what his punishment would be. The sentence of the court was that he serve a year's imprisonment, that he be bound to his good behaviour for seven years and that he be fined £1,000 and be committed to prison until he paid it. Clifford did not have £1,000. The other four defendants were fined and committed to prison until they had paid up. Captain James Purcell and Robert Punsey* were each fined £500, and John Canner (Connor?) and Nicholas Richards were fined £100 each. Ann Siderfin was not satisfied with this. She vowed that she would 'sue them again for her own damage'. It was a despondent Robert Clifford who was led off to Fleet prison on that day, probably failing to reflect that many men would suffer worse penalties for taking a woman to France for a week.

Only two of the men named as being responsible for the abduction managed to get away unpunished, Dorneson and Sarsfield. Sarsfield seemed to lead a charmed life. Three weeks after the others had heard their sentences read out in court, another of his petitions was placed before the king, this time for land. He still had not received the £58 backpay for his service under Justin MacCarthy and so instead unsuccessfully asked the king for 'a parcel of land under fifty acres in Kent escheated to the crown as having belonged to Constance Michell, an alien'.[21]

As if this was not enough to draw attention to himself, a mere six weeks after sentence was passed on his friends, Sarsfield decided to emulate Clifford.

> Last Saturday (24th March 1683) Captain Sarsfield, the tall Irishman, ran away with Lady Herbert, widow to Lord Herbert of Cherbury. . . He carried her that night to Captain Parsons's house at Enfield Chase where on her refusing marriage and promising not to prosecute him, he brought her back on Sunday.[22]

Being then thirty one years old, Elizabeth Herbert (Betty to her friends)[23] was a few years older than Sarsfield. The second daughter of Lord Chandos, she had married Lord Herbert ten years before. He had been nineteen years older than her and had died in 1678. Sarsfield had probably met her through Herbert's son who had served with him in Monmouth's Regiment. Lady Herbert was in her day a very desirable woman and was yet to marry twice more. She and Sarsfield had been very close, and she had visited him several times when he 'lay ill of his hurts', but he had not been without rivals one of whom was Lord Cholmondeley. Whether or not this lord had anything to do with it or not, Lady Herbert had rather lost interest in Sarsfield and this explains his desperate plan to get her to marry him. Sadly for him he only succeeded in hardening her heart against him. Women reach an age when they do not react kindly to being kidnapped in the night and held prisoner. Lady Herbert was furious. Only in exasperation to get Sarsfield to release her did she sign a note promising not to prosecute him or Parsons, but as soon as she had been set free on Sunday 25 March 1683 she resolved to do something about

---

* Robert Punsey was released by royal warrant after he had spent a year in prison. His part in the abduction had been both small and innocent. He had been employed as Lord Dumbarton's groom when 'airing his lordship's horses on Hounslow Heath he did at the desire of several gentlemen he had often seen at his lordship's house conduct them to Richmond Ferry.' He had in fact done no more than show them the way.[20]

her treatment. And she was not a woman to shy away from litigation. 'She has taken out a warrant from the Lord Chief Justice on him', it was recorded, 'but notwithstanding (that) the Town says it will be a marriage and that all this is an artifice. Wagers are laid on it and it appears there was a great familiarity between them.'

As he had her signed promise not to prosecute him, and as no one seemed to take the matter very seriously, Sarsfield had little fear of joining Clifford in Fleet prison. In fact he had more serious matters to worry about as shortly after this 'taking away' he was again severely wounded in a duel, although it is no longer known who his opponent was. His wounds were such that he thought that he was going to die. He asked for his friend and accomplice Captain Sir John Parsons and gave him for safekeeping the note signed by Lady Herbert that protected them both from prosecution.

John Parsons, a baronet and a Middle Temple man who had like Sarsfield once held a commission in the short-lived Dongan's regiment, took Lady Herbert's warrant very seriously. Although no doubt concerned about the sad plight that Sarsfield found himself in, he was most relieved to have the note in his possession. It was his insurance against prosecution. And when Sarsfield recovered from his wounds, Parsons was determined not to give the note back.

Sarsfield wanted the note so badly that he eventually went to find Parsons a couple of weeks later to demand its return. Parsons refused. The only use that Sarsfield could possibly have for the note would be to give it back to Lady Herbert, and he knew that Sarsfield 'was so fond' that if she asked him for it he would hand it over. Parsons did not mind Sarsfield being prosecuted, but where did that leave him? He told Sarsfield that he would either keep the note himself or else, for both their sakes, he would 'seal it up in a third gentleman's hands.'

Sarsfield insisted, but Parsons stood his ground. The argument became heated and Sarsfield, although perhaps London's least successful duellist, challenged him to a duel. The outcome was recorded by the gossip, Frank Gwyn:

> On Sunday morning [29th April 1683] they fought behind Montague House. Sarsfield is run through the body a little above the belly into the lungs, and Sir John into the lungs. They were both thought desperate, but today their surgeon, who dined with us, tells me he has much hope of them both.

Both of them recovered. The only fatality was their friendship.

On a national level, 1683 saw many changes. In June the dubious 'Rye House Plot' was uncovered. Its supposed object was to assassinate the king and his Catholic brother, the duke of York, and to crown the duke of Monmouth. Monmouth, Shaftesbury and Lord Grey fled abroad to escape the consequences. A number of Catholics were released from prison, and by 1684 the detestable Oates, once hailed as the man who 'by awakening us out of sleep was an instrument in the hands of God for our preservation',[24] was fined £100,000 for referring to the Catholic duke of York as a traitor. He was then thrown into the debtors' side of the King's Bench prison until he paid. It was intended to be a life sentence.

While Sarsfield lay in London recovering from his latest wound he received the news that his eight-year old nephew, Charles, had died in Paris on 3 July 1683. Patrick Sarsfield was now entitled to be the master of Lucan. His years of waste were now over. In mid August he returned to Dublin with Francis Sarsfield, a Middle Temple lawyer and a member of the Limerick branch of the family.[25] In September his late brother's will was at last proved. But the lawyers had not finished yet. The Fanshawes were still able to pursue their claim on behalf of Sarsfield's niece, Charlotte, and even by the new year Sarsfield still had not got possession. The king noted ruefully, 'our said gracious intentions were still being frustrated by Theophilus Jones.' In the meanwhile, the Sarsfields suffered. They still had to finance the legal battle and there was little income. To raise money, Patrick Sarsfield in 1684 sold Maudlin Castle and Sarsfield's Mill in Clare, Co. Kildare along with sixty acres to Francis Sarsfield for £500.[26] That same year, the greatest obstacle to Sarsfield gaining possession of Lucan was removed: old Sir Theophilus breathed his last.

Sarsfield's movements in 1684 are not known, but an incident took place in London on 7 April, the Sunday after Easter, which leads one to suspect that he returned to England.

> Captain Clifford sometime since convicted of a great misdemeanour in stealing and carrying away Mrs Siderfin into France for which he received £1,000 damages, as also Mrs Siderfin recovered £1,500 in a special action, and there in the Fleet prison having since lain for some time, some gentlemen came under pretence to see him, but rescued him, and carried him away, notwithstanding the endeavours of the officers.[27]

CHAPTER III

James II

Monsters of *Roman* and *Hybernian* Race
With *Phangs* and *Claws* infect the *wasted Place.*
Thomas Shadwell, 'A Congratulatory Poem on His Highness
the Prince of Orange's coming into England', 1689

ON 6 FEBRUARY 1685, Charles II died having suffered a stroke. He was succeeded by James II, the first avowedly Roman Catholic monarch to be crowned in over a century. Although some hostility was inevitable, he had come to the throne at the most favourable time. England was staunchly royalist and had a small standing army and a capable fleet, and Ireland and Scotland were quiet. However, the exiled Whigs were spurred into immediate and precipitate action. Their worst fears had been realised: there was a Roman Catholic king on the throne. Confident that the horror of a Catholic monarchy would swing the country behind him, the duke of Monmouth set sail for England.

He landed in Lyme Regis on 11 June accompanied by Sarsfield's old enemy, Lord Grey of Warke. Monmouth issued a proclamation claiming that James had both poisoned Charles II and started the Great Fire of London in 1666. He also announced, not for the first time, that his mother had been secretly married to the late king and that as the legitimate son of Charles II he was also his lawful successor. He resolved 'to pursue the said James of York as a mortal and bloody enemy'.[1] But he and his supporters had misjudged the country's response. His enthusiastic reception was confined to the west. Parliament dutifully passed an act of attainder condemning the Protestant pretender to death. Nevertheless, the rebellion rapidly gained strength as 'King' Monmouth marched north with the intention of setting himself up in Bristol, the western capital. Within a week of his landing he had beaten the Somersetshire militia out of Axminster and had made a triumphant entry into the county town of Taunton.

In London the response was rapid. On 19 June James gave the command of the army to Lord Feversham who on the next day led his men out of the capital along the west road.

Monmouth's rebellion presented Sarsfield with his greatest opportunity yet. He lost no time in volunteering his services to the king. Along with the young Lord Newburgh and two others he was accepted as a 'gentleman volunteer' to serve under Colonel Theophilus Oglethorpe in a mixed force of some fifty dragoons and cavalrymen. As the royal army left London, Oglethorpe's party sped on ahead to reconnoitre the enemy.

3 King James II by Nicholas Largillière.

Sarsfield did not have to wait long to see action. On the night of 25 June Monmouth and his rag-tag army of volunteers, now some six thousand strong, were sheltering from the rain in Keynsham, a village five miles from Bristol. Although the royal army was still too far away to assist, Oglethorpe decided to act.

Reinforced by a militia troop and forty horsemen he ordered a night attack on Keynsham. After dark they charged into the village, firing and shouting, and charged straight out again as the rebels poured into the streets shooting in all directions. Fourteen of Monmouth's men were killed in the mêlée, including a captain of horse. Oglethorpe lost six men, and both his 'gentlemen volunteers' were wounded. Lord Newburgh was unlucky enough to be 'shot into the belly', although he was later to recover, and Sarsfield had his hand slashed.[2]

The next few days passed quickly. Sarsfield remained in Oglethorpe's patrol which was kept busy following Monmouth's army and sending messages back to Feversham. Wet and weary, they passed through Frome, Shepton Mallet and Wells, and on 3 July watched the rebels march into Bridgwater.

On that same day, Feversham's army camped four miles away in the village of Westonzoyland. Although desertions had begun to weaken the rebel army, numerically the two sides were not uneven. The duke had some four thousand men and Feversham a thousand less, but Monmouth was well aware of the difference in quality between his men and the professional soldiers that would face them. It was clear to him that his only hope was to launch a surprise night attack on the royal army's camp.

While Feversham's men camped down in Westonzoyland, and Monmouth prepared to march out of Bridgwater, Sarsfield waited with Oglethorpe and his patrol on the steep slopes of Knowle Hill to the north.

At ten that night the entire rebel army silently moved out of Bridgwater and headed straight for Oglethorpe's patrol on Knowle Hill. So quiet were Monmouth's men that they remained undetected even though they passed to within half a mile of the horsemen before turning off the road and marching across Sedgemoor towards Feversham's camp. Between them and Westonzoyland lay three deep irrigation ditches. The rebels were guided across the first two of these with ease by a local herdsman who for one guinea had agreed to lead Monmouth all the way to Westonzoyland. A heavy mist hung over the moor, and as the rebels tramped forwards they could see nothing through the dark gloom, and hear nothing but the sound of their own feet in the coarse grass. Just after one o'clock Oglethorpe learnt that the rebels had left Bridgwater. His patrol mounted up and headed cautiously down the hill. They found no sentries on the road. The town was deserted, but just audible through the gloom they could hear the distant popping of musketry.

Monmouth's infantry advanced to within thirty yards of the Bussex Rhine, the last ditch between them and the royal army. Although their orders were march up to its brink in silence, his men began firing too early and were halted by the continuous fire they brought down on themselves.

In the meantime, Oglethorpe with Sarsfield and the rest came galloping down the Bridgwater road, well aware that their news was of no value whatsoever. Feversham ordered them to the other end of the line to protect the infantry from Grey's horse which was still felt to be a threat. Reinforced by fifty horse guards Oglethorpe's patrol was sent around behind the royal army and then over a makeshift bridge on the Bussex Rhine.

No sooner were they over than they met Grey's cavalry. The skirmish was over in seconds. In fact the contact was so fleeting and the visibility was so bad that it was thought that they had simply chased off a small patrol. Monmouth's left flank was now exposed and ripe for an attack, but Feversham wanted his horse to hold back in case Grey returned. The horse guards obeyed and remained in position, but Oglethorpe ordered his men to wheel to the left and charge.

The rebels were now in a hopeless position, but they stood firm. As Oglethorpe's cavalry came at them from out of the mist they opened fire. The pikemen kept their ground. Most of the horsemen pulled up and withdrew after firing their carbines, but a few spurred their horses on and plunged into the rebel ranks. Sarsfield was one of these. As if he was giving vent to the accumulated frustration of all his idle years, he ploughed into the footmen, slashing and swearing at those who leapt out of the darkness to meet him. He was surrounded and clubbed off his horse with the butt end of a musket and left for dead. The battle still had over an hour to run, in fact the slaughter had hardly begun, but Sarsfield was unconscious to the events around him. He spent this time lying in the enemy lines.[4]

In the last hour of darkness Feversham decided that his men had taken enough punishment. He ordered a general advance. With drums beating and colours flying his six infantry battalions marched forward into the Bussex Rhine. They waded through the knee-deep mire and scrambled up the other side to face the rebels. When they found themselves on flat ground with no obstacles between them and the enemy, there was no holding them back. With a great roar the infantry broke into a trot and then a charge. The rebels did not wait for the impact. They broke and ran.

Before the battle the rebels had been led carefully across the Langmoor Rhine, the second irrigation ditch, by their local guide. As they approached it for the second time, in full flight, they plunged in wherever they could and waded across. The sides were steep and slippery after the recent wet weather. While they floundered about in the mud, or tried to scale the other side, the soldiers lined up along the brink and fired volleys into their backs. Many of those who succeeded in scrambling out were chased through the thick corn on the other side and butchered. By sunrise hardly 'ten to a dozen' rebels were left together in one fighting body. While it was still dark Monmouth had stripped off his armour and fled with Grey and a few others, leaving his humbler followers to their fate.

Three days later Feversham sent a report to the earl of Sunderland, the Secretary of State. He wrote:

I do not believe that we have lost fifty men killed in that place, and nearly two hundred wounded. There was only one ensign killed two captains, six lieutenants and six ensigns wounded and some volunteers of whom my Lord Dumblane was one, but so slightly that he remained mounted.

'Sarsfield', he went on, 'was also wounded in several places but not mortally. I am assured that the enemy have been killed in thousands and nearly three hundred prisoners taken.'[5]

The total rebel casualties in the battle will never be known for certain. On the actual waste of Sedgemoor they were probably only as few as four hundred, but in the rout towards Bridgwater another fifteen hundred fell. The king noted these facts with satisfaction, and observed that his men had 'showed themselves to be old troops, and what difference there is between such and new raised men.'

Within two days of the battle both Grey and Monmouth were arrested by the Sussex militia. The duke, disguised as a shepherd, was found sleeping in a copse. According to his captors he was 'trembling with cold and apprehension'. Although he tried everything in his power to get a pardon, his pleas fell upon deaf ears. He even wrote a letter to the king wishing him 'a long and happy reign', and in a private interview with James he begged for his life. When all his efforts had failed he issued his last declaration which read: 'I declare that the title of king was forced upon me and that it was very much contrary to my opinion when I was proclaimed.'[6]

On 15 June 1685 he was decapitated on Tower Hill before a silent crowd. His courage returned to him at the end and he announced: 'I die with a clear conscience; I have wronged no man.'*[7]

One hundred and fifty or so of his followers were also executed and eight hundred were transported into slavery on the West Indian plantations. The second most senior rebel, Lord Grey, secured himself a pardon for forty thousand pounds.**

Despite his wounds, Monmouth's rebellion proved to be a great success for Sarsfield. Before the campaign no one of any influence had even heard of him. After Sedgemoor his name was known where it counted most. Even the king noted in his diary exactly how he had been knocked off his horse.[8] Sarsfield's reward of a commission and rapid promotion was not long in coming. After six years without a position in either military or civilian life he was given a captaincy in Richard Hamilton's regiment of dragoons on the Irish establishment. His commission was backdated to the date on which he had volunteered so that he would receive pay for the period he had spent in arms. However, as James's immediate intention was to increase the number of Roman Catholics

*   He then turned to the executioner and said: 'Do not hack me as you did my Lord Russell.'
**   Grey's political career was far from over. King William made him the earl of Tankerville, and he lived to serve on the Privy Council and as the first commissioner of the Treasury and as lord privy seal before his death in 1702.

in the English army, Sarsfield was never given the opportunity to take up his new post in Ireland. On 26 July 1685 he was transferred to Lord Dover's newly raised regiment of horse and was promoted to the rank of major. As the colonel was both a Roman Catholic and something of a favourite with the king, 'Dover's Horse' was given every assistance. Sarsfield was in his element. Within three months he was promoted to the rank of lieutenant-colonel and took over the day to day running of the regiment.[9]

Having set in motion his policy of increasing the number of Catholics in his officer corps, James needed to protect them. Most of his new officers had not taken the oath of allegiance as it was still administered in the same form as it had been in Charles's reign. These officers were also open to prosecution under the penal laws that were still in force. In November 1685 both Sarsfield and Dover were named in the king's 'pardon and dispensation from all penalties etc incurred as a result of various acts passed against certain popish recusants and signifying the royal pleasure that no proceedings should be taken against them thereafter under the said act'.[10] Two months later James issued a warrant to the attorney general to prepare a bill that would exempt a list of named people, Sarsfield included, from taking the oath of allegiance and supremacy.

The changes within the army were rapid, particularly in Ireland where the policy to 'Catholicize' the army was more rigorously implemented. The process was speeded up in England by the rapid promotion of Roman Catholics, often over the heads of more experienced Protestants, and even by the introduction of Irish officers. It was even rumoured in 1686, perhaps provocatively, that Sarsfield was to be sent to Ireland as a brigadier.[11]

On 18 April 1686 a new Roman Catholic chapel was opened in London's Lime Street by James Stamford, the envoy of the elector palatine. In those difficult times this was a most unpopular move with the majority of Londoners, especially as the chapel was to be run by the much hated Jesuits. The king was well aware that there could be trouble and had promised that Lord Dover's regiment would be stationed in London at the time of the chapel's consecration.[12] This precaution in itself proved to be insufficient as a crowd soon formed outside intent on breaking in and smashing the place up. The trained bands, the city of London's militiamen, had been posted at the door to prevent any damage, but they were soon pushed aside by the mob who broke in and set about destroying the furniture, the crucifix and the organ. Sarsfield's men arrived to find the militia standing helplessly (and perhaps apathetically) aside. The mob was turned out back into the street and dispersed before the chapel suffered any structural damage.[13]

Although there is no record of who it was that led Lord Dover's regiment in its only recorded action, as he was the commanding officer it is very likely to have been Sarsfield. As the regiment was based in London for the very purpose of dealing with such an incident, Sarsfield would certainly have directed his officers as to how such a situation should be handled. James employed Sarsfield and this Catholic regiment, in effect, to keep the capital in awe of him. The crown was not to be dictated to by the London mob. This incident convinced the king of the necessity of basing Roman Catholic regiments in London. When it came to establishing Catholic rights Protestant troops, regular or otherwise, may well behave as did the militiamen in Lime Street.* He resolved to upgrade Lord Dover's regiment of horse and incorporate it in the horse guards. In May 1686 Dover's horse was disbanded and the Catholic officers were transferred to the newly raised 4th troop. Lieutenant-Colonel Sarsfield became their new commanding officer. The colonel was a Protestant but a trusted one. He was the thirty-six year old John Churchill who later, as the duke of Marlborough, was to become the most successful general of his age.

Although James's army reforms were highly unpopular with all but a few of his Protestant officers, they were carefully implemented so as to discourage any active opposition. So well was this done that the first serious incident of open opposition within the army did not come until 1688, the last year of James's reign. The duke of Berwick's regiment, then based in the important naval town of Portsmouth, was instructed to keep its numbers up to full strength by accepting Irishmen into the ranks. This was strongly opposed by everyone in the regiment except the Roman Catholic duke of Berwick himself. Seven of his officers bluntly refused to allow any Irish Catholics into their companies as they feared that the Irish recruits heralded the start of a policy to purge the army of Protestants. The ringleader, Captain John Beaumont, declared that he and his fellow officers 'did not think it consistent with their honours to have foreigners imposed upon them'. When it became clear that they were going to be punished Beaumont and the others hurriedly signed over a hundred passports for their troops and incited them to desert. In view of this the court martial which sat on 11 September 1688 was remarkably lenient in that it did no more than cashier the seven guilty officers.[15]

Within a week, Sarsfield was given his first staff duties. The duke of Berwick's regiment, once the mainstay of the Portsmouth garrison, was now short not only of men but of officers. Sarsfield, freshly promoted to the rank of colonel, was sent with all speed to Dublin to ask the lord deputy of Ireland, Lord Tyrconnell, for Irish troops to fill the gaps.[16] Tyrconnell sent Sarsfield straight back to London with the message that there were no troops to spare. To emphasise this Tyrconnell wrote to the king shortly afterwards requesting instead that troops should be sent to Ireland.[17] In the meantime the situation in Portsmouth worsened as the government's solution to the manpower problem was to reinforce the garrison with the all-Irish regiment of Colonel MacElligott. 'Some think', wrote the Dutch ambassador darkly, 'that there are other reasons for sending a newly recruited Irish regiment to Portsmouth.'[18]

*   He was so incensed at the behaviour of the militiamen that he had their captain arrested. It was reported that the trained bands had shouted to the crowd to find out what they were up to. 'Only pulling down Popery', came the reply. 'If that be all, we cannot in conscience hinder', said the militiamen.[14]

King James's reign came to an end in December 1688. Although at that time he was not universally unpopular, he had lost the support necessary to ensure his survival in a time of crisis. The loyalty and love that his subjects had shown him during the western rebellion had disappeared in the space of three years. The savagery with which Monmouth's followers had been persecuted had shocked the country. The army and the government were being placed increasingly into the hands of Roman Catholics. The effects of Catholicism could be seen elsewhere. In 1685, the eighty-seven year old edict of Nantes which had promised limited toleration to French Protestants, was revoked by Louis XIV and London was subsequently flooded by thousands of Huguenot refugees. With them came the most horrific tales of persecution, forced conversion, torture and murder. To the Englishman of 1688 Roman Catholicism, that old superstition, had two offspring—despotism and terror. Worrying tales came also from Ireland where James's government was in the hands of Richard Talbot, the earl of Tyrconnell. Tyrconnell, or 'Lying Dick Talbot' as he was known in England, had shown the English what they might expect from a Catholic regime as he set about purging the government, the city corporations, the army and the judiciary of Protestants.

On 7 May 1688 King James issued his Declaration of Indulgence setting out his policy of religious toleration. A week later he ordered that the bishops should distribute copies of it in their dioceses and ensure that it was read in every church in the country on two successive Sundays. This was too much for the church establishment. Most of the bishops refused to do any such thing. Seven of them, including the archbishop of Canterbury, printed and circulated a petition to the king explaining their reservations. James had them arrested for seditious libel and put in the Tower. The country was outraged.

Two days later the queen gave birth to her only son, James Francis Edward. The rumour was circulated that the baby was the son of a miller and had been smuggled into the queen's bedchamber in a warming pan. It was a Jesuit plot to ensure a Catholic succession. Public feeling could not have been more inflamed. On top of this James began recalling his subjects from the Dutch brigade, those British regiments in the pay of the prince of Orange, and fears were expressed that there was to be an Anglo-French alliance that would bring about such changes in the world as could never again be altered.

In July 1688 William, the prince of Orange, accepted after much deliberation an invitation from some leading Englishmen to invade their country. They promised him their support if he led a rebellion against James on the grounds that he was next in the line of succession; next in line because he was married to James's eldest daughter and because the new prince of Wales was an imposter.

> The people are so generally dissatisfied with the present conduct of the government in relation to their religion, liberties, and properties (all of which have been greatly invaded), and they are in such expectation of their prospects being daily worse, that your Highness may be assured there are nineteen parts of twenty in the people throughout the kingdom

who are desirous of a change; and who, we believe would willingly contribute to it if they had such a protection to countenance their rising as
could secure them from being destroyed.[19]

It was impressed upon William that he had a duty to ensure the liberties of
England and to protect the Protestant religion. He accepted, although those
reasons were not to him the most important ones. The very survival of the Dutch
republic was at stake. France was again preparing for war and if England either
held back from the fighting or sided with the French, the Netherlands could be
overrun. It was to save his own country that William agreed to the overthrow
of his father-in-law.

On Thursday 11 November 1688 Prince William set sail for England leaving
behind him assurances to the Holy Roman Emperor that he intended neither to
drive James from his throne nor to harm the Roman Catholics. As luck would
have it, a 'Protestant wind' blew the Dutch fleet straight to its objective at Torbay
and prevented its interception by the powerful English navy. On the 15th William
of Orange set foot on English soil at the head of a cosmopolitan army of fifteen
thousand men. Within two days the English army had set up its headquarters at
Salisbury and King James was riding west to do battle.

To the king the great test would be the loyalty of his troops. Many were
clearly sympathetic to the aims of the revolutionary party and would be happier
serving against James rather than for him. Even as the Dutch fleet swept down
the Channel news reached London of soldiers and militiamen refusing to obey
their officers and deserting their posts. A taste of what was to come was given
almost immediately it was known that William's army had landed. The colonel
of the royal regiment of dragoons, Lord Cornbury, marched his men over to the
other side and offered his services to the prince of Orange. The problem was
that his men had not been told of their colonel's intentions, especially as many
of them were Catholics and had no intention of deserting. The second most
senior officer in the regiment at the time was Major Robert Clifford, who by
now had certainly got the authorities to forget the Siderfin affair. Much to his
credit he, with one other officer and most of the dragoons, fought his way out
of the enemy's hands and made for the royal camp at Salisbury. For this show of
loyalty, Clifford was rewarded by James with promotion to colonel of dragoons.[20]

While the main body of James's army gathered in Salisbury, patrols and scouts
scoured the country to the west to keep the king informed of the invaders'
movements. One such patrol of fifty dragoons from Bernard Howard's regiment
returned to Salisbury on Monday 19 November. Their lieutenant bought back the
vague information that there was a body of men in or around the village of Bruton
in Somerset, just five miles north of Wincanton. Nothing was known of these
men, but no other patrol was meant to be in that area. General Kirke was
justifiably irritated at having been given such an unsatisfactory report and was
determined to find out what was going on. He sent for Sarsfield.[22]

Next morning Sarsfield set out with seventy of his horse guards and fifty others, mostly from the 4th troop of horse grenadier guards led by another Irish-man, Henry Luttrell, the rest being a small detachment of dragoons commanded by Cornet John Richmond Webb. This small mounted force moved with all possible speed directly to Bruton some thirty miles away. When they arrived the village showed no signs of having harboured any troops, nor could they get any information from the local inhabitants. While the men rested a trooper from the horse guards who knew the area well changed out of his uniform into civilian clothes and rode off to see what he could discover. It was not long before he returned with the news that a group of infantrymen had marched into Wincanton on the previous day. Sarsfield's men mounted up and rode off to investigate.

The men that they were seeking were some thirty Scots from Colonel Mackay's regiment of foot, a regiment that had formed part of the Scots brigade in Holland. It had been shipped to England by the prince of Orange as part of his invasion force. The patrol was led by the recently promoted Lieutenant Campbell, an experienced soldier who had already served for twelve years as a sergeant.[23] His instructions were to collect horses from the surrounding area and then to wait in Wincanton until the main body of the army caught up with him. The Scots had spent the previous night in the village and were well settled in. In fact they would have been completely surprised had it not been for a miller who had spotted the approaching column and had run into the village to give the alarm.

Campbell had to think quickly. He had no idea how many troops were approaching the village. The countryside around Wincanton in those days was one of dense woodland broken by small thickly hedged fields. Although it is a hill-top village there was no vantage point from which Campbell could watch the approach of Sarsfield's men, and when he first received the warning, they were no more than a few hundred yards away. He did not know that the approaching force was six times more numerous that his own. His options were limited. He could either run for it, or he could wait and see. As at this stage he did not even know whether Sarsfield's patrol was hostile, he decided in favour of the second option. He led his band of men out of the village towards the approaching horse guards. His plan was simply to deny a potential enemy access to Wincanton by placing his troops in an ambush alongside the narrow lane that led to Bruton. He left twelve men in the village itself to protect the horses that had been rounded up. A few others were posted in a small but well hedged garden that bordered the lane just outside the village, and Campbell hid the rest of his men further out behind a hedge on the other side of the road. To get to Wincanton the horse guards would have to run the gauntlet of this hedge, get past the garden that would be bristling with muskets, and then enter the village to be confronted with more of his men sniping from the windows.

As Sarsfield's patrol came into view Campbell and five others stepped into the lane. The Scots had orders not to fire as there was a possibility that the horsemen coming towards them were deserters from the royal army; it was only five days since Lord Cornbury had brought his men over to the prince of Orange.

When the leading trooper was only a stone's throw away, Campbell called out for them to stop where they were.

> 'Stand! For who are ye?'
> 'I am for King James', replied Sarsfield. 'Who are you for?'
> 'I am for the prince of Orange!'
> 'God damn you!' came the reply, 'I'll prince you!'

The horse guards braced themselves. Campbell shouted to his men to open fire. He stepped forward and shot a trooper 'in at the mouth and through the brains, so he dropped down dead'. The dragoons and grenadiers dismounted as soon as the firing had started and began looking for places where they could break through the hedge. Sarsfield tried to get the horse guards to charge towards the village. The narrow lane was blocked by fallen men and loose and shying horses and those who were trying to get a clear shot back at the Scots. Campbell was shot dead. The men who had been with him in the lane managed to get into the garden where one of the ambush parties was waiting. The horse guards surged forward waving their sabres and carbines. Campbell's body was trampled underfoot. They could not get into the garden, but the hedge on the other side of the road was dead and so a few of them managed to get into the field opposite. The Scotsmen there were now in serious trouble. Grenades were being thrown over the hedge at them and shot was coming through it. Luttrell's grenadiers and the dragoons had broken through the hedge at the upper end of the field and were firing directly at them. Worse still, an obliging yokel had opened a gate at the other end of the field through which Sarsfield was able to lead a large body of the horse guards.

But Providence favoured the weak. The fighting was confined to the eastern end of the village. The miller who had first warned Campbell of Sarsfield's approach now warned Sarsfield of the approach of the Dutch reinforcements. With great bravery he ran from the village shouting 'The Dutch! The Dutch!' and 'Away for your lives! Save yourselves, the enemies are at hand!' Sarsfield and those horse guards with him were able to see that the village street was crammed with people. With victory in their grasp, the king's men suddenly lost their confidence. Sarsfield could see the danger. If he was attacked now his men would be in complete disarray. They could not form up while under fire from the Scots behind the hedge. He had to make a quick decision. He decided to pull his man back out of musket range and regroup. This saved the Scots. As the horse guards retreated away from the village, the Scots ran back into it. If any of them actually believed that there were any Dutch reinforcements they were to be disappointed. The Scots ran through the village and out the other side, making good their escape.

It was probably some time before Sarsfield advanced again as in the panic some of his troopers had galloped off, so precious time was wasted in calling them all back. When he eventually led his men back across the fields to the village, except for six of them who had already been taken prisoner, the Scots had vanished. Three horse guards had been shot dead, and another had been shot through the thigh. Cornet Webb of the queen's regiment of dragoons was seriously wounded by a shot 'between his back-bones and his reins'. Including Lieutenant Campbell, twelve of the Scots had been killed in the lane and in the field. The dead of both sides were buried together in one mass grave. Sarsfield returned to Salisbury that same day, taking with him the seventeen or so horses that had been rounded up by Campbell. The unfortunate Webb was left behind in the village to be treated, as he was too badly wounded to be moved.*

As the prince of Orange's invasion force moved eastwards the Wincanton skirmish was the only test of arms that it had, to face. Many confused rumours reached London of fighting elsewhere, but these were either very minor incidents or else were purely fictitious events. Some actually heard news of the king's defeat at Wincanton and that 'the king's army was retreating towards the capital with the prince's army pursuing it'. Such reports generated the fear that the Irish soldiers would sack the city before they fled to find shipping to take them to the continent. On the other hand Lord Preston was informed that Sarsfield had beaten off four hundred of the enemy. The Dutch envoy in London, Van Dychveld, recorded that 'the court and the Catholics divulged with great satisfaction in every direction that forty of his highness's (i.e. William's) men should have been met by a party of the king's troops and that seventeen of ours should have been killed and six taken prisoners'.[25]

It has often been suggested that had James pushed on quickly he would have forced the prince of Orange into a battle, and that once blood had been shed between Englishmen and foreigners there would have been a general rallying around the king. But James was pessimistic. He felt that his army would not stand by him and that the North would rise up against him. Although it was a decision much regretted by his friends, he gave the order to return to London.

The king may well have been right. Colonel Ambrose Norton later confessed to being part of a plot hatched by some of James's most trusted officers. If the king advanced to Warminster as had been his initial intention, a group of officers were going to take him as a prisoner directly to the prince of Orange. The king's escort was going to be carefully selected to include the plotters amongst whom were General Percy Kirke, Sir John Lanier, Colonel Norton and Captain Cornelius Wood. Another conspirator was the second in command of the army, Lord Churchill. It was planned that he should sit with the king in the royal

---

* John Richmond Webb was to live to achieve great things. He served as a brigadier at Blenheim, as a major-general at Ramillies and Oudenarde, and as a lieutenant-general at Malplaquet. After the victory of Wynendael in 1708 where he commanded the English army, his fame was such that a poet was to write of him:

    'The past out-done, what future shall dare claim

    Or rank his own with WEBB's immortal name?'[24]

coach. The main concern of these men was that their kidnapping would be frustrated by 'Dumbarton, Sarsfield or any other of the papist officers'. In the event of a rescue attempt the two outriders, Colonel Norton and Captain Wood, were to draw their pistols and shoot the king dead. If they failed, Churchill, equipped with a pocket pistol and a dagger, was to finish the job.[26]

Before James took his fateful decision to go back to London there had been no more than a few desertions from the royal camp. (One of the Scots who had survived the Wincanton skirmish had even deserted to the king.) Even the most anti-Catholic of James's soldiers were aware that if the army did fight the Dutch it could well win, and then anyone who had previously deserted would most certainly be hanged. Those who, despite this sobering thought, had resolved to make their way westwards to join the prince of Orange still had to slip past the many loyal troops who had been deliberately posted to stop any desertion. Sarsfield was particularly noted for his alertness.[27] Every soldier knew that there would be only one punishment if they were caught and rumours were circulated that Sarsfield had already had some deserters hanged.

But things changed once James moved his army back to Andover. The whole army lost its spirit. His officers began to disappear, often taking large bodies of men with them. One of the first to go was young Lord Colchester who was a lieutenant in Sarsfield's troop of horse guards. On 24 November the army's second in command, Lord Churchill, deserted with the duke of Grafton. On the 25th they were followed by the young duke of Ormonde and James's second son-in-law, Prince George of Denmark.

Throughout this time Sarsfield worked desperately to staunch the flow. Even those who had fought alongside him at Wincanton were now leaving. Officers were deserting with their men often on the pretence that they were going on some important mission. Groups of officers would leave at night and persuade or order the guards to follow them. One group of deserters brought back by Sarsfield claimed that their officers had threatened to hang them if they did not desert and march to the prince's army. Sarsfield spent the night of the 23rd chasing around Wiltshire with twenty of his men in the hope of catching one of his own junior officers, Ambrose Cave, who had managed to slip away with some of the horse guards even though he was under suspicion.[28] Sarsfield's task became impossible. The English army was disintegrating.

The Dutch advance was slow as William was above all else anxious to avoid a confrontation. His enemies melted away before him, especially once it became clear that James was not going to stand and fight. It was not long before his supporters began to panic. On 2 December 1688, the diarist John Evelyn noted that 'the Papists in office lay down their commissions and fly. Universal consternation amongst them; it looks like a revolution.' And so it was. James made a pretence at negotiation to gain some time but at three in the morning on 11 December he slipped out of Whitehall to find a ship for France. On the 12th England had no government and London found itself in a state of anarchy. 'The prentices go together and were falling upon all Mass houses and committing many irregular things.'[29] Lime Street chapel which had once been protected by Sarsfield was wrecked and the mob made off in mock procession holding the candlesticks aloft. Leading Catholics were arrested without authority and were held to await the formation of a new government, 'but none were killed, no houses burnt, nor were any robberies committed'.[30] Thankful that there had been no bloodletting, William entered London on 18 December to the enthusiastic cheers of the common people. James reached France for Christmas and never set foot in Britain again.

The reign of James II had brought about great changes in Ireland, but they were changes that could only be sustained so long as they were upheld by the English government. Shortly after his accession to the throne, James had elevated Richard Talbot to the peerage as the earl of Tyrconnell. Dick Talbot, then aged fifty-five (three years older than James), had once commanded James's regiment when they were in exile during the interregnum. James rewarded him with the rank of lieutenant-general and the task of reforming the Irish army, which he did by steadily removing the Protestants. His success was such that he was appointed the lord deputy of Ireland in January 1687, and he set about creating a Catholic state. The army, the government, the corporations and the judiciary were purged of Protestants. By 1688 even the Protestant city of Londonderry, which had only a small Catholic population, was obliged to accept a Catholic mayor and council. Tyrconnell then set about preparing for an Irish parliament that would pass new laws to settle the land question once and for all. These plans were interrupted by the English Revolution.

William's position in early 1689 was far from settled. It was by no means clear that the English would welcome or even accept the change of king. In Scotland civil war was inevitable. It was feared that the French were standing by to strike, and Tyrconnell's party was firmly in control in Dublin. Fighting, although only on a small scale, had already broken out in the northern part of Ireland. Those Protestants in the south were sure to be overwhelmed if it came to a civil war, and it was at best uncertain as to whether the Protestants in the north would be able to hold out until help came; indeed, it was doubtful that help could be sent. Outside England there was little for the Williamites to celebrate.

William's English supporters did not see Ireland as a remote or obscure country. It had an important place in the imagination of the seventeenth century Englishman. Catholicism itself was epitomised by the ignorant and backward Irish. Ireland was a place where the very existence of the Protestants was being threatened by wild popish barbarians. Tyrconnell's government had committed great wrongs that needed righting. James had even been chased off his throne to the whistled tune of a mock-Irish song:

> A foolish ballad was made at the time, treating the Papists, and chiefly
> the Irish, in a very ridiculous manner, which had a burden, said to be Irish
> words, Lero Lero Lillibulero, that made an impression on the army that

cannot be well imagined by those who saw it not. The whole army, and at last all people both in city and country, were singing it perpetually. And perhaps never had so slight a thing had so great an effect.[31]

While James's deputy ruled in Dublin, the London government had reason to regret the last verse:

> Now now de damn Heretics all go down,
> Lillibulero Bullen a la.
> By Chreest and St Patrick the Nation's our own,
> Lillibulero Bullen a la, Lero, lero, lero, lero,
> Lillibulero Bullen a la.

It was with some relief then that William's government learnt of a letter written to Sir John Temple by an Irish judge. It suggested that Tyrconnell saw himself as being in a desperate situation. He would, in the judge's opinion, be willing to give up the government of Ireland without a struggle. It was resolved to contact Tyrconnell as soon as possible to give him the chance to surrender his position peacefully. It would have been useful to have sent the fleet to lie off Dublin as a show of strength, but William did not trust the English navy and so a less threatening approach had to be adopted.[32] Tyrconnell had to be told that the Catholics of Ireland would enjoy the same freedoms that they had enjoyed under Charles II, and that King William needed his assurance that he would allow such troops into Dublin as the king felt necessary for the security of the kingdom. It was hoped that a leading Irishman who would be trusted by Tyrconnell could be persuaded to go to Dublin and assure him of William's good intentions.

The first choice for this delicate mission was Sarsfield. It was known that he was respected in the army, that he had been favoured by King James, and that he had travelled to Dublin on a mission to Tyrconnell before. All that he would have to do would be to travel to Ireland and promise to return within three weeks if he was unsuccessful. Sarsfield would do no such thing. His loyalty to King James was unshakeable. He let William know that he was willing to obey his commands and even to fight for him against the king of France, but under no circumstances would he help deprive his lawful sovereign of one of his kingdoms. It was a predictable answer, and not one that caused William any concern.[33]

In those early days after James's flight all matters to do with Ireland were influenced by the Temple family. The idea to send such a mission to Ireland came from Sir John Temple, the Irish solicitor general. His brother, the great statesman Sir William Temple, was a personal friend of the new king, and Sir William's eldest son, John Temple was at that time a bright and rising young politician. All the family had a wide experience of Irish affairs, so when the young John suggested an alternative to Sarsfield he was carefully listened to. The most suitable person to be sent to treat with Tyrconnell, he said, was Major-General Richard Hamilton.

The government liked the idea. Hamilton was then on the Isle of Wight where most of the Irish troops were being kept until things settled down. Hamilton was Irish and 'he was a Papist, but was believed to be a man of honour, and he had certainly great credit with the earl of Tyrconnell'.[34] In fact the two men were very well known to each other as Tyrconnell's wife was the widow of Hamilton's brother. Better still, Hamilton apparently had none of Sarsfield's qualms and agreed straight away to the undertaking. He declared that he was confident that he could win Tyrconnell over and promised to return to London in three weeks' time if he did not. The government let Hamilton go, and Hamilton broke his promise. Whether he had initially intended to keep his word or whether he was just desperate to escape from England is not known, but by the time he reached Dublin all thoughts of his mission were gone. An Irish Protestant noted that 'the Papists lit bonfires when Dick Hamilton came over; they said he was worth ten thousand men'.[35] Tyrconnell greeted him with open arms. The Irish army that had until then been leaderless, now had an experienced new general.

In the meantime Sarsfield remained in London. Given the mood of the time, he was in an unenviable position. On Christmas Eve the House of Lords had ordered that 'all popish officers that shall give bail in six days [are] to appear [on] the first day of the term, and to be of good behaviour in the interim' and those who did not were to be arrested.[36] It was not an order that could be ignored. On 7 January 1689 Sarsfield's troop of horse guards was paid off and disbanded, and those men who wanted to remain in the army were incorporated into a new regiment commanded by Lord Colchester who had been the first of the horse guards officers to desert the king.[37]

Sarsfield was again out of work, and in the eyes of the new government he was most certainly unemployable. He was reported to William for expressing his violent views. William was told that as Sarsfield was 'a man of a desperate and daring nature it might be advisable to secure him for fear he might assassinate his person'. William was unimpressed with the news: 'Let him do it if he dares' was his answer.[38] There were too many dangerous people about to try to seize them all. William was concerned that matters should proceed quietly. Sarsfield and many other officers who were clearly unsuited for the new service were issued with passes to travel to France. Sarsfield went to join his king.

Encouraged by Hamilton's arrival, Tyrconnell set about dealing with the opposition. He packed off the Protestant leader, Lord Mountjoy, to France to 'negotiate' with King James, and sent a secret letter along with him that ensured that Mountjoy was put straight into the Bastille.[39] Messages were sent to France demanding arms and money. The Jacobite cause that had been so easily pushed aside in England was preparing for war in Ireland. Above Dublin Castle flew a flag embroidered with the words: 'Now or Never! Now and Forever!'

Young John Temple was made to feel personally responsible for having put Hamilton's name forward. He received an anonymous message promising that his family would pay for the blood that would be lost in recovering Ireland.

Although he was still trusted by the king and had since been made William's secretary of war, this error of judgment weighed heavily on his conscience. On 19 April 1689, while being rowed up the Thames to Whitehall, he scribbled a note which read: 'My folly in undertaking what I cannot perform has done the king great prejudice which cannot be stopped any other way but this. May his undertakings prosper! May he find a blessing!' And with that he leapt into the water and drowned.[40]

Away from his enemies James was a changed man. It was as if the French air had given him fresh spirit, and he wasted little time in preparing his return. He had hoped to invade England at the head of a French army, but the French rejected the idea. This made it easy for Tyrconnell to persuade him to go to Ireland, and from January 1689 preparations were made to receive him. By mid February Sarsfield was in France, and with Lord Dumbarton, the duke of Berwick and a great many other loyal officers who had recently fled England, he worked to build up the nucleus of an invasion force.[41] Although they had few soldiers with them, it was common knowledge that there would be a plentiful supply of willing men in Ireland.

CHAPTER IV

Return to Ireland

Play, piper — play, piper,
Come lasses, dance and sing,
And old harpers strike up
To harp for the King.
He is come—he is come,
Let us make Ireland ring
With a loud shout of welcome,
May God save the King.
King James's Welcome to Ireland, 1689[1]

BY THE BEGINNING OF 1689 Tyrconnell's position in Dublin was stable. He wrote to James in January that he had seven new regiments ready and had given out commissions to raise forty six others. The Irish army would soon number forty thousand men. But the good news ended there. The men had no arms, uniforms or pay and there was no way to maintain them 'unless by letting them live on the spoils of the people, which in six months' time will destroy both nation and army'.[2] An urgent remedy was needed, the king must arrange for French supplies and money to be shipped to Ireland. And there were other problems that called for speed, and firm attention. The Protestants in Sligo and Ulster had declared for King William. Even before James had fled from England, Tyrconnell's troops had been refused entry to Londonderry. The north was now clearly preparing for war. The massacres of 1641 were not yet fifty years old and Tyrconnell's rule had revived old fears. Ships scudded across the Northern Channel taking Protestant families to Scotland and returned laden with arms. Ireland was on the brink.

The Irish eagerly awaited their king's arrival. Rumours abounded of invading French armies and of landings by Sarsfield. At one time he was reported to be in Killiney Bay and at another to be in Waterford.[3] The reports were premature, but Ireland was confident that help was at hand. The new government in London was criticised for letting such important prisoners go. Sarsfield and the rest should have been confined on the Isle of Wight. 'The indulgence and generosity of his Majesty and his minsters in suffering the Lord Dongan, Colonel Sarsfield and many others of note to have their liberty has produced most ungrateful effects on the other side by increasing the insolency of those in Ireland towards the Protestants.'[4]

At the end of January 1689 Tyrconnell was galvanised into action by the news that James was coming to Ireland. There was now no question of him treating with the Protestants in Ireland or with the English. As he looked to the north he knew that he must crush those who had already declared for William. By the time that James arrived, he hoped to have reduced the whole country to his obedience. The principal centres of Protestant resistance were Sligo, Enniskillen, Londonderry and Hillsborough from where the Williamites effectively controlled the whole of Ulster. They had already struck the first blows by burning down several fortified houses thought likely to be of use to their enemies. Tyrconnell ordered Hamilton to march to the north, and Sarsfield's old commander Justin MacCarthy was sent to Co. Cork to disarm the isolated Protestants of Bandon.

In early March Hamilton marched out of Dublin at the head of three thousand men, the cream of the Irish army. The news of his march sped ahead of him. The new Protestant leader, Lord MountAlexander, hurriedly set about gathering together militiamen from Antrim, Lisburn and Belfast and marched to reinforce Hillsborough, the key to eastern Ulster. He was not quick enough.

Hamilton arrived in Co. Down on 11 March. On the next day, without waiting for MountAlexander's reinforcements, Sir Arthur Rawdon rode out from Hillsborough with the entire garrison of five hundred men to meet the Irish. Rawdon had grossly underestimated the size and the spirit of Hamilton's army. He only discovered his mistake when it was too late to stop. The two forces met at Dromore and the fighting was over in minutes. Rawdon led the remnants of his force in headlong flight back to Hillsborough from what has since been remembered as the 'Break of Dromore'.[5] The hundred or so Williamites whose corpses lay strewn between the two towns were the first casualties in a bloody civil war that was to lay waste to the country for the next two and a half years.

The shock of this rout was so great that Hillsborough was deserted by the time that Hamilton arrived. The Antrim reinforcements retreated to the River Bann without firing a shot and MountAlexander took ship to Scotland. The battle for the north seemed all but won.

Meanwhile King James was in Brest poised to set sail for Ireland. He had left St Germain on 13 February. King Louis had seen him off with the words 'The best that I can say to you is that we shall never see each other again'.[6] Accompanied by a bodyguard of French cavalry and most of the English, Scots and Irish who had fled England to serve him, the king reached the coast on the 23rd. And there he waited for the weather to break.[7]

The French allocation of twenty two ships was not large enough to carry all James's men at once. It was decided that the fleet would make two voyages, the first with the king and the officers, and the second with the stores, the ammunition and some two thousand soldiers. King Louis also provided James with an experienced general to direct the coming campaign. He was Lieutenant-General Conrad Rosen, a fiery-tempered (and some said mad), ill-mannered, and unpopular Latvian who had served the French crown for forty years. A contingent of French officers accompanied him, lured on by the promise of promotion, as did the French king's special ambassador, Count d'Avaux.[8]

4 Richard Talbot, duke of Tyrconnell.

As if to ensure a quiet voyage, these officers from four nations were segregated on the ships.[9] The *Furieux,* for example, carried only Scots; the *Faucon* only English; the *Entreprenant* (with one exception) carried only Frenchmen, whereas the Irish officers travelled on the *Apollon, Sage, Neptune* and *Duc*. Sarsfield sailed on this last ship in the company of his cousin, Sir Randal MacDonnell, Sir Neal O'Neill, an Antrim landowner, Colonel Roger MacElligott, and a number of subalterns from MacElligott's regiment. At the time of the revolution MacElligott's Irish regiment was still in Portsmouth. The men had subsequently been disarmed and interned on the Isle of Wight. The plan had been to ship them off to Germany to fight for the Holy Roman Emperor but most of them, MacElligott included, had escaped on the way and gone to France from where they now found themselves going home.

King James set sail on the *Saint Michel* with his two illegitimate sons, James Fitzjames, the duke of Berwick, and Henry Fitzjames, the grand prior. He was also accompanied by his closest advisors, the Scotsman Lord Melfort and the Englishman Lord Thomas Howard, and keeping a watchful eye on them all was the French ambassador, Count d'Avaux. On the same day that Hamilton scattered the king's enemies at Dromore, 10 March, the wind changed to the south west and the fleet left harbour. The three-day crossing was a smooth one untroubled by either the weather or the English fleet. The only ship that the convoy met with was an English merchantman. On 12 March they lay at anchor off Kinsale harbour. The townspeople thronged along the quayside to greet the king who was rowed ashore to a tumultuous welcome from the crowd and a three gun salute from the fort. His officers followed him and dined ashore, little thinking, perhaps, that many of them would never dine in another country again.

The king spent three days in Kinsale to recover from the voyage and on the fourth he rode to Cork where he was again met by joyous crowds in 'their rude and barbarous manner, by bagpipes, dancing [and by] throwing their mantles under his horse's feet'.[10] He was also met by Tyrconnell, who was rewarded for his good work with a dukedom, and by a group of Protestant clergymen led by the bishops of Chester and Cork.

Just before James's arrival in Kinsale, Sarsfield's old commander, Justin MacCarthy, quietly took the town of Bandon from the 'nest of rebels' that had held it. He had simply marched his men in through the open gates while the townspeople were engaged in their Sunday services. This bloodless coup was ruined on the following day, 'Black Monday', when eight of the Irish soldiers left to guard the town were killed and the rest were chased out. The Protestants raised a flag on which were written the words 'No Surrender'. It was a futile gesture. They had few arms, no supplies, no hope of relief and MacCarthy's force was simply too powerful. He re-entered the town and rounded up the culprits, but instead of hanging them there and then, he took them to Cork so that they might explain their behaviour to the king.

This humane action, as it was intended to be, caused a certain amount of irritation. MacCarthy's nephew and second in command, the twenty year old earl of Clancarty, was said to be in favour of making an example of the Bandon Protestants.[11] The story was that he set about gathering support for the idea of punishing the rebels harshly. Sarsfield refused to side with him on the ground that he preferred to leave their fate to the king's discretion, but Clancarty did get James's son, the duke of Berwick, to support him. James was unimpressed. 'To the first [Clancarty] he said, he was a young man. And to the latter [Berwick] that he was a fool.'[12] When MacCarthy got the Bandonians to petition the king for mercy, James seized the opportunity to show his intended goodwill to all his Protestant subjects and forgave them. 'You may now see', he said, 'you have a gracious king'.[13] Grateful though they no doubt were to James, the people of Bandon were perhaps more impressed by Clancarty's attitude. Shortly afterwards, thirty of them took ship and fled to Bristol.[14]

From Cork James travelled to Dublin where he arrived on Palm Sunday, 24 March. The crowds were the largest he had seen in Ireland. He made a triumphant entry into the city and on hearing the pipers playing 'The King Enjoys His Own Again' as he entered the castle, he was so overcome by emotion that he wept.[15] The next day he issued a proclamation promising freedom of religion for all and announced that he was calling an Irish parliament to sit on 7 May.

While James was in Dublin Castle, one of his most pressing tasks was to reorganise the army to accommodate the wealth of professional soldiers that he had brought over from France. This was not difficult as Tyrconnell had of necessity appointed men to positions well above their level of experience or ability. Even so, there was such a shortage of professional officers that even the newly arrived men found themselves promoted to ranks that they had never before held. At the instigation of Tyrconnell and d'Avaux, Sarsfield was promoted to brigadier, despite James's objections. According to d'Avaux, although James thought that Sarsfield was a very good man, he said that he had nothing in his head.* But despite his mixed opinion the king not only agreed to Sarsfield's promotion, he also gave him the colonelcy of the best cavalry regiment in the Irish army.[16] This regiment had until then been commanded by a German Protestant, Colonel Theodore Russell, who subsequently fled to the north to join the rebels.

Sarsfield's task as a brigadier in those early days of the war was purely administrative. He was to tour the country and disband any regiments or parts of regiments that were too large to be supplied either with arms or money. The Irish army had grown very rapidly during the first three months of 1689. Many men had banded together, often under a local worthy or senior member of their family as a captain, and they now formed themselves into regiments with anything as many as thirty companies. Although William's government was greatly concerned by reports that Tyrconnell commanded fifty thousand soldiers,

---

* 'Le Roy disant que c'estoit un fort brave homme, mais qui n'avoit point de teste.'

the ill-trained Irish volunteers had become something of a joke.[17] Many of the companies did not possess a single musket. The men were armed with clubs, knives and pikes. They had no uniforms and often no shoes. More importantly, they often had no food nor any pay to buy some. It was decided to reduce the army to thirty-five thousand men as that was considered, somewhat optimistically, to be the maximum number that the government could reasonably be expected to support.

Sarsfield's instructions were to visit the towns where new regiments had been raised and to reduce their numbers by dismissing those men he felt less well suited to fight for their king and country. The plan was to reduce each regiment to thirteen companies, the standard number for the Irish establishment.

In mid April he arrived in Birr in King's County[18] (now Offaly). The situation in that small town was not dissimilar to that in many others in mid-Ireland away from the centres of Protestant resistance. There had been a social revolution on a local scale. The Protestant landowner was under lock and key in his own dungeon, and the Protestant traders lived in fear, unable to resist or to claim compensation when their goods were commandeered. There had been a break-down of law and order in the countryside and the Protestant farmers had been forced to come into the town for their own safety. The new power in the area was both Irish and Catholic.

The castle and townland of Birr was owned by Sir Lawrence Parsons, a second generation Irishman of English Protestant stock. During Tyrconnell's viceroyalty, Parsons had left for England with his wife and children after his wife had been accused by a servant of making a treasonable remark, a charge which would have been laughed at two years earlier. But in the changed political climate it was a very dangerous accusation. When he left Birr, Parsons appointed one Hewar Oxburgh, who had worked for the Parsons family for half a century, to manage the estate in his absence. Oxburgh was to receive the rents on the estate, pay off Parsons's debts and send Parsons five hundred pounds a year. But after the first year, Parsons had only received two hundred pounds and so, leaving his family in Cheshire, he returned to Birr. On his arrival in April 1688 he found many changes. His estate manager was now not only the colonel of a new regiment, but the sheriff of King's County 'and was grown and swollen to such a height of pride he scarce owned his master'.

Parsons demanded to know what had become of his money. It transpired that Oxburgh had not even been paying off Parsons's debts. Instead, he had spent the rents on raising a regiment of foot and a troop of horse and on paying the troops as Tyrconnell had sent no money for three months. Parsons, who had returned to Birr to dismiss Oxburgh, now found him immovable. Oxburgh told Parsons that 'if there were any wars in Ireland, he must expect no favour'. Parsons laughed at him.

In the first months of 1689, when Ireland was on the brink of civil war, a powerful gang of tories terrorised the countryside around Birr. One of the results was that eighty local Protestants came into the town to seek Parsons's

Map I: A General Map of Ireland, 1689–91
based on a map in J.G. Simms, *Jacobite Ireland*

protection. He did what he could and sheltered them in the castle. Oxburgh then made his move. He told Parsons that he, as sheriff of the county and a colonel in the king's army, intended to garrison the castle with his regiment. Parsons understandably wanted nothing of the sort and locked him out, but Oxburgh was determined. That night he set his regiment to undermine the walls. Parsons had no choice but to agree to Oxburgh's terms and allow his men in. Parsons and four others were locked up, and when a month later the assizes were sitting at Philipstown,* Oxburgh had Parsons taken there to be tried on a charge of high treason for keeping a garrison against the king.

The judge was Sir Henry Lynch, 'a passionate, furious, bigoted papist'. He directed the jury to find Parsons guilty, called him 'a notorious villain', and sentenced him to be hanged, drawn and quartered. Parsons was returned to Birr as a convict, granted a temporary reprieve and left to await the outcome of his appeal.

The twenty-two companies of Hewar Oxburgh's regiment, now swollen to over fifteen hundred men, were in April 1689 quartered in Birr. Two of the companies were garrisoned in the castle. Additionally, in the town, there was a troop of horse commanded by Oxburgh's son John and an independent foot company, commanded by a Lieutenant-Colonel Grace. Birr, then a small village, had the appearance of a military camp.

A few days after Parsons's return to Birr, Oxburgh received the news that Tyrconnell was going to visit the town. Parsons's cousin, who had been allowed to remain in the castle, was ordered out to make way for the lord lieutenant. Oxburgh had some oxen and sheep belonging to local Protestants slaughtered for the feast. The regiment prepared itself for the inspection. The camp and the town were in a state of excitement.

But sadly for Oxburgh, Tyrconnell did not come. Brigadier Sarsfield rode in instead, and Oxburgh's initial disappointment was to be exacerbated when he learnt the purpose of the visit. Worse still, not only had he come to Birr to trim down the regiment, but Sarsfield showed an unexpected interest in those unhappy prisoners now held in the castle. As one of them noted, he 'carried himself very liberally to all people, and made no distinction between Protestants and Papists but courteously treated them alike'.

Word of this soon got back to Sir Lawrence Parsons in his dungeon and he quickly scribbled a message to Sarsfield begging for a short interview. This Sarsfield granted him. Parsons told him that he needed help. He was a condemned man sentenced by a biased judge to a gruesome fate for a crime that both he and his accusers knew he was innocent of (all but innocent any-way). There had been a suggestion that there would be an exchange of prisoners between Ireland and England, and that he might be released. Parsons asked Sarsfield if he would help him, and Sarsfield was sympathetic. He would do what he could. He even enquired about the conditions of Parsons's imprisonment and was told that Parsons was not fed or clothed by his captors but had to rely

---

*   Daingean, Co. Offaly, thirty-three miles away.

on the charity of his neighbours for his food. And his neighbours could ill afford it. Sarsfield was 'seemingly much concerned' at this situation and spoke to Oxburgh. Why was Parsons not being fed? Oxburgh pointed out that he had received insufficient pay from Dublin for his own men. Who was going to pay for the prisoners? Was Oxburgh to pay out of his own pocket for food for the king's enemies? Sarsfield told him to give Parsons a weekly allowance for his food, and an order would be made out and sent to Dublin to reimburse the colonel.*

Sarsfield then set about the main business of his visit. The twenty two companies of Oxburgh's Regiment were paraded on a meadow in Birr, some fifteen hundred men in ragged ranks. Despite the great number of officers and ladies present to watch the review, it was a dismal spectacle. Most of the men were unarmed and without uniforms. Many had no shoes. Sarsfield set about dismissing almost a third of them. Those that looked the fittest or the best equipped were to stay, the rest were to go. By the time that he had finished the necessary thirteen companies were all that remained.

A very peculiar incident then took place. During the parade, the rumour got about that the regiment was to be sent to Derry. On hearing this, two of the privates who had been chosen to remain in arms threw down their weapons, broke ranks and ran off. 'Colonel Sarsfield seeing it, threw off his jackboots, ran after them, and bringing them back commanded them immediately to be shot.' There can have been few stranger sights on a parade ground than that of the tall brigadier sprinting barefoot across the grass in front of a whole regiment to collar a couple of fleeing deserters. This spectacle was followed by that of Mrs Oxburgh and her daughters running from their coach in all their finery, falling on their knees before Sarsfield and begging for the lives of the miserable duo. Sarsfield had a quick temper, but not a bad one. 'The charming beauties so melted this hero's heart he forgave the men.' And so ended the great parade at Birr.

From Birr, Sarsfield travelled the sixteen miles to Portumna on the Shannon, the seat of Lord Clanricarde. Clanricarde's young half-brother, Lord Galway, who was not yet twenty, had raised the biggest regiment in Connaught. It was made up of perhaps as many as four thousand men divided into fifty-six un-trained, ill-disciplined, unpaid and ill-equipped companies. Sarsfield dealt with them as he had done with Oxburgh's troops. He dismissed them all except those he judged to be the fittest and best equipped, again leaving thirteen companies only. Clanricarde's family naturally bore Sarsfield no ill will for this. A large regiment had been a means of showing the king their loyalty, but it had become a crippling financial liability. Sarsfield's visit had been most welcome.

The disbanded men generally drifted off home, mostly relieved that they were safe, for the moment at least, from having to march across Ireland and face the guns of Derry, although also perhaps disappointed at being denied a soldier's pay. Many of them had only volunteered within the last two months. There had

---

* 'This was promised to be done, but not thought on afterwards.'

been no fighting in the vicinity, and their homes were as they had left them. But the short and generally inadequate experience of military life had an un-settling effect on many of those now dismissed. A whole new world had been opened up them. Banditry became a national pastime. As the Protestant chronicler of Birr wrote:

> These disbanded men of both regiments and all the others that were laid aside throughout the kingdom were ordered by the priest of every parish to arm themselves with half-pikes and skeans from whence they were called rapparees: *rapparee* signifying in Irish a half-pike as I have been informed. These wild and savage creatures having been long idle, could not betake themselves to their work again, at which they were never good, but being encouraged by the priests they armed themselves with half-pikes and skeans and what other weapons they could get, and in great numbers rose all over the kingdom and robbed, spoiled, plundered, and murdered their English neighbours where any opposition was made and they overcame. These outrages were complained of to the late King James, upon which there was in every county Commissioners of Oyer and Terminer* appointed who did sometimes hang such notorious villains against whom there was such pregnant proof (that) justice could not for shame be denied; but if there was any the least failure of evidence, both judge and jury being red letter men,** the fellow escaped and often after the judge and jury had done their duty, if any of the Irish army met with the criminal they rescued him.

Although this anonymous writer was especially concerned with the suffering of his fellow Protestants, they were not the only ones to suffer. The very poor, and there were a great many of them, had nothing to lose and saw the rapparees as no great evil. The soldiers often sympathised as but for their better fortune they could well be reduced to leading a similar life style. But those Catholics who did have property were as likely to be robbed as the Protestants. Banditry rarely discriminates, and although at a later stage of the war the rapparees were used to good effect against the enemy, in 1689 in territory well away from the Protestant militia and the war, they could not claim to be anything other than bandits. Notwithstanding this, the sympathy that many of the Irish had for them ran deep. Oxburgh, for instance, was often threatening to hang rapparees. When on one occasion he did actually decide to make an example of one of them by doing just that, his wife was so furious that she refused to sleep in the same bed as him.§

The war in Ulster had then entered its second stage. The shock of Dromore had thrown the Williamites into disarray. Hamilton's forces swept through Down and Antrim without meeting any organised resistance. Few Protestants felt that the Irish could be stopped. The entire aristocracy of the north and most of the officers took ship to Scotland.

---

*   A judicial panel 'to hear and to determine'.
**   Roman Catholics, saints' days in the Roman Missal being printed in red.
§   The chronicler explains that she was a Coghlan and 'a great upholder of the Irish'.

The only obstacle between Hamilton and western Ulster was the River Bann. The command structure of the Williamite forces had broken down and the remaining officers were quarrelling as to how the campaign should be conducted. They concentrated their forces at Coleraine and beat off an Irish attack. Their defence on this occasion was so well conducted that the Irish only escaped heavy casualties because the Williamites had so effectively barricaded themselves inside the town that they could not get out to give chase.

It was only a temporary triumph, but it showed that the Irish could be beaten. Within two days Hamilton's men crossed the river in boats at Toome and Portglenone and marched up the western bank. Rather than be trapped in Coleraine, the defenders fled to Derry, their leaders accusing each other of stupidity or cowardice. There was a second flight of officers to Scotland. In fact, anyone who could afford to left. The governor of Londonderry, Colonel Robert Lundy, was caught up in the general indecision and panic. He made a last attempt to stop Hamilton on the River Finn. He divided his men to prevent a crossing at each of the likely fords, but it was too late. The Irish were confident of success, especially now that they had been joined by those experienced officers who had accompanied the king from France. They swept the Protestant troops aside at Clady and Lifford. This was the Battle of the Fords. It was as much of a rout as Dromore had been. Only at Castlefinn was the crossing frustrated, but being out-flanked even there the Ulstermen had to withdraw to the safety of the walls of Derry. Lundy sent his English reinforcements away by sea. By the time that the Irish army stood before the walls, the Williamite leadership in Ireland had disappeared. There was only one man of the rank of colonel in the country, and that was Lundy. The next most senior officers, Michelburne and Baker, were two recently appointed majors. The Irish-born Baker had no wartime experience and had only recently been prevented from fleeing to Scotland when his own men opened fire on him.[19] The forty-one year old Michelburne had been in the army since he was a boy, but most of his military career had been in the ranks.

While Sarsfield was in the midlands disbanding the companies that James's government could not afford to equip, the king appeared before Londonderry. He wanted to avoid more bloodshed and felt that his presence would induce his misguided Protestant subjects to negotiate. But the city was so divided that Lundy could not control his men. They opened fire on the king, narrowly missing him. Lundy, who had been willing to treat, now had to be guarded in his room for his own safety. The violent faction in the city regarded him as a traitor. He, the most experienced Protestant officer in Ireland, was forced to creep out of the city at night disguised as a private soldier and to sail for Scotland. Londonderry shifted quickly from anarchy to a popular election of leaders, and for the next three months its destiny was placed in the hands of five unlikely men— George Walker, a boastful, speechifying country parson: Henry Baker, an inexperienced garrison lieutenant: Adam Murray, a young Donegal farmer: Hugh Hamill, a Tyrone lawyer: and John Michelburne, a quick-tempered and foulmouthed sergeant from Horsted Keynes in Sussex.[20] So began the most celebrated siege in the history of the British Isles.

CHAPTER V

Sligo

Tyrconnell: Thus far the cause has with success been crowned
And great Saint Patrick blessed his sacred ground;
He's been his own loved countrymen's defence
And chased the English toads and serpents hence.

The Royal Voyage, I.i., 1690

SLIGO HAD BEEN EVACUATED, on Lundy's orders, even before Richard Hamilton had left Dublin. This decision was later much regretted by the Williamites as Sligo was, apart from Derry, the only town in their hands that was sufficiently fortified to withstand an attack from the Irish army. Those few men of Sligo who could afford to took ships for Scotland, but the majority of them took the road to Enniskillen where they were joined by farmers from all over the north west.

Enniskillen was not a walled town. In early 1689 its only fortified building was the small castle that had been built by the Maguires in the previous century. It would crumble to dust under the fire of field artillery, let alone siege guns. Despite this, the very number of refugees in the town had increased its importance. Enniskillen had become the capital of a Protestant country. The newly swollen population unanimously elected as their governor the half-Swedish Gustavus Hamilton, one of the few remaining local men of any wealth.[1] Confident in that there was no effective opposition in the counties of Donegal and Fermanagh, he decided that attack was the best form of defence. Troops of horsemen from Enniskillen now rode about the countryside at will destroying anything that might be of use to their enemies, and driving back all the cattle that they came across.

The Irish in Donegal and Fermanagh lay low. They were isolated, leaderless and very few of them were armed. Wherever they assembled and resolved to hold a village or a fortified house for King James, they were attacked and chased off by rough riders from Enniskillen. The Dublin government was too preoccupied with eastern Ulster to support them other than by sending a small force under Lord Galmoy into the area in March. As he had too few men to take on the Enniskilleners, Galmoy had attempted to frighten them into surrendering. He sent the news before him that he intended to hang the minister of Enniskillen 'higher than Haman was'*[2] and to put the entire population to the sword if he was resisted. He attacked Crom Castle, an outpost on Upper Lough Erne, but was forced to withdraw from even this modest objective as he had no cannon.

* Which was on a gibbet fifty cubits high (Esther vii, 10).

His expedition was in every way a miserable failure in that it served only to increase the Enniskilleners' confidence and to instill into them a fresh sense of outrage. Galmoy had parleyed with the Enniskilleners over the possible exchange of Captain Woolstan Dixie, who he had taken prisoner, and Captain Brian Maguire, an Irish officer then being held in Enniskillen. Captain Maguire was released, but Dixie, who had been captured in possession of a commission to raise troops for King William, was tried for treason, found guilty and then hanged on a signpost. Reports reached Enniskillen that he had then been decapitated and that his head had been given to the Irish soldiers to use as a football in the market place at Belturbet.[3] If the Enniskilleners had been wavering before Galmoy's visit, he left them united and determined.

While James, irritated and disappointed by his failure at Londonderry, travelled to Dublin, Sarsfield was leaving Athlone. He had been ordered by Tyrconnell to march northwards and to secure Sligo, 'the gateway to Connaught'. To do this he was given the largest body of soldiers that he had yet commanded: two thousand men divided into thirty-five foot companies and four troops of dragoons and cavalry.[4]

Sarsfield's force entered Sligo unopposed on about 1 May 1689. Waiting for him was a motley group of volunteers led by a local lawyer, Counsellor Terence MacDonogh. MacDonogh, or 'Blind' MacDonogh as he was known (he only had one eye),[5] had been active since the Protestant Association had evacuated the town but had been able to do little more than sit tight in Sligo and wait for reinforcements. The few men that he commanded were locally recruited and untrained. They could never have held Sligo against an attack from Ulster and were not even capable of challenging the foraging parties that rode out from Ballyshannon. But Sarsfield's arrival changed all that and the Enniskilleners now found themselves caught between the new garrison at Sligo and the royal army outside Derry.

James returned to Dublin partly because the opening of Parliament was due to take place in the King's Inns on 7 May. Tyrconnell had already arranged the distribution of the election writs to the sheriffs and mayors throughout the counties and boroughs in those parts of the country under Dublin's control. With these had been sent letters from Tyrconnell recommending the candidates to be elected. This was not to be a contested general election. Throughout the weeks after James's arrival in the country, Dublin clerks had been busily choosing the representatives who were to sit in the House of Commons. Although his military commitments were to ensure that he would never attend, Patrick Sarsfield was nominated and elected as one of the two members for Co. Dublin. Blind MacDonogh was elected to sit for the borough of Sligo, and in Birr the sheriff of King's County, Hewar Oxburgh, was instructed to arrange his own election, which he did.[6]

James was to be much criticised for calling an Irish Parliament. He wanted to raise taxes to pay for the war in the north and the invasion of Scotland, and so as to allay the fears of his Protestant subjects he wanted to ensure that the Irish rallied behind him in a quiet and legitimate fashion. But his new Parliament proved to be far from conciliatory. No time was wasted in repealing King Charles's Act of Settlement, passing an act of attainder naming some two and a half thousand people as traitors, and legislating for the confiscation of their land. The Parliament was in every way ill timed. Even as the Lords and Commons debated less aggressive subjects such as debasing the coinage and ensuring liberty of conscience, the fiercest fighting to date was taking place around the walls of Derry.

Sarsfield was one of those who had no time for the Parliament. As soon as he had entered Sligo and met MacDonogh he set about making preparations for the second part of his mission. His objective was that part of the River Erne that flows between Lower Lough Erne and the sea. There his troops would be able to prevent supply ships from getting in or out of Enniskillen. This had been the great fear of the Enniskilleners from the start and as early as December 1688 the governor, Gustavus Hamilton, had garrisoned and fortified the town of Ballyshannon at the river's mouth. The threat now posed to this vital line of communication was so serious that all other activity ceased while Enniskillen concentrated on Sarsfield.

In particular, Sarsfield's presence put a stop to those 'insolences' committed by a body of rough riders led by a very able young commander, Lieutenant-Colonel Thomas Lloyd. Lloyd had recently demolished the Irish posts at Augher and Trillick so successfully that he was known in Enniskillen as the 'Little Cromwell'. The son of a Roscommon settler, Lloyd may well have been known to Sarsfield as he had begun his military career in 1685 as a cornet in Sarsfield's company of Richard Hamilton's dragoons, a regiment in which Sarsfield had nominally served for only a few days.[7] Although still not yet twenty-five, he was to prove to be a very dangerous opponent. A contemporary of Lloyd's later wrote of him that he was:

> A good sort of man, he was vigilant, careful, active, of a great soul, very observing, slipped no opportunity that offered to gain his end, and besides a man of unwearied industry and good intelligence, and for his personal valour, few went beyond him.[8]

Leaving Sligo well garrisoned, Sarsfield made for Ballyshannon. It was, he was told, a small place and he should be able to take it with ease. He was misled. He reached the town on 4 May to find that the garrison was ready for him. His every move had been watched by vedettes posted across the countryside. By the time his men had blocked the roads from Ballyshannon the garrison commander, Captain Henry Folliot, had sent riders off to Enniskillen for help.

Ballyshannon was surprisingly well fortified. It contained two strongholds. The first of these, the fort, possessed two thick outer walls surrounded by a

5 A Prospect of Sligo painted by Thomas Phillips in 1685. Note the Stone Fort in the centre of the town, and the Earth Fort on the high ground to the right of the picture.

twenty-five foot wide ditch flooded with twelve feet of water. The defenders had thrown up sturdy earthworks to enable them to cover the approaches with their muskets and cannons. The only means of access was by drawbridge. Inside the defences stood an imposing old keep which was itself surrounded by another moat which in places measured forty feet across.[9] The second strong point, the church, was also surrounded by a sturdy and well defended wall. It was situated in a commanding position overlooking the town, and it is there that Folliot placed his heavy ordnance.[10]

For Sarsfield, the extent of these defences was an unwelcome discovery. The Enniskillen raiders had been so successful in keeping the Irish at bay that MacDonogh's intelligence had proved to be all but useless. He had only brought two small field guns from Sligo, not to conduct a siege but to fire on the shipping that might attempt to slip up the narrow waterway. Sarsfield could not concentrate on the river while sandwiched between the enemy garrisons at Ballyshannon and Enniskillen.

Sarsfield summoned Folliot to surrender the town and all the cattle that had been herded inside. Folliot's answer was predictable. Confident in his sturdy defences, his superior firepower and in the knowledge that the whole of Enniskillen would soon descend on Sarsfield like a swarm of hornets he refused to budge.

Sarsfield's problems were not confined to Ballyshannon. He was now in hostile country. Four miles away on the Enniskillen road lies Belleek and five miles beyond is Castle Caldwell, then held by Sir James Caldwell. The bridge at Belleek, then described as being 'a great pass between the provinces of Connaught and Ulster'[11] had been broken down. Sir James had collected his men on the north bank of the Erne and had thrown up breastworks at all the fords to prevent anyone crossing, and Castle Caldwell was barricaded and garrisoned with four hundred well equipped and provisioned men. Sarsfield could not afford to ignore Caldwell and so was obliged to divide his forces between Ballyshannon and Belleek.

He detached almost all of his mounted troops and sent them off together with some infantry along the road to Belleek. The rest of his infantry remained around Ballyshannon, although they could do little more than keep Folliot's garrison in check. As he feared that he did not have enough men to withstand a determined sally from the town he had his two cannons mounted on Fish Island, a flat sandy islet in the estuary where they could not be overrun. From there they could fire both on any shipping that might try to enter the river and also on the town to remind Folliot that he was supposed to be under siege. The cannons and the sixty troops on the island were left under the eager command and watchful eye of Terence MacDonogh

When Gustavus Hamilton received Folliot's message he acted immediately. He drew men in from his outposts and gathered them in the town. By nightfall on the 6th he had assembled a strike force of a thousand men and in the early hours of the morning Lloyd set out to relieve Ballyshannon. He took with him twelve infantry companies and some troops of Enniskillen horse who acted as outriders and scouts. They marched along the south side of Lough Erne, past the ruined village and castle of Tully where nearly fifty years before wild Rory Maguire had massacred the Scottish settlers, and along that narrow and dangerous stretch of land that lies between the Magho Cliffs and the brown waters of the lough.

The road from Enniskillen ran through Belleek, then a small village at the northwestern end of the lough. That part of the village that was on the north bank of the Erne was occupied by Caldwell's men. Belleek was then almost encircled by bog and water. The level of the lough in the seventeenth century was considerably higher than now and the flat land around it was wholly undrained. The land to the south was one large bog of the worst type that stretched from Lough Erne to the sea and down to the Drowes River by Tullaghan. Although there were scattered settlements on the higher ground, most of this area was so wet that the road had been built upon a long and narrow causeway between the bog and the water. It appeared to be an easy place to defend. Sarsfield had a bridge on the causeway broken down and erected a barricade on his side behind which he placed his musketeers. His cavalry, which was a mixture of both regular soldiers and MacDonogh's Sligo volunteers, stood well back on firmer ground.

Lloyd arrived in the late afternoon.[12] Although his force outnumbered the Irish who had been sent to meet him, he was dismayed at what he saw. He drew up his infantry at the edge of the bog just out of musket range. While they rested and listened to the jeers of the Irish on the barricade, his mounted scouts probed the bog inland. They confirmed the obvious. It was deep and it stretched inland for a very long way. Lloyd was not in a good position. If he could get his men to file along the causeway they would be mown down without being able to return any effective fire. If he retraced his steps to find a way around the bog he could be marching all night. If he advanced directly across the bog it would be slow going and he would risk losing many men as the Irish would pick them off as they floundered about within musket shot of the Irish. However costly it would be, the last option seemed to him to be the best. He ordered his men to start clearing the scrub and to set about bundling wood into faggots to throw in front of the column as they advanced. The Irish could see what was happening and were ready for them.

Then the unexpected happened. Lloyd's troopers who had been scouring the area for an end to the bog picked up a local man who claimed to know a way across the bog. He was brought to Lloyd. The preparations for a frontal attack were abandoned. Captain Acheson led a company of men off as pathfinders and the rest followed him inland. For a short while it seemed as if they had given up. The Irish on the barricade cheered. But their cheers died away as they saw the enemy in column picking their way diagonally away from them across the bog. Suddenly the strong defensive position behind the bridge on the causeway became very unimportant. The enemy were bypassing it. The horsemen mounted up and moved inland to stop the crossing, leaving the infantrymen on the barricade to block the road.

They had acted too late. The Irish were on a peninsula sticking into the bog. The Enniskilleners had succeeded in crossing the bog and had now formed up on the firm ground. One minute the Irish had been unassailable. The next they were face to face with their enemies and were outnumbered. Orders were issued for the men on the barricade to move back to Ballyshannon, and the cavalry prepared to cover their retreat. But panic reached them first.

The men on the barricade ran for it. Sarsfield's horsemen were unwilling to engage the Enniskilleners alone. They retreated to cover the infantry. Just then, they suffered another blow. Sir James Caldwell had led three hundred of his men across the river in boats, with their horses swimming alongside them. They now entered the fray behind the Irish. The Enniskillen horse charged, caught the Irish in disarray, and scattered them. The running battle, in fact a rout, continued as far as Ballyshannon and as many miles inland. Sir James Caldwell later claimed to have led the Enniskillen horse in hot pursuit all the way to Bundrowes. Sarsfield, along with the others, was forced to dig in his spurs.* Only dusk stopped the fighting.

While Lloyd's horse divided into small skirmishing groups, the Enniskillen infantry made haste for Ballyshannon. As they approached, Sarsfield hurriedly ordered his men to abandon their positions and march off towards Sligo. The whole episode had happened so quickly that many of the men outside

---

* Sarsfield's position in this skirmish is unclear. Neither of the two Enniskillen accounts of Andrew Hamilton and William McCarmick make any mention of his presence, but as he was in overall command he would have at least been involved in the final stages of the action. It could well be that he was nearer Ballyshannon than Belleek when Lloyd and Acheson made their way across the bog.

Ballyshannon were taken completely by surprise. Most of them got away but those who had been posted on Fish Island were stranded. Blind MacDonogh, cursing his bad luck, surrendered with his sixty men. Lloyd was not interested in taking prisoners. He selected the better dressed of them, including MacDonogh, to take back to Enniskillen and he had the rest stripped naked and set free. In that state, even in May, it is a long cold night's walk to Sligo from Bally-shannon. The Enniskilleners looked disdainfully at what they had captured. The clothing, stores and equipment were 'beggarly'. The only worthwhile prizes were the two field guns that had kept Folliot's head below the castle walls.

And so it was that on the same day that King James opened the Irish Parliament, the honourable member for Dublin was riding for his life from the king's enemies, and the honourable member for Sligo was being led off to captivity.

Lloyd's losses were negligible. His success was so complete that the action came to be known as 'the Break of Belleek'. Sarsfield had lost heavily, not only in men and equipment, but in face. It was the Enniskilleners' best performance to date, and their first engagement with Irish troops other than those that they had caught in isolated outposts. Morale in Enniskillen was greatly boosted and exaggerated reports reached London. One news sheet declared that 'Sarsfield and five or six more narrowly escaped, the rest being most killed and about two hundred taken'.[13] Another pronounced Sarsfield to be among the dead. As a Jacobite noted, the Enniskilleners 'were much puffed up with their success against Sarsfield'.*[14]

Notwithstanding this, the strategic effects of the skirmish were minimal. Sarsfield remained in occupation of Sligo where he still threatened the Erne. Although they had chased him off, it was by no means certain that the Enniskilleners could continue to hold the line. By the next day Sarsfield had reorganised his men in a forward camp in a stone walled deer-park on Sir William Gore's estate at Manorhamilton, just seventeen miles from Enniskillen. He still remained as great a threat to western Ulster as ever. He had suffered a temporary set-back, and he was determined that his enemies would be made to realise that their success was no more than that. His horsemen harried Belleek and the road along the Erne and a few days later he sent a summons to Sir James at Castle Caldwell to surrender. Sir James later boasted that his answer was 'that the Protestants were then divided from the Papists like the sheep from the goats, and that I would defend the river whilst I had a man to stand by me'.[15] Sarsfield was not destined to have happy memories of Belleek.

Of those who had been taken prisoner by Lloyd the most important by far was Terence MacDonogh who had led the Sligo men since the beginning of the war. His capture along with a number of local men on Fish Island had a serious

* So varying were the reports of this skirmish that Dr J. G. Simms in his standard work on the war was misled into describing two different skirmishes on the Erne (see *Jacobite Ireland*, pp. 114, 115).

Map II: The Upper Shannon and Fermanagh

effect on Irish morale in Sligo. The feeling amongst the local volunteers was such that Sarsfield felt obliged to treat with the enemy. He sent a drummer to Enniskillen to ask for an exchange of prisoners.[16]

Sarsfield's problem was that he had very few prisoners, whereas the garrison of Enniskillen held not only several of his men but also those Irishmen they had captured in other raids, and in any event Gustavus Hamilton was reluctant to treat with the Irish after what had happened to Woolston Dixie at the hands of Lord Galmoy, that 'infamous wretch whom no titles could honour'.[17] However, Sarsfield did have one bargaining strength. Several Protestant land-owners from Connaught had been arrested and held at the beginning of the war for their part in forming the Protestant Associations. They now suffered the same fate as Sir Lawrence Parsons in Birr, and amongst them was Sir Thomas Southwell, who had been the sheriff of Kerry, Limerick and Clare, and who was now imprisoned in Galway gaol. Men such as Southwell were to the Protestants every bit as important as Blind MacDonogh was to the Sligo Catholics. Hamilton arranged for a list of all his prisoners to be drawn up and had it sent to Sarsfield with the message that he would only consider bargaining when he received a list of those held by the Irish.

This reply caused Sarsfield some concern. His own list did not make very long reading. He was not empowered to release people like Southwell from Galway and he was unwilling to ask the government to hand over important prisoners to him so that he could set them free. But the Sligo men were insistent that they should have MacDonogh back. Sarsfield was pushed into adopting a plan that had the result of further embittering the Enniskilleners against the Irish. He had all the Protestants in the county of Sligo rounded up. They were arrested and brought to Sligo regardless of whether they were Williamites or not, regardless of whether or not they had been granted the crown's protection, and regardless of age or sex. All of them were brought to Sligo gaol.

By mid-June the operation was complete. Sarsfield again sent a messenger to the governor of Enniskillen, this time with a full list of all those Protestants now interned in Sligo. They would be released in exchange for MacDonogh and the rest of the captured Irish. Gustavus Hamilton was furious. He sent the messenger back and refused to discuss the matter. The Protestants in Sligo had not been 'taken as prisoners of war, but [had been] forced out of their own private dwellings to be serviceable in redeeming those that we had taken in actual arms.'[18]

Sarsfield did not let the matter rest there. Conditions in Sligo were not particularly good and the gaol was now crowded.* He did not intend to allow

---

*   The Irish also made free with the property of those protestants who had fled to Enniskillen or beyond the seas. Sarsfield was petitioned by Captain Hugh MacDermot, other-wise known by the ancient title of the prince of Coolavin, who had been obliged to pay out about £100 from his own pocket to buy clothing and food for the Sligo garrison. It was agreed that he should be reimbursed from the confiscated goods that were being held in the town.[19]

anyone to die of cold or hunger, but the prisoners were not exactly kept in comfortable conditions. It was suggested to their wives that they were all going to be starved and the women were then released and sent off to walk over the hills to Enniskillen with their letters and petitions for the governor. They were in a bad state when they arrived. They pleaded with Hamilton to release MacDonogh and the others for the sake of their husbands. Hamilton's first reaction was anger. He was damned if he was going to give in to this sort of trickery. But the mood of the garrison was against him. The people of Enniskillen were greatly moved by the pathetic sight of the barefoot Sligo women. Hamilton was forced to concede. He arranged for an exchange of prisoners on Sarsfield's terms.

Hamilton was cautious to the end as he was quite sure that he had every reason to distrust Sarsfield. The prisoners were marched out of Enniskillen under the eyes of a watchful cavalry escort. The man placed in charge, Lieutenant-Colonel Francis Gore, knew the area well as he was a cousin of the Gore who owned the deer park at Manorhamilton where Sarsfield had set up his field headquarters. He led them eight miles in the direction of Sarsfield's camp where he was met by an escort bringing the prisoners from Sligo, and the change over took place without incident. The Irish got MacDonogh back, and the Enniskilleners received into their ranks the welcome addition of enough aggrieved men to form a new company.

In the meantime Lloyd had not been idle. Sarsfield had more to worry about than rounding up prisoners. Now that Ballyshannon was no longer in immediate danger, the Enniskillen raiding parties rode out in all southerly directions. Lloyd firstly led a force into Co. Cavan where he successfully attacked and captured the two Irish strong points at Redhill House and Bellanacargy Castle. He then continued his raid deep into Irish territory and was rumoured to have got to within forty miles of Dublin. The Irish were at a loss to stop him. He attacked any party of Irish troops he came across, destroyed crops and supplies, burnt houses and barns, and rounded up as much cattle and horses as he could. In Dublin it was not clear whether or not a whole army was approaching. Rumours abounded that sixteen thousand Protestant troops were advancing on the capital. Security measures were taken to prevent the Protestants from rising up to receive them. A terror gripped the administration in Dublin Castle. The garrison was weakened and at half strength following the persistent calls for troops for Derry. But Lloyd was in no position to attempt such an enormous task, and he turned back to Enniskillen where his men were desperately needed. He reputedly took with him three thousand head of cattle, two thousand sheep and some five hundred horses loaded with meal. Whatever deprivations the defenders of Londonderry were to suffer, the Enniskilleners were not going to have to resort to eating their cats.

During Lloyd's absence, Gustavus Hamilton had been busy in Enniskillen preparing for his grand design; the relief of Derry. Throughout May and early June the Enniskilleners toiled away with spades and picks building fortifications.

There grew up around the town a system of forts, palisades and trenches. Hamilton's plan was to march out of the town with the majority of his troops and attack the Irish army at Derry in the rear. The newly fortified Enniskillen was to be garrisoned by a small force under Lloyd. This choice was perhaps not the best as Lloyd was nothing if not a raider, whereas Hamilton's achievements had been in overseeing the town's defence and administration. That observation aside, one fact was inescapable, neither man had the necessary experience or training to be able to carry out successfully such an ambitious plan. Nonetheless, when Lloyd returned, Hamilton marched out.

He got as far as Omagh, not even half way to Londonderry. A small Irish garrison had been posted there in a fortified house from where they could cover the barricaded road with their guns. They were not strong enough to sally out and beat off Hamilton but they had to be dislodged if the road to Londonderry was to be cleared. The governor of Enniskillen sent a trumpeter to summon them to surrender. The Irish would not even listen. They told the unfortunate messenger that if he came back a second time they would shoot him on the spot. Hamilton had no artillery with him so he could not blast them out. He set his men about the task of sniping while he considered the problem. It was not one that he could solve. Intelligence came in that the Irish had sent for assistance and that Irish troops led by Lord Clancarty were approaching from the south east on their way to join the main Irish army. This force, he was told, was made up of (at least) two foot regiments and a regiment each of dragoons and of horse. And it was drawing near.

Hamilton lost heart. He could not gamble the whole Protestant interest in Ulster on this adventure. If, while he was sandwiched between Clancarty and the Irish at Omagh, Sarsfield left Manorhamilton and attacked Enniskillen, all could be lost. He ordered a withdrawal, and led his men back to base.

It was a bad plan anyway. He would have led his small force against the best part of the Irish army commanded by James's best officers. The Irish would have known of his approach even if he had succeeded in taking Omagh, and they had enough men to keep Derry bottled up and to attack him at the same time. This episode illustrates the importance of Sarsfield's position at Manorhamilton to the conduct of the siege of Derry. Without his being able to threaten Enniskillen, the besieging army would have found its supply routes difficult to maintain against attacks from Lloyd's raiding parties, and it could even have come under direct attack itself. The siege, difficult though it was, may well have been rendered impossible. The Irish war effort in that case would have had have to been directed at Enniskillen instead, and the war would have taken a very different course.

A few days later the twenty-one year old Clancarty reached the Irish camp outside Londonderry. He immediately prepared himself for a night attack by getting himself drunk and then launched his fresh men against the Butcher's Gate. It was a disastrous attempt. A hundred men were slaughtered to no effect.

General Rosen, who was now the most senior professional soldier in the Irish army, decided against making any more assaults on the city, and his men prepared themselves for a long uneventful blockade where they hoped famine and disease would do their work for them.

To King James, the siege of Derry was of strategic importance. The war that he was now conducting in Ireland was not for Ireland alone, it was for the British Isles. He needed to secure Ireland so that he could take his largely Irish army across the sea to Scotland. He had high hopes of being successful there and he would then be in a position to march into England. The prize that shone in the imagination of all those officers who had come with him from France was London rather than Londonderry. But this last city had proved to be the ruination of many hopes. There were enough rebels within its thick walls to retake Ulster. Coupled with the garrison of Enniskillen they could threaten the whole of Ireland. James's supporters in Scotland desperately needed Irish reinforcements if they were to prevail, but those Irish reinforcements could not be spared while Derry held out. The dreams that the Jacobite officers had of spending Christmas in London had been shattered. If they were lucky, they might still spend Christmas in Edinburgh, but as each day went by even this hope faded. The English were preparing fleets to relieve Ulster. With Derry blockaded and surrounded, James's advisors looked to the one place where English ships could still be welcomed. They decided to take Enniskillen.

The task was initially given to James's nineteen year old son, the duke of Berwick. He led a force to Trillick, some twelve miles from Enniskillen and speedily set about taking the small rebel outpost there. Rather than risk a full attack on Enniskillen itself, he detached Henry Luttrell with his dragoons to attack the town and test its defences. Just outside Enniskillen stood a mill, and it was this building that Luttrell first made for. As it was less than half a mile from the town's outworks, the mill was in range of the defenders' cannons. The gunners waited for Luttrell to reach his objective and then opened fire. Luttrell's dragoons turned and scattered. But the Enniskilleners who leapt onto the parapet to cheer were to be disappointed. The Irish horsemen formed up again just out of range and prepared themselves to meet an attack by the rebel cavalry that was sallying out to meet them. Luttrell ordered the charge and this time it was the Enniskilleners who broke and fled. In fact, so rattled were the defenders by the unexpected professionalism of the Irish, that they all withdrew back to the town and contented themselves in keeping Luttrell at bay with their cannons. The Irish were very pleased with the action and took three officers and twenty-three men back to Trillick as prisoners, boasting that they had killed fifty of their enemies.

Berwick was also very pleased with Luttrell's success but still did not want to risk a full attack on Enniskillen. The town, he reasoned, would fall if it was starved of supplies, and the way to starve it was to prevent any shipping getting up the Erne from England. If this was to be done, it would have to be done quickly as reports had been received that an English fleet was at sea. Berwick sent a message to Sarsfield instructing him to press Ballyshannon a second time and to prevent any shipping entering the Erne. In the meanwhile he would take his men along the northern bank of the Lough to join forces with him.

Sarsfield immediately marched his men to a new camp some five miles from Ballyshannon. Once again Folliot found himself under the threat of siege. Sarsfield waited as he did not have enough men to advance without reinforcements. His total command was now somewhat less than three thousand infantrymen and perhaps two hundred horsemen.

Berwick never came. Shortly after sending his message to Sarsfield, he received instructions from General Rosen. The English fleet had been located in Lough Swilly in Co. Donegal. The supply ships were loaded down with troops and materials for the relief of Londonderry and every available Irish soldier was needed to reintensify the blockade and to prevent an English landing on the Enishowen peninsula. Berwick marched north, and the threat to Enniskillen receded.

An oddity of this period is Sarsfield's already high reputation in the country. When Berwick wrote an affectionate letter to him on the subject of a joint attack on Ballyshannon he addressed Sarsfield as 'Dear Notorious'.[*20] Notorious for what?, one might ask. For being chased away from Ballyshannon? Sarsfield's record in Ireland had not been a great one, but now that he was one of few Irish commanders with an independent command, much was expected of him by his countrymen.

Berwick's departure was immediately felt in the area as with him out of the way, the Enniskilleners could afford to march against Sarsfield, and soon it became clear that they were preparing to do just that. From his camp outside Tullaghan Sarsfield wrote to Major General Anthony Hamilton[**] at Belturbet to suggest that as the enemy could launch an attack on either of them it would be better if they joined forces.[21] His own position was certainly under direct threat. In a letter to Tyrconnell he carefully described an attempt to dislodge him that took place on 18 July 1689.[22]

Sarsfield's camp was on the coast on the western side of the Drowes, the river that flows from Lough Melvin to the sea. In the morning nearly a thousand enemy horsemen led by Sir Gerald Irvine[23], a veteran of the English civil wars, had approached along the shoreline, while another large party of horse and foot

---

*   Deare Notorious

     This is to give you notice that Marecharl Rosen or I will march within three or four days from this place to Balishannon, so that if you looke out sharp this way, you may see us laying on these rebelly and cowring rogues which may give you also an opportunity of attacking on that side of the water to make a divertion. I am afraid the siege of Derry will be raised, and I thank god that I have not nor ever will give my consent unto it. I will say no more this till I meet you at Balishannon. In the meantime, I remain, Deare Notorious,

          Your kind Friend and servant
          Berwick

**   One of Richard Hamilton's two brothers who were to serve as major-generals in the Irish army. The third (and youngest) was John.

crossed over by the fords about a mile inland. Sarsfield was not unduly worried by any of this. Of the mixed force on his right, he noted that:

> The foot continued in the wood by the waterside to make good a retreat for the horse who could receive no hurt from me no more than I from them the ground being so bad on that side, craggy in some places and bog in others.

Sarsfield formed up his cavalry as a 'grandguard' between the enemy infantry and his camp and ordered a battalion of foot to wait behind them. He had already ordered his three field guns into position to face the enemy cavalry on the beach.

> When all was secure on the right I went to the battery upon the left where I made our biggest gun play upon their horse and with every shot made them shift their ground from place to place till at last they withdrew on all sides. They tell me there were some few killed but how many I cannot tell for they were carried off, the truth is we could not well miss them they being very near and really more in number than I could believe.

Sir Gerald Irvine led his men back to Enniskillen, having achieved nothing. On the next day Sarsfield wrote of a further threat:

> I had an account that all the people of Enniskillen are marched last night five miles this side in their way here. I am so well posted that I do not fear them were they double the number, all I apprehend is that they will march the other side (of) the mountain and burn Sligo.

This is a typical example of the optimistic letters that Sarsfield would write throughout the war. On this occasion, despite the great danger he was in, his only complaint was his shortage of 'good horse', and not being aware of the happenings on Lough Swilly, he continued to make plans for the siege of Ballyshannon and for the capture of Enniskillen. He sent messages to Cavan to his old commander, Justin MacCarthy, who had recently been raised to the peerage as Viscount Mountcashel. He told them that he was confident that Ballyshannon would not hold him up for long, and that the way would be open for him to attack Enniskillen from the west. Berwick, he wrote, would march along the Erne and attack from the east. If Mountcashel could join up with Berwick, their success would be guaranteed.

The events that were to follow were beyond Sarsfield's control. As Berwick had withdrawn to Londonderry, Mountcashel was ordered by King James to advance on Enniskillen alone. Mountcashel did not wait. Without wasting any time, he marched towards his objective at the head of his four thousand men. He commanded, it must be said, the worst part of the Irish army. He had very few professional or experienced men with him as all the best troops were being used before the walls of Derry. But nonetheless, the one thing that concerned him was speed. He wanted a forced march straight to the gates of Enniskillen and then a speedy victory. But although he joined forces with Anthony Hamilton, no effort was made to coordinate his attack with an advance by Sarsfield. He did not even ask him for reinforcements. Sarsfield in the meanwhile was waiting for the replies to his dispatches. He did not blockade the Erne, and did not attack Ballyshannon. While he held back, the enemy received intelligence of Mountcashel's advance and five hundred men were sent as reinforcements to Enniskillen from Ballyshannon.

The only obstacle that stood between Mountcashel and Enniskillen was Crom Castle. This sturdy building was well fortified and had already withstood one attempt on it earlier in the year. It would have been so easy for Mountcashel to march straight past and on to Enniskillen, but such was not the military wisdom of the day, and he ordered an attack. As soon as the defending troops in the outworks opened fire on his men, he lost control. His men, wild with ungovernable enthusiasm, threw themselves forward, overran the outworks and chased the defenders back into the castle. This was just what the defenders expected. As the Irish drew near they let loose a tremendous volley of musketry and cannons. Lead balls and cartridge shot ripped through the disorganised mass of charging men. They fell back, realising their mistake too late. They had cannons but had not used them. There was no breach in the walls and no way of getting in. The slaughter had been for nothing. Squinting and cursing his poor eyesight, demanding a running commentary of events from his staff, and howling in exasperation at his troops, Mountcashel sat astride his horse on a nearby vantage point. Unfortunately for him, this was only a foretaste of what was to come. That evening, while the Irish settled down around Crom, Enniskillen was a hive of activity. Messages had already been received from the castle. As there had been no indication that Sarsfield was on the move, a council of war decided to strike the first blow and not wait for the Irish to get any closer.

Mountcashel's failure to give Sarsfield good warning of his plans would cost him dearly. English ships had been sailing up the lough and landing supplies in Enniskillen. They had brought weapons, powder, ammunition, clothing, shoes and blankets, and most important of all they had brought an excellent English professional soldier, Colonel William Wolseley. The Enniskilleners had never been in a better position to fight.

At dawn on the next morning, 31 July 1689, Wolseley's second in command, Lieutenant-Colonel William Berry left Enniskillen with all the horsemen he could muster and sped off towards Crom. Wolseley followed with the infantry, trudging through the dust on a glorious Sunday morning in their new scarlet uniforms.

The Irish vedettes on the Enniskillen road sped back to Mountcashel with the news of Berry's approach, and the camp prepared for action. Crom was forgotten about. Major-General Anthony Hamilton ordered his regiment of dragoons to mount up and rode off to block Berry's advance. At Lisnaskea he met the first rebel horsemen and undaunted made straight for them. Berry retreated and with wild yells the Irish gave chase, straight into the ambush that Berry had prepared for them. The Irish dragoons wheeled about and scattered with the Enniskilleners close behind, picking them off with horse pistols and slashing at their backs with sabres. It was later said of Anthony Hamilton that he did not pull up his horse until he reached Navan, sixty miles away. His dragoons were completely routed and made no attempt to return to Mountcashel. This setback was considerably more serious than the previous day's fiasco at Crom as Mountcashel's infantry had now been left to fight alone.

Mountcashel's heart was full of foreboding as he led his army to Newtown-butler.[24] There was still no news from Sarsfield, and he resolved to fight alone. He knew that his men were not the best but they were enthusiastic. If he could find a good defensive position they would be good on the counterattack, and Newtownbutler provided him with just such a position.

The village of Newtownbutler lies on low ground. To its south was a bog, and south of the bog was a steep wooded hill. The road from Enniskillen ran through all three. Mountcashel ordered the village to be burnt and he lined his men up on the hill. Where the road ran through the bog it was supported by a narrow causeway where no more than two men could ride abreast and at the southern end of this causeway he placed his cannon.

Wolseley approached the burning village with caution. Although he had joined forces again with Berry's horsemen, as he came in view of the hill he realised how outnumbered he was. He had two thousand men, Mountcashel had twice that number. He was not frightened of fighting those to the front, but he feared being attacked by Sarsfield in the rear. The rumour spread that the plume of smoke rising from Newtownbutler was a signal to Sarsfield's brigade to join Mountcashel. Wolseley called a general council of war. Was he to fight or was he to retire to defend Enniskillen? The men knew what they wanted. They wanted to fight. The small army pushed through the village and formed up on the blackened smoking ground. There was only one way to get to the Irish and that way was through the bog.

The battle at Newtownbutler was a brief affair. As the hot weather had partly dried it up, the bog proved not to be a very difficult obstacle. After a general shout of 'No Popery', the infantry advanced, albeit slowly, straight through the middle. The Irish fired volleys at them, but the Enniskilleners did not break. The front Irish rank on the left did. Wolseley's infantry rushed and took the guns so that Berry could lead his men over the causeway. Those horsemen still with Mountcashel turned and fled the field. More infantry waded through the bog, and the Irish army became seized with a general panic. They turned and ran.

After half an hour, Mountcashel's army no longer existed. Scattered groups and individuals ran back down the road. Berry's horsemen soon overtook them and cut them down. The only escape was through the bogs or into the loughs where many of them drowned. Parties of Enniskilleners moved through the woods seeking out fugitives and killing them. The slaughter continued into the night.

Mountcashel did not flee. He sheltered in a small copse near the front while the advance passed him by. Then, with five or six of his officers alongside him, he spurred his horse forward at the guns that were now in the enemy's hands. The guards presumed that he was an Enniskillener and allowed him to close with them. He pulled out his pistol and fired. Seven or eight of the guards promptly fired back. Mountcashel's horse was shot under him and he was seriously wounded in several places. A guard ran forward to club his brains out, but was stopped when one of the Irish officers shouted out to him who the wounded man was. As Mountcashel was led away a prisoner, he told his captors that he was unwilling to outlive that day and was sorry to have survived. It was noted of him that 'he did all a brave man could do'.[25]

The Irish casualties at Newtownbutler were high. Perhaps as many as a thousand Irishmen were killed by the Enniskilleners, the vast majority of them in the rout. All the Irish cannon and baggage was captured and five hundred prisoners were taken. Colonel Wolseley's force was reported to have suffered less than one hundred casualties. Although the Enniskilleners were far from finished in this war, this was their finest hour. Their reputation for bravery was now established. As one impressed officer wrote, 'I have seen 'em like masty dogs run against bullets.'[26]

In Mountcashel's pocket was found the letter from Sarsfield outlining his plan for the attack on Enniskillen.[27] The letter made it clear that Sarsfield was prepared to advance, and may have already done so. What a blow it would have been for Wolseley if he had managed to defeat Mountcashel only to find Enniskillen burnt and sacked in his absence. He lost no time in getting back. His men were allowed no rest until they collapsed, exhausted, within the town's defences. 'If Sarsfield continues in his camp until Tuesday', said Wolseley, 'I'll visit him'.[28]

It was not long before Sarsfield heard of the disaster at Newtownbutler. It was idle even to contemplate a lone attempt on Enniskillen when the carefully laid plan had been for a three pronged attack, and in the meantime his men were doing no good exposing themselves to danger around Ballyshannon. This was clear even in Dublin, and James issued orders that he pull back.[29] He withdrew all the way to the security of Sligo. Captain Folliot kept a careful eye on his movements and sent runners to Enniskillen with the news that the Irish had gone and that a ship loaded with arms and ammunition had arrived from General Kirke's fleet.

On 4 August 1689 Enniskillen had another reason to rejoice. The news arrived that Derry had been relieved from the sea. General Kirke's ships had broken through the boom on the Foyle and had reached the city with supplies and reinforcements. The Irish advances had that year reached their high water mark and now the tide was rolling back. 'And thus', wrote an Ulsterman, 'having defeated Lieutenant-General MacCarthy's party and taken him prisoner, Sarsfield fled, and the siege of Derry being raised, our fears were now at an end'.[30]

But for Sarsfield the worst indignity was yet to come. As soon as Folliot's dispatch arrived, Wolseley sent three troops of horse and some companies of infantry to Ballyshannon under the command of Colonel Zachariah Tiffin. Tiffin's task was to take over the defence of that town, reinforce it with his new men and to arrange for a strong escort to accompany Kirke's ammunition ship up to Enniskillen. This he did without incident, but after a few days it became clear that the Irish had not even maintained a token presence; not even the occasional patrol. Tiffin's second in command was his son-in-law Lieutenant-Colonel Francis Gore who, being a local man, was the ideal officer to seek out Sarsfield's position.

Gore was instructed to reconnoitre as far as Sligo to find out what Sarsfield was up to, how many men he had, what condition they were in and where they were. Tiffin wanted to know whether it was possible to retake Sligo with the thousand or so men now based in or around Ballyshannon. Gore's reconnaissance patrol was made up of three troops of Enniskillen horse and three companies of infantry. While his mounted patrols swept the country ahead, his musketeers marched straight for Sligo.

When he got to within some six or seven miles of Sligo, Gore had the most extraordinary stroke of luck.[31] His scouts captured an Irish straggler. There was nothing unusual about that, but when the man was brought before Gore, the lieutenant-colonel recognised him immediately.

It was the son of his Irish nurse. They had played together as children and had grown up together. The poor man had clearly been brought up in mortal fear of Francis Gore who now feigned great rage that a former employee and member of his household should take up arms against him. He immediately sentenced him to be hanged. The prisoner was terrified. He fell to his knees to grovel for his life and began blubbing that if Gore spared him he would remain faithful and loyal evermore. This was just what Gore expected. He knew the wretched fellow very well indeed. He would forgive him, he said, if he performed one task for him. In fact he would not only pardon him, but would reward him as well.

The task that had to be carried out was no more than a simple errand. He was to go quickly to the Irish garrison at Sligo and was to inform five or six Irish officers, who in happier times had all been Gore's personal friends, that they were in serious danger. Gore told the prisoner that his small force was merely an advance guard. A day's march behind him was an army of twenty thousand men drawn from the garrisons of Enniskillen and Londonderry and a newly arrived English army off Kirke's ships. The heavy hand of King William was about to fall on Sligo. Gore also made it clear that on no account was this message to be given to anyone except the named officers.

The prisoner readily agreed to do whatever he was asked. He would have sold his soul to the devil to avoid being strung up. He promised Gore that he would be back on the following day, and took his leave.

Gore's plan was entirely successful. His messenger broadcast his secret to everyone that he met on the road. Within a few hours Sligo was thrown into panic by the news that an English army was due to arrive in the morning. The townspeople scrambled for their possessions and set out on the road to Roscommon, Athlone and Galway. Soldiers began to disappear.

Sarsfield had the rumour-monger arrested and brought before a council of officers. The explanation that they were given made things worse. Each of the officers named by the messenger confirmed that in the past they had been on friendly terms with Gore. When this news got out there was no holding the troops. Sarsfield marched into the market place and had the drums beaten for a muster parade. No one turned up. He was left there with a handful of men and officers and his personal servants. To the south his men were already in full flight. There was nothing he could do but follow. Pausing only to direct those that were still with him to break the artillery carriages[32] and salvage what they could, he mounted up and rode off to Athlone.

> And thus Colonel Sarsfield and his whole party left Sligo to us; without seeing an enemy.[33]

A few hours later Francis Gore at the head of his three hundred conquering troops rode into the strongest town in north Connaught and captured fourteen cannons, a mortar and the bulk of the garrison's provisions.[34] He had taken Sligo with the same ease that Sarsfield had fifteen weeks earlier. It was the second time that year that the town had changed hands without a shot being fired.

On 18 August Sarsfield reached Dublin and reported to King James on the situation in Connaught.[35] Perhaps fortunate in that there were no experienced officers to replace him, he survived the interview. The king did not criticise him for what had happened in Sligo and accepted his explanation that he 'was obliged to quit that post when the Enniskilleners marched towards him'.[36]

From the Irish view point, the war had taken a very bad turn. Less than a month earlier they had all but taken the country. Enniskillen had been hard pressed and the defence of Londonderry was ready to crumble. Since then the rebels had broken out, pushed two armies back, destroyed a third and taken a major fortified town. But worst of all, while Sarsfield was still in Sligo, an English force of twelve regiments had set sail from Hoylake, near Chester. With them sailed the new commander of the Williamite army in Ireland, Friedrich Herman, duke of Schomberg, one of the most experienced generals in Europe. By the time that Sarsfield had reported to the king in Dublin, this new English army had already taken Bangor and Belfast, and was preparing to attack Carrickfergus, the only sizeable fortress in Co. Antrim. Meanwhile eleven more regiments were preparing to embark at Hoylake. Schomberg's army posed a threat far more serious than that offered by Wolseley, Tiffin, Gore and Lloyd. The loss of Sligo was now an unimportant detail of the war. James acted as quickly as he could to block Schomberg's southward advance. He set off for Drogheda to establish his headquarters and sent his son, Berwick, to Newry to make the area as inhospitable as possible for the English. This Berwick did. He burnt the town and the countryside, drove away all the livestock and confiscated or destroyed any stores that could be of use to the enemy. When Schomberg reached Newry he found it completely desolated.

Both Schomberg and James behaved cautiously. Schomberg was criticised for not pushing straight down to Dublin before winter set in. James was criticised for not marching northwards and striking a blow before Schomberg reached Dundalk. Neither of them wanted to engage the other as neither felt ready and as a result both their armies suffered far more than they would have done in a pitched battle. The October rains came and both sides fell victim to a devastating outbreak of dysentery ('the bloody flux') which was encouraged by inadequate clothing, shelter, sanitation and food. The most active men on both sides were the chaplains who conducted the services for the dead. The English came no further than Dundalk where they dug in. The Irish camped in front of them, their commanders ready to lead a dash southwards back to Dublin should the English fleet try to land another army behind them.

CHAPTER VI

The Attack on Sligo

King James: How now, Sarsfield, how goes the world? Are your men in heart?

Sarsfield: Lusty and brave, sir. They have all vowed to save your majesty the expense of belly-timber and to feed upon nothing but Danes and Dutchmen as long as there is one alive, and as for the Inniskilling men, they have sworn to dry 'em up in their chimneys for relishing bits i' the winter.

The Royal Flight, I.i, 1690

NOW THAT JAMES had blocked Schomberg's path and stopped the English advance in the east, he wanted Sligo retaken. If the English could not be driven out of Ireland before winter, they were at least to spend it bottled up in Ulster and he did not want to give them the opportunity of marching through Connaught in the spring. In any event, a victory in Connaught would restore the morale of the disheartened Irish army now shivering in the rain in Co. Louth. The problem was that if Sligo was to be taken, it had to be taken soon while there was still only a small Williamite presence there. It would not be long before whole regiments from the English army would be marching westwards to find winter quarters.

As Sligo was to be retaken quickly, James was satisfied that Sarsfield should lead the expedition. No other senior officer had his recent knowledge of the area. The king allowed him three thousand men who were all that could be spared from the main army. Sarsfield's orders were necessarily vague. He was 'to go to Sligo to preserve the inhabitants under His Majesty's obedience and check the excursions from Enniskillen'.[1]

In the meantime, Tiffin had not been idle. He arranged for the forts in Sligo to be strengthened and on 10 September 1689 he was joined by Ulster's darling, 'The Little Cromwell', Colonel Thomas Lloyd. Lloyd's task was, as one would expect, not to sit in Sligo but to drive southwards into Irish held territory. And that is what he did.

When he had gone to Dublin, Sarsfield had left his main force at Roscommon under the orders of Colonel Charles O'Kelly, the most experienced officer under his command. But although O'Kelly's military experience stretched back to the 1640s, his career had been indifferent and he was now almost seventy years old. Indeed, his most obvious quality was a simple desire to strike a blow against the enemy. While Sarsfield was away, his scouts brought back frequent reports that the country between Roscommon and Sligo was free of enemy troops. The temptation was too much for O'Kelly. He decided to march northwards to retake some of the unoccupied territory so as to prevent Tiffin from moving south. In the first week of September 1689, before Lloyd had left Ulster, O'Kelly set up camp in a deer-park outside Boyle, twenty-five miles from Sligo.

Tiffin was initially concerned at the return of Irish troops to the area, but after a few days it became quite clear that O'Kelly was not planning to come any closer. It also became apparent that O'Kelly had made an unfortunate move. The only reinforcements that he could call upon were in Athlone but his advance had taken him forty-five miles from there into an area in which there was still an enemy presence. Having done that, he even failed to get his men to dig in. In fact the only defensive precaution he took, apart from day time patrols, was to place a few ineffectual sentries as lookouts on the Sligo road where it ran through the Curlew Mountains. He in effect offered himself as an easy target for Lloyd.

On 19 September 1689, Lloyd rode out of Sligo at the head of three hundred horsemen and one hundred and fifty footsoldiers. In the early hours of the morning he reached the 'Castle of the Curlews', a tumbledown relic of the Elizabethan wars, and the village of Ballinafad four miles from Boyle. All that separated him from O'Kelly were the Curlew Mountains. He halted his column and sent out a small fighting patrol of twenty infantrymen and a troop of dragoons. In those dark hours before sunrise they scoured the Curlews and found O'Kelly's vedettes. One was killed and three were captured and, most importantly, no word got through to O'Kelly who with the rest of his force was fast asleep in Boyle. Within two hours Lloyd was on the move again. As the sun began to show itself on the miserably wet and misty morning of the 20th, his force was formed up in battle order overlooking O'Kelly's tents.

As soon as the alarm was raised, the Irish camp sprang to life. Men struggled to dress and arm themselves. O'Kelly and his officers desperately tried to get the men into some order. While the latecomers were still arriving, those who were ready first were straining their eyes into the mist to see what was going to happen. Something happened very quickly. Lloyd charged. The Irish had still not formed up to meet him. As the Enniskillen horsemen came thundering at them out of the mist, the Irish infantry took to their heels. Most of them did not even wait to fire before they hared off into the woods and the bogs along the Boyle River. The Irish cavalry turned about and raced away along the Roscommon road with O'Kelly in hot pursuit, cursing at their backs.

At the 'Break of the Boyle' the Irish perhaps lost as many as two hundred men, more than they had lost at Belleek and Ballyshannon together. Their flight had been so sudden that they lost all their stores and supplies and even O'Kelly's portmanteau containing up to date details of the disposition and numbers of all the Irish troops in Connaught. Lloyd's losses were minimal and he did not stop at Boyle. He did what he was best at and raided as far south as he dared. His men chased O'Kelly to within sight of Roscommon and then went on the rampage. They rounded up a 'vast prey of black cattle, sheep and horses, with all the growth of the country'.[2] Anything of value that they could carry off was looted, and that which they could not carry was burnt.

The only other post of consequence in the area held by the Irish was at Jamestown, fifteen miles to the east of Boyle. The fort commanded a crossing over the Shannon and was held by a garrison of eighty men. Lloyd rode directly to them and demanded their surrender. To his annoyance the Irish refused and Lloyd sent messengers back for reinforcements. The garrison did not wait, and on the night after his arrival they disappeared into the darkness. 'The Little Cromwell' triumphantly rode back to Sligo with 'a considerable booty'.[3] He had become to the Enniskilleners all that Sarsfield would later be to the Irish.*

When the news of the victory at Boyle reached the English army head-quarters in Dundalk, Schomberg was delighted. His troops were living in the most miserable and damp conditions and he felt that this was exactly the sort of news that would cheer them up. As his army had recently been joined by three battalions from Enniskillen, he had them formed up in front of the Irish lines while he rode up and down their ranks waving his hat over his head. He then ordered all his artillery and the guns on board the English ships on the river to open fire.[5]

Mystified by these scenes of jubilation the Irish were at first rather perturbed, thinking that it signified the arrival of new troops or a great victor. But Boyle? Jamestown? —few of them had ever heard of these places. When they finally discovered what the fuss was about, they were completely uncon-cerned and returned to their rotting tents to get out of the rain. But Schomberg made the most of it, and had it put about that four thousand Irishmen had been killed at Boyle. Certainly he was not believed in the Irish camp, and just as he could exaggerate a victory, so could others minimise a defeat. The French minister of war was informed by his ordnance officer in Ireland that the incident had left only a dozen Irish soldiers dead.

Schomberg's optimism was certainly misplaced. Although there was a victory to celebrate, Lloyd had done no more than carry out a successful raid. Within four days of the fight at Boyle he had withdrawn to Sligo leaving no more than a token presence in Boyle and Jamestown. The Irish had been chased away, but there was little to prevent them from returning. Many of the Enniskilleners simply refused to stay in Connaught while they had valuable cattle to drive back to their farms in Fermanagh and Tyrone. What, after all, was the point of rounding up Irish cattle if you could not take them home with you? This was to prove to be a perennial problem with Enniskillen troops throughout the war. Their officers often found themselves powerless to stop the desertions. Although the Enniskilleners earned a reputation for being tremendous fighters, good horse-men, and good shots, their discipline was little better than that of the rawest Irish recruits.

The news of the victory at Boyle was swiftly followed by a letter to Schomberg from Lloyd.[6] His forces were, he wrote, too far stretched. He asked permission to pull back out of Jamestown as it was too far away from Sligo and he could

---

*   'Under whose conduct we never failed accomplishing what we designed, but without him could not nor ever did anything.' So wrote one of the Enniskilleners of Thomas Lloyd.[4]

not defend it properly if he had to hold Boyle and cover the Shannon crossing at Drumsna as well. He told Schomberg that unless he was able to concentrate his forces, he would lose everything that had been gained. Lloyd was not the man to sit behind wooden stockades and mud walls with nothing to do but smoke and play cards until the Irish took the initiative. He was not a regular soldier. He only had one military skill and that he performed excellently. He raided; he travelled light, moved quickly and attacked where he was not expected.

Schomberg was the opposite. He was not used to dealing with small campaigns such as the one in Connaught. He had commanded armies numbering more than all the soldiers in Ireland put together. He had fought battles in which more men had been shattered by shot and ball than now sat huddled around Dundalk. To him, war was about land. One took it, and one held it. Lloyd, he ordered, was not to give up 'one foot of ground'.[7] He was to stand and fight until he was reinforced, and reinforcements, he was assured, were on the way.

Some reinforcements did come. A company of Huguenot infantry was sent to Sligo as were a few odd companies of horse under the experienced, although ageing, Colonel Theodore Russell.[8] A German by birth, he had begun his military career in the Portuguese war over twenty-five years earlier. Before Tyrconnell came to power he had been the governor of Galway and the commander of the finest cavalry regiment on the Irish establishment. After the Revolution, Russell had begged James to be allowed to stay on and serve him, but his colonelcy was given to Sarsfield and Russell promptly joined the other side. His defection was later much regretted by the Irish, as it was feared that he would use his close contacts in Galway and his detailed knowledge of its defences to lead a Williamite expedition to seize the town. But his instructions were now merely to take over the command in Jamestown and he rode directly there, leaving most of his troops to follow as soon as they could be got ready. Some of them arrived so late that they need not have bothered.

The equally important task of commanding the garrison at Boyle was given to a popular local landowner, Captain 'Laird' Weir, 'a valiant, brave fellow'.[9] Lloyd remained in the Enniskilleners' main prize, Sligo, where, after the departure of Colonels Tiffin and Gore, he was the most senior officer.

In early October 1689, Sarsfield set out on the most important mission of his career to date. He had the command of two foot battalions which had been detached from the royal camp in Louth on 31 September. They were the infantry regiments of Colonel Oliver O'Gara and Colonel Charles Moore, Sarsfield's uncle. When Sarsfield marched out of Athlone at their head, he also had with him Sir Neal O'Neill's regiment of Dragoons and Colonel Henry Luttrell with his cavalry regiment. This force was smaller than Mountcashel's had been but it was all that could be spared. If Sarsfield wanted more men, he would have to recruit them on the way and he was given the king's commission to do just that.

Recruiting was not a problem. Many Irishmen were willing to enlist in exchange for the first wages (or at least the promise of the first wages) that they had ever received in their lives. The war had already displaced so many people in the area, especially after Lloyd's raid, that enlistment offered them their only chance of regular food. Within two days of leaving Athlone, Sarsfield's force was swollen by the addition of two thousand new recruits.

Three main centres of enemy concentration lay in front of Sarsfield: Sligo, Boyle and Jamestown. The garrison in Jamestown was small. Colonel Russell, the recently arrived commander there, held the town in the hope that when he was attacked he would be able to summon speedy relief from Boyle. Without outside help he knew, and Lloyd knew, that the fort was untenable. It commanded a good pass over the Shannon, but the river could just as easily be crossed at Drumsna, which was undefended and less than two miles away.

Sarsfield was also aware of Russell's difficulties. He firstly ordered O'Kelly ahead with two hundred infantrymen and the remnants of his troops from the Break of Boyle to block the road that leads from Jamestown to Boyle. He then ordered Captain Ulick Burke to march off with another body of infantry and to block the road between Boyle and Sligo. This Burke did by setting up an ambush in the Curlews.

On 12 October Sarsfield reached Roscommon at the head of his main force. This was the last Jacobite post before he entered the no-man's land that stretched between him and Boyle. There he made a third detachment by sending off Henry Luttrell, who had fought with him at Wincanton, with a hundred and seventy horsemen to scour the area for enemy troops and prevent them from destroying the shelter and forage that the main force would need.

News travelled quickly. It was clear to the Williamites that the Irish were planning a last push before winter set in. Lloyd was told that bodies of troops were travelling across the country. No news came back to Sligo of any attacks. He decided to inspect the situation for himself and so rode out on the 13th October with a small mounted force along the road to Boyle. His intelligence had failed him. He rode straight into Burke's ambush in the Curlews and was driven back with loss. He attempted a counter-attack, but he was outgunned and in the open. Lucky perhaps to survive, he was forced to return to Sligo. This was his first defeat.

Meanwhile Captain Weir, the commanding officer in Boyle, was on a foraging patrol some fourteen miles to the south with two hundred men. He was also surprised, this time by Luttrell. As had been demonstrated in the Enniskillen raid, Luttrell's regiment of horse was among the finest in the country. Weir's irregular cavalry was completely outclassed and chased back to the River Boyle. As darkness fell, Weir decided that the best policy would be to abandon Boyle altogether and to get back to Lloyd in Sligo where he could collect more men and then return to sort out the Irish properly. In the dark of night he found the Sligo road and galloped through the Curlews. Burke's ambush party was waiting for him. Weir, his lieutenant and fifteen troopers were shot dead.* The remaining men turned about and made for Boyle which was all but deserted. As there was nothing to be gained by staying there, they rode out that same night for Jamestown. As O'Kelly was blocking the road, they were forced to ride by a tortuous cross country route in the darkness, but succeeded in joining Russell's garrison before dawn.

Russell's position in Jamestown was now useless. He had already learnt that the road to Boyle was blocked and that men from Sarsfield's main force had been reconnoitring the town. Weir's men now brought him the news that the Irish were in force north of Boyle, and that Boyle was deserted and probably by now lost. There was only one thing to do in Jamestown, and that was to get out. In the cold October dawn, Russell's garrison marched out along the eastern bank of the Shannon hoping to get to Sligo by a long, safe and roundabout route. Alas for him, Sarsfield was close by. What had started as an orderly withdrawal was soon transformed into a furious pursuit. Russell's troops, including Weir's men whose mounts were worn out, were mercilessly chased. 'They were forced like hard hunted deer', wrote a jubilant Irish pamphleteer, 'to swim three rivers in which there were eighty drowned and several killed.'[10]

Sarsfield did not waste much time on Russell. It only needed a few troops of cavalry to keep him on the move. He was now in a great hurry to get to Sligo as soon as possible so that Lloyd could neither prepare himself for the attack nor receive any reinforcements. His cavalry covered the thirty four miles from Jamestown to Ballysadare in a day while his infantrymen were flogged along behind. Delaying neither in Jamestown nor Boyle, he collected Charles O'Kelly and Ulick Burke on the way and that evening allowed his men to rest in Ballysadare, just five miles from Sligo. His advance had been so rapid that by the time he allowed his men to rest that night the only Williamite troops left in Connaught were those in Sligo itself. Sarsfield had not done a thing wrong. He had lost no time in his advance and he had prevented his divided enemies from regrouping. His ambush party and Luttrell's aggressive patrolling had met with great success and now, just two days after leaving Roscommon, he was ready to attack Sligo. His return had been even more rapid than his departure.

In the early hours of the morning of 15 October 1689, Russell arrived at Sligo. His force was depleted and exhausted. Throughout the night last minute preparations had been made to defend the town, mostly by the company of Huguenots who had recently arrived there. Lloyd had led a small force of his own men out of the town to Ballysadare to block Sarsfield's advance. All that now separated them was the broken down arches of Ballysadare Bridge.

---

* 'The Irish had thrown up an entrenchment across the road, at the foot of the Curlew Hills, about two miles from Boyle, in order to cut off his retreat towards Sligo. The entrenchment was stormed by Weir. Both he and Lieutenant Cathcart fell; the former mortally wounded by a random shot. After the war, Lord Kingston ordered a monument to be erected on the height, opposite to where Weir fell. The remains of the monument may still be seen'. W. G. Wood-Martin, *Sligo and the Enniskilleners from 1688-91*, Dublin 1882.

The broken bridge was a problem. There was no way of repairing it while the Enniskilleners occupied the far bank. The water that separated the two forces ran deep and fast, and the only way round was to march back inland around Lough Gill. But just as it seemed that all Sarsfield's efforts to ensure speed in the advance were to be wasted, he was visited with the same luck that had once visited Lloyd at Belleek. A countryman came and volunteered the information that he knew of a crossing place inland. Sarsfield again acted quickly. While the main body of his men paraded in view of the bridge and his cannon opened fire on Lloyd's men on the other side, he issued orders to Luttrell. Luttrell was to take three hundred footsoldiers and a hundred and seventy horsemen across the ford to attack the Enniskilleners in the rear. The 'Little Cromwell' was to be taught a severe lesson.

In the meantime, Lloyd had sent a message to Sligo demanding reinforcements. This was received by the recently arrived Theodore Russell who as the senior officer in the town elected to ride out with his exhausted horsemen. As Russell wearily approached Ballysadare he came across Luttrell in front of him, between him and Lloyd. Luttrell had put himself in a weak position as his dragoons and infantry were still struggling through the ford. He had ridden on ahead with only seventy troopers from his own cavalry regiment. Lloyd had in the meantime been told that the Irish had crossed the river upstream and so had abandoned his defence of the bridge and was returning to Sligo. Luttrell was consequently caught between these two converging groups.

He decided to make the best of a bad situation. He formed his seventy men into two lines, one facing towards Russell and one facing south towards Lloyd. Without waiting to be surrounded he led the north facing line and charged at Russell. It was a good choice. Russell's men and their horses were still badly in need of rest. They had not had a full night's sleep since before they left Jamestown and they had spent the intervening hours in great discomfort. If they had not quite been to hell they had certainly experienced fire and high water. They simply did not have the stomach for any more. They panicked and scattered back towards Sligo with Luttrell in pursuit.

Sarsfield's musketeers moved down to the bridge and crossed over. They were followed by the engineers who with joists and planks managed to patch up the broken span so that it was not long before all Sarsfield's men were marching to Luttrell's assistance. Not that Luttrell needed any help; Russell had fled and Lloyd had led his men around him and straight back to the safety of Sligo's defences.

Although Sligo had the makings of a strong town, Lloyd's problem was that most of his troops had been withdrawn to join Schomberg's army in the east. The high earth wall that ringed the town was too long for the remaining defenders to man. Sarsfield outnumbered them by about three to one. When he reached Sligo he needed no plan. He just ordered a general advance and his officers led his five thousand men forward in a rush on the outer defences. Without waiting to receive them, Russell led all the horse in headlong flight out of the town and

6 A contemporary Dutch print of Sarsfield's troops storming the defences of Sligo. Note that the artist has scurrilously depicted the Irish planting a French flag on a captured bastion.

across the river onto the Ballyshannon road. Luttrell chased him to the bridge where he ordered his men to take up positions to prevent the Williamites returning. He need not have bothered. Russell had already told the others in Sligo that he was going straight to Ballyshannon and that they were best advised to do the same.

There were three separate forts inside Sligo. The earth fort (also known as the sod fort), the stone fort, and the castle. The best and most modern of these was the earth fort. It stood in a commanding position on the north side of Sligo overlooking the town and the highway and it was to this haven that Lloyd took his men.

It was there that he paid the price for his appalling lack of preparation. The fort was stocked with neither ammunition nor powder nor provisions. Even if he had taken only the most rudimentary precautions the Irish would have been at great pains to winkle him out, especially as there was a good well in the fort. But then Lloyd was no defender of fortresses, and he was not prepared even to try after this unhappy discovery. Before the Irish could consolidate their hold on Sligo, he made up his mind to fight his way out. And this he did. His men swarmed out of the gates firing at the still disorganised groups of Irishmen in their way. Nothing could be done to prevent the Enniskilleners getting on to the Ballyshannon road and marching off after Russell. Behind him, Lloyd left his

French reinforcements who were still fighting as he crossed the bridge. Not wanting to start a fresh adventure before the town was truly his, Sarsfield made no effort to give chase, He ordered Luttrell to remain in the town and to break down the central arch of the bridge to prevent another break-out. For company, Lloyd's troops had only the few scouts that shadowed them along the road, just to ensure that they really were going.

The Frenchmen left in Sligo were four hundred Huguenot troops from Mellonière's regiment of grenadiers commanded by Captain Saint-Sauveur. They were defending the southern half of the town when Sarsfield rushed them, so they fell back into the old Fitzgerald castle, described as being 'one of the oldest in Ireland'.[11] They had no sooner got in when Saint-Sauveur realised that it was untenable. The ricketty old walls were a death trap for the men inside. In the confusion that followed the storming of the walls, the Frenchmen were able to charge out of the castle and make for the stone fort which they were able to reach and shut themselves inside. In with them staggered one of Russell's officers, Major Henry Wood, who was clasping a cask of powder.

As the strongest fort in the town, the earth fort, had not been provisioned, and as Saint-Sauveur did not know that the old castle was untenable until he was actually inside it, it is difficult not to reflect on how complacent and incompetent Lloyd had been as a garrison commander. Considering the natural defensive strength of Sligo and Sarsfield's lack of siege artillery, Lloyd should have been able to hold out for a very long time and wait for relief from Enniskillen. He had just lost the whole province of Connaught, including one of the most strongly fortified towns in the country and it was unquestionably his own fault. His subsequent disgrace can have come as no surprise. He was ordered to rejoin the army at Dundalk, and there he contracted dysentery and died.

Saint-Sauveur's position was bad from the outset. He was trapped with four hundred men inside a fort designed to accommodate fifty. The fort, although new, was small. It was no more than a rectangle of vertical walls inside which there was a small barracks, a stable and a guard house.[12] Although Sarsfield had not brought any siege artillery to Sligo, after the capture of the earth fort he had been able to drag several cannons across the town to use against the stone walls. Even though Saint-Sauveur had a limited supply of gunpowder thanks to the last minute enterprise of Major Wood, without food or water he could not hold out indefinitely. The chances of being relieved were slim, especially as any force that came from the north would have to pass under the guns of the earth fort. He also had little chance of breaking out. The south and east sides of the fort looked into the town and the Irish had barricaded the streets against him and posted musketeers in the houses. To the north lay the earth fort and the River Garvogue which flows through the town from Lough Gill. The river was too deep for his men to cross and the bridge had been broken by Luttrell. The only clear avenue of escape was to the west, across the barren peninsula to Strandhill and Sligo Bay. It led nowhere, but even this route of escape was soon denied to him as Sarsfield had trenches dug so that his musketeers could get close enough to the wall to be effective. Saint-Sauveur's four hundred men were now trapped by Sarsfield's five thousand.

Although things were bad for Saint-Sauveur, Sarsfield's situation was not without its worries. He did not know what was going on to the north. There were strong garrisons still at Ballyshannon and Enniskillen, and Russell had got away with all the horse from Sligo. If they were to mount an expedition against him he could be in difficulties, especially while the stone fort was still in enemy hands. And for all Sarsfield knew, the garrison may have had provisions, powder and ammunition to last them for months.

Saint-Sauveur, of course, did not know how much Sarsfield knew about the Williamite troops in Fermanagh. But Saint-Sauveur knew that they were depleted. The garrisons of Ballyshannon and Enniskillen were no longer able to do anything more than defend themselves. The cream of their forces had been sent over to south east Ulster and Dundalk. Help was going to be a long time in coming. The men inside the fort felt deserted and even betrayed. They were also miserable because it was raining heavily and there was inadequate shelter within the walls. Saint-Sauveur knew that it was only a matter of time before he would have to surrender, but he also knew that if he wanted good terms, he would have to convince Sarsfield otherwise.

During the first full day of the siege, Sarsfield inspected his newly acquired cannons, some of which he would have recognised from his last visit. Only light field guns were left and he could not even afford to bring them all to bear on the fort as some were needed in the earth fort to prevent an attack from the north. The larger pieces of ordnance had been taken from Sligo by the Williamites over a month ago to be transported to where the important part of the war was to be fought. It was clear that if he relied on the guns that he now had, it would take a long time to batter down the walls. With this in mind, he consented to the construction of the most extraordinary military machine to be seen in the war—a sow.

A sow is a medieval siege engine that had once been widely used in Ireland, but times had changed and no such contraption had been seen since the siege of Ballyahy Castle forty-eight years earlier. Sows varied in shape and size, but were built for the common purpose of getting men safely up to an enemy's walls. Sarsfield's sow was a tall rectangular box built on wheels, like a mobile tower, inside which there was a ladder. It was designed to be pushed up against the fort's wall so that troops could climb up through it and over the parapet. It is not known whose bright idea this device was, but the unknown engineer constructed it as follows: the sturdy wooden framework was made of whole timbers bound with iron hoops. These were then draped with two layers of cow hide and another two layers of sheep skin which together rendered the inside musket-proof. The rear end of the sow was left open so that troops could enter and then run up a wide ladder to the top. It was built to be higher than the fort's wall and at the top was a door which was to be opened when the machine was alongside the fort. The sow was mounted on wagon wheels and iron axles and was to be pushed by a team of men at the back.

Machines such as this had been widely used in medieval times but were particularly vulnerable to cannon fire, as one direct hit on the wooden frame would send the whole thing toppling over. However, there were no cannons in the fort and since he had an engineer who was keen to build such a machine and as he was anxious to end the siege as soon as he possibly could, Sarsfield was willing to try out the idea. That night, under cover of darkness, he arranged for the sow to be pushed towards the fort.

Although the French sentries were understandably surprised at what they saw creaking and wobbling towards them out of the gloom, they were ready to receive it. It was a dark night, but their field of visibility had been improved by Saint-Sauveur's practical good sense in arranging for torches to be placed around the fort's parapet to prevent any surprises. The torches were made of tall fir staffs, the ends of which had been dipped in turpentine and lit.

Once the sow was up against the wall, the French tried to push it back. They slashed and cut at the skin and fired through the holes. The men inside quickly discovered that the sow was very far from being bullet proof. They leapt out the back and ran as fast as they could into the outer darkness. Two or three men, as well as the engineer, were shot dead. This ancient stratagem had proved to be a complete disaster.

It seems that the attempt was in all probability doomed to failure from the start. The sow could never have been manoeuvred to the wall without being spotted, and once the garrison had been alerted the door would open to a crowd of French musketeers who would kill anyone who showed themselves. Those coming up the ladder would be knocked back by falling bodies and the entrance would be choked with the dead and wounded. Perhaps its only practical use would have been to get a mine up to the fort.

The sow came to rest a few yards from the wall, just too far for a man to jump. But Saint-Sauveur was going to take no chances with it and ordered its destruction. Wood chippings and kindling were thrown over the wall and piled up against the side of the machine. A man was lowered by a rope over the parapet with a torch and a bottle of turpentine. Within a few minutes the last sow ever to be seen in the British Isles was engulfed in flames.

The Frenchman who had been lowered over the edge had not volunteered merely for the glory. His mind now turned to more mundane matters. Although he was under fire, in the open and in the glare of the burning timber, he refused to return to the fort until he had stripped one of the dead Irishmen of his possessions. This done he ran to the wall and was hoisted up while the Irish musketeers did their best to shoot him. A lucky musket ball went clean through the rope when he was half way up and he fell straight back down again. While his comrades inside rushed to get a fresh rope he set about stripping a second corpse, which he successfully did before he was hauled back to safety with twice as much loot.

During that night, Sarsfield brought up some small cannon under cover of darkness to fire at the fort. Even if the balls did not have much effect on the walls, at least the Frenchmen were prevented from sleeping. The trouble came with the morning light. One of the cannons had been placed in a street leading to the fort, completely exposed to fire from the walls and this had not escaped Saint-Sauveur's notice. When the light was good enough, on a given signal a file of musketeers fired a volley from the wall at the group of men around the gun. Eight out of ten of them, some being officers, were shot dead.

Despite these minor defensive successes the French were in a bad way by the third day. They had now all but finished Major Wood's powder and they had no food. They only had rainwater to drink. Sarsfield of course did not know this and so was relieved that when he sent a messenger to demand a surrender, Saint-Sauveur agreed to treat. The terms that Sarsfield offered were generous and were readily accepted. The whole Huguenot force was to be given a safe passage to Ballyshannon. They could march out with their muskets at the ready, their drums beating and their colours flying. The terms were drawn up and signed by Saint-Sauveur and Sarsfield. Relief was the only feeling felt by each commander on that day, 21 of October 1689. Sarsfield knew that he could now defend Sligo properly and Saint-Sauveur knew that he would not starve, especially as at midday Sarsfield entertained Major Wood and all the French officers at his table. The respect that Sarsfield had amongst the Williamites was enhanced by this gesture. The Protestant news-sheets ensured that it became common knowledge that Sarsfield, that most civilised of Irishmen, had treated his enemy kindly and had cheerfully kept all the agreed articles.[13]

That afternoon, Major Wood and the four hundred Huguenots led by Captain Saint-Sauveur marched out of the stone fort across the patched-up bridge and out of Sligo. As they passed, Sarsfield stood on the bridge holding a bag of guineas in his hand. He addressed them in French; any man who would come and serve under King James would be given a horse, arms and five guineas advance pay. It was not a successful offer. It is reported that the men marched on saying (no doubt in broken English) that 'they would never fight for Papishes'.[14] Only one man took up Sarsfield's offer under the glaring eyes of his comrades, but he deserted the next day and rode to Ballyshannon a horse and five guineas richer.

Saint-Sauveur and his men were subsequently sent to join the main army at Dundalk. There they suffered terribly through the Irish winter from the effects of the fever that raged through both armies. Saint-Sauveur died shortly after-wards of this sickness in Lisburn.

Now that Sligo was again in his hands, Sarsfield's involvement with the town was over. Although he had commanded the expedition, the man with the king's commission to be governor of Sligo was Henry Luttrell whose first task was to fortify the town properly. Although Tiffin had made a start, the little that he had achieved had been wasted by Lloyd's extraordinary negligence. Under the direction of the engineer, Robert Burton,[15] the reconstruction of Sligo's defences was performed admirably. The town was encircled by a new system of trenches and palisades and a redoubt was constructed on the Ballyshannon road. The earth fort was transformed into one of the strongest in the country. Its defences were laid out in geometric patterns with deep ditches, gun platforms, palisades and a covered sally-port to defend the strong outworks.

When Sarsfield left Sligo for Dublin, he left it better defended than ever before. At no time had the garrison been so large, and never before had such preparations been set under way for its future defence. Sligo, the town that had changed hands three times that year, two of those without any fight at all, was to prove to be a very different prospect in the future.

In just seven days, while the Irish army was shivering in its camp in Louth, Sarsfield had swept the victors of Newtownbutler out of Connaught. The king was delighted with this achievement, and Ireland had found a new hero.

CHAPTER VII

Inactivity

Tyrconnell: Though that sly fox their general posts himself where none can touch him, 'tis full out as well. Distempers will their business do, and save our swords the labour. They already drop, provision comes but slowly, our thick fogs please not their queasy stomachs; they'll begin to wish for home.

The Royal Voyage, IV.i., 1690

King James: What fellow is that with a crow's nest about his chops, and a mouth as wide as a sawpit?

Tyrconnell: Why sir, have you forgot your friend, Teague O'Regan, your designed Governor of Charlemont?

The Royal Flight, II.ii., 1690

WITH NO FORAGE for the horses, little food for the men, and the roads having all but disintegrated under the wet assault of an Irish winter, the fighting ground to a halt as the season advanced. Marshal Schomberg had perhaps lost his best chance of pushing south when in September he encamped the English army outside Dundalk. It was soon clear that the longer he stayed there the less able his army was to move. The effects of the cold and the damp and dysentery were such that after two months over half his men were dead or unfit for service. He had been urged by William to push on, but he was reluctant to do so. He felt that too much was at stake and that if he did take a chance and attack the Irish army, which he believed to be numerically superior to his own, he risked losing the whole country. So when winter came he moved his men north into winter quarters. 'This was censured by some, but better judges thought the managing this campaign as he did as one of the greatest parts of his life.'[1]

Despite, or perhaps because of, the generally inert state of Ireland, one event did take place that winter that was to Sarsfield of the greatest importance. He married Lady Honora Burke, the youngest daughter of the late earl of Clanricarde.[2] She was half-sister to the living earl and his brother Lord Bophin, and she was Lord Galway's sister, Lord Mountcashel's niece and Lord Clancarty's cousin. She was in fact a woman of an impeccable Irish pedigree, far grander, it must be said, than that of the Sarsfields. It is also notable that she was only fifteen years old,[3] nearly twenty years younger than he was. Although there was nothing particularly unusual about such an age difference in those times, she was a long way from the merry widows that Sarsfield had chased in London.

In all probability they were married at the Clanricarde family seat at Portumna, then the most impressive building on the Shannon. There is no record of their courtship, although it is most likely that he met her for the first time when he visited Portumna earlier in the year after he had reformed Oxburgh's regiment in Birr. There is also no record of her character at the time of her marriage or of their life together, but many flattering things were written of her when she was in her early twenties and much admired for her beauty and sense of fashion. But pretty though she no doubt was, she was very young and one suspects a marriage forged more out of duty than sentiment.

Throughout the winter months of 1689/90 the great majority of troops on both sides, Sarsfield included, was not engaged in any fighting. Both armies were by then in a very bad way. Supplies were irregular and their clothing was inadequate. They were ill-housed and ill-fed. The Irish made some small attempts to disrupt the peace in Ulster, notably by Major-General Boisseleau's raid on Newry in November and by the capture of Keenagh Castle in Co. Longford by Brigadier Nugent in January, but nothing was done to alter the strategic map. James was anxious that his men should save their efforts for the coming campaign in the spring. But on the other side, Schomberg grew more anxious with each passing day to have something to show for his pains.

In February, Brigadier William Wolseley, the hero of Newtownbutler, was ordered to march from Belturbet and to take Cavan, one of the most northerly Irish garrisons. Wolseley and his Enniskilleners chased Berwick's troops away from the town, but were unable to capture the fort held by Brigadier John Wauchope. While the Enniskilleners got down to the important business of looting, Wauchope ordered a sally that put his enemies 'in the greatest confusion in the world'.[4] Wolseley withdrew, unable to hold the town while the fort was in Irish hands and unable to attack the fort without cannons. Wauchope, who was greatly outnumbered, was left to watch helplessly as the town, which contained a large stock of supplies and his magazine, burnt down around him. The losses that Wolseley inflicted on Berwick gave him grounds for describing his raid as a victory (although Wauchope reportedly only lost nine men),[5] but it was a wasteful affair that gained little (apart from the £5,000 in brass money that was taken from the town) and cost the Enniskilleners over a hundred casualties.

Berwick rode back to Dublin to report. His defeat outside Cavan had been an alarming affair and for him a near fatal one. He deputised Sarsfield to take his place,[6] and there Sarsfield remained for some six weeks. The frontier region at the time consisted of a wide band of open and devastated country, devoid of cattle and all but devoid of population. The inhabitants had driven their livestock away to behind the protective lines of one or other of the armies, and even there many had been robbed of all that they possessed. There were no firm lines either side of this invisible frontier. The Williamites and the Irish soldiers were mostly congregated in garrisons. They patrolled in small groups and tested each other's defences. The difficulties of travelling over the wet

7 Lady Honora Burke

terrain precluded any long range raiding parties and most troops were pulled back to safe winter quarters leaving a scattered series of small posts on the frontier. Sarsfield's task was to keep his men patrolling so that the enemy could not launch any surprise attacks, and to ensure that the larger frontier posts such as Cavan were properly fortified. To the north the enemy were doing the same. No one intended any serious activity west of Newry, but neither side knew the intentions of the other.

Holding on to Cavan soon showed itself to be a pointless task. Now that Wolseley had burnt down the town, the men were operating without sufficient shelter or adequate supplies. It was tiresome, unpleasant work, especially in the wet and windy month of March, and the strain began to tell. Sarsfield decided to abandon Cavan altogether, and in early April he returned to Dublin to report, and there he took to his sick bed.[7]

His illness was not serious, and he was not indisposed for long. Shortly after Sarsfield's arrival in Dublin, Lawrence Parsons, for so long a prisoner in his own castle at Birr, was also brought to the capital.[8] Since he had been sentenced to death in the previous year he had been reprieved some four or five times, and it was with some relief on his part that he was brought to Dublin where the rule of law remained, if not unblemished, at least substantially intact. Despite the reprieves, Parsons was still a convicted felon, and was to be thrown into prison with the other criminals. As he had no friends amongst the new Dublin elite he, perhaps rather ambitiously, decided to contact the only Irishman who had shown him any kindness since his return to the country. He instructed his solicitor, Robert Deey, to go to 'his old friend' Colonel Sarsfield 'and prevail with him to let him not be sent to a common gaol'. Luckily perhaps, Deey knew Sarsfield and was able to approach him with the news of Sir Lawrence's arrival and predicament. Sarsfield agreed to help and gave Deey permission to write to the town major to let him know that Sir Lawrence had Sarsfield's authority to lodge in Deey's house. And so thanks to Sarsfield a 'notorious villain', who a year before had been found by a jury to be guilty of treason and rebellion, was given liberty to walk the streets of Dublin while the country was still in the grip of a bloody civil war.

Ever since he first set foot in France, James had asked Louis for French troops to help him win his kingdoms back. And ever since the request was first made, the French had been reluctant to allow any such thing. The only acceptable solution to the problem had been suggested by d'Avaux, Louis's ambassador to James, before the Irish expedition had left Brest. It was known that there were plenty of men willing to be soldiers in Ireland; Tyrconnell had on paper an army so large that it could not possibly be adequately equipped or armed. The answer was simply to send Irishmen to fight in France, and replace them with Frenchmen. King Louis's army would then remain the same size and James in exchange would get the benefit of well trained and experienced French troops.

James was naturally more concerned to get French help than to help France, but he was keenly aware of his desperate need for experienced troops. The only way to get them was to go along with d'Avaux's suggestion, and so he ordered his officers to allocate men to an Irish brigade to serve in France. It was not a difficult choice as because of the acute shortage of muskets some Irish regiments were still unarmed, and so six battalions were selected primarily because James could not afford to equip them. In return the French would send him over six experienced battalions armed to the teeth. But then came the rub: the French were happy to accept several thousand fit young men into their army, but they also needed men to officer them and above all a man to command the brigade. It was essential to the plan. Most of the Irish soldiers destined for France could not speak any English, let alone French. Irish officers would be a necessary part of the bargain, and in particular an experienced Irish soldier would be needed to command the brigade.

In mid October 1689, the French ambassador approached James:[9]

> I asked the King of England's permission to allow a certain person called Sarsfield to go to France as one of the colonels and to command this corps. Sarsfield is not a man of noble birth like my lords Galway or MacCarthy but he is a gentleman who has distinguished himself by his ability and whose reputation in this kingdom is greater than that of any man I know. He is brave but above all he has a sense of honour and integrity in all that he does. He is a man on whom the King can count and who will never leave his service.
>
> I think he will be very useful because he is a man who would always be at the head of his troops and who would take great care of them, and if MacCarthy could not leave prison, you would always have a good commander in Sarsfield, who other first class colonels would keenly obey, something they would not do for anyone else.

But James was far from pleased with the interest that d'Avaux showed in Sarsfield, especially following his success at Sligo:

> The King is now so pleased with him that when I asked him for Sarsfield he told me that I wanted to take all his officers away from him, that he would not give him to me, and that I was unreasonable, and he stormed around the room three times in a temper.

However, James replied to d'Avaux with another suggestion. He would release his son, the duke of Berwick, to command the Irish brigade. D'Avaux was certainly unimpressed. Although he felt that Berwick was brave, he felt that he was a bad officer and that he lacked common sense. This in itself may have been a fair comment on Berwick at the age of twenty, but it is not a good description of the marshal duke of Berwick who at the age of thirty-seven would win the Battle of Alamanza. Interestingly enough, d'Avaux's damming description of Berwick is even worse than Berwick's later assessment of Sarsfield: 'He was a man of huge stature, but without sense, [although] very good natured and very brave.'*[10] But then, d'Avaux never had cause to clash with Sarsfield as Berwick did, and d'Avaux's experience of both Berwick and Sarsfield took place when d'Avaux was an experienced diplomat and Berwick was twenty. It is perhaps not surprising that they held such very different views of Sarsfield.

D'Avaux in the meantime was also considering the problem of which colonels should be sent to command the regiments in the Irish brigade.[11] Lord Dungan, Lord Clancarty and Lord O'Brien were all considered, as was Sarsfield's cousin, Dominic Sarsfield, Lord Kilmallock.** But James was unhappy in every case. The suspicion began to arise in d'Avaux's mind that the colonels that he was likely to get would not be of 'la première qualité'. And worse still, the matter of a brigade commander was still not resolved although it was greatly hoped that Mountcashel would be exchanged for Lord Mountjoy, the Protestant leader who was still languishing in the Bastille after trying to treat with King James.

Luckily for d'Avaux, the problem of finding a commander for the Irish brigade was solved in an unexpected fashion. Mountcashel escaped. Although he had been on parole in Enniskillen, he had it revoked when he told his captors that he intended to escape. They locked him up again and he bribed his gaoler and made his way back to Dublin at the end of December 1689. When he received the offer of the command of an Irish brigade in the French service, he did not hesitate. As he had once written to Louvois, the French minster of war, the command of the Irish brigade was 'the thing I most desire in the world . . . . If they should send another, it would cause me the greatest grief and I would think only of spending the rest of my life in retirement.'

On 12 March 1690, a year after James had first set foot in Ireland, a French transport fleet arrived in Cork. It carried the six thousand men of the French brigade. To James's concern it turned out that of the six battalions only three were French. One was made up of Walloons and the other two were formed from (chiefly Protestant) Germans who had until recently been prisoners of war in French camps. But at least they were all trained soldiers and that is what the Irish needed more than anything. The king was pleased to find that they were commanded by his old friend, Antonin Nompar de Caumont, comte de Lauzun. The fifty-eight year old Lauzun was a diminutive and unpopular courtier who had fled to London following a court scandal in France. He then lived in England until the Revolution where he found great favour with his royal host. But his new appointment pleased no one except the king. When the fleet left it took off Mountcashel's Irish brigade and, to James's approval, both the interfering d'Avaux, who was not prepared to work with Lauzun, and the fearsome Rosen, with whom nobody wanted to serve.

*   'Patrice Sarsfield étoit né gentilhomme et avoit hérité de son frere aîné d'environ deux mille livres sterling de rente. C'étoit un homme d'une taille prodigieuse, sans esprit, de très bon naturel, et très brave'.
**   Dominic Sarsfield, Viscount Kilmallock, came from the Limerick branch of the family and had married Sarsfield's youngest sister, Frances. He served throughout the war as the colonel of a cavalry regiment.

8 Frederick, duke of Schomberg, from a painting by Kneller.

   Throughout the spring of 1690 the English army in Ireland was resupplied
and reinforced. Although disease had reduced it to less than half of its original
fighting strength, by the second week of May, after the daily arrival of troop-
ships packed with English, Dutch and German soldiers the Williamite army in
Ireland was stronger than it had been since the days of Cromwell. Schomberg
prepared to move.

   The first target of Schomberg's new-found strength and subsequent confidence
was the isolated Irish stronghold of Charlemont. Tyrconnell described it as
being 'a small fort in the province of Ulster, which had been long since quitted
were it not in expectation to have brought off the artillery and some ammunition that lay there'.[13] The small but strong fort of Charlemont was situated on
the edge of a bog and looked down on the River Blackwater and the Armagh-
Dungannon road. It had been under attack since November 1689, but throughout the winter a steady flow of supplies had been carried in during the nights
across the large bog on the south side. Schomberg was determined to put a stop
to the resistance.[14] In early 1690 he had sent a messenger to invite the veteran
Irish commander of the garrison, the eccentric Colonel O'Regan, to surrender.
The messenger returned with orders to 'tell his master from Teague O'Regan that
he's an old knave and by Saint Patrick he shall not have the town at all'.
(Unsurprisingly perhaps, as one witness commented, as by that time there was
nothing left of the town.)

   As the Williamites applied more pressure, O'Regan was forced to reassess
his position. In early May five hundred Irish troops crossed the bog to bring
him supplies, but they were then unable to break out again. The supplies that
they brought lasted less than a fortnight. On 12 May, O'Regan agreed to
surrender the fort if he and his whole garrison could march out with all their
provisions and weapons to Dundalk. The duke of Schomberg was present at
the time and as he was anxious to push on he agreed to accept a surrender on
those terms. He then waited to supervise the evacuation.

   To many of the newly arrived continental troops that Schomberg had with
him, the defenders of Charlemont were the first Irish troops they had seen. They
watched the proceedings with great interest. The eight hundred men were badly
clothed and in poor physical condition, and with them were two hundred women
and children.

> The Duke seeing so many women and children asked the reason of keeping
> such a number in the garrison, which no doubt destroyed their provisions.
> He was answered that the Irish were very hospitable and that they all
> fared alike, but the greatest reason was the soldiers would not stay in the
> garrison without their wives and mistresses. The Duke replied that there
> was more love than policy in it.

More striking than the poverty of the garrison was the spectacle of Teague
O'Regan who rode out to lead his men to Dundalk.

Old Teague, the governor, was mounted upon an old stoned horse, and he was very lame with scratches, spavin, ring-bones, and other infirmities: but withal so vicious that he would fall kicking and screaming if anybody came near him. Teague himself had a great bunch upon his back, a plain red coat, an old weatherbeaten wig hanging down at full length, a little narrow white beaver cocked up, a yellow cravat string (but that was all on one side), his boots with a thousand wrinkles on them, and though it was a very hot day yet he had a great muff hanging about him, and to crown all, was almost tipsy with brandy. Thus mounted and equipped, he approached the Duke with a compliment, but his horse would not allow him to make it a long one, for he fell to work presently and the Duke had scarce time to make him a civil return. The Duke smiled afterwards and said, Teague's horse was very mad, and himself very drunk.

So ended the long siege of Charlemont. Schomberg looked to the south. James received O'Regan at Dundalk as a hero and knighted him.

While the Irish marched out of Charlemont, Colonel Wolseley's Enniskilleners completed their last push of the spring. For the second time in the war they successfully attacked and forced the surrender of the fort at Bellanacargy in Northern Cavan. This was described by Wolseley as being 'the strongest place I have seen in Ireland'. He also reported, perhaps rather coyly, that he had been shot in the belly.[15] The Reverend Mr Story, less coyly, carefully noted that Wolseley had been shot in the scrotum. Apart from a few weak outposts that no one had yet bothered to chase out, the nine counties of Ulster were now free of King James's soldiers.

On the Irish side the spring of 1690 was spent marching troops from their winter quarters to Dublin. They had been scattered all over the country and based in every major town—in Bantry, Kinsale, Cork and Youghal right up to Sligo and the borders of Ulster in the north. Sarsfield's own regiment, for instance, was divided into its squadrons which were scattered across the country in Shrule, Athlone, Longford and Navan.[16] It was no mean task to gather them together to join the main army around Dublin, but there was fortunately no need to rush. As Tyrconnell wrote to the queen of England in Paris:

We are impatient until the grass be of such a growth as that our horses may be able to feed upon it, which will not be until mid-May at least, that we might attempt something upon our enemies. And if they had not forage brought out of England (which I think is hardly possible), they must lie idle as well as we until then.[17]

By late May James was all but ready to do battle. In order that he could block the roads from the north and north-west he divided the main part of his army between Trim, Kells and Ardee. He posted Brigadier Cairney to Dundalk, and ordered Lieutenant General Lery de Girardin to scour the countryside round about. At the same time he sent Sarsfield with three thousand men to Finnea.[18] Finnea is some twenty miles south of Cavan and lies on the low ground between Loughs Kinale and Sheelin. Through the village and past the small fort ran the road from Cavan to Mullingar and nearby lay the road to Longford and Kells. This gave the village a tactical importance beyond its size, and it had been the site of two battles in the civil war four decades earlier. It was not known where the English intended to launch their campaign. James and his advisors felt that they would advance on one of two routes. They would either try to march along a coastal route from Newry to Dundalk, Drogheda and Dublin, or they would approach the capital from the northwest through Cavan and Kells, Trim or Mullingar. Sarsfield's brigade was some thirty miles in front of the main concentrations of Irish infantry. His task was to block or at least delay any advance from the Cavan area.

Nothing was happening in Finnea. Sarsfield's patrols moved north but the Williamites showed little signs of activity throughout the whole area. Only in late June was he able to send any definite news. The English were pulling out of Belturbet and marching to Armagh. They were gathering in the east.[19] On 14 June 1690 the prince of Orange landed at Carrickfergus with fifteen thousand men to join Schomberg's army. The man of action had arrived. He was determined to act quickly. Schomberg's plan of a two-pronged attack on Dublin from Cavan and Armagh was rejected and William set about concentrating his army around him. He intended to get to Dublin by the most direct route.

The feverish activity in the English camp acted as a spur to the Irish. James recalled Sarsfield. The French generals were anxious to bring their forces together, and by 25 June Sarsfield had joined the main army at Ardee. For the time being his days as an independent commander were over, and for the first time in his life Brigadier Sarsfield prepared to command a brigade of cavalry in a pitched battle.

CHAPTER VIII

The Boyne

July the First, of a morning clear, one thousand six hundred and ninety,
King William did his men prepare, of thousands he had thirty;
To fight King James and all his foes, encamped near the Boyne Water,
He little feared though two to one, their multitudes to scatter.

The Boyne Water

Sarsfield: Curse o' my stars, that I must be detached that day—I
would have wrested victory out of heretic Fortune's hands
The Royal Flight, III.iii., 1690

IN MID JUNE, James rode northwards to do battle. He had planned to fight outside Dundalk by holding the Moyry pass between Dundalk and Newry, but Lauzun was unhappy about the idea. He felt that the Irish army was too far away from Dublin and its supplies and there was a danger of being outflanked by a second Williamite force advancing from Armagh. It was decided to pull back to the south and to take up a defensive position on the River Boyne. Consequently the Irish began their campaign by surrendering Co. Louth to the enemy.

Once across the Boyne James turned to face the north. The river was not impassible, but it was a useful line of defence. His enemies had more men, but he had the advantage of choosing the ground. In his own words, 'there was not any situation more favourable' than the Boyne. Both Tyrconnell and Lauzun were opposed to his plan, but James was determined to decide things there. 'If he continued all his retreating, he would have lost all without striking a stroke, and would have been driven fairly into the sea.'

James's intention was to fight a defensive battle. He hoped firstly that William would actually launch an attack and not just try to outflank him, and secondly that William's attack would be at Oldbridge. As the latter was less certain than the former, it was necessary to keep a large reserve of men to race to whatever part of the river that a crossing was attempted.

James took up his position on the hill of Donore. Two miles to his east was the town of Drogheda, which he garrisoned with thirteen hundred men commanded by Lord Iveagh to guard Drogheda Bridge. Between Drogheda and the vicinity of Oldbridge, just below Donore, there were no crossing points. James's right flank was safe. Some four miles west of Oldbridge was the next crossing point, the narrow ford of Rosnaree and three miles west of that was the broken down bridge of Slane. Meandering between Oldbridge and Slane lay some ten miles of the River Boyne. As William's army was some ten thousand men stronger than his, James's plan was to confine the battle to narrow and defined passes. He could not risk an open battle.

William was equally concerned that James should stand and fight. His fear was that the Irish army would draw off to the west to prolong the war indefinitely. But if James did that, he would leave Dublin open, and for that reason William was confident that there would be a battle. 'We are of the opinion that the Boyne is the walls of Dublin', wrote his secretary.[1] When William stood on a hill overlooking the Boyne on the morning of Monday 30 June he was relieved to see that the Irish had camped along the south bank between Oldbridge and Drogheda.

William did not want to attack on that day. He wanted to plan and prepare his attack and in any case he felt that Mondays were unlucky. He could see only part of the Irish camp and did not know where James had positioned the rest of his men. In fact neither king had a clear view of the other's army. The Williamites marched down 'and spread themselves along the side of the hills where they encamped, but so as we could not discover them all, a great part being covered by the high grounds.'

At about noon William's army marched into view. Some of the foremost regiments were made to stand in parade order within range of the Irish cannons. 'Indeed, 'twas madness to expose so many good men to slaughter without needs, for we had not artillery yet come to answer theirs.' Eventually the Williamite troops were allowed to retire out of range.

Sometime after three o'clock, William decided to go down to the river with his staff to inspect the ground. He rode down towards Oldbridge and just out of musket shot from the Irish positions he inspected the preparations that the Irish had made on the south bank. There was not much to see. The stone houses in the village were loopholed for troops to fire out of and there were several entrenchments mostly still unfinished. He then rode on to what is now known as King William's Glen and with his entourage of officers he dismounted. There they sat down on the ground in full view of the Irish on the south bank and started a picnic. The Irish that watched them through prospective glasses were not merely curious. They could not believe their luck.

> Whilst His Majesty sat on the grass . . . a party of about fifty horse advanced very slowly and stood upon a ploughed field over against us for near half an hour. This small party brought two field pieces amongst them, dropping them by a hedge, in the ploughed land, undiscovered.[2]

The rumour later spread among the English that amongst these horsemen were 'five gentlemen of the Irish army', including Tyrconnell, Lauzun, Berwick and Sarsfield. Unlikely though it is, it is perhaps no less likely than the fact that William had chosen to take most of his senior staff officers for a picnic in full view of his enemies. However, no mention is made of the presence of the 'five gentlemen' in any Jacobite account.

9 King William III, by Jan Wyck.

> They did not offer to fire till his Majesty was mounted and then, he and
> the rest riding softly the same way back, their gunner fired a piece which
> killed us two horses and a man, about a hundred yards above where the
> King was, but immediately came a second which had almost been a fatal
> one, for it grazed upon the bank of the river, and in the rising slanted
> upon the King's right shoulder, took out a piece of coat and tore the skin
> and flesh and afterwards broke the head of a gentleman's pistol.[3]

William was rushed off to have his wound dressed. Those around him thought
that it was a fatal shot, and those on the south bank optimistically spread the
rumour that they had killed the prince of Orange. The news of his death was later
to reach Paris where there was an orgy of premature celebrations.

William was very lucky indeed. His wound was not a serious one: he had a
nasty graze on his shoulder the size of the palm of a hand. While he was being
bandaged his secretary for Ireland, Robert Southwell, spoke to him:

> I told him he had now paid his tribute to the war. He answered cheerfully:
> 'And tomorrow we'll have our revenge.'[4]

In the early hours of the morning the Williamite drums beat the muster. The
army was on the move. The drums were heard in the Irish camp, but as there
was a thick mist across the Boyne valley it was not possible to tell what was
going on. William had the night before decided on his battle plan. He was going
to send Count Schomberg, the second son of his commander-in-chief, with a
small force of some eight thousand men to cross the river upstream at Rosnaree
or Slane. He hoped that his manoeuvre would draw off a large part of the Irish
army. Once the count's men were over the river he intended to make a full frontal
attack on the main Irish position at Oldbridge. As dawn broke, it was clear to
the Irish that a part of the Williamite army was marching westwards. It was
difficult to assess how many of them had been detached as most of the English
army was hidden from view, and those that were marching soon disappeared
behind the hill on which stands the bronze age tumulus of Newgrange.

Count Schomberg reached Rosnaree at eight o'clock on what was a beautiful
sunny summer's morning. 'A Joyful day. Excessive hot.'[5] On the other side of
the river was one regiment of dragoons and three field guns. These men, commanded by Sir Neal O'Neill, numbered less than five hundred. The fighting
that followed was a one sided affair. The Irish tried to hold the ford, and did so
for half an hour while the Williamites prepared to cross, but when the attack
came it was all over in minutes. The dragoons were swept aside by overwhelming numbers. Those that could galloped from the field, taking with them the
mortally wounded O'Neill.

By ten o'clock William had received the news. His men were across the
Boyne. He detached Lieutenant-General James Douglas with a cavalry brigade
to join Count Schomberg.

The French were the first to hear of the attack on O'Neill's position, and
Lauzun immediately arrived at a false conclusion. The main enemy thrust was

going to be Rosnaree, he told James. They conferred, and Lauzun marched off with his French brigade, six guns and some cavalry to meet Count Schomberg. The Jacobite army was now split. James also formed the opinion that the main attack was to be at Rosnaree and that if he did not respond he would be encircled or cut off from the Dublin road. He issued the fatal order that most of his army was to follow Lauzun and take up positions to stop Count Schomberg. The mounted brigades of Sarsfield and Maxwell rode westwards, followed by Cairney's and Wauchope's infantry who had been positioned between Oldbridge and Drogheda. As they marched they could see to their north Douglas's brigade marching towards Slane.

Although firmly established on the south bank near Rosnaree, Count Schomberg was in some difficulty. As his troops marched forward the ground got boggier. When Lauzun's brigade appeared to his front and positioned itself along a hillside, he still had not made any significant progress. Writing of the bog, one of his officers commented: 'I thought the Devil himself could not have got through.'[6] Lauzun's only concern was to block Schomberg's way, and now that he had ground to a standstill, the French just waited and watched. The first reinforcements to reach the French were those commanded by Thomas Maxwell and Patrick Sarsfield. Like Schomberg, they desperately began sending out men to test the ground between them. By late morning, James was with them. The majority of the Irish army was now facing the enemy across a bog some four miles from Oldbridge.

Tyrconnell was left at Oldbridge. He had a battery of field guns, three cavalry regiments, two troops of horse guards and seven infantry battalions. In all he had less than seven and a half thousand men. Even his reserves had marched off with the king. Facing him, mostly hidden behind high ground and in the woods, was half of King William's army. The Irish in Oldbridge were outnumbered by more than two to one.

At a quarter past ten, William ordered the advance. Count Solms at the head of the three battalions of the Dutch guards, their blue uniforms looking splendid in the bright sunshine, moved down to the Boyne at Oldbridge with their colours flying, their drums beating and their fifes playing the tune of Lillibulero. As they reached the river their drums stopped and the men marched in, holding their muskets and powder over their heads as the water came above their waists. They were veteran troops and knew what to expect.

The Irish infantry was lined up in battalions to meet them. Each battalion stood four men deep and was divided into its thirteen companies, and each company was divided into its four platoons. As the Dutch emerged from the river, less than fifty yards from King James's guards who held the centre at Oldbridge, the Irish opened fire. The first platoon in each company fired a volley, and this was followed a few seconds later by a volley from each second platoon, and then from each third platoon. The front rank of the whole company had until then remained silent but now they fired a volley along the whole length of

10 A contemporary Dutch print showing Irish cavalry charging into the village

ldbridge. Schomberg's death is shown at the right of the picture.

the line. By this time the first platoons had reloaded and were again in the firing position.* The smoke from the powder was now blinding, and many of the troops could no longer see the enemy. But they had been trained to fire to their front and so there was a continuous blind discharge, soon added to by a thunderous reply from the Dutch who were marching forward, firing all the way, into the Irish positions. As they closed, Major Thomas Arthur of King James's guards stepped forward and ran the leading Dutch officer through the body. The troops fell to hand to hand fighting. Mortally wounded, Arthur was trampled underfoot. The fighting was fierce and soon became muddled. Outnumbered, the Irish regiment of guards began to give ground. 'The Jacobite resistance to the Dutch was strong, the fighting was so hot that many old soldiers said that they never saw brisker work.'

Behind the Dutch guards the two Ulster infantry regiments marched down to the river, Colonel John Michelburne's Londonderry regiment and Colonel Gustavus Hamilton's Enniskillen regiment. To their left the two Huguenot battalions of Caillimote and Cambron began to advance along with the English regiments commanded by Colonels Hanmer and St John: and behind them came the Dutch regiment led by Count Nassau, William's cousin.

Once Tyrconnell could see what was happening he immediately ordered his cavalry into action. If the Dutch guards were not thrown back over the Boyne, the next seven infantry regiments would form up alongside them and then his men would be outnumbered. The young duke of Berwick led the thousand horsemen down to Oldbridge and ordered the charge. Across the river William showed himself to be worried for perhaps the first and last time that day. His secretary recalled him watching his Dutch guards:

> The King was in a good deal of apprehension for them, there not being any hedge or ditch for them or any of our horse to support them, and I was so near His Majesty as to hear him say softly to himself, 'My poor guards, my poor guards', but when he saw them stand their ground and fire by platoons so that the horse were forced to run away in great disorder, he breathed out as people used to after holding their breath upon a fright or suspense and said he had seen his guards do that which he had never seen foot do in his life.[7]

But it was not going to be easy. The Irish guards were threatening to charge the Dutch again and General Hamilton ordered the Irish infantry forward to meet the Huguenot and English regiments. He failed. The infantry battalion that he was leading refused to advance, and then turned and fled. They took with them any chance that James may have had of winning the battle.

* Well trained soldiers were able to loose off a shot about every fifteen seconds, so that a well drilled company of men would be able to keep up an almost continual fire to their front. The loading of the flintlock musket was by paper cartridge which contained both the ball and the charge. Each soldier held the ball through the paper, bit off the other end of the cartridge and then poured the powder down the barrel. The ball was then dropped down after it, and the cartridge paper was then stuffed into the muzzle and then tightly rammed home with the ramrod which was then put back into its 'pipes'.

Only the Irish cavalry could now save the day. Hamilton returned with his squadron of horse and rode straight into the first Huguenot regiment to emerge from the river, and then directed another squadron into Nassau's and Hanmer's regiments. The fighting reached its greatest pitch: 'There was nothing to be seen but smoke and dust nor anything to be heard but one continued fire for nigh half an hour.' Nassau and Hanmer were chased back into the river. The Huguenots suffered severe losses as they had no *chevaux de frise** to protect them from cavalry attacks. Colonel Caillimote was mortally wounded. As he was carried back over the Boyne he urged his men on with the words 'A la gloire, mes enfants, à la gloire!' Although by then the two Ulster regiments were across the river, the Huguenots looked less than steady. The duke of Schomberg rode with his staff to their front and urged them on 'Allons, Messieurs, voilà vos persecuteurs', he bellowed, pointing to a fresh wave of Irish cavalry led by Dominic Sheldon, Berwick and John Parker.

It was the last great charge of the day. Wurtemberg had already moved his Danish brigade through the river to the left of the English. For the second time, the earth shook under the hooves of a thousand horses as the Irish cavalry came screaming down the hill. Although the Williamite infantry suffered terribly and some of their formations broke and ran back into the river, they were now too numerous to be dislodged, and the Irish were beaten off. Berwick's horse was killed under him and he was helped off the field, dazed and bruised. Parker was seriously wounded, and for the second time that day, Sheldon had his horse shot under him.

But on the other side, Schomberg was dead. He had been caught in the open by the cavalry and as the Irish swept by he was twice hacked by sabres and was then shot in the neck. A man riding near him reported that in the confusion the fatal shot had come from the panicky Huguenots behind him,[8] but the Irish version of events makes better reading:

> One Master Bryen O'Tool of the Guards discovering his former acquaintance Marshal Schomberg near the village of Oldbridge, resolved to sacrifice his life to the making him away, upon which he with a few of the Guards and a few of Tyrconnell's horse made up to him and O'Tool with his pistol shot the Marshal dead. But soon after, fighting like a lion, he was slain.[9]

Killed in the same attack was the Reverend Mr George Walker, who had been the civil governor of Londonderry during the siege. He had been urging Michelburne's regiment on when the Irish charged. He was shot in the belly and died within minutes, after which (according to Story) some irreverent 'Scotch-Irish' stripped him of his expensive clothes and pocketed his belongings.

---

* These were long spiked wooden poles carried by infantrymen. They were locked together to make a barrier to stop cavalry charges; they were so called (tr: Friesian cavalry) because they were first used in Friesland.

The Williamites were very impressed with the Irish cavalry. 'The enemy's horse fought wonderfully bravely as ever men could do', wrote Lieutenant General Douglas. They did 'very bold things'.[10] But Tyrconnell had shot his bolt. He had nothing left to impress them with.

Further down the river Baron Ginckel ordered the first of the cavalry regiments to swim their horses across under the cover of heavy artillery fire from the north bank. Now that his troops were established in and around Oldbridge, William himself led his Dutch cavalry through the water. It was not a simple crossing. His horse got bogged down and William had to dismount and wade through the thick mud. Wearing his star and garter as if to advertise his presence to the enemy he remounted and led the largest cavalry force on the field up towards Donore. It was at this point that Tyrconnell decided that the battle was lost. He was now heavily outnumbered and was being attacked on two sides. After instructing Hamilton to stay behind and delay the enemy with the remnants of the cavalry he rode off to direct the retreat to Duleek and beyond. It would have been foolhardy to have done anything else.

James was still four miles away facing Count Schomberg. He was completely unaware of what had been going on at Oldbridge until two o'clock when a breathless messenger from Tyrconnell came galloping up to him. 'The enemy have forced the pass at Oldbridge', he said. 'The right wing is beaten.'

This was devastating news, and James was now a desperate man. He whispered in Lauzun's ear. There was, he told the Frenchman, nothing to be done but to charge Count Schomberg straight away before the troops get to hear about what has happened on the right. That was now the only way to save the day— to smash William's right wing in return. As Lauzun later wrote: 'His Majesty was determined to fight the battle.' King James issued orders quickly. He sent the Marquis de la Hoguette to the head of the French infantry. He ordered his dragoons to dismount and to form ranks in the gaps between the squadrons of horse. And he ordered Lauzun to advance. There was now a great need for hurry.

In his memoirs, King James recorded what happened next:

> Just as they were beginning to move, Sarsfield and Maxwell, who had been to view the ground betwixt the two armies said it was impossible for the horse to charge the enemy by reason of two double ditches with high banks and a little brook betwixt them that ran along the small valley that divided the two armies.

Sarsfield's reconnaissance was correct. Schomberg's men had already marched into the bog from the other side. It proved to be so swampy that they were forced to pull back. 'I thought I should never have got out of it'',[11] recalled one. As James looked ahead he could see that Schomberg's dragoons were outflanking him further to the south and were threatening to cut him off from the Dublin road. He soon lost sight of them but could see the dust rising between the hills. If he could not use his cavalry it would a long protracted fight using infantry alone, and infantry squelching through thick bog at that. He no longer had the time.

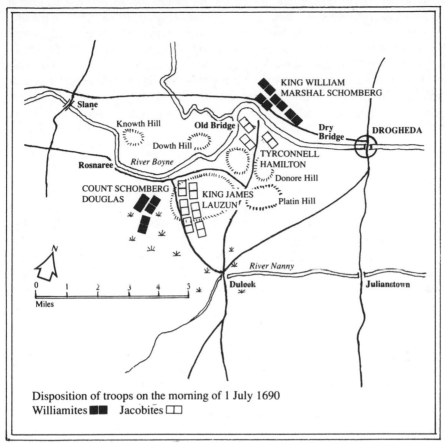

Disposition of troops on the morning of 1 July 1690
Williamites ■■ Jacobites ☐☐

Map III: The Battle of the Boyne

It quickly became apparent that he was no longer able to deceive his men as to what was happening at Oldbridge as galloping towards them came the remains of Tyrconnell's cavalry 'scattered and wounded'. Lauzun put pressure on James to go to Dublin. If they did not withdraw now they would be cut off. James did not want to go. He had steeled himself to stand and fight and as he had not even seen any fighting, he was unwilling to leave. But when the extent of the action at Oldbridge became known, that the entire corps led by William and old duke Schomberg had crossed the Boyne and chased away Tyrconnell's troops, Lauzun's entreaties prevailed. The order was given to march to Duleek and the Irish infantry moved off in good order, irritated that they had not been able to fight.

But matters then took a turn for the worse. As they marched, the infantry became gripped by panic. Horsemen from Oldbridge knocked them off the road in their haste to get away. The obvious show of fear in others was infectious even though no enemy was in sight. The orderly retreat became a rout that the officers were powerless to stop. 'Viewing the hills about us I perceived them covered with soldiers of several regiments all scattered like sheep flying before the wolf, but so thick they seemed to cover the sides and tops of the hill', recalled Lieutenant John Stevens of the Grand Prior's regiment, itself now broken up.

> The shame of our Regiment's dishonour only afflicted me before, but now all the horror of a routed army, just before so vigorous and desirous of battle, and broken without scarce a stroke from the enemy, so perplexed my soul that I envied the few dead and only grieved that I lived to be a spectator of so dismal and lamentable a tragedy.[12]

In the middle of all this James was ushered out of danger. Lauzun told de la Hoguette that nothing mattered now but saving the king, and that he was to stick by him and take the six hundred men of Sarsfield's cavalry regiment to escort him to Dublin and beyond. Lauzun personally urged the king to go to France as if he was captured, it would be the ruination of everything.

Meanwhile at Donore, the Irish infantry had left the field. The flight was led by a rabble of men who had broken ranks and who were making off with all the speed that they could for Duleek on the Dublin road. They were followed in a more orderly fashion by the regiment of guards who in turn were covered by Richard Hamilton with the mounted troops. Behind them there was still a great mixture of men left on the field, and not all the Irish had given up the fight. At one stage Ginckel's Dutch cavalry was forced to retreat when attacked by Dominic Sheldon, but there was no holding the general advance. Hamilton fell back on Donore itself and ordered his dragoons to dismount and to occupy the old churchyard on top of the hill.

William was anxious to press forward and was now concerned that his attack was loosing its momentum. He rode up to the nearest mounted regiment, the

Enniskilleners. 'Gentlemen', he called out to them, 'You shall be my guards today. I have heard much of you. Let me see something of you.' He led them up the hill and directed their charge. The confusion at Donore was desperate. The Enniskilleners attacked from one angle and the Dutch from another. The Irish held their ground, and in the ensuing confusion William's attack was beaten off. The Enniskilleners

> did very bravely at first, but espying another great party whom they took for the enemy just ready to surround them, they began to fly and did actively put in disorder the Dutch horse and all others that stood in their way. The place was unfortunately full of holes and dung pits and the passages narrow; but above all the dust and smoke quite blinded them. His Majesty was here in the crowd of all, drawing his sword and animating them that fled to follow him. His danger was great among the enemy's guns which killed thirty of the Enniskilleners on the spot.[13]

Hamilton's cavalry again posed a threat, and while the Enniskilleners and Dutch prepared another attack, the last of the Irish infantry withdrew from Donore and doubled along the road to the south. The Williamites formed up to chase after them and, for the last time, Hamilton ordered his horsemen to turn about and charge. The Irish cavalry force was now greatly depleted. Some of the regiments had all but ceased to exist. Parker's regiment, for instance, had suffered ninety per cent casualties and had only thirty men left. Notwithstanding this, Hamilton knew where his duty lay. The Irish horse spurred up the hill and charged straight into the pursuing horsemen. For the second time in an hour the Enniskilleners were beaten off and again with heavy losses. In these short engagements with Hamilton's men, a quarter of them were killed. The Williamites fell back to reorganise, and the Irish were gone, too weak to repeat the performance.

In this, the final action of any importance that day, Richard Hamilton, wounded and exhausted, was taken prisoner. He came face to face with William, the man whose commission he had betrayed a year and half earlier when he agreed to treat with Tyrconnell on his behalf. William spoke to him kindly and ordered that his wounds be treated. He asked Hamilton whether he thought the Irish cavalry would try another attack. 'Yes, upon my honour', he answered 'I believe they will for they have a good body of horse still.' '*Your* honour?' retorted the Dutchman.

Hamilton was a disappointed man. It is fair to say that no one had fought harder than he had on that day. Although he had been let down badly by his infantry he had led his cavalry in attack after attack. But despite all his efforts the Irish had been beaten and he was bloodied and a prisoner. He told his captors, probably with some bitterness, that he had been waiting for Sarsfield to come to his relief with eleven battalions of foot and three more cavalry regiments.[14] But Sarsfield, as recounted above, was occupied elsewhere and never received any such order. The fact of the matter was that once Lauzun and James had left Oldbridge, the battle was effectively lost as soon as the Dutch guards entered the water. No reinforcement from Sarsfield or anyone else would have made any difference to the final outcome. Hamilton's achievement was that he had directed some of the fiercest fighting of the battle and had enabled the Irish army to slip away.

The fighting was certainly fierce and confused, especially around Donore itself. There were no national uniforms in 1690, as each regiment was dressed in its own. Although many English, Irish and continental regiments were dressed in distinctive colours—blue, brown, white, grey or yellow; most regiments on both sides wore red coats. When the fighting got to be at its fiercest and most muddled it was very difficult to tell who was on which side. In an attempt to remedy this problem orders were issued on the night before the Boyne that the Williamite soldiers would each wear a green sprig of leaves in their hats, as this was what the Dutch did when fighting on the continent. The French traditionally fought with white cockades in their hats and so the Irish were issued with orders to do the same. As it was be an expensive task to find some twenty thousand new cockades, the overwhelming majority of them pinned a piece of white paper into their hats instead. Consequently, it was the English rather than the the Irish who were 'wearing of the green' at the Boyne.

Despite these precautions mistakes were most certainly made, especially in the confusion around Donore. Perhaps the worst incident was when the Enniskilleners were beaten off by Hamilton's men for the second time. They found themselves confronted with Colonel Donop's Danish cavalry and both regiments charged each other. The Huguenot Isaac Dumont de Bostaquet wrote of another incident when he was about to run a man through. The man shouted to him: 'I'm an Inniskillinger' and just in time, Dumont noticed the sprig of green in his hat. Potentially the most serious accident of all was that recorded by Southwell: 'One of the Inniskillingers came with his pistol cocked to His Majesty until he called out: 'What, are you angry with your friends?' The truth is the clothes of friends and foes are so much alike.'[15] Why it was that the men of Enniskillen were especially prone to being involved in these errors of judgement is a matter for conjecture.

The pursuing Williamites were in some disarray themselves. There was little co-ordination in their movements and they did not know the land in front of them. In his journal the Huguenot cavalryman Gideon Bonnivert recorded an Irish ambush at nine o'clock that night:

> Having too hotly pursued them we were almost upon them when they faced about as if they had been willing to receive us, but we having left our foot and cannon behind, considering how late it was, made haste. They fired for an hour and a half small shot very thick upon us, for they had hid parties in bushes.[16]

Lauzun's French brigade, which had not been involved in the fighting, acted as a rearguard and effectively prevented any pursuit. It was getting to be too dangerous to advance as the light faded, despite William's desire to push on, and no great effort was made to break through. As night fell the fighting died out. The Williamites had no tents with them and so were forced to sleep where they were in the fields. The Irish continued their retreat southwards.

'I still think the slaughter on the place was not 1,000 men of the enemy, nor half as many of ours, but the consequence has been of great extent.'[17] So wrote William's secretary three days later in Swords. The Boyne was certainly not a great battle in terms of men killed. Plunket referred to it as a skirmish. But it was a great victory for King William. He had fooled King James. He had made him divert his strength to miles away from where the battle was to be fought, and a general deserves more credit for achieving his ends with little rather than great carnage.

James's strategy had been dangerous from the start. He gave William the chance to dictate the terms of the battle. Every important move at the Boyne was made by William first and then followed by an Irish reaction. James was manoeuvred into a defeat that lost him not only the field of battle but also Dublin, and the consequences of that were great.

Much has been written of James's behaviour to the effect that he ran away in a cowardly fashion, but such an assessment does not stand up to close scrutiny. He intended to fight and he wanted to fight, but he was quite simply outmanoeuvred. On the other hand the only criticism of William was that he exposed himself to too much danger. This was certainly so: at Donore one musket ball shot the heel off his boot and another shattered one of his pistols. His behaviour on that day said much of his character. At the end of the battle 'after he had been seventeen hours in constant fatigue with all the stiffness that his wound gave him, he expressed neither joy nor any sort of vanity, only he looked cheerful.'[18] However carefully one looks at the events of the Boyne it is difficult to imagine, even with the advantage of hindsight, how any man could have bettered his performance.

CHAPTER IX

The Retreat to Limerick

'Some few desperadoes, with Jesuits, priests and friars, are got on the other side of the River Shannon and would have the people believe that river more consecrated than the Boyne, and that their charms and masses will be more available than their other artillery was at the last engagement with them. Tyrconnell and Sarsfield are said to be at the head of them, but their own lieutenant general as well as we, are of opinion they will not fight, but we believe the war to be at an end'.

London Newsletter, 19 July 1690[1]

MUCH OF THE IRISH ARMY had disintegrated. Scattered groups of men, separated from their officers, made for Dublin but although in many cases the command structure had broken down completely, it was only a temporary break from authority. On the northern outskirts of the capital the troops began to reform into their companies. Regimental colours were placed on high ground to attract the stragglers and the officers then marched the men around the city and onto the Limerick road. 'Indeed,' wrote O'Kelly, 'tis admirable how every individual person, both officer and soldier, came hither without any orders and even without the conduct of any of their chief commanders as if they had been all guided to Limerick by some secret instinct of nature.'[2]

In Dublin a provisional government was set up by Robert Fitzgerald to await the coming of William and to prevent the Protestants from sacking the town. Without his efforts there would have been complete anarchy. But there was no stopping the celebrations and the houses of many Catholics, including Sarsfield's, were broken into and ransacked.

Within a fortnight of the Boyne Tyrconnell and most of the Irish army had reached Limerick. The retreat had been disorganised and no provision had been made to supply or feed the troops on the way. Consequently, the troops had swept across the countryside stealing what they could. The Irish army now collecting outside Limerick had clearly suffered far more from the flight than from the fighting. The infantry were in an especially bad state. Their clothes and shoes were ragged and they had thrown away their equipment and often their muskets to lighten their loads. The senior officers were exasperated. Stevens related how when his regiment was reviewed by Brigadier Wauchope outside Limerick, of the seven hundred men on parade, five hundred of them had lost their weapons. Wauchope was furious. He considered shooting a few of them to teach the others to keep hold of their arms, but as there were so many of them to choose from it was thought impractical. Instead 'it was only declared to them how well they deserved to die.'[3]

'Limerick is a very good seaport, badly fortified, but with an advantageous situation as it is surrounded by a number of impassable bogs.'[4] So wrote a French observer a few months before. The city's peace-time population of about twelve thousand people was substantial even by English standards and perhaps made Limerick the third largest city in Ireland.* Limerick stands on the Shannon and in those days consisted of two distinct towns, the English town on King's Island and the Irish town on the southern bank of the Shannon. These two halves of the city were connected by Ball's Bridge, a plain medieval construction. Although both towns were walled, the walls were old and could not be expected to stand up to a concentrated cannonade as they were 'far from being thick'. There were no ramparts nor any place on the walls to position cannons, and apart from a small palisade in front of part of the walls there were no other fortifications. If Limerick was to put up a fight, there was a lot of work to be done.

The news of James's flight from Ireland was met with great joy by the Protestants in Dublin. It seemed that at last the war was nearing its end. On 7 July 1690, William issued a declaration from Finglas offering amnesty to all the Irish now in arms except the leaders of the Jacobite party provided that they surrendered before the 1st August. It was not the best of moves.

> This was a foolish edict and the first of its kind, I believe, that ever had been; for commonly a prince entering into a country in order to conquer it doth in the first place encourage the principal persons to submit unto him, and when these are gained the rest do follow in course. I suppose the Prince of Orange was persuaded to go against reason in favour of his great officers who would have the Irish Catholic lords of lands to be rejected of all expectation of recovering their estates.[5]

William knew that the Irish intended to concentrate their main forces along and behind the Shannon and he knew that the Irish army was regrouping at Limerick, but Limerick was not his first objective. His victory at the Boyne had been soured by the news that he received two days later in Swords: the Anglo-Dutch fleet had been defeated by the French in a great sea battle off Beachy Head in Sussex. The first reports that he had received made things seem very bad. The French were now masters of the Channel, and would be in a position to prevent supplies reaching him from England. As it was, he had barely enough powder and ammunition to continue the war in Ireland Worse still, the threat of a French invasion of England in his absence grew by the day. William resolved to return to London.

* By comparison, Dublin, then the second largest city in the British Isles had a population of about sixty thousand and the second city of Ireland, Cork, had a population of twenty-five thousand. Londonderry housed less than a tenth of that last figure. Every other city in the British Isles was then, as now, dwarfed by London which even at that time had a population of several hundred thousand. The next two largest English cities at the end of the 17th century were Bristol and Norwich each with some thirty thousand inhabitants.

However, before he left Ireland, William wanted to ensure that his gains were secure. As he studied the map his eyes fell on Waterford. That was where he would finish his campaign. With that town taken he would control the entire eastern seaboard of Ireland and he would have a port with which to supply his army as it marched into Munster. He sent detachments on ahead to take the smaller towns. The Irish did not try to stop them. Colonel Eppinger found Wexford deserted and Count Schomberg marched quietly into Clonmel to learn that Sarsfield had just left for Limerick with 'a large body of horse'.[6] The Irish had clearly given up Leinster. William marched south, crossing the Liffey at Kilcullen, the Barrow at Carlow, and the Nore at Bennettsbridge.

The mail that William received from the Cabinet Council in London was insistent. He must return and leave Ireland to his generals. On 17 July he wrote back: 'We are now within twenty four miles of Waterford which pretends to hold out, but we believe that all the other seaport towns in Munster may take example by what we shall do therein. We therefore hold it absolutely necessary for us in person here to remain for six or seven days in the army for the better settlement of all things.'[7] When he reached Carrick-on-Suir, only sixteen miles from his objective, he sent Lieutenant-General Percy Kirke on ahead to finish the campaign. To Kirke it must have seemed a daunting task. Waterford was apparently well defended and garrisoned and the governor, Colonel Barrett, gave every impression that he was going to hold out. But he was isolated and far from help. On 23 July he was ready to talk. 'The garrison of Waterford', wrote Davies, 'sent this day very saucy proposals of capitulation'. The proposals were at first turned down, but William did not want any delays. He changed his mind and allowed Barret the terms that he had demanded. Two days later the garrison was permitted to march out with their all weapons and to go to Mallow. William personally came to watch the garrison depart. 'They were but three scurvy regiments,' it was noted, and '(the most) sorry wretched fellows I ever saw'.[8]

Only one Leinster stronghold now remained in Irish hands, Duncannon, the powerful fortress overlooking Waterford harbour. When Colonel Abraham Eppinger had first summoned it to surrender on 21 July the governor, Colonel Michael 'Brute' Burke had said that he would defend the fort to his last man. But as the days went by he too began to feel isolated. On the 26th when he saw Admiral Sir Cloudsley Shovell's squadron of sixteen frigates sailing into Waterford harbour he changed his mind.[9] To the great relief of the English, Burke surrendered on the next day on the terms that he and his men could march to Limerick with all their arms and baggage.

William made haste to leave. With Ulster and Leinster now secured, and with the knowledge that there was no opposition to his army in western Munster he rode off to Dublin. He left the conduct of the war in the hands of Count Solms with instructions to march on Limerick. But on reaching Dublin, or rather Chapelizod, William was met with news that made him change his mind. His fleet had not been destroyed, the French had gained little at Beachy Head, and there had been no invasion. He later learnt that there had been only a wasteful raid on the Devonshire fishing village of Teignmouth, a place that he had never even heard of. Messengers were sent to Solms. The king was returning to finish the Irish war in person.

Had the battle of the Boyne not been an English victory; had the English been sent reeling back through Dundalk to Belfast or Carrickfergus rather than the Irish through Dublin to Limerick, the leadership of the Irish army would never have been questioned. As it was, defeat soured the relationship between King James's viceroy and those under him and there was a powerful body of opinion that wanted him to resign. Sarsfield had never got on with Tyrconnell. Their personalities were very different. Tyrconnell was sixty years old, domineering and experienced. He was also contemptuous of those who presumed to express opinions contrary to his own and he felt no inclination to relinquish any of his authority. Sarsfield was young, not yet forty. He was popular and he knew it. He was a frustrated man of action, a professional and aggressive soldier who resented being dictated to by a man who had become more used to bullying council meetings and issuing proclamations than to leading bodies of armed men. And there were others, perhaps craftier men than Sarsfield, who agreed with him and told him so. More than that, they suggested to Sarsfield that he should be the power in the kingdom, not this old man whose bumbling had brought them all to so much misery.

The greatest concern among the Jacobite officers was the lack of preparation being undertaken to defend Limerick. It seemed that now they had gathered there they were doing little more than waiting for the English to arrive. The senior officers eventually selected five of their number to go to Tyrconnell and demand a general council of war to decide some form of strategy for the inevitable defensive campaign that was approaching. Tyrconnell agreed and a general council of war was called to discuss 'what was to be done in this desperate state of our affairs'.[10]

When the officers were gathered together, Tyrconnell addressed them. He laid his cards on the table straight away. Brandishing a piece of paper he told the assembly that he had in his hand a declaration that the city of Limerick could not hold out for more than three days once the English arrived. Although the declaration was signed by only three Irishmen, it did bear the signatures of Lauzun and all but one of the senior French officers.

There was an immediate, deafening uproar. Although the Irish had been forced to retreat they did not feel beaten yet. Few of them had even had the opportunity of fighting at all. They were furious at the viceroy's suggestion and shouted him down. The feeling against Tyrconnell was all but unanimous. The officers resolved to 'suffer the utmost extremities rather than submit to the usurper and to hold out what was left to the last'. The fury was greatest amongst those who would before long be using every opportunity to challenge Tyrconnell: Sarsfield, Nicholas Purcell, Gordon O'Neill and the two Luttrell brothers. They in turn were backed by the only Frenchman not to have signed Tyrconnell's declaration, Major General Boisseleau, a haughty and proud man if ever there was one.

Tyrconnell was not intimidated. They could not bully him. He was the toughest man there, and he was not going to be overruled by a group of men whose lack of experience in war was glaring when contrasted to that of the French veterans who had signed the declaration. But he had now lost the confidence of his officer corps. The council of war ended and the malcontents, many of whom had disliked Tyrconnell from the start, set out to poison the men against their commander in chief. Exaggerated accounts of what had taken place in the meeting were spread throughout the army. Tyrconnell had suggested, it was rumoured, that if they did not surrender they should at least hamstring the horses to prevent the English capturing them, and then they should all retire behind the walls of the stronger cities and castles until help came from France.

One should bear in mind that Tyrconnell's most vivid experience of a town under siege had been as a young man when he had helped to defend Drogheda against Cromwell. The governor of the town had refused to surrender on the terms that had been offered and Cromwell's men had stormed in with orders to spare no one. They slaughtered both the garrison and the civilian population. Tyrconnell, although so badly wounded that he was left for dead, was one of the handful of Irishmen who lived to tell the tale. The rules of war had not changed in the intervening years and he now feared that the Irish were wasting whatever chances they had of being offered any decent terms. The longer they held out, the more their bargaining position would deteriorate.

But his reasoning did not convince Sarsfield who became one of the most vocal of those determined to banish defeatism from the army. Limerick, he told his men, was a strong city. The enemy, who had yet to march all the way from Waterford, would not be able to take it from them. Although the English had established themselves in Dublin the Irish still had the two main ports on the south coast, Cork and Kinsale, and they had both been well fortified. They also had the three main ports on the west coast; Limerick, Galway and Sligo. They had the French as allies and the French navy would be able to keep them supplied. The French navy would also land a great army in England[11] and would prevent the English getting any supplies from across the Irish Sea. The Williamite government in England was already tottering and an uprising of loyal subjects was expected daily. In Scotland there was a great civil war likely to spill over the border at any time. In all probability the Irish would not have to hold out for very long as the English would be forced to withdraw to attempt, hopelessly, to deal with more pressing problems. This was no time to be a Williamite rebel and this was no time for Ireland to surrender. Soon it would be the English that would be begging for favourable terms.

While Tyrconnell was out of the city, a second council of war was called. It was at this meeting that Sarsfield first established himself as the leader of the opposition to Tyrconnell, and he found that he had the support of the over-whelming majority of the senior officers in the army. Not only was he much liked and trusted as the hero of Sligo, but he was also able to bridge the cultural divide in the army. His popularity owed much to his background. He was able to call on the support of both the Palesmen and the large number of Gaelic officers now to be found in the army. His alliance with the Gaels ran very deep. He was related by birth to several Gaelic families and by marriage to the MacCarthys, and he had established very close friendships with several leading Gaels such as Randal MacDonnell, Gordon O'Neill and Oliver O'Gara. Both the 'Old English' and the Gaels could claim Sarsfield as their own. Tyrconnell on the other hand represented the Catholic 'Old English' ruling order of Ireland who had dominated the country before the 1641 rebellion in much the same way as the 'New English' ascendancy was to do in later years. Although Tyrconnell had set out to deal with the Cromwellians as harshly as they had dealt with his people, he never had any intention of surrendering power to the Gaels. Not only did he share with most other people in the country a dislike for the Ulster Gaels,* he did not care much for any of 'the O's and the Mac's'.[13] But in order to re-establish the 'Old English' he had been obliged to rely heavily on them to the extent that a third of his colonels were Gaels. And it was now these men, along with most of the Palesmen, who were clamouring for his removal.

Sarsfield's first concern was to ensure that the defence of Limerick would be properly handled, and that they would get French support. He and his sup-porters suspected that having made the pessimistic declaration, Tyrconnell and Lauzun could no longer be trusted to stand against the English, and it was feared that they would misrepresent matters to the French government who in turn would cease to supply them. Although many wild and aggressive solutions were no doubt discussed, the unofficial council of war finally agreed on two resolutions that were to be put to Tyrconnell.

Firstly, two 'persons of quality' were to be chosen by the council of war and sent on a mission to France to correct any misunderstanding that there might be as to the position and loyalty of the Irish army. Secondly, the command of the Irish army should be given to Sarsfield. The nature of these resolutions and the clumsy way in which they were put to him did nothing to improve Tyrconnell's temper on his return. He would not have any of it. It was not for an unconstitu-tional council of war to send missions abroad, he said. It was the viceroy's prerogative, and he would choose who to send and when to send them. And as for Sarsfield? He would not hear of it. But he was too wily a politician not to see that he had played his hand very badly, and he could plainly see how dangerous his position now was. He announced that he intended to take every

---

* After the Williamites had established themselves in the North, especially after the arrival of Schomberg's army, thousands of refugees flooded southwards. Resentment soon built up against this 'rabble that destroyed the country, ruined the inhabitants and prevented the regular forces from drawing that subsistence that they might otherwise have had from the people.'[12]

step to ensure that Limerick would be able to defend itself, and he promoted Sarsfield to the rank of major-general.

This was not enough to satisfy his officers. They met in groups and encouraged one another in the violence of their opinions against Tyrconnell. They spoke to their junior officers and told them of the row in the meeting and of his refusal to adopt their proposals. Dick Talbot, they told them, has had his day. He was no longer fit to lead them. Their main concern was that he would surrender to the English despite their protests. In certain quarters it was not difficult to convince people that Tyrconnell was a traitor. Ways were sought as to how they could rid themselves of this burdensome viceroy. Men whose loyalty to the crown's authority as vested in the king's deputy would never have been doubted, became conspirators after the councils of war. Junior officers were enlisted to the cause and they rallied the troops with the same zest and fire that had enabled the young militia captains in Londonderry to force their governor to flee. The chief conspirators were careful, but once it became clear to them that they represented the feelings of most of the officers and men, a plan began to form.

The first problem to overcome was the choice of Tyrconnell's replacement. The most obvious candidate was the king's son, the duke of Berwick. Sarsfield and the conspirators greatly feared being deserted by King James. It was of paramount importance to them that any action taken by them would be recognised in France as a legitimate expression of loyalty to the crown. It was reasoned that if Berwick took Tyrconnell's place, the king would be forced to support his son. They would also be able to count on French patronage by making it clear to Louis' government that they were the war party, the party of no surrender. Although Berwick was not the ideal replacement, being barely out of his teens, he was not without military experience, and he certainly would not consider a surrender on any terms short of the reinstatement of his father in the Court of St James.

The difficulty was in sounding Berwick out. They would risk everything if he suspected that there was a plot afoot. Unless there really was no alternative, Berwick was to be kept in the dark. The plan was then to present him with a *fait accompli.*

At that time, the French still garrisoned Limerick. They had suffered very few casualties at the Boyne and having shown a high degree of discipline in their retreat they were still well equipped. The Irish infantry, badly equipped, often unarmed, badly shod and clothed, were camped outside the Irish town in the county of Limerick. This was on the same side of the river that the English would advance from. The conspirators could be sure of one thing: Tyrconnell would have to issue orders for the Irish to march into Limerick, through the Irish town, across Ball's Bridge, through the English town, and across Thomond Bridge into Co. Clare where they would have the Shannon between them and the enemy. With this in mind the vague plan to remove Tyrconnell took on a definite shape.

When legitimately ordered to march, the Irish would do so. The front of the

11 A Prospect of Limerick painted by Thomas Phillips in 1685.
Thomond Bridge and the Castle are shown at the left of the picture, St Mary's Cathedral is in
the centre, and Ball's Bridge and the Irish town are on the right.

column would pass through the city gates into the city. Once a great body of men
was inside, a signal would be given to seize the gates and keys, and allow the
rest of the troops in. When this was done a drum would be beaten as a signal to
the Irish to seize and disarm the un-suspecting Frenchmen and throw them out
of the city. The French, unarmed, could then go to Galway and ship themselves
back to France which is what they were expected to do anyway. The Irish would
have taken possession of Limerick, deposed Tyrconnell, and rearmed themselves
in one fell swoop. The war against the English could then be pursued with vigour.

This was to be no small putsch. It involved thousands of men and would rely
on the cooperation of hundreds of officer who would have to be briefed befor-
hand. The plotters set about swearing others to secrecy, but it was an impossible
task. The plan was too ambitious and Tyrconnell still had his own supporters.
One of the officers who was let in on the secret, Colonel Mark Talbot, owed
Tyrconnell particular loyalty as he was the viceroy's natural son. He went
straight to his father and told him all that he knew.

Tyrconnell had to protect himself, but he had to be careful as he knew that
there would be the most terrible trouble if the French got to hear of the plot.
There could be no question of doing anything publicly. He could not arrest the
ringleaders or do anything that might provoke a revolt. He was an experienced
man and acted sensibly. He let the ringleaders know that he knew. He kept
them out of Limerick when he ordered the troops to march through the city to
the Clare side. He briefed his trusted officers to ensure that nothing would happen
and then before the conspirators could alter their plans he issued the order for
the army to move. When the troops later marched straight through the city,
many were straining their ears for the signal that never came.

That did not end the matter. The conspirators were still at liberty and still
hoped to rid themselves of Tyrconnell. They turned to a less dramatic plan. In a
secret meeting Sarsfield volunteered to approach Berwick. He was to let the

young duke know of their intentions and to get him to agree to take Tyrconnell's place.

Sarsfield did his best. He went alone to Berwick and swore him to secrecy. Berwick was astounded at what Sarsfield had to say: that he represented a body of officers who were convinced of Tyrconnell's treachery—that they had resolved to put him under arrest and to continue the war that the plotters were the only men truly loyal to Berwick's father; and that they wanted Berwick to lead them in their treachery. The young man would have none of it. To act against the viceroy was to act against King James. It was high treason. But Berwick knew how dangerous things were. He could not even speak of the plot. He told Sarsfield that if he heard anything more of it he would tell both Tyrconnell and the king. This threat, he later wrote 'prevented the execution of the design'.

Although the French never learnt of the severity of the plan against them, they were very suspicious of the Irish. Their commander, Count Lauzun, certainly had no intention of staying in Limerick. He was not impressed with the defences. The walls, he let it be known, could be beaten down with roasted apples.[14] He wrote to France saying that he feared that both he and Tyrconnell were likely to be made prisoners of war. His best chance was to go to Galway where he could prepare to ship his troops home. The Irish could keep Limerick and delay the English advance although he knew that they would not stop it. Besides, he had no desire to stay garrisoned with or near the Irish. 'They hate us so much', he wrote, 'that we fear that they may play some dirty trick on us'.[15] He issued the order to march for Galway, and his men left Limerick, fully armed, well equipped and with high hopes that they were going to embark for France.

Now that he had been forced into continuing the war, Tyrconnell resolved to make the best of things. He garrisoned Limerick with some fourteen thousand men, four thousand of whom were formed into unarmed labour battalions. He had his wife and several other ladies, possibly including Lady Honora Sarsfield in the group, shipped off to France for their safety. The in-fighting and the bitter arguments had invigorated him but there was little point in him remaining in Limerick. He arranged to have his government transferred to Galway.

With the French out of the way, the Irish set to work. There was much to be done. Brigadier John Wauchope took command[16] of the city and set about improving the defences. Not surprisingly, his attempts to keep out the women and children were largely unsuccessful.

The most important task was to build defensive works outside the walls. The idea was firstly to dig a great open ditch around the Irish town. The earth that was thrown up by this was then used to build a series of earthen forts or bastions up against the medieval city walls. These bastions were reinforced with timber and rubble and were faced with stone so that they would not only serve as forts in their own right, but they would also screen the base of the walls from direct artillery fire. The measurements of the Limerick defences are not known, but as they were so hurriedly thrown up it is likely that they were both irregular and generally less imposing than would otherwise have been the case.

Although a ditch should be as deep as possible, twenty feet would usually serve the purpose, and ideally it would have been forty feet wide. Breastworks were then set up on both sides of the ditch and several small earthworks were built outside it. The result was that the English would be faced with a hard fight to even get to the city walls.

While William was still engaged at Waterford, another English army had been trying to establish a foothold in Connaught. Major-General James Douglas had been detached with orders to take Athlone and to secure the bridge over the Shannon. The garrison at Athlone was commanded by a peppery old Irish colonel, Richard Grace. Grace had fought throughout the civil war in the 1640s and after the Cromwellian victory had, as had thousands of Irishmen, joined the Spanish service as a mercenary. Competent though no doubt he was, he was best known for an incident that took place in 1653 when he commanded an Irish regiment in the defence of Gerona, then being besieged by the French. On that famous occasion he had simply led his men out of the town and joined the enemy. But, if Douglas was hoping for a repeat performance, he was to be disappointed. He arrived outside the town on 17 July 1690 and summoned Grace to surrender. Grace showed no such inclination. 'These are my terms', he said, firing his pistol. 'These only will I give or receive, and when my provisions are consumed, I will defend until I eat my old boots.'[17]

Douglas had an impossible task. His only hope had been to intimidate Grace, but Grace was quite confident that he was in a very strong position. The town was walled, the bridge had been dismantled, and the castle was strong enough to withstand any cannonade that Douglas's field guns could offer. And as Douglas could not even cross the river to surround the town there was no likelihood of him being able to force Grace into any culinary adventures.

Tyrconnell was especially concerned that Douglas should be prevented from taking Athlone. It was a strong and valuable town and was the gateway to Connaught. To the Irish it was more important than Sligo. As soon as news came that Douglas was attacking the town, preparations were made to reinforce Grace's garrison. Grateful for the opportunity of getting him away from the cabals of Limerick, Tyrconnell appointed Sarsfield to lead the expedition. He hurriedly collected the cavalry together and made arrangements to prepare as large as force as he could. On 28 July he rode out of Limerick with three and a half thousand horsemen northwards to Athlone via Loughrea. That same day an artillery train, four cannons and a large escort of dragoons and cavalry followed him. They also had to take the longer Loughrea road as even in the height of summer it was the only road to Athlone that was suitable for wagons and draughthorses. When the infantry followed they marched by the direct route that was passable for soldiers on foot although even so they would have to pick their way through bogs.[18]

The attack on Athlone did not last for more than a week. In fact before Sarsfield had left Limerick, Douglas had already marched back to Mullingar having wasted all his ammunition.[19] He was concerned even then by rumours that Sarsfield was on his way to relieve Athlone with fifteen thousand men. The rumours were both premature and exaggerated, but Douglas was in an unfavourable position. He did not have the power to prevent Sarsfield crossing the Shannon into Leinster at any of the fords or bridges south of Athlone and so he ran the risk of being caught between Grace's garrison on the one side and Sarsfield's supposedly massive army on the other. He did the sensible thing and left.

To add to Douglas's discomfort, his expedition had been badly provisioned and, despite his reputation as a strict disciplinarian, the effect on his hungry troops was all too predictable. One of his colonels, William Wolseley, the hero of Newtownbutler, was disgusted at the consequences: 'I am uneasy here with the disorders of our own men which has been great in our march to all without distinction that it is a shame to speak of it, and it was not in my power nor the other colonels to prevent it, having neither bread nor money to give them, which had I had, I would have hanged them to the last man.'[20] Woe to the inhabitants of mid Ireland! What the English did not steal, the Irish did. The rapparees 'have stripped the whole country of all the sheep and cattle so that we are like to have no provisions but what we have out of the stores'.[21]

William's advance had been better controlled, mostly perhaps because he so disapproved of his soldiers misbehaving. It was morosely noted that 'The King is very strict and will suffer none to plunder, so that this part of the army will be very poor because we are forced to be honest.' Anyone who was caught looting was strung up by the roadside to serve as an example to the others. Indeed, William's feelings on the subject were so strong that he personally beat one soldier with his cane for robbing on old Irishwoman, and then had him hanged.[22]

King William was not unduly concerned that Douglas had been unable to take Athlone. As his secretary noted: 'His Majesty seems not to doubt that the taking of Limerick will make Athlone easily fall in.'[23] ' Limerick was both further away and larger than Athlone and was a project for which he knew he needed as many men as possible. He had arranged for his comptroller of artillery, Willem Meesters, to take all the artillery and stores collected in Drogheda southwards to Dublin. He now issued instructions for Meesters to march to Kilkenny to await further orders. In Kilkenny Meesters was met by Captain Thomas Poultney who then commanded the two squadrons of Colonel Villiers's regiment of horse. Poultney also had his orders—to take the colonel's squadron and to escort the artillery from Kilkenny to the army at Limerick.[24] From Chapelizod William sent orders to Douglas to secure Mullingar and to march southwards leaving garrisons at Castle Forbes, Philipstown Fort, Birr Castle and Roscrea and to leave behind him a sufficient number of dragoons 'to scour the country and to hinder the enemy from breaking in between the places abovementioned'.[25]

Tyrconnell also knew what William's intentions were. He ordered back the Irish infantry, artillery and most of the cavalry, but left Sarsfield with instructions to watch and harry Douglas's progress. The English made slow progress southwards on the east bank of the Shannon. Sarsfield rode alongside them on the west bank, his only concern being to prevent Douglas from either crossing over onto his side or from securing any of the crossing points.

When it was safe to suppose that Douglas had no intention of forcing a crossing, Sarsfield returned to Limerick. He arrived there in the morning of 8 August at the same time that Douglas met up with King William and the English army at Caherconlish, eight miles away on the road to Tipperary. The mood in Limerick was still for holding out. Tyrconnell had done what he could and had appointed an experienced Frenchman as governor.* Although not yet forty, Alexandre de Rainier de Droue de Boisseleau had spent his whole life in the French army and was no stranger to the perils of war. At the battle of Saint Denys he had been one of only two officers in his regiment to escape death or serious injury. He had participated in the sieges of Tournai, Douai, Lille, Maastricht, Artois, Valenciennes, Cambrai and Luxembourg.[27] After twenty-two years of soldiering he had reached the rank of major and had been posted to Ireland where he now held King James's commission as a major-general. No other officer attached to the Irish army was as well schooled in siege warfare, and only a few had his experience of war.

---

* According to Lauzun, this was not a popular choice: 'Since this time three or four malcontents named Wauchope, Dorrington and Luttrell have made factions and have written letters saying that a Frenchman will betray them, which has much embarrassed the duke of Tyrconnell as there are many people under these gentlemen who are united in their hatred of France.'[26]

CHAPTER X

Sarsfield's Ride

Twas the calm hush of night: all silently we sped
From the city's battered walls, Patrick Sarsfield at our head;
Nor wondered why 'twas so, for we knew his heart was true
And he'd ask from us but all that Irishmen should do.
William Rooney, 'Sarsfield's Ride'[1]

In Ballyneety
He left not a bomb nor a copper pontoon
Nor anything bigger than a coin
Of their brass equipment
That he did not blow away
Like a candle's flame
In the open air.   Daibhi Ó Bruadair[2]

KING WILLIAM'S approach to Limerick was necessarily cautious, for although the Irish army had been defeated, it had not been destroyed. The Irish knew of his approach and had been preparing the city's fortifications for what was to come. He knew that a large force had been collected inside the city's walls and he was told that another large force, which included the French brigade, had garrisoned Galway. But he only had inaccurate estimates of the enemy's strength in these places. He also knew that the Irish cavalry were encamped in Co. Clare between the two cities, and that the Irish had garrisoned all the small forts and castles at the crossing points on the Shannon and throughout the counties of Limerick, Kerry and Cork.

The nearer the English got to Limerick, the more desolate the countryside became. They were horrified at what they saw. Under Berwick's supervision, the Irish had burnt every house and barn along the way and had removed or burnt the crops.[3] As the English advanced, the Irish withdrew, blocking the roads behind them to gain time. Although no serious attempt was made to halt them, the English were wary. Hedges were cut, cover was burnt and woods combed to prevent ambushes. There were several minor skirmishes between the advance guards and the Irish patrols. Irish horsemen shadowed William's army. The English knew that they were in very hostile country. The cover was so close and the hedges so thick that they could hear their enemies talking 'with their damned Irish brogue on their tongues',* but could not see them. 'Ye toads, are ye there? We'll be with you presently', shouted back the English.[4]

---

* Predictably, as Wurtemburg noted, 'The Irish shouted many insults at the English' as William's army neared Limerick.[3]

And so they were. On 8 August 1690 the vanguard of the English army chased an Irish reception party into the city and William's men formed up on Singland Hill overlooking Limerick. The king sent a trumpeter with a summons to the commander of the garrison to send out delegates to hear the terms that he would offer them on their surrender. Boisseleau sent back a note to William's Secretary of State for Ireland, Robert Southwell. 'I am surprised, sir,' the message read, 'at the letter that you wrote to me. I am best able to deserve the Prince of Orange's esteem by a vigorous defence by the king's troops whom I have the honour to command.'[5] Once these formalities were over, the siege began. The Irish guns opened fire from the city walls. The English were unimpressed. 'Tis not doubted they will alter their sentiments so soon as the heavy cannon comes up, which is expected the next day being but eight miles behind.'[6]

William's tactical options were limited. He could either remain on the south side of the city and attack the Irish town knowing that fresh supplies and reinforcements were available to Boisseleau from Co. Clare, or he could try and surround the city by crossing the Shannon upstream and attacking from both sides. The danger of the latter course was that his besieging army would be divided. That part of it in Clare would be under the grave threat of an attack by the Irish cavalry and the Franco-Irish force at Galway. In addition to that, either part of the army could well be unable to cope with a concentrated sally from one part of the town. If such a plan was to be carried out, a crossing point would need to be established as near to the city as possible. For that very purpose, pontoon boats were being brought across the country with the siege artillery and William issued orders for such a crossing to be found.

On the next day, 9 August, a small party of dragoons were sent up the Shannon to secure the ford at Annaghbeg, only two miles up river from Limerick. As they neared the water's edge they drew heavy fire from three Irish regiments that had been positioned on the north bank. The English saw that there could be no possibility of them getting to the other side in any order as nature had strewn large boulders across the ford and the Irish had covered it with a field battery. 'Everyone believed that five hundred men would have made a stop to our army.'[7] The English dragoons settled down for the day to watch the Irish and to wait for reinforcements. There was every indication that there was going to be a battle.

In Limerick the Irish waited to see how and when the English would attack. Tyrconnell's plan of defence was unimaginative. The army would retire into garrisons, the two largest being Limerick and Galway. The cavalry would remain at large in Co. Clare. The English were to act, the Irish were to react.

Many of the leading officers were dissatisfied with the plan. They wanted the Irish to do something positive. Berwick, still only twenty years old, was particularly critical. Filled with the confidence of youth, he proposed leading the entire cavalry force, all three and a half thousand men, on a raid directed at the unwalled city of Dublin. His plan was to attack and destroy every magazine and garrison on the way, and to race back across the country to Athlone and Sligo once William had detached men to deal with him.

Tyrconnell was unimpressed. He was not going to be dictated to on strategic matters by a boy. In any case, Berwick's plan was a foolish one. The cavalry was needed in Clare to prevent the English from attacking Limerick from both sides. Also there were still many English troops scattered across the country and Berwick could easily be held up. The plan was too dangerous, and was rejected. Rejected, Berwick wrote later, because Tyrconnell was jealous. He was jealous because he was too old and fat to lead such a raid himself.

Shortly after the English army had arrived in the outskirts of Limerick, a second plan was suggested. It was just as ambitious as the first but it involved fewer men. This plan was said to be Sarsfield's.[8] It had been noted that the prince of Orange was still in the habit, as he had been at the Boyne, of riding about in the company only of his staff and runners. A squadron of determined men could, with luck, intercept him and carry him off. That would end the siege, and perhaps the war, in one fell swoop.

None of the Irish sources mention this plan, and it is unlikely that Sarsfield ever made any attempt to carry it out. However, such an attempt was made but perhaps without Sarsfield's or any other senior officer's authority. The following is an extract from a letter written to Christian V of Denmark from one of his representatives with the Danish brigade outside Limerick:

> A few days ago a squadron of the enemy might easily have carried him (William) off. He had gone attended by only seven or eight persons to reconnoitre the fortifications on the banks of the river, to the right of the camp. He was perceived by the enemy's cavalry. A squadron was detached and sent to cross the river at a ford which is near and to cut off the king. This might easily have been done without attracting the attention of those who were about the king. Fortunately, however, the late duke of Schomberg's equerry, who was on a slight eminence between the camp and the spot where the king was now standing, saw the enemy's manoeuvre and came at full speed to warn the king. He at first laughed at the equerry's advice, so that the latter, who knew that there was but little time to lose, began to swear and to address him in language so coarse that the respect that I owe your Majesty does not allow me to repeat it. Thereupon the king who had left his saddle remounted his horse and barely had time to escape in safety. The enemy, who had already passed a part of the river, fired their carbines at him, and Count Schomberg, who was at his Majesty's side, had his horse shot under him.[9]

A French artilleryman deserted from the English camp on the second day of the siege and surrendered himself to the Irish. He gave them information[10] that was to prove to be of great importance. The prince had insisted that the army march to Limerick with as much speed as possible. There had not been time to prepare and bring along all the supplies and equipment necessary for a siege. The only cannons that the prince had with him at the time were light field guns designed to shatter ranks of soldiers with grapeshot, but clearly inadequate for the task of battering down thick stone walls. All the heavy siege guns were a few days behind the main army as was the army's supply of gunpowder. The artillery train was winding its way westwards from Cashel under the direction of Willem Meesters, the prince's comptroller of artillery, a brilliant engineer and a siege specialist.*

Sarsfield was determined to take the opportunity. If he could capture or destroy the siege train the English army would be sitting outside the walls of Limerick for nothing. He had to move quickly. He left Limerick that very day and galloped off along the Galway road to the cavalry camp at Clare Castle to find Tyrconnell. Sarsfield's immediate problem was twofold. Less than half the cavalry was now gathered together at Clare, the rest had either been detached to the garrisons in Munster or to the city of Galway and three whole regiments were still outside Limerick at Annaghbeg. For a raid deep into enemy territory he would need the best mounted men available even if it meant taking men from their posts on the Shannon. This presented him with the second problem of getting permission to do just that. The cavalry was nominally led by Berwick but in real terms was commanded by Major-General Sheldon. However the commander in chief of the army was Tyrconnell and Sarsfield certainly had no authority to desert his post in Limerick and to demand detachments from other commands without the viceroy's permission.

Fortunately, the idea of a raid appealed to Tyrconnell. Sarsfield would need only a fraction of the cavalry that Berwick had wanted for his raid on Dublin, and even if Sarsfield was unsuccessful in reaching the artillery train the expedition could return. There seemed to be much to gain and little to lose. The English had not yet had time to secure the countryside and certainly had not yet been able to reach and post guards on every crossing point on the river between Limerick and Athlone. Sarsfield would be able to return within three days. Tyrconnell gave his blessing to the enterprise. It was now or never.

Sarsfield began his preparations straight away. He not only needed to draw the best men from the cavalry camp, he also needed the men from Annaghbeg. While the cavalrymen in Clare checked their equipment and prepared to move out, messengers were sent off to Annaghbeg where the Irish had made laborious preparations to prevent a crossing. Once his orders were received, the defences were abandoned as without cavalry the position was untenable. The horsemen made rapid preparations to ride out. The infantry and the gunners collected their equipment together and marched back to Limerick. Speed was now all important. For every minute that they lost, the artillery train drew closer to the English army. By midnight Annaghbeg was deserted.

---

* Meesters, the most highly paid artilleryman ever employed by the English army, received £3 per diem—overtunce that received by a colonel of infantry.[11]

The Williamite troops at Annaghbeg had begun their preparations to storm across the river. Reinforcements had arrived under the command of Generals Ginckel and Kirke. At first light a survey of the far bank proved it to be deserted. General Ginckel, William's second most senior Dutch officer, cautiously led a cavalry regiment into the water and up onto the northern bank. There was no sign of the enemy. The English inspected the deserted fortifications. There was no clue as to why the Irish had allowed them to cross the river without a fight. At first, no one's mind turned to suspicion. The English were just grateful that they had managed to cross the river with such ease, and by the end of the day some five thousand of them were in Co. Clare.

For his plan to succeed, Sarsfield needed to find out at the earliest opportunity where the artillery train was, and he had to keep well out of the way of English patrols. The next day, 10 August 1690, scouts were no doubt sent across the Shannon to ride towards Clonmel from where the artillery train would make its way to Limerick. The cavalry was gathered together and rested and that afternoon, within a day of Sarsfield having first decided to intercept the artillery, his force of some six hundred horsemen were ready to go. That evening they made for the ford at Killaloe, about twelve miles upstream from Limerick, where they crossed the river without mishap and disappeared into the Silvermine mountains. As dawn broke, Sarsfield's men were resting in a temporary camp, tradition says on the wooded slopes of Keeper Hill, and his scouts scoured the countryside questioning local people about the enemy's movements, getting local guides, and keeping a watchful eye on the main road to Limerick for any sign of the approaching wagons.

Sarsfield was not the only one who could command the services of spies and informers and his own movements had also noticed by unfriendly eyes. During the day, Monday 11 August, a local Protestant landowner, Manus O'Brien,* appeared in the English camp with the news that a sizeable body of Irish horsemen had crossed the Shannon during the night at Killaloe. He was not believed. One senior officer even took O'Brien aside and began questioning him about the cattle in the area. Exasperated, O'Brien complained openly that King William's staff cared more about cows than their king's honour. Although no one had any real cause to believe the word of an unknown Irishman, Count Schomberg, to his credit, did at least think it worth taking precautions. He wanted to dispatch the regiment of Huguenot cavalry to join the artillery train, but he was overruled by Portland and Solms who made light of the matter. It was stretching belief, said Portland, that Sarsfield would try anything in Tipperary as it is 'such difficult, close country'.[13]

O'Brien was insistent. He had seen the Irish cross the river and he knew that it was important. Hours went by before, amongst the bustle and chaos of the camp, he found an officer who knew him. He told his tale afresh and was taken to the king. But even William was slow to act decisively. He did not send the

---

*   Accompanied, according to Ferrar, by one Mr Bevin.[12]

Huguenot cavalry off to meet the artillery, as Schomberg suggested. Instead he made arrangements for O'Brien's story to be verified. A Huguenot cavalry sergeant was ordered to take a patrol up to the river to Killaloe to have a look.[14]

Although no one was willing to issue commands on the basis of a rumour, there were reasons to take O'Brien's story seriously. Why, for instance, had the Irish pulled back from Annaghbeg ford? It could not have been because they thought it untenable as it clearly was a formidable defensive position. It may merely have been that Tyrconnell needed to concentrate all his forces in Limerick, but suspicions began to form. Independent intelligence had already suggested that the withdrawal was related to 'some design to be conducted by Sarsfield on this side, and that he was gone to the ford at Killaloe, nine miles up, to effect it'.[15] O'Brien's evidence was certainly not uncorroborated.

More time was wasted. The Huguenot sergeant rode off into the country in search of some evidence of enemy movement. There was plenty of evidence. It was quite clear what had happened. Turning his horse, he rode back as fast as he could with the news.

William heard the report, but had weightier matters on his mind. He was planning the siege. He instructed his close friend and advisor, Hans Willem Bentinck, the earl of Portland, to arrange for a mounted force to search for Sarsfield and protect the artillery. Portland in turn instructed Sir John Lanier to arrange matters. Lanier was in no hurry. Although he received his instructions to ride out in the morning of Monday 11 August, when William returned to the camp in the afternoon, he found that Lanier was still preparing his men.

The 11th was a nerve-wracking day for Sarsfield. He knew that the English must be looking for him and he did not know how big the cavalry escort would be. It must have been an enormous relief when his scouts brought him the news that the artillery train had spent the night outside Cashel and was now moving along the road to Tipperary. Indeed, it would have been impossible for the English to keep its whereabouts a secret. From the first wagon to the last it stretched for over two miles. The weather had been very hot and dry and the dust raised by the one hundred or more wagons and the cavalry escort hung high over the road. For miles around the air resounded with the clanking of the artillery and the rumble of the wheels. The day wore on and nothing happened. Most importantly, no troops joined the train from the English camp. Sarsfield's men were undisturbed by enemy patrols. As the afternoon turned to evening it seemed unbelievable that the English were taking no precautions. The wagons wound their way slowly through the village of Cullen and as dusk fell they stopped on the road by the ruins of Ballyneety Castle. In the darkness, Sarsfield's spies were able to report that the English had lit fires. They were settling down for the night.

Late in the evening just before midnight, there was an alarm when six troops of horsemen approached from Limerick. They were a detachment of Enniskillen Dragoons commanded by Sir Albert Cunningham who had been sent out at night not to reinforce Poultney but to act as an escort for another convoy that was waiting in Carrick. As the Irish watched, Cunningham's men threaded their way past the wagons and disappeared along the Tipperary road into the night.

Sarsfield knew that he now had to act quickly. There was a great risk that he would be interrupted by more troops riding out of Limerick. As soon as the dragoons had gone, and it was safe to move, he issued his orders.

Captain James Fitzgerald was detached with an ambush party after Cunningham to prevent him returning, and Sarsfield led the rest of his force off to Ballyneety.

That is all that the written sources of the time tell us of 'Sarsfield's Ride', but tradition adds much more. Sarsfield was guided throughout his ride by a man named Galloping Hogan, a local rapparee. Hogan certainly was no fictional character although apart from the fact that he was a particularly audacious bandit chief nothing is known of him except that for the next year he made a great nuisance of himself to the English. Writing the best part of two centuries later, Maurice Lenihan preserved the local tradition of Hogan as being: 'a well educated, popular man, and a brave rapparee. Hogan knew every pass and defile—was familiar with every track and roadway—with every ford and bog.'* Tradition also has it that when Sarsfield set off on the night of 10 August, 'a fine harvest moon lent light to the landscape'. The almanacs agree on this point, there was a full moon throughout Sarsfield's Ride.[16]

While riding out to Killaloe, Sarsfield's party took from his home at Ballycorny Bridge a local Protestant named Cecil. Whether Cecil was kidnapped to act as a local guide, or whether he was taken as a prisoner to prevent him from raising the alarm, is no longer clear. Once over the Shannon at Killaloe, Sarsfield was startled by the appearance of a body of men near Laobadiha Bridge. The suspicion crossed his mind that Hogan had betrayed him, but the men turned out to be Hogan's band of rapparees who had been instructed by their leader to join Sarsfield's force. Laobadiha Bridge spans what is now known as 'Hogan's Glen', a deep thickly wooded gully about a mile and a half from Killaloe Bridge, and it is in this gully that the rapparees hid and stored their loot.**

Tradition has also preserved the route of 'Sarsfield's Ride'. He rode first to Glennagross and then down to Ballyvalley Ford outside Killaloe where he crossed the river, and then inland to Laobadiha Bridge. He was then led into the

---

* It is unlikely that the Tipperary highwayman was well educated. Story (p. 236) wrote of an incident in the following year: 'Towards the latter end of September two lieutenants of the Irish Army having deserted and having got our General's pass to go home, they were met withal by Hogan and his party and stripped of what they had, but neither himself nor any of his crew could read the pass, else it's probable they would have sent them the same way they sometimes did our militia when they fell into their power.'

** Accordingly to Lenihan, Laobadiha (or Labadhy, as he spells it) in Irish signifies 'the bed of the rogues'.

12 A contemporary Dutch print of siege artillery on the move.

thickly wooded Silvermine Mountains, along the west side of Keeper Hill through Ballyhourigan wood and then up the Doonane valley to Toor and between the hills to Rear Cross below Mother Mountain and then down the Bilboa valley and across the hills to Glengar. It is not known where he camped during the day, but one would very much suspect that it would have been in the area of Glengar which is at the southern end of the thickly wooded range of hills that he had crossed. From there he could look across to the other side of the Mulkear Valley where the road ran from Cashel to Limerick.

After dark on the 11th, Sarsfield's men came down from the hills and crossed the low country to Toem, through Monard to Cullen, and from Cullen they moved as quietly as they could towards Derk, a mile away from Ballyneety. One suspects that tradition is confused on this last detail of the itinerary as to get to Derk from Cullen Sarsfield would have to bypass Ballyneety first, and it is there the English had encamped, near 'the Hill of Ballyneety',* a remarkable conical eminence which may be seen from a great distance'.[17]

The artillery train was in silence as Sarsfield approached. It was badly positioned and badly guarded. It was made up of somewhat more than a hundred carts and wagons and included eight eighteen-pounder guns. The only soldiers with the train were the twelve fusiliers that guarded the guns and a few artillery-men. The cavalry escort of eighty troopers from Colonel Edward Villiers's regiment of horse had bedded themselves down away from the wagon encampment. It was not for them to mix with the civilians in the convoy. The officer

---

* Now known as Sarsfield's Rock, it is well signposted and juts up next to Templebredan parish church. It is not to be confused with the village of Ballyneety, which is only six miles from Limerick.

commanding the escort, Captain Thomas Poultney, had neither posted vedettes nor sent out any patrols. The camp's security was left in the hands of the fusiliers and the artillerymen. There were only ten guards awake that night, and they were more concerned with watching the horses that had been put out to grass than with guarding against an attack.

Most of the wagons were drawn up in a meadow next to the ruins of Ballyneety Castle. The castle had been destroyed nearly two hundred years before by the Earl of Kildare, but could still have been used as a defensive position. Even at the beginning of the nineteenth century it was described as 'a stately heap of ruins, with here and there a wall nearly entire'.[18] George Story later remarked that it would have been so easy for the soldiers to draw the guns and the wagons into and around the ruined walls 'if they had feared the least danger'. But Poultney did not fear the least danger. He was no more than twenty miles from the English army and it would take him less than a day to deliver the artillery safely to the camp. There were other groups of English troops either camped or moving along the road that night and the army and the river Shannon lay between him and the Irish. In any event it would need a large force to deal with the cavalry escort under his command. The seventeen miles from Cashel had been through a far more worrisome and difficult stretch of country, and now he felt as if he was home. Although there were some earthen walls and ditches along one side of the camp, no attempt was made to convert them into a defensive line.

Sarsfield attacked at about midnight. A body of five hundred heavily armed horsemen, clanging and blundering about in the dark, was not the perfect instrument of surprise but tradition has it that the Irish knew the password, and that the password was 'Sarsfield'.* Armed with this information Sarsfield led the attack. 'When the clouds gathered heavily for a few moments, Sarsfield, at the head of his men, accompanied by Galloping Hogan with Cecil near him, cautiously proceeded down the hill'.[20] As Sarsfield approached the camp he was challenged by a sentry and was able to give the word. When they were in the camp he was challenged a second time. 'Sarsfield is the word', came the reply, 'and Sarsfield is the man!'[21]

The surprise to the escort could hardly have been more complete. The camp was awakened by the thundering of hooves. The guards opened fire. Poultney struggled to put on his boots. His men fumbled in the dark for their weapons. The cavalrymen tried to make for their horses, but the Irish were upon them. Poultney emerged from his tent and shouted for the bugler to sound 'To Horse'. He

*   Tradition tells us that one of Sarsfield's troopers was given this information by a woman. Either it was an old woman who had been bathing her feet in a stream and who was then taken to an inn and plied with drink before supplying this valuable information; or else it was the wife of a Williamite soldier who had been found by a straggling Irish trooper with a lame horse. He took pity on her unenviable position, got her on her way and was rewarded with the password. It would seem more probable that Sarsfield's men had simply heard the artillery guard challenging Cunningham's dragoons an hour earlier.[19]

desperately tried to get his men to form up but it was hopeless. Sarsfield's men swept through the camp firing their carbines and lashing out with their sabres at anything that moved. For the troopers of Villiers's regiment it was every man for himself. They ran, many of them barefoot, all of them half dressed, into the woods. The train was in pandemonium. No one could recognise friend or foe. The Irish galloped in and out shouting loudly so that they would not mistake each other for the English. The wagoners, all civilians, hid where they could. There were many camp followers with them, including women and children whose screams added to the confusion. The fighting was over in a couple of minutes. The escort and most of the wagoners had disappeared.

For the English it had been the most terrifying awakening. Two minutes before they had been sleeping peacefully. Now they were sprinting off in all directions into the darkness. Their commander, Thomas Poultney, was unable to do anything to save the situation. He escaped by running for dear life across a corn field. The Dutch engineer, Willem Meesters, perhaps the most important person in the convoy, escaped death by flinging himself into a bed of nettles. There he lay undetected until the fighting had died down and he was able to slip away into the night.*

Once it became clear that the English were not going to stay around to defend their cannons the killing stopped. The Irish made little effort to search the ditches and hedgerows for soldiers that might be concealed in the dark. No one was keen to stick his head into the bushes and run the risk of meeting a musket ball coming in the opposite direction. Some of the English managed to hide in the midst of the camp area throughout. So close were they to Sarsfield's men that they were able to name the Irish officers present. Prisoners were not an important part of Sarsfield's plan, but there was one man he very much wanted to meet. Those few prisoners that were brought in were asked the same question: where was Willem Meesters? No one knew.

Nearby in a peasant's cabin lay a sick man. The Irish burst in and dragged him out of bed. They discovered that he was an English lieutenant from Colonel Erle's regiment of foot and that he had been left behind to recover while his men had marched on to Limerick. Fever or no fever, he was stripped and taken off to Sarsfield. He was the only officer to be captured in the raid. He found the Irish leader in a courteous and elated mood. The success of this raid, Sarsfield told him, is the ruination of Prince William's plans for Limerick. If it had failed, he, Sarsfield, would have looked upon the war as having been lost and would have returned to France. The lieutenant was not badly treated and was allowed to return to his bed.

Sarsfield's plan was simple. He ordered his men to burn everything. They dismounted and began rummaging about in the wagons. There were great quantities of gunpowder, bombs, cannon-balls, matches, ramrods, chains, spikes, picks and spades. There was three days supply of bread and flour for

* King William later said that the loss would have been 'irrepairable' had Meesters been captured.

the whole army. There were metal pontoon boats for bridging the Shannon. His men set about their task with great energy. They began pushing the wagons together and overturning them. They ran through Poultney's tents tearing everything down and pocketing everything of interest. They took the picks and spades and began beating holes in the bottoms of the pontoons. The camp fires were fuelled with more and more inflammable material. The powder kegs were broken open.

One difficulty remained. How were the guns to be destroyed? The answer, according to a French report of the raid, was not long in coming. A captured artilleryman was hauled up before Sarsfield. Having seen the carnage he was easily persuaded to trade his life and freedom for some technical advice. A cannon is best destroyed, he told them, if it is overcharged with powder and is then fired while the barrel is in a vertical position with the muzzle buried in the ground. The men set to work. The cannons were stuffed to their brims with gunpowder. They were manhandled into shallow pits so that they stood on their noses in the meadow like eight great posts. Fuses were jammed into touch holes and generous trails of gunpowder were poured on the ground so that they would explode one after the other.

While this went on, other men busied themselves elsewhere. Since the initial shooting the loudest noise was the frenzied clanging of as some of the troopers set about inflicting as much damage as they could on the metal-bottomed pontoons. Most of the men set to work looting, overturning and wrecking the wagons while others occupied themselves by collecting the hundreds of horses together and loading them with the saddles and tackle from the escort. Others merely stood guard, straining their eyes and ears into the night for any suggestion that the English were about to descend on them in force.

Four miles away in the hamlet of Dromkeen a group of English army officers were asleep in their beds. They and their troops had been marching behind the main body of William's army, and Dromkeen with its large and old mansion was a convenient place to bed down for the night. It was also one of the few substantial houses in the area that had not yet been burnt down by Berwick. One of these officers was a forty-one year old army chaplain from Cork, Rowland Davies, who had been keeping a careful diary of his experiences in the war. At three in the morning, he wrote, they were woken up by 'the firing of two great cannon' that made the house tremble. They waited, but nothing happened. Half an hour later they were alarmed again, this time by a near naked trooper from Poultney's cavalry escort. The Irish, he shouted, have attacked the artillery train, destroyed the escort and taken all the cannon and the money. Davies and the officers with him mounted up and rode towards the English camp at Limerick to raise the alarm.

They need not have bothered as the camp was wide awake. From Limerick the guards had seen the flashes of the explosions and had heard the distant rumbling as their supply of gunpowder went up in flames. No one who saw it

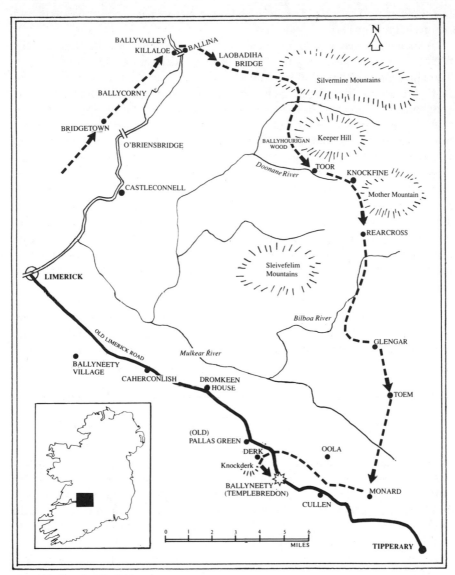

Map IV: Sarsfield's Ride

or who was told of it needed any prompting as to what it could be. Sarsfield had found the artillery.

Although Lanier was finally ordered to set out and meet the train at nine o'clock that night, he did not finally leave the English camp until after midnight. The Huguenot cavalry, reliable as always, were ready to go straight away, but the rest of Lanier's force took their time in preparing for the night ride. The Frenchmen had to wait for the best part of four hours.[22] So long was the delay that it is quite possible that when Lanier did eventually lead his five hundred horsemen out of the camp, Sarsfield had already attacked the train and was busying himself in organising its destruction. Despite this, Lanier did not take the direct route and was still over five miles from Ballyneety when he heard the explosions. He was forced to make an instant decision. Should he go straight to Ballyneety, or should he make for the Shannon and cut off Sarsfield's retreat? The Irish, he knew, had crossed at Killaloe. They would make for the river to escape into Co. Clare and to do that they would ride away from Ballyneety to the north or northeast. Lanier was approaching Ballyneety from the northwest. It was too late to save the artillery train, but he could reach Killaloe before the Irish and cut them off. Lanier was right about one thing: by the time Sarsfield had allowed his position to be given away by the tremendous explosions, he was riding off as fast as he could out of the area. But Lanier's second assumption was wrong. Sarsfield did not intend to strike out straight for the Shannon, nor did he intend to return to Clare by the same route. Lanier led his cavalry at breakneck speed through the night to Killaloe. There he waited. And no one came.

Sir Albert Cunningham's six troops of dragoons who had passed the convoy before the attack had not heard the fighting, but there was no mistaking the explosions. They turned their horses and made their way straight for Captain Fitzgerald's ambush, but before they could reach it they had an extraordinary stroke of luck. They came across an Irish deserter who told them exactly where Fitzgerald's men were waiting. Cunningham did not hesitate; he knew where his duty lay and forewarned, he spotted the Irish before they could launch an attack and he charged them. The ambush party turned and raced off into the night. In the melée the unfortunate Fitzgerald and fifteen of his men were killed. The fighting over, Cunningham cautiously led his men on towards Ballyneety.

In those early hours of the morning after the explosion, every available mounted unit was out to catch Sarsfield. Colonel Villiers made for O'Briensbridge, but had no luck. Other units rode off into the country. The Shannon was made impassible from Limerick to Lough Derg. At first light Scravenmoer crossed the river to scour the other side to prevent Sarsfield getting back to Limerick. He also found nothing.

As dawn began to break, the first English troops arrived at Ballyneety. These were the troops who had been quartered at Dromkeen. They were met by a desolate sight. 'There we found many men killed', wrote Rowland

Davies. 'I believe fifty, and of them most were of the train.' The Irish had burnt everything they could; all the bread and flour, and most of the carriages. The barrels of two of the eight cannons were split; the others had survived as the second cannon to explode had done so with such violence that it blew the next two in line onto their sides so that they did not fire into the ground. Their carriages had been wrecked by fire, but six of the guns could still be used.

The burnt grass was still smoking. Pieces of the wagons and debris from their loads were scattered in the fields roundabout where they had been flung by the explosions. Most pitiful of all were the bodies, scorched and gashed. And amongst them were women and children. Richard Kane, then a subaltern in Lord Meath's regiment of foot, later wrote:

> This was a well managed affair of Sarsfield's and would have redounded much to his honour had he not sullied it with so much cruelty, for though there was not the least opposition, yet he put man, woman and child to the sword. However, we cannot suppose so gallant a man as Sarsfield certainly was could be guilty of giving such orders. It is rather to be presumed that at such a juncture it was not in his power to restrain the natural barbarity of his men.[23]

Robert Parker, then a sergeant in the same regiment, wrote much the same. The Reverend Samuel Mullenaux, who wrote a journal of the siege of Limerick, went further: 'The women and children that belonged to the wagoners they murdered most barbarously in their beds'. Dumont de Bostaquet recorded the scene with more shocking imagery: 'He cut the throats of everyone, including the women.' In his *True and Impartial History of the War*,* 'J.S.' wrote that Sarsfield had slaughtered the wagoners 'not sparing their wives, with their children in their arms'. And Dean Harrison, who was in Dublin at the time, capped all other accounts by passing on the information that the Irish had burnt the carriages and thrown 'the women and children alive into the fire'. So the story spread to England and to Europe.

There can be no doubt that these reports were exaggerated. The only recorded eyewitness account of the scene at Ballyneety that morning was that of Rowland Davies. He was an observant and sensitive man. If he had seen dead women and children at the scene he certainly would have recorded the fact, but his journal makes no mention of the subject. He may not have seen all the bodies, but he did see most of them. He noted about fifty bodies whereas the final tally was nearer sixty.** His silence on this point must lead us to the conclusion that there was no general slaughter of wives and infants.

George Story, who did not go to Ballyneety but who was in the camp outside Limerick, wrote the fullest account of Sarsfield's raid relying on eyewitness accounts of the scene. He also made no mention of women and children, but did record that some 'country people that were bringing

---

*   Which was occasionally truthful but never impartial.
** Only Robert Southwell gave a higher figure. He wrote of there being eighty dead.

13 Sarsfield's Rock as seen from the site of Ballyneety Castle,
and (below) the Hill of Derk as seen from Sarsfield's Rock.

provisions to the camp' were killed. There is no evidence that Kane, Parker, Mullenaux, Dumont, 'J.S.' or Dean Harrison's informant went to Ballyneety. They merely, in good faith or otherwise, related the tale that later went around the English camp, a tale that Story perhaps did not think reliable enough to record. In times of conflict there are no shortages of horrifying tales that reflect on the savagery of the enemy, but this particular allegation of cruelty is not a strong one. Although there may well have been several women killed in the confusion as the Irish swept through the camp in the darkness, nothing occurred that in the context of war could be described as an atrocity.

The cost to the English in terms of lives lost was not great. Of the bodies he saw, Davies wrote that 'most were of the train;', that is, civilians. No mention was made by anyone of any casualties suffered by Sarsfield's men, and the general impression is that, with the exception of Fitzgerald and his ambush party, the Irish got away without loss. The artillery guards certainly suffered. Of the ten on duty that night, only three survived. Some of the troopers from Villiers's regiment were cut down as they sprinted to their horses and one of their officers, Lieutenant William Bell, was killed. The total military casualties are unlikely to have numbered more than twenty. Most of the dead were wagoners who had been sleeping with their wagons some distance away from the soldiers. Even so, the vast majority of them managed to escape with their lives while the Irish fell to their more pressing tasks with picks and torches.

A much more serious loss to the English army was in materials and horses. Apart from the two split cannons and the gun carriages, up to one hundred wagons had been severely damaged or destroyed. A hundred and twenty barrels containing twelve thousand pounds of powder had been burnt as had great quantities of match, grenades and bombs. Three thousand cannonballs had been scattered or lost and the Irish had broken or taken the thousands of tools needed for digging the trenches. Three days' urgently needed supply of bread and flour had been ruined by fire. Many of the forty nine boats for building a pontoon bridge over the Shannon had been damaged or destroyed, and five hundred artillery horses had been driven away or slaughtered.

If the destruction was not complete it was because the train had been halted in such a haphazard fashion. Many of the carts and wagons had been scattered around the fields and the roads. The Irish just did not have the time to destroy them all. Considering how badly paid the Irish soldiers were, there is a degree of irony in the following extract from Davies's diary: 'The money wagon was not touched by the enemy, but some of our own men, as I believe, took out some of the bags. The rest were secured.'

When Sir Albert Cunningham reached Ballyneety after dawn, the money and the remaining six cannons were the only things left that were worth guarding.

The most important effect of Sarsfield's raid was that it bought time for the Irish garrison at Limerick. It prevented King William from launching an immediate attack. Although his men were fully occupied in building earthworks, making fascines and digging trenches, while the Irish were still protected by the walls of Limerick there could be no move. Breaches had to be blown in the walls so that the infantry could charge though, and those could only be made after a concentrated and sustained cannonade. Such a cannonade needed not only cannons but a good stock of powder, and powder was now in short supply. Hundreds of barrels had to be carted across the country from Dublin and Waterford. The defences of the whole kingdom were now put under strain as the next ammunition convoy from England had yet to leave the Thames. William simply did not have the means to attack. On the day after the raid, Sir Robert Southwell wrote sagely: 'In this affair we have much to lament. We lose admirable weather which will not always last.'

The loss of the two cannons was less important. In fact, within a couple of days, two more had arrived from Waterford where every available wagon had been sent to make good the losses. Troops were posted along the route to prevent another attack. On 18 August a replacement artillery train arrived complete with heavier siege guns than the two that had been destroyed. But the weather broke on the 25th.

The second effect of the Ballyneety raid was on the morale of the two armies. Inside Limerick the success was greeted with great jubilation. Boisseleau had bonfires lit throughout the city and treated the English to a particularly fierce cannonade from the walls.[24] The Irish, who had been so despondent on the day before, were revived. The effect on the English was equally predictable. 'This news', wrote George Story, 'was very unwelcome to everyone in the camp.' The Huguenot officer, Dumont de Bostaquet, added: 'It put the king and the army in one great consternation'. The soldiers could do no more than wait outside the walls while the Irish shot at them. On top of that, the loss of the bread wagons was felt straight away. Dumont recorded bread being sold for four times its normal price. Another correspondent wrote on the day after Sarsfield's attack that he had not had any bread for three days and could not even buy a sixpenny loaf for half a crown. 'I pray God things may not prove scarcer.' 'Without fresh guns we can do no good against Limerick', he went on, 'many are of the opinion that it will be both a bloody and tedious task taking it.'[25]

The low spirits in the English camp soon turned to anger. 'What smarts most is this', wrote Southwell, 'that it was in our power to have prevented all. We had noticed on the 10th at night that the desertion of the ford (at Annaghbeg) was for some design to be conducted by Sarsfield on this side'. By the 11th it was widely accepted that Sarsfield had crossed the river and was looking for the artillery and still nothing had been done. People looked for a scapegoat. Portland, Solms, Lanier and Poultney each received some of the blame. The very vocal Schomberg was particularly angry with Portland and Solms for not sending Sir John Lanier out earlier.[26] Lanier had not only set out late but went the wrong way and, wrote Richard Kane, 'when he was on his march he loitered away the time by making unnecessary halts which gave time to Sarsfield to do his business and return without the loss of a man'. He added darkly: 'Sir John, who had once been a great favourite of King James's, was shrewdly suspected of treachery. He ought to have been hanged.' Bishop Burnet noted that 'the general observation made of him (Lanier) - and of most of those officers who had served King James and were now on the king's side—was that they had a greater mind to make themselves rich by the continuance of the war of Ireland than their master great and safe by the speedy conclusion of it.'

Although the 'general observation' repeated by Burnet was a nonsense, it was generally accepted that Sarsfield's success had been made possible by the failure of Portland and Solms to provide more security for the artillery, by Lanier's late departure from the camp and by Poultney's false sense of security. In England, it was this last error that was most talked of. 'Limerick still holds out', wrote John Evelyn in his London diary, 'we having received some loss very considerable by the negligence of Sir William Poultney's son, who was to guard the cannon'.

Although it can be assumed that Poultney never forgot the terror of that night, his military career did not suffer. He left Colonel Villiers's regiment, joined the life guards and later rose to the rank of brigadier-general. Lanier's career was similarly unaffected as he was later promoted to lieutenant-general. His immediate superior, Count Solms, who was 'very ill and confined to bed' at the time,[27] also escaped any official blame. The suspicion must then form that the man William considered to be responsible was the one man who he could easily forgive, his life-long friend, Willem Bentinck, the earl of Portland.

The English soon found that they had been quite wrong to suppose that Sarsfield would ride hell for leather back to the Shannon. This caused them some more concern. Wagon loads of other supplies were still winding their way towards Limerick and a train of empty wagons had left the camp to go to Waterford. Suddenly nothing was safe. 'We hear now at night that Sarsfield is still hunting our roads, so that our bread carts being in danger we are sending out a fresh party to find him out.'

Sarsfield's raid had touched a raw nerve. Whereas before the destruction of the artillery train it was not even considered worth discussing whether the Irish would dare to make lightning cavalry raids on the English lines of communication, it was now the greatest fear. The English in the camp outside Limerick felt isolated. Now it seemed to them that the Irish had abundant opportunities to cause mischief. Rumours came in that Colonel MacElligott and young Clancarty were at the head of eight thousand men in Co. Cork 'ranging' across the countryside. An Irish deserter brought in news that Berwick and Sheldon had led three thousand cavalry off to Loughrea in Co. Galway to rendezvous with Sarsfield. They planned, the deserter informed his interrogators, to ride to Athlone, cross the Shannon and ravage all of Leinster up to Dublin. A wilder rumour also gained some credence in the camp: a French naval force was already on its way to Dublin. The ships were carrying some twenty thousand soldiers who were going to burn down the capital. From all over Ireland came fresh rumours of uprisings and of bands of Irish troops and rapparees burning towns. As Southwell noted: 'All these different swarms of rovers and flying parties of the enemy, mixed of soldiers and rapparees, seem yet to move under one common design of drawing us away from the siege of this place or to weaken us so by detachments as to make it a winter's work.'

Daily the English braced themselves for another raid. It was a worrying week. Only on 18 August did it become known that Sarsfield had gone, but news travelled slowly. Four days later the new garrison at Cullen braced itself for an attack when it was rumoured that Sarsfield was coming for them with three thousand men. He never came because he was nowhere near. William learnt that Sarsfield had led his men northwards to Portumna on 14 August. There he had recrossed the Shannon over onto his brother-in-law's land driving with him the draught horses from Ballyneety. If there was any relief at that news, it was dispelled by the reports that followed. Sarsfield had made directly for Loughrea where he had met up with Berwick, Sheldon and the Irish cavalry as had been predicted. The race to take Limerick was now on, before Sarsfield struck out for Dublin. For the first time since the crossing of the Boyne, the English were doubtful of their success.

CHAPTER XI

The Siege of Limerick

The city of Limerick, the siege of which was begun under his majesty King William himself, the year after I went into the army—lies, an' please your honours in the middle of a devilish wet, swampy country.—'Tis quite surrounded, said my uncle Toby, with the Shannon, and is, by its situation, one of the strongest fortified places in Ireland. 'Tis all cut through, an' please your reverence said the corporal, with drains and bogs: and besides, there was such a quantity of rain fell during the siege, the whole country was like a puddle.

> Lawrence Sterne, *The Life and Opinions of Tristram Shandy, Gentleman*, 1761, v, ch. 40

HOWEVER DESPONDENT the English had been when they first heard the news of Sarsfield's raid, they were soon spurred to vigorous activity. Although the bombardment of the walls could not begin, they concentrated on preparing for that happy day. Whole regiments spent their days collecting wood and cutting and binding branches into fascines and gabions. Others spent their nights digging trenches ever closer to the Irish defences and throwing up earthworks to house the heavy artillery that was yet to arrive. It was frustrating and dangerous work. The Irish gunners were able to shoot at them at will and with impunity. The only comforting thought that the English had was that when their replacement artillery did arrive there was a certainty that the Irish would get an ample return of fire.

King William's men were now facing the Irish town of Limerick on the south bank of the river. As the English town is situated on an island in the Shannon it was out of their reach. The Irish town was approximately diamond shaped with corners that pointed north, south, east and west. The western sides of the town were covered by the cannons in the English town and faced out over a bog that stretched to the river. Consequently, the English concentrated their efforts on the sides that faced to the south east and the north east. Outside these walls were the new earthworks and the open ditch, and half a mile away on the high ground overlooking this side of the city were the ruined reminders of a siege that had taken place nearly forty years before: Ireton's Fort to the east and Cromwell's Fort to the south east. An old earthwork known as the Danish Fort lay to the south and it was in and behind these old strong-points that King William's army camped, just out of cannonshot from the walls.

Each night the English dug trenches closer to the city. Each night the Irish sallied out to attack them. The besiegers had as their first objective those relatively small defensive works that had been so recently built by the Irish between the open ditch and the English camp. Attacks were made on two of the smaller forts on 17 August, but nothing serious could be achieved until the new siege train arrived. On that day Southwell wrote to the secretary of state in London: 'Since my last we have done little except getting and mounting the six pieces left at the surprise of our artillery.' The six guns, most of them without their carriages, had arrived in the camp on Friday 15 August. This was the first of the days of public fasting and prayer set aside by King William so that his army might make peace with the Lord and enjoy divine favour in the difficult and dangerous days that lay ahead.[1] On the following Monday six twenty-four-pounders and a fresh supply of powder and ball arrived from Carrick. The bombardment began.

Over the next few days and nights the fighting outside the walls intensified as the English set about destroying or capturing the various outworks that prevented them from getting the guns as close as they would have liked. The most serious of these clashes took place on the afternoon of the 20th when an attack was made on the 'Yellow Fort', a new earthwork situated outside the southern extremity of the Irish town wall, just at the point where the firm ground gave way to the bog. The defence of the fort was entrusted to a Colonel Fitzgerald with one hundred and fifty men. They were all but wiped out when a force of Danes and Brandenburgers stormed in with orders to kill everyone in sight, which they did, except for the one prisoner they took, Captain John Barrett, and those of the Irish who had managed to run away.* The continental troops had barely gained the position when they were in turn chased out by Sarsfield's brother-in-law, Lord Kilmallock, who charged into them at the head of three hundred horsemen. The Williamites launched a second attack, but this time with cavalry, and in turn forced Kilmallock to withdraw. Although the Williamites were left in possession of the fort, it had cost them dearly. It had been the bloodiest fight since the Boyne.

The capture of the Yellow Fort changed little, but it allowed the gunners to edge their pieces nearer to the southern walls. On the 22nd Boisseleau was given another opportunity to surrender or else 'to expect nothing but fire and sword'.[3] When he refused William ordered the biggest cannonade yet. He had his forty field guns, siege pieces and mortars lined up to the east of the Irish town. Despite it being the second of his fasting days he sent brandy to encourage the gunners.[4] They responded by smashing down a tower on the walls over the Black Battery, the largest of those bastions that had been built up against the Irish town walls. The tower crashed down on the defenders below, burying several of them.[5] The walls were weakening, and the siege gunners now concentrated their fire on an area of wall just north of the Black Battery.

On 24 August Meesters, his nettle stings now forgotten, came to the conclusion that the gun positions were still too far back. That night, under the cover of darkness, he had the heavy cannons wheeled forward, protected from musket fire by woolsacks. By dawn the siege artillery was within eighty yards of the wall.

---

*   In London it was reported that when the Irish called for quarter, they 'were answered they should have the same Sarsfield gave the waggoners'[2].

On the following day, the weather broke. 'This morning it began to pour down at such a furious rate that some of the trenches had been two feet deep,' wrote Sir Robert Southwell. 'I find by this one day's fierce rain a strange damp as to our success among many of our chief officers and that our army must draw off or be ruined if the rain should hold.' King William became despondent and hinted that he was going to return to England. The soldiers were soaked through and miserable. The downpour even prevented the newly sited cannons from firing until the mid afternoon.

As the Williamite staff officers stood huddled together in their great coats surveying the sodden ground between them and Limerick, they contemplated a new problem. To ensure that the walls got the full benefit of his twenty four pounders, Meesters had advanced them as near as he dared, to within musket shot but outside the throwing range of the Irish grenadiers. This made good military sense in dry weather, but between the high ground of the English camp and the high ground on which Limerick was built there was a flat area now all but flooded. If the rain continued the guns would be left stranded between the city and a wide belt of water and bog. Even after one day it was clear that it was going to be no small task to retrieve the guns. Conditions had become very bad very quickly. The forward trenches had filled with water and had been abandoned and the heavy rain had turned the road surfaces to thick mud. The countryside was fast becoming a quagmire. To the Williamite generals it was clear that their careful plan for an assault would have to be abandoned. They would now have to move quickly, even precipitately.

At three o'clock in the afternoon the cannonade started at last. Every piece of artillery opened fire. The mortars sent incendiaries and explosives into the city, while the siege pieces concentrated on a section of wall on the north eastern side of the Irish town and the field guns fired at targets along the whole length of the Irish town walls. After Meesters's batteries had fired some three hundred shots the wall gave way. The breach was not a large one but it augured well. The weather did not. The day ended as it had begun, 'so extremely wet no man could stir.'[6]

On the next day William called a council of war. Opinion was divided as to what should be done. His plan was to push forward to the edge of the open ditch, 'the counterscarp', and then to dig in and prepare for a major assault once the wall had been mined or the breach had been widened. Wurtemburg strongly advised him to order no such thing. He insisted that the breach should be first enlarged so that sixteen men could charge in abreast, and that would take two more days of battering. There were great difficulties in making a lodgment on the counterscarp as it was so close to the walls and to the bastions that had been thrown up between the walls and the ditch. The Irish would be able to hurl down a continuous stream of rocks and grenades on them. But William could not afford another two days, and Meesters was running out of ammunition for the heavy guns. He decided to take the risk and follow his own plan.

All that day the cannon pounded at the walls around the breach. The Irish desperately tried to slow down the rate of damage by hanging woolsacks over the ramparts, but they were next to useless. The continuous bombardment gave them no opportunity to repair the damage. Boisseleau set his face against the inevitable and made other preparations. Inside the city he had an inner wall built around the breach, and he had cannons placed in the streets to cover it. When the storming party came they were going to be warmly received.

The next day was 27 August 1690. The sun returned. 'The day itself was excessive hot.' The breach was not as wide as the English would have liked but, with ammunition for the siege guns running low, it would have to do. Boisseleau stated that it was forty two yards wide, Story remembered it as being much narrower at only twelve yards.* But the breach in the wall was not the objective. The plan was that the troops would charge to the edge of the counterscarp and hold it. They would be led by a forlorn hope of grenadiers commanded by a hundred Huguenot officers eager, as always, to be revenged on any Catholic for what their families had suffered in France. The wall could be dealt with on the next day.

At half past three in the afternoon three cannons fired to give the signal for the attack. The first wave of five hundred grenadiers and the hundred Huguenot officers leapt out of the forward trenches and sprinted towards the counterscarp. The Irish musketeers were ready for them and opened fire as they drew near. The grenadiers fired their flintlocks as they ran, and when they reached the Irish outworks they threw their grenades over them to clear the way. 'In less than two minutes the noise was so terrible that one would have thought the very sky ready to rend in sunder. This was seconded with dust, smoke and all the terrors that the art of man could invent to ruin and undo each other.'[7]

As the grenadiers charged, the artillery opened fire on the Irish defences. The violence of the attack was too great for most of the defenders on the counterscarp and they ran. The only ways of escape were by leaping from the counterscarp into the open ditch and then running to the Black Battery or back into the town through the breach. There was a period of panic and confusion. It seemed as if the Irish town was going to fall. Irish troops could be seen racing away over Ball's Bridge, but those manning the main defences held their ground. Having reached the counterscarp the grenadiers were in an exposed position. The Irish left on the walls kept up a steady fire at them and the guns in the Black Battery raked them from the flank. The grenadiers charged on. They threw themselves into the ditch, splashed their way through it, clambered up the other side and chased after the Irish who had fled through the breach.

Inside the city there were scenes of frantic activity. The timing of the attack had thrown Boisseleau. He personally rushed his men into position. The Irish

---

*   One is tempted to suggest that the breach was probably forty-two yards wide at the top of the wall, and twelve yards wide at the bottom. Berwick who was not present at the siege later wrote, perhaps for reasons of hyperbole, that the breach was two hundred yards across. But then he also wrote, 'I can affirm that not a single drop of rain fell for above a month before or for three weeks after.'

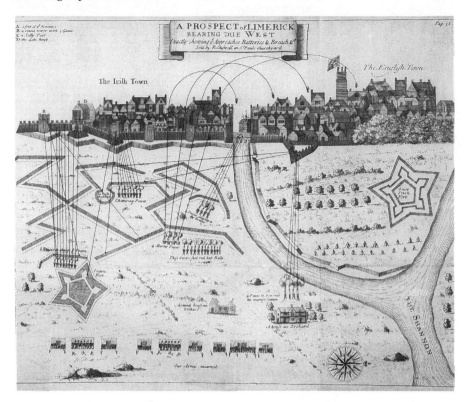

14 A Prospect of Limerick Bearing Due West, from George Story's
A Continuation of the Impartial History of the Wars of Ireland.

were not sure who to fire at. The breach was obscured by the smoke from the
grenades and the musketry. They could see red coats coming through the gap,
but it was not clear whether or not they were their own men falling back from
the defences outside. The grenadiers burst in. Men blundered into the city not
knowing what to expect. The first man over the rubble was Captain Farlow
who commanded the grenadier company in Stewart's regiment. He was shot
dead on the spot. His men charged through behind him; into Boisseleau's trap.
Behind the grenadiers, eight regiments were now running forward to take the
counterscarp. There they were held back by their officers. They had been instructed to go no further, but the Danish Green regiment who were to hold the
counterscarp in front of the breach could not be restrained. They charged in
behind the grenadiers.

There was a most terrible slaughter inside the walls. The grenadiers and the
green-coated Danes found themselves flanked on three sides by ranks of Irish
troops protected by Boisseleau's retrenchments. The Irish were ordered to hold
their fire 'until the pound was full'. Then whole regiments fired volleys at the
grenadiers. The cannon were loaded with cartridge shot. Many of the grenadiers

charged on to get out of the trap, but they were heavily outnumbered. The Irish were everywhere. Firing from windows, from behind walls, from barricades in the streets. At no time when they were inside the city did the English get the opportunity to form up. Those who were not shot down ran forward in uncoordinated groups. Men lay amongst the dead desperately trying to reload their muskets. What cover there was in there was being used by the Irish.

Pitching grenades in all directions, a group of grenadiers managed to smash through the Irish barricade and charge down the streets into the main square. None of them came back[8]. In the pound both sides were blinded by the smoke from the powder and the burning houses. The Irish used every weapon at their disposal. Bottles and stones rained down on the English. Out of this fierce fight grew the legend of the Limerick women,* best related by Maurice Lenihan a century and a half later:

> John Street, Broad Street, Mungret Street, every street of the Irish town down to Ball's Bridge were crowded with those detested freebooters and vagabonds, the ruffian rabble soldiers of the bloody minded contriver of the massacre of Glencoe! Burning with insatiable revenge, the women, forgetting their nature, called aloud on husbands, sons and brothers to rally—and showed the example themselves . . . Imagine the worn and wasted figures of those maids and matrons who, forgetful of the gentler influences which reigned predominant in the female breast, lost for the moment the amenities of their nature, wild with the excitement of battle —and nerving their arms to hurl death on the heads of the most odious foemen that ever challenged an oppressed and outraged people to combat.

The grenadiers and those Danes who had followed them were in a hopeless position. They were not being supported with fresh men, they were running out of grenades and ammunition, and they were taking fearful casualties. They began to give ground, but behind them the Danes were attempting to form a lodgment in the rubble. Despite the concentrated fire from inside the breach, for a while it seemed as if they would succeed. The grenadiers fell back and joined them in the ruins of the wall from where they kept the Irish back with a rapid and deadly fire. But it was not to last. A regiment of dragoons led by Colonel Mark Talbot sallied out of St John's Gate and ran the gauntlet of the attacking troops on the counterscarp to get to the breach and attack it from the outside. Inside, Boisseleau ordered a general advance. The assault was now clearly over. For the surviving grenadiers there was now only one realistic option to take. They ran.

On the counterscarp things were not going well for the English either. They were crouching behind the limited protection of the fascines that they had brought with them. They were under continuous fire from the walls. The cannons from a fort over on King's Island flanked the counterscarp and were able to fire

---

*   A Danish report read as follows: 'The very women, prone as they are to violent passions, have since become furious. It was noticed that during the attack on the counterscarp they caused as much, indeed more damage than the garrison by throwing huge stones on the assailants of whom a great number thus perished.'[9]

straight along the English positions with impunity. The Irish in the Black Battery were blazing away on the other flank, and once Boisseleau's men had regained the breach they wheeled their guns into it and raked the counterscarp with cartridge shot. Throughout all this hundreds of unarmed Irish soldiers from the labour battalions kept up a steady hail of stones from the wall. Desperately, the engineers tried to organise parties of men to start digging, but with the enemy so close it proved to be an impossible task.

One of William's continental battalions, the Brandenburg Regiment, was ordered to storm the Black Battery. This they did. Under covering artillery fire the Germans charged across the open, over the counterscarp and into the ditch from where they swarmed into the Irish redoubt. Their successful assault was a disaster. There was a sudden and tremendous explosion. The defenders' magazine had caught fire. Attacker and defender were blown to bits, 'the men, faggots, stones and whatnot flying into the air with a most terrible noise'.[10] Those Germans still advancing were bowled over by the blast and were left choking and coughing in the dense smoke. Those who could turned and fled, confused and shaken and convinced that the works had been mined.

Elsewhere along the walls the fighting was as fierce as ever. The Williamites were suffering terribly. Had the action gone on for only five minutes, it would have been an experience that no man present would have remembered without horror. It lasted for hours. 'From half an hour after three until seven there was one continued fire of both great and small shot without any intermission: insomuch that the smoke that went from the town reached in one continuous cloud to the top of a mountain at least six miles off.'[11] The officers on the counterscarp could see how useless their position was, and they could see that it was not going to improve. 'As the engineers were now mostly dead or wounded the lodgment on the counterscarp made no progress and many men were killed.'[12] It was requested that they be ordered to charge the breach again as the only way to save the situation. Solms told the King not to. It was too late, he said, they must stick to the original plan. But as the minutes went by it became ever clearer that the original plan was a failure.

As the afternoon turned to evening, orders were issued to call the troops back. Those still in the English camp were met with a dismal sight. 'When our men drew off, some were brought up dead, and some without a leg; others wanted arms, and some were blind with powder, especially a great many of the poor Brandenburgers looked like furies with the misfortune of gunpowder', wrote George Story. 'The king stood nigh Cromwell's fort all the time and, the business being over, he went to his camp very much concerned, as indeed was the whole army, for you might have seen a mixture of anger and sorrow in everybody's countenance'.[13]

The Williamite losses had been very severe. The army had been decimated in one day. As Southwell wrote to King William's Secretary of State: 'I have no good news to tell your lordship but rather we were yesterday unfortunate in the loss of many brave men.'[14] Wurtemburg estimated the number of dead and wounded as being 2,324, but that did not take account of the Brandenburg Regiment 'which was almost entirely destroyed'.[15] The total loss to the Williamites was nearly three thousand casualties, and that included some of their best troops. The Danes, Huguenots and Germans had suffered particularly badly, and very few of the grenadiers who had entered the breach had returned unscathed. While the infantry had been digging in on the counterscarp under fire, there had been a disproportionate number of officers shot. The Huguenots had lost two hundred officers alone. The Irish losses were mild by comparison, their highest estimate was four hundred.

The next day brought more misery to the English. The artillery made a last effort to widen the breach, but without much success. It started to rain again. A drummer was sent to Limerick to seek permission to bury the dead, but was answered so haughtily by Boisseleau that nothing was done. The next day was Friday 29 August. It was the third of William's days of fasting. He called a council of war. He wanted to try another attack and to storm the breach properly. He would even lead the attack himself. The mood of the army was certainly behind him, but his staff officers were not. The whole campaign was getting to be too risky. If they suffered another set back they would leave Limerick a defeated army. The weather was worsening. If they did not get the guns away now they would never do so, and if they remained encamped around Limerick they would fall victims to the 'bloody flux' that had all but destroyed Schomberg's army at Dundalk.* The conditions for the troops were already very bad, there were no more cannon balls and the supply of powder was running low. It was decided to abandon the siege and march off to winter quarters.

> God grant that our passage may be better than the success which we have met in this cursed siege during which we have all been on the point of perishing from the fetid exhalations of the bogs and of the filth of the army.[16]

On 30 August William rode off towards Waterford, a frustrated and disappointed man. He had taken a risk and he had failed. Before leaving, he told Wurtemburg that he wished he had taken his advice. On the following day the army withdrew to Caherconlish. 'We have had a temporary setback in Ireland with the raising of the siege of Limerick', wrote Wurtemburg.[17] 'The English army marched off from Limerick with some precipitation', recalled one of the joyful defenders, 'as fearing pursuit from the Irish'. The cannons were hauled

---

*   Corporal Trim who served with ('his honour') Captain Toby Shandy in the besieg-ing army at Limerick, spoke of the weather so: ''twas that, and nothing else, which brought on the flux, and which had like to have killed both his honour and myself: now there was no such thing, after the first ten days, continued the corporal, for a soldier to lie dry in his tent, without cutting a ditch round it, to draw off the water; -nor was that enough, for those who could afford it, as his honour could, without setting fire every night to a pewter dish full of brandy, which took off the damp of the air, and made the inside of the tent as warm as a stove' (Lawrence Sterne, *Tristam Shandy*, v, ch. 40).

through the mud by teams of oxen. There was a shortage of draught horses and carts as so much transport had been needed to take the wounded to Cashel and beyond. Large quantities of military stores, including grenades and bombs, had to be left behind. What the English could not take with them they burnt.[18]

Within a week the army was twenty five miles away in Tipperary and began to divide itself into winter garrisons. For many of the soldiers the real misery was just beginning. 'We were very hard put to it while the siege lasted before Limerick', wrote Lieutenant James Lonyne of Babington's regiment, 'now they (the soldiers) are in a starving condition; they want bread, shoes, stockings; they have no forage for horse nor iron to shoe them'.[19]

William set sail from Duncannon and left Ireland for ever on 5 September 1690. His last acts were to appoint three Lord Justices to govern the country, to appoint Solms commander-in-chief of the army and to order the commissary of stores in Waterford to supply Colonel Villiers's regiment with seventy carbines to replace those lost at Ballyneety.[20]

William's repulse before Limerick was the greatest Irish victory of the war. His army suffered some five thousand casualties during the campaign, five times as many as the Irish had lost at the Boyne. This victory would not have been gained without Sarsfield. He was not in Limerick during the fighting, but the Ballyneety raid had greatly affected the conduct of the siege. William had been forced to risk a desperate attempt on the counterscarp because he knew that he was running out of time. Precious days of battering the walls had been lost when the weather broke, and the ammunition and powder was insufficient for the task. If William had been allowed those extra days and the ammunition denied him by Sarsfield's raid, there would most certainly have been both a far bigger breach and a carefully planned attack. Limerick could well have fallen at the first assault.

The English were not slow to recognise this. 'The ill success at Limerick was well known to be owing to the want of ammunition occasioned by Sarsfield falling upon the artillery', wrote King William's Secretary at War, George Clarke, 'so that after a fruitless attempt on a breach which we had not powder and shot to make larger, the King left the army'. One could say more than that, and Lenihan did:

> 'Mullenaux and Story fully sustain this account of the magnificent achievement of Sarsfield, and indeed all the writers of the time and since agree in declaring that there never was a nobler or a bolder instance of successful strategy at any period, or under any combination of circumstances'.

CHAPTER XII

Birr Castle

The Lords Justices have received an account that Colonel Sarsfield is
not dead, as was given out, but is come on this side the Shannon with
diverse regiments of horse and foot with intent to surprise some of our
men in their quarters.

London Newsletter, 23 October 1690[1]

NOW THAT WILLIAM had left Ireland, Tyrconnell decided to do the same.
Unlike William he was resolved to return. Tyrconnell wanted to go to France
to report to James. His reasons were twofold: firstly, now that he smelt the possibility of military success, he wanted fresh supplies and officers, and secondly
he wanted new instructions and his authority to be confirmed. He recognised
that his situation in Ireland was such that he would have to go to James in person
and explain exactly what had happened. This was not a mission that he could
delegate.

He knew that his position was difficult in that a sizeable proportion of his
officer corps loathed him. If he remained in Ireland, he could well be inviting
a mutiny. He had no fear of Sarsfield alone, but Sarsfield's head was being
turned by the more ambitious and devious of 'les mutins', as he described them.
He could not keep Sarsfield away from the Luttrell brothers, Nicholas Purcell
or Gordon O'Neill, and those four flattered Sarsfield that he was the only man
fit to lead Ireland. Sarsfield had begun to believe them. His war had been a
successful one. Indeed, it could be argued that he alone had salvaged the war.
His name struck fear into the hearts of Englishmen far more experienced than
he. Even to Tyrconnell it was quite plain that Sarsfield was the 'Darling of the
Army' and Tyrconnell feared, as Berwick later wrote, that after the Ballyneety
raid Sarsfield 'considered himself to be the greatest general in the world'.[2]
Tyrconnell felt gravely threatened by Sarsfield's faction and needed fresh
authority in order to crush them. He could not rely on his letters or his envoys
to successfully convey his belief that the king's interest required that all authority in Ireland should be vested in him. The king, and the French court, would
need to hear the message from his own lips. Support me, he would say, and the
war can be won.

Another man keen to go to France was Lauzun who throughout the siege of
Limerick had remained in Galway with his French brigade. He felt that he could
do no good in Ireland and he was fed up with having been cut off from French
society. He had only stopped in Galway so as not to discourage the defenders
of Limerick. He could not risk it being said that the Irish army had collapsed

because of his departure. Each day he and his men had anxiously, perhaps eagerly, awaited the news from Limerick, knowing that if King William was victorious they could immediately begin embarking on the transport ships that lay at anchor in the bay.

During their time in Galway, Tyrconnell and Lauzun had seen a lot of one another. Tyrconnell's treatment of the little Frenchman was masterly. He confided in Lauzun and told him how uneasy he was. He was, he said, tired of all the infighting in the Irish army. He felt that the situation was altogether hopeless. Even if by some fluke Limerick did hold out until the winter, it would mean nothing. The English would only be back in the spring in greater numbers. Tyrconnell made it plain that he would be going to France in any event. He felt old and would rather end his days in the palace at Saint-Germain than in being chased around Connaught. This was all music to Lauzun's ears. If he and Tyrconnell went to France together and made a joint report, far from being criticised for deserting Ireland, Lauzun would be congratulated for salvaging the French brigade from a stricken country.[3]

Tyrconnell even discussed how Ireland would be governed after their departure. All civil affairs were to be left in the hands of the lord justices and the army was to be commanded by Galmoy and Sarsfield.[4] Although the mention of Sarsfield may have aroused Lauzun's suspicions as to the credibility of anything that Tyrconnell had said, this made good sense to him. After all, and despite Tyrconnell's differences with his commanders, Galmoy was the most distinguished nobleman in the army and Sarsfield was both popular and competent.

Tyrconnell's talk of giving up encouraged Lauzun to expand his own plans. He began thinking of not only shipping away the French brigade but also taking the cream of the Irish cavalry and the Galway garrison. He also began to entertain hopes that Sarsfield, Galmoy and Sheldon would also go with him with perhaps the intention of serving in Mountcashel's Irish brigade. Sarsfield had naturally spent some time in Galway while they awaited the outcome of the siege of Limerick, and Lauzun was able to ask him that important question: If Limerick fell would he come to France? Sarsfield was non-committal, but from what he said Lauzun formed the opinion that he probably would. Sarsfield was however quite adamant in his answer to the second question; if Limerick held out, he would stay on and continue the war regardless of French aid even if it meant pursuing a guerrilla war throughout the winter without a regular army.[5]

In the event, Limerick did hold out and Tyrconnell appointed a new administration to govern in his absence. Lauzun was not involved in any of the decisions that were taken in this respect and consequently did not look too closely at the arrangements that were made. If he had done, he would have noticed that Tyrconnell had set about ensuring that his rivals would be prevented from improving their position while he was away. The reins of government were handed over to the one man he felt that he could trust, the duke of Berwick. Just before his departure, he had a letter drawn up by Sir Ignatius White, his secretary, making Berwick commander-in-chief of His Majesty's forces during the viceroy's absence. The commission ended with the words 'and we do hereby command all officers to be obedient to you as their chief commander'.[6]

Berwick was to rule Ireland as a vice-viceroy. He was to preside over a military council of twelve men, eleven of whom had, at least in part, been selected for their loyalty to Tyrconnell. The twelfth man was Sarsfield who, although he would perhaps prove to be troublesome, was now so much of a national hero that he could not be left off the council. Indeed, the pressure on Tyrconnell to recognise Sarsfield was such that he had felt obliged to make him up to the rank of major-general even before the Ballyneety raid. This promotion had made good sense to the viceroy as, overbearing and irritable though he was, he certainly was not the petty and vindictive man that his enemies represented him to be. Sarsfield, he knew, was not only very popular but had great qualities of leadership and it would not serve Tyrconnell's purpose to waste these obvious talents.

In the second week of September, Tyrconnell and Lauzun took the same ship for Brest. With them sailed a convoy of transport ships carrying the French brigade and Boisseleau, who was allowed home as a reward for his defence of Limerick. Having left everything in order, Tyrconnell was able to concentrate on Lauzun again. They had plenty of time to talk and plenty of time to agree their story and they did just that. Ireland was lost. The Irish were too dispirited and ill-disciplined to continue the campaign against the English and their continental allies. Any supplies of equipment or men from France would be wasted. His Most Catholic Majesty should not be tempted to throw good money after bad. Having now shipped off their own troops, the French should now make arrangements to bring away the best equipped Irish regiments.

On their arrival at Brest, Tyrconnell was feeling his years. He needed to rest after the tiring voyage. He urged Lauzun to go on ahead of him and to let the French court know of the true state of affairs in Ireland. Lauzun did so. He reported directly firstly to King Louis and then to King James and he painted them both a very dismal picture. Although he had saved the Irish army at the Boyne, the Irish were now tired of war. The situation was hopeless. Limerick itself would have been surrendered had it not been for his encouragement and for the energy of Tyrconnell, who was the only Irishman who had held out for war. In fact, Lauzun had nothing but good to say of Tyrconnell, and nothing but bad to say of King Louis's hopes in Ireland.

A few days later, Tyrconnell arrived in Paris,[7] much refreshed after his rest. So refreshed in fact, that he was no longer the tired and dispirited man that Lauzun had known for the past month. He was the Dick Talbot of old, vigorous and triumphant, and quite determined to set the record straight in the reports he would make to the two kings. Lauzun, he said, had let him down. Ireland was in a desperate state, but so much could have been done if only Lauzun could have been persuaded to stay in Limerick, or indeed, to do anything worthwhile at all for either of the kings. But notwithstanding the French general's obvious distaste for war, their majesties should be clear on one thing. The Irish were willing to fight. All they needed was the means to do so .

Lauzun was devastated. He, who had lived on his wits for years in the most sophisticated court in Europe, had been betrayed, fooled and outwitted by an Irishman, by a country bumpkin. Not only that, but he had known Tyrconnell's reputation for years and had still allowed himself to fall into the trap. And there was nothing that he could do to remedy the situation as he had already used his considerable powers of persuasion to impress upon the two kings and their ministers how brave and loyal Tyrconnell had shown himself to be. It was now too late to change his story. Lying Dick Talbot had found another victim. Lauzun, again out of royal favour, was left to reflect on his part in making Tyrconnell a hero and thereby ensuring French support for the coming campaign in Ireland.

Once they had withdrawn from Limerick, the English took steps to consolidate their position in Ireland. Their priority was in finding secure and dry winter quarters. The Irish on the other hand, and for the first time that year, had more aggressive plans. Berwick, urged on by Sarsfield and the rest of the Council, was anxious to take as much land back from the English before the weather put a stop to all campaigning. Except for the short-lived occupation of Annaghbeg, William's men had not penetrated to beyond the Shannon. Connaught was firmly in Irish hands and as the English had failed to take Athlone, the Irish were confined not by the river itself but by the string of garrisons that had been established by General Douglas stretching southwards from Mullingar. The Irish intention was now to push the English line back further from the river. Within days of Tyrconnell's departure, most of the Irish army was marching northwards and Berwick had set his sights on the first of these garrisons. He was to personally lead an attack on Birr.

Except for the fact that it was now garrisoned by a company of Colonel Zachariah Tiffin's Inniskilling regiment of foot, Birr had not changed since Sarsfield's visit in the previous year. The war had passed it by. After the Boyne, the Irish troops then stationed there had marched off to Athlone and Birr had subsequently become a link in Douglas's chain of garrisons along the east side of the Shannon. The castle was then occupied by a hundred men under the command of Captain John Curry, a veteran of the fruitless attack on Athlone.

On the morning of 16 September 1690 a party of Irish horsemen appeared on Burkeshill, just four hundred yards or so from the castle. This in itself was not an unusual event. According to John Phillips who was in the castle at the time,

> We took no great notice, being often alarmed and daily used to that sight, but in a short time we perceived the party, by little and little, to increase more and more; upon which we began to look about us and beat drum for gathering in the soldiers who were scattered in the town, and put ourselves immediately in a posture of defence.

The sentries who had been posted on Burkeshill came running back to the castle. Curry had only three officers with him, the two most junior of these he kept in town. Ensign Ball was sent running off to barricade himself into the church with twenty musketeers so they could occupy the steeple, and Ensign Hamilton was kept with Curry in the castle. Lieutenant Richard Newstead was sent off down the lane towards Burkeshill with twenty Enniskilleners to find out what was going on. While he did this, the Protestants of Birr were rushing for the safety of the castle. Newstead, in blocking the lane, was able to hold a shouted conversation with Dick Oxburgh, one of Colonel Hewar Oxburgh's sons, who was commanding a troop of Irish horsemen. Captain Oxburgh told Newstead that the duke of Berwick, Lord Galway and Colonel Sarsfield were approaching Birr with a train of artillery to see to the castle. As they spoke, Newstead could see the main column advancing, and so made his way straight back to the safety of the castle walls.

As if they were on a parade ground the Irish marched towards the town with colours flying, trumpets sounding, drums beating and bagpipes playing. They formed up on Burkeshill and sent their horsemen ahead to ride around the town and herd up the cattle while some of their foot soldiers began plundering the houses that were out of musket shot. When it was clear that all the opposition was confined to the castle and the church, the main body moved forward. Those townspeople who had elected to take refuge in the castle now looked out and saw a body of men that they had hoped to have seen the last of Colonel Hewar Oxburgh and his infantry were back in Birr.

> They summoned the castle and promised fair quarter if it were peaceably surrendered, but if they took it by storm no quarter was to be given to either man, woman or child. This summons Captain Curry answered with great gallantry, courage and resolution, and sent them word he would not surrender till the castle was beaten down or he had one man left.

He also hoisted over the castle a red flag, that international signal for 'No Surrender'.

It is not clear whether Berwick actually intended to capture Birr and hold it, or whether the intention was merely to burn it and withdraw. Judging by the amount of troops he had with him, it was clear that he was at least prepared to take the former course of action. It certainly was not an impossible task. Strangely enough, at the last siege of Birr in 1646 Sarsfield's grandfather Rory O'Moore had been one of the Irish commanders. On that occasion, the garrison's surrender had been greatly facilitated by the correspondence he had held with 'his much honoured and highly esteemed the Lady Anne Parsons' who was inside the castle. The siege had then lasted five days.[9]

The problem that Berwick now faced at Birr was simply that he was too early. The English army had not yet been broken up for the winter and marched off into garrisons. General Kirke commanded a large force in Roscrea, a mere twelve miles away, and any attack on Birr was certain to attract his attention. For that reason Berwick brought with him not only enough men for the attack, but also men to fight off the reinforcements. In his memoirs, in which he makes no reference to Sarsfield at Birr, he says that he brought all his cavalry and seven battalions. This would amount perhaps to some three thousand horseman and four and a half thousand foot soldiers. The defenders of Birr estimated the Irish to number about ten thousand, but however many there were it is clear that only a minority of them were actually engaged in the attack. The cavalry kept their distance and most of the infantry never entered the village. An English report clearly stated that Sarsfield had kept his main force well away and left no more than a hundred and sixty men to conduct the siege of Birr Castle.[10]

The attack on Birr began with the Irish artillery being drawn up on the green just out of effective musket range. They had only three cannons, only one of which was of a calibre big enough to usefully serve as a battering piece, and that was only a twelve-pounder. The other two were small field guns, a six and a three-pounder. Having received Curry's reply to the summons, the cannon opened fire. The first shot augured well. It smashed its way straight through the castle roof sending the wooden tiles flying in all directions. The Irish let out a whoop of delight as they heard the loud clatter of wood on stone as the shingles fell down inside the building. But if they thought that the castle was about to fall down, they were to be disappointed.

Captain Curry's position inside the castle was certainly awkward. It was no more than a fortified manor. Although built of stone, its walls were not designed to withstand a strong and prolonged cannonade. If the Irish did get in or were to force his men to come out, he would have no hope of beating them off. There were simply too many of them. His only hope lay in the knowledge that Kirke was at Roscrea. As the English cavalry could reach him in little over an hour and the English infantry were less than three hours away, Curry had good reason to believe that he needed to hold out for no more than a day before a relief column would reach him. The only question was whether or not the castle walls would last that long.

Conditions inside the castle were cramped and dangerous:

> The Lord Galway and several other officers got into the market house, which fronts the Castle, and with their fusees shot sharply at the windows and doors of the Castle so that the besieged could not, without apparent danger of their lives, stir in any of the front rooms.

The Irish in fact surrounded the castle and took what cover they could in and around the buildings and 'lay pelting at us under the hedges'. John Phillips wrote that:

> From two of the clock till after sunset the small shot on both sides and their great guns never ceased but continued without intermission like a continual thunder, only now and then with a little comical discourse and scolding would happen from our men, bidding them go home and dig their potatoes and calling them rapparees which they took as a great affront.

Not that the Irish were behind in the exchange of words, although the only recorded insults they hurled at the besieged were 'rogues', 'traitors and rebels'; these doubtlessly being the only words fit to put on paper.

In this short and fruitless siege, Berwick's men were said to have suffered very heavy casualties.

> The besieged lost but one man in this action, and the enemy lost at least sixty men, as was confessed by two wounded men they left behind them when they broke the siege. These wounded men Captain Curry ordered be taken care of and cured. The person who was killed on the besieged side was the sergeant who, contrary to the command of Ensign Ball, his officer; went up into the steeple of the church to look at the enemy where he foolishly exposed his body to their view and was shot dead.

Also, one of the Irish guns burst in the late afternoon and killed a gunner. Although there is no Irish record of their losses on that day, one suspects that the number was much lower than sixty. In any event, the defenders of Birr would not have been in a good position to make an accurate estimate as, with the exception of the two wounded men, the Irish took all their dead and wounded away with them.

By nightfall there still had been no significant damage to the castle. The walls had not been breached in any place and all the damage done on the inside was caused either by the cannonballs that had come in through the windows and smashed through internal walls, or by the besieged themselves who were ordered by Curry to rip the lead of the roof to make bullets with and to pull down 'two coach houses, a hen house, a slaughter house, a bake house and a bolting house within the walls of the castle and uncover a large stable and turf house to prevent the enemies firing them'.

Although Sarsfield was present at the siege, he did not take any active part in it. Berwick later wrote that he alone was responsible for directing the operations and that his failure was due to 'the unskillfullness of my gunners who never could bring their guns to bear upon the castle'. Indeed, as John Phillips noted, 'when they played their great guns, they commonly fired all three at a time and as good luck would have it, played at the flanker next them, which we judged to be the strongest part of the house'.* Galway, Sarsfield's brother-in-law, was the only other senior officer named as being directly involved in the siege.

While the fighting was continuing it can be surmised that Sarsfield was commanding the cavalry and keeping an eye on those foot battalions waiting outside the village. His immediate concern was with whoever might appear along the road from Roscrea rather than the attack on the castle, but according to the Birr chronicler he did at least try to influence the conduct of the siege, and may well have been responsible for it having been called off.

---

*   The damage to this flanker, the east wing of the castle, is still evident and bears witness to how scattered and inaccurate the cannon fire was.

Before I quit this relation, I beg the reader's leave to acquaint him how Colonel Sarsfield and Colonel Oxburgh (formerly Sir Lawrence's servant and his father's servant before and since the wars of '41) behaved themselves in the siege as I have been informed by one who was in the action and heard the passage. When the enemy came to besiege the castle at Birr, Colonel Sarsfield made a speech to the officers and desired them to consider what they were going to do. He told them it was a place of no strength and not worth their keeping if they had it, and if they took it they could not expect to hold it long, it being in an open country and the English army around them who would certainly retake it soon to their great loss. He further added the house had cost Sir Lawrence a great deal of money and since it would do them no good it was a pity to destroy the gentleman's castle. To this Colonel Oxburgh furiously replied; Sir Lawrence was a traitor, that King James had given him the estate (and) that he would sacrifice the castle to His Majesty's service and therefore prayed they would lay it in rubbish, or make the rebels submit. To this noble Colonel Oxburgh's advice and desire the enemy adhered as hath been related, and rejected Colonel Sarsfield's advice to their loss both of men, ammunition and honour as hath been declared.

This is the third occasion in the Birr manuscript that the anonymous chronicler makes mention of Sarsfield's kind consideration towards Sir Lawrence Parsons, a man who he had never met until the war had begun and who had constantly sided with Sarsfield's enemies. The esteem in which Sarsfield was held by Protestants, which almost bordered on affection, is one of the curiosities of the war. To the English it was as if Sarsfield had been fighting on the wrong side.

The Irish certainly had not prospered by their raid on Birr. During the following weeks they made successful raids on other midland towns, but at Birr they had been handicapped by the proximity of General Kirke. The garrison had not beaten them off, they had withdrawn from the area because they knew that Kirke was marching straight for them.

On the same day that Berwick attacked Birr, word had got through to Roscrea. As soon as he could Kirke marched his infantry towards Birr and three miles out of town he joined forces with Sir John Lanier's cavalry. Kirke knew nothing of Berwick or Galway, but was told that Sarsfield was at Birr with a large force. This is another indication that it was Sarsfield who commanded the Irish cavalry that day while Berwick spent the afternoon cursing and swearing at his inept gunners. The combination of Sarsfield and the Irish cavalry made Kirke hesitate. He did not want to advance until his own cavalry was reinforced. He sent urgent messages to General Douglas who was stationed over thirty miles away at Portlaoise. In the meanwhile Curry was left to his fate.

If it is correct that Sarsfield was opposed to the idea of destroying Sir Lawrence Parsons's home, according to O'Kelly he certainly was not inclined to return over the Shannon either. He wanted to attack Kirke's force. If Kirke was chased away, Birr castle would no doubt surrender without further ado. However, it would seem that Berwick had been taking more cautious advice from others, and was unwilling to risk a battle. Despite Sarsfield's objections, he ordered his men to withdraw.

That night the Irish cleverly kept both Curry and Kirke guessing. They collected the town's supply of cut peat that had been drying at the bottom of Burkeshill and carried it to the top where they set it alight. The fires on Burkeshill gave the impression that they were camping there and were either going to attack in the morning or were preparing faggots so that there would be a night attack. There was to be no sleep for the garrison. Curry ordered several doors and loose boards in the castle to be split up into thin strips which were dipped in tallow and lit. These were then thrown over the walls to provide enough light to prevent a surprise attack. To let the Irish know that they were awake and ready, the Enniskilleners fired random shots into the town throughout the night. Only at first light did they learn that Berwick had gone.

> Praise be God who hath delivered us from the hand of our enemies and may we never forget the Sixteenth of September which I hope we shall live to observe here as an anniversary day of Jubilee.

Although Berwick and Sarsfield were no longer sieging Birr, they had not fled in any panic. The main Irish force had withdrawn only three miles towards Banagher, but they had kept their patrols active right up to Birr. On the day after the siege, Phillips wrote; 'Some small parties did often appear about the town to alarm us and tire us out and indeed we could hardly rest for their frequent alarms all that day, which were almost every two hours.'

On the second day after the siege, Thursday 18 September 1690, the reinforcements were at last hesitantly led into Birr by General Douglas. He was later followed by the even more hesitant General Kirke and Sir John Lanier. After this liberation, Birr would never be the same again. Up to that date the town had come through the war relatively unscathed. Berwick, and it was unlike him not to do so, had not burnt it down. The Irish had of course looted everything that they could carry away (including the glass from the windows) and they had driven off all the cattle, but the only lasting damage caused by them to the buildings was the shot marks on the castle walls. But now the town was to be all but destroyed. Kirke wanted to garrison the place with several thousand men and so had all the houses around the castle pulled down to make room for his new fortifications. To ensure a wide field of fire, he had the orchards, hedges and ditches levelled. If the Irish had razed the town to the ground, they would only have saved Kirke's men a lot of hard work.

On the Friday or Saturday, Sarsfield and Berwick recrossed the Shannon at Banagher. There they had taken a stone arch out of the bridge and replaced it with a wooden draw bridge. A strong Irish garrison was posted in some newly thrown up earthworks to guard both sides of the bridge. The position was so strong that Douglas decided against any pursuit.

With so much of the eastern midlands weakly garrisoned it was clearly not a wise move to spend time on one of the few places that was going to be strongly defended. Birr was simply no longer worth bothering about and Sarsfield's interest turned to the north. Before the Irish withdrew, there were several small clashes between their patrols and the English scouts, and although both sides probably claimed these as minor victories nothing happened of any importance. There was certainly no incident as startling as that described in the hopeful London newsletter dated 2 October 1690:

> Lieutenant-General Douglas and Sir John Lanier had fought Colonel Sarsfield and killed 2,000 of the Irish, and killed Colonel Sarsfield as is reported.[11]

CHAPTER XIII

Berwick's Government

Berwick: Come, Colonel, there's no help for no remedy, 'tis my royal
father's misfortune to work with bad tools, and the best artist in the
world can never make a silk purse of a sow's ear.

Sarsfield: However, there's life in a muscle still: the heretics have not done
all their work yet, we have something still left that will hold 'em
play for some time, and if we can get fresh succours from France
we may be able to turn the scales, or else at least to make an
honourable composition for ourselves.

The Royal Flight, 1690

WHILE WILLIAM was still in Ireland and marching towards Limerick, the
Privy Council in London had approved a bold plan set before them by their
youngest lieutenant-general, John Churchill, earl of Marlborough. Give me, he
told them, five thousand men, ships to carry them and a naval escort, and I will
take those two ports still in Irish hands on the south coast of Ireland. I will
capture Cork and Kinsale. Messages were sent to William who despite his dislike
of Marlborough, agreed. His approval may have been largely due to the fact that
the proposal came to him at a particularly disturbing time in the campaign. He
had only just been able to assess the damage caused by Sarsfield's raid at
Ballyneety.

On 23 September 1690, a week after the attack on Birr Castle, Marlborough
landed his troops at Passage West, eight miles from Cork. The city, the second
largest in the country, was garrisoned by four and a half thousand men commanded by Colonel Roger MacElligott.

While Marlborough's British troops arrived by sea, a continental force of
another five thousand men under Generals Wurtemburg and Von Tettau had
marched south to assist them. All were concerned that the campaign should be
over quickly as it was feared that the Irish would detach a large force which
would seek to forge its way south from Limerick to relieve the besieged towns.
Five days after Marlborough's arrival, the Cork garrison surrendered. It had been
simultaneously attacked by Marlborough from the south and by Wurtemburg
from the north. For the first time in the war the Williamites were confident
enough to offer no special conditions to a major Irish garrison. MacElligott and
all his men, including the young earl of Clancarty, were made prisoners of war.

Two days later, Marlborough's advance guard reached Kinsale, the busiest
port in Ireland. Again, no favourable terms were offered. A trumpeter announced
that if the garrison surrendered immediately they would be made prisoners of

war. If they did not, they would all be hanged. Both the forts in the town hoisted red flags. The garrison commander, the seventy year old Sir Edward Scott, was resolved to fight despite the fact that his garrison numbered less than two thousand men. Fifteen days later he surrendered, but only after Marlborough had agreed to allow him to march to Limerick with the entire garrison. So ended Marlborough's month in Ireland, and with proof perhaps that he was destined for great things, he returned with his men to London.*

During this month, the new Williamite commander-in-chief in Ireland, Godard van Reede, Baron de Ginckel, had been anxious to protect Marlborough's force from any Irish reinforcements that might march from Limerick. He arranged for his cavalry to be deployed around Mallow. Rumours abounded as to what the Irish were doing. During the siege of Kinsale, Berwick had attempted to mount an expedition, but he had too few men for the task. Most of the Irish army was with Sarsfield in the midlands establishing itself on the eastern bank of the Shannon. He contented himself instead by burning as many villages and houses as he could to the south of Limerick.

However, one minor clash did take place in the Mallow area while Sarsfield was still threatening Birr. A hundred and fifty Danish cavalrymen and dragoons commanded by Major Von Viettinghoff were reported to have caught a large band of rapparees and to have killed five hundred of them without losing a single man. Although even those figures were doubtlessly exaggerated, by the time the story was repeated in a London pamphlet the petty skirmish had become a great victory. It was not fought between Von Viettinghoff and a band of rapparees, but between General Scravenmoer and Sarsfield. Scravenmoer, it was reported, was outnumbered by two to one. Sarsfield 'being buoyed up and flushed with his late attempt of seizing the cannon' tried to cut him off. Scravenmoer crushed the Irish force. Over two thousand Irish soldiers were killed. 'Sarsfield with only five of his party escaped in the fight'. No doubt it was with great pleasure that Londoners read the despatch. 'We have sufficiently given him a *Rowland* for his *Oliver.*'[1]

Although Berwick's rule in Ireland had begun with a frantic effort to take the military initiative, he was unable to sustain this policy. Not least because it was not working. His failure at Birr and subsequent retreat had seriously affected the morale of the Irish army, and his scorched earth policy in northern Munster, an activity which he seemed to relish, had not won him any friends on either side.

> The enemy under the duke of Berwick has carried out frightful burnings while we were occupied with Kinsale. He has done damage to the country to the value of several millions and has burnt down more than twelve fine towns and very many beautiful castles, including Charleville, which was

---

* Marlborough was Berwick's uncle, Berwick being the eldest son of Arabella Churchill, Marlborough's sister. (Arabella Churchill had since married Charles Godfrey, Lord Grey's second in the Albemarle duel.) It is also a curious fact that Marlborough was married to Lady Tyrconnell's sister.

the finest in Ireland, and all such places in the counties of Cork and Tipperary. A message has been sent to the duke of Berwick to intimidate him saying that, if he continued burning, the Irish prisoners, including the officers of whom there are great numbers, would be burned alive.[2]

By this time, Berwick's position was far from secure. The government that he led was Tyrconnell's, and it was held to be collectively responsible for the military failures of September and October 1690. Sarsfield and those others who had opposed Tyrconnell were now taking steps to remove his appointees. After the loss of Cork and Kinsale, it was with a certain amount of apprehension that Berwick returned to Limerick.

In Berwick's absence a general council was held in Limerick without either his permission or knowledge. The prime point of discussion was the legality of his position. According to Colonel O'Kelly the council was attended by 'the nobility, bishops, and prime officers of the army'.[3] They listened to a series of Irish lawyers advancing the view that Berwick's government was so manifestly unlawful that any contrary opinion was unarguable. The law of Ireland was such that the government could only be vested in the king or in his viceroy or in a deputy holding his position by royal authority. Both the king and viceroy had now left the country, and the king had not appointed a new deputy in their absence. It mattered not that Tyrconnell had appointed Berwick as his deputy as Tyrconnell was not empowered to do so. Berwick's appointment simply had no legal foundation.

Having heard this irrefutable assertion, the council debated what action should then be taken. It was clearly accepted that, as Berwick was acting without authority, it was up to this general assembly of free Irishmen to decide on whatever policy they felt best for their own preservation and for the good of the country. And as the general assembly of free Irishmen did not include Tyrconnell's partisans, the policy chosen as being in the best interests of the nation was to take immediate steps to remove Tyrconnell's appointees from the council of war and to ensure that Tyrconnell did not return. Berwick in himself was not a problem; he was in fact the very figurehead that the general assembly needed. It was known that King James 'had a fond affection for the youth', and Berwick's loyalty to his father had not manifested itself in any irreversible hostility towards Sarsfield's party. It was decided to ask Berwick to agree to, or in reality to force Berwick to allow, the sending of a delegation to Saint-Germain to put the feelings of the general assembly to King James.

Sarsfield was again chosen as the one to approach Berwick. When, two months before, he had spoken to him on the subject of the coup, it had been a cautious and secretive mission. Now it was an open affair. He took with him the Englishman William Dorrington and the quieter of the two Luttrell brothers, Simon. Sarsfield had been careful in his choice of delegates. Dorrington had been the architect of Tyrconnell's army in the years before the war, and Simon Luttrell had been the governor of Dublin earlier in the year. They were both experienced and efficient men, and with Sarsfield they made up a delegation whose purpose was not to

15 James Fitzjames, duke of Berwick.

frighten Berwick into submission, but rather to quietly explain to him what it was that they wanted and why he should go along with them. They were confident of persuading him. They wanted only one thing and that was that they should be able to send certain nominees to Paris 'as they had reason to suspect that Tyrconnell would not represent their wants with sufficient force'. Even Berwick knew that this was a gross understatement of their case.

Berwick was furious. He was furious in the way that he had been when Sarsfield last approached him. But now he could do nothing. Tyrconnell had been able to stand up to Sarsfield. The viceroy was old and experienced enough to be able to cajole and bully senior officers into taking his side. He could dominate domineering men, and men feared him. But Berwick was different. He was too young to dominate anyone of consequence and he did not have Tyrconnell's personal following. He was only twenty years old. People that would have toed Tyrconnell's line when Tyrconnell was there to glare at them, could make excuses now that the viceroy was gone. Whereas Tyrconnell had roared, Berwick could only squeak. How dare they, how dare the Irish hold an assembly without telling him, the governor-general? He was astonished that they had the nerve to do such a thing and as for Sarsfield, he had already been warned once and here he was again, proposing fresh mutiny against the viceroy who held King James's commission. There were to be no more general assemblies, he declared. Sarsfield, Luttrell and Dorrington listened politely, deferentially even. They held all the cards. They were confident both in the power that they now possessed and in the correctness of their assertions. To them Berwick was a weak appointee who desperately needed their support to keep his position, a position they knew to be unlawful. He was just a token of government, a very useful token, but no more. If Berwick was to leave, the situation in Ireland would not deteriorate. Berwick suspected that he was beaten. Even the composition of the delegation told him that. Sarsfield he would have suspected, but never Dorrington. He did the one thing that they would have allowed him. He told them to come back tomorrow morning and he would tell them what he, as Governor-General, had decided.

If in the evening Berwick suspected his position as being hopeless, he certainly knew it by the morning. His advisers left him in no doubt. He called a further general assembly, and perhaps an even bigger one so as to include all the senior officers, the nobility and bishops, and he repeated in a quieter and more eloquent fashion his disapproval of the holding of unauthorised assemblies.

> . . . but to show how well I was inclined, I said that to oblige them I was willing to send such persons as they should approve of to France to represent their real condition and necessities. I proposed to them the bishop of Cork, the two Luttrells and Colonel Purcell. My choice was unanimously approved.

Berwick later wrote of the occasion as if he had graciously thrown the Irish a small sop to prevent them from feeling too wounded after his disapproving tirade. In fact, he had given way completely. They had only wanted one thing and they had got it. They had found a way in which they could destroy Tyrconnell. The men that had been chosen to go to France were the very men who would feel most at ease before the king. The Luttrells were among the wealthiest landowners in Co. Dublin and Purcell, apart from being a wealthy landowner, was also first cousin to the Hamilton brothers and a nephew of the duke of Ormonde and had spent much of his life in court society. Berwick's position was also much weakened. He was no longer seen as the power in the land. The real authority lay with the general council and the voice of the general council was increasingly Sarsfield's.

The struggle did not end there. Berwick was not going to give up immediately. He was a proud young man, and his pride had certainly taken a beating. Although he would one day be a great man, he was then wholly dependent on those who had been instructed to guide him. Tyrconnell's partisans now saw in him their one hope. Directly after Berwick's address, Sarsfield had returned to Athlone. Berwick and his advisers reasoned that the other Irish officers would soon do the same. As the officers turned their attention to their military commands, the general assembly ceased to exist. Berwick again found himself in command and now greatly resented the way that he had been treated by Sarsfield. He decided to delay the delegation. As each day passed there was an increased chance that fresh orders would come from King James, or perhaps, as O'Kelly thought, even a viceroy's commission for Berwick, 'which would put an end to all disputes about that legality of power'. And as winter drew on there was an increased likelihood that the ships would be stormbound in Galway. Berwick withheld his permission for the delegation to sail. 'This unexpected tergiversation of the young man highly incensed the nation.'[4]

Messages were sent to Sarsfield, and he returned to Limerick. His partisans were no longer in a mood to compromise. They resolved to form a new government and this time to exclude Berwick altogether and to replace all Tyrconnell's nominees. Their anger prevented discretion and their plans were discovered by the very people they intended to oust. Berwick's advisers saw the danger; they would have to comply with the assembly's wishes. It was a time for subtlety rather than confrontation. Berwick signed the credentials for the agents 'seemingly without any reluctance'. He even gave in to their further demands in that he agreed to the addition of two bishops and eight peers, all of whom had been left out by Tyrconnell, onto the executive council so that Sarsfield's party would be in the majority. He even agreed that his councils of war would be made up of all the general officers and not just Tyrconnell's appointees. By the time that Sarsfield had returned to Limerick, everything was in order and running to plan.

Berwick made one last attempt to frustrate the delegation. He made arrangements to send Brigadier Thomas Maxwell, 'a cunning Scotsman', to France as well. Maxwell was one of Tyrconnell's appointees and was, according to O'Kelly, one of the few that exerted a strong influence over Berwick. Maxwell was instructed to report to James and let him know of the pressure that Berwick had been placed under. He was also to ensure that James did not let the delegates back to Ireland, especially those 'two most dangerous incendiaries', Brigadier Henry Luttrell and Colonel Nicholas Purcell. Indeed, Berwick later wrote that he had chosen these two men for the deputation only because he wanted to get them out of the way. Without them, he hoped, Sarsfield would truckle under and concentrate on the war with the English.

It was almost a fatal voyage for Thomas Maxwell. He found himself with the Luttrells, Purcell and the bishop sitting out the stormy weather in Galway.

The others were suspicious of his presence and when they all got on board they turned on him. It was quite clear to them that the Scot was going to France with some secret communication from Berwick and they correctly suspected that that communication related to them. Henry Luttrell and Nicholas Purcell had every intention of having Maxwell thrown over the side. They were only prevented from doing so by the intervention of the bishop of Cork, who Berwick described as 'a prelate of distinguished piety', and by Simon Luttrell, who Berwick wrote of as being 'of an obliging disposition and a man of honour'. Maxwell was indeed very lucky to have such paragons of virtue on board with him.

The delegation had a lot of work to do. Within a day or so of their departure from Galway, a message arrived from the king in France. His Irish subjects, it read, could not give any greater proof of their fidelity to him than by their ready submission and obedience to Tyrconnell and by their exact observance of his orders. It was an unwelcome indication to Sarsfield of how Tyrconnell was faring in France. The message also contained instructions forbidding anyone to leave Ireland. It was of course too late; the very birds that Tyrconnell had wanted to cage had flown.

The storms that delayed the delegation affected the whole country. The commanders no longer thought of military adventure. Berwick was forced to concentrate on consolidating his position. His army was divided into its winter quarters to cover the areas around the five main towns in Irish hands; Sligo, Athlone, Galway, Limerick and Killarney. Of these the most important throughout the winter was Athlone. The army group there was commanded by Sarsfield. His responsibility lay in a series of posts stretching along the Shannon from Jamestown to Portumna, nearly a hundred miles of river.

The month of November in 1690 saw both the Irish and the Williamites scrambling for positions along the east bank of the Shannon. After his ill-fated expedition to Athlone in the summer, Douglas had secured the garrison towns in Offaly and Westmeath. His men were still in Mullingar and the forts and castles at Newtown Forbes, Daingean, Birr and Roscrea, but there were too few of them to control the countryside. Sarsfield's troops moved into this vacuum and took up positions deep into Offaly between the English garrisons, establishing a string of Irish garrisons on the east bank from Nenagh up to Ballymore. The last of these, which had been garrisoned by the English since Douglas's withdrawal from Athlone, was to become the most important of Sarsfield's bases in Leinster.

When old Schomberg had commanded the Williamite army in Ireland in the winter before the Boyne, his main concern had been to keep his troops as warm and as comfortable as possible. His continued inactivity into the spring had prompted William to cross the water and lead the army in person. Within three weeks of setting foot in Ireland, William had won the Battle of the Boyne and taken Dublin. Now, the following winter, William was again in England but he was adamant that the Schomberg mentality should not reassert itself in his absence. He had a war to fight in Europe and he needed men for that war. Every effort was to be made to gain a strategic advantage for the coming campaign. In particular, a crossing on the Shannon should be secured so that in the spring the army could march straight into Connaught.

Now that the French had left, it was felt that the Irish army could well collapse if the pressure on it was maintained. Ginckel accordingly gave each of his four regional commanders an objective. Douglas, based at Cavan with eight thousand men, was to make an attempt on Sligo. To his south at Mullingar were six thousand men commanded by Kirke and Lanier. They were to try to secure a bridgehead over the Shannon. From Cashel Ginckel himself intended to accompany Scravenmoer in an attack on Limerick, and from Cork General von Tettau was to raid deep into Kerry with three and a half thousand men to destroy the Irish winter quarters there.

Sarsfield was well aware of the unexpected activity on the other side of the Shannon, and he knew what the Williamites were intending. He busied himself in fortifying all the crossing places. Earthworks were thrown up on both banks wherever there was a bridge or a ford. He was determined that the English would have to fight to get to the river, let alone across it. He supervised defence works at Portumna, Meelick, Banagher, Shannonbridge, Lanesborough and Jamestown and posted in them whatever regiments he could. His own base at Athlone was also the scene of fresh engineering works. Stationed there was not only the biggest garrison on the Shannon above Limerick, but also a flying column of two thousand men with whom he could react to an attack on any of the other crossing points.

At the beginning of December 1690, two of the four Williamite forces were on the march. Generals Ginckel and Scravenmoer moved on Limerick in the hope that the Irish had weakened their defences during the winter months. They were disappointed. Major General Dorrington, who was the city's governor, had been alerted and was ready for them. Ginckel saw no point in making a serious attempt on the city, especially as the state of the roads had prevented him from bringing any cannons. To the south, General von Tettau was advancing into Kerry, and so Ginckel's men marched off to join him. It was a miserable expedition. The Irish burnt everything in the path of the English army and then melted away before them, taking their cattle and supplies with them. When it became clear that Ginckel was marching on the strategically unimportant town of Killarney, the Irish burnt it down to deny the English any shelter. This gained nothing as it was exactly what the English would have done in any event. By the time they reached Killarney, Ginckel's men were exhausted, and it was decided to return to Cork. Kerry had nothing to offer them except the opportunity of a long and fruitless chase around the Derrynasaggart Mountains and MacGillycuddy's Reeks. As the English withdrew to the east, the Irish advanced to take up their original positions.

The Irish, and Sarsfield in particular, knew of Ginckel's plans and the mere fact that such plans existed brought fresh divisions to the Irish camp. 'In truth', wrote Sarsfield, 'it does not appear that the enemy would choose to attempt in the heart of winter an enterprise which they were incapable of carrying out in the finest part of summer if they were not encouraged by some traitors amongst us.'5 It was a dismal thought, but one that preyed much on his mind.

Sarsfield's fear of traitors was not an irrational one. Three hundred years after the event it is less easy to judge how far certain Irishmen may have been willing to go to assist King William's army, but there were certainly those who would have been happy to see peace at almost any price. Irish trade was now centred in two towns, Limerick and Galway. The other towns controlled by the Irish were either too small or, in the cases of Athlone and Sligo, were now little more than garrisons. Limerick was where the government, nominally at least, sat but the most important town and port in Jacobite Ireland was Galway and therein lay the problem. Throughout the seventeenth century Galway had established itself as one of Ireland's prime mercantile towns and, unlike Limerick and Cork, it had only a very small Protestant population. The wealthy merchants who had built their substantial stone houses in sight of the bustling dock yards were all Catholic Irishmen. It was the premier Gaelic city. The men who built Galway and who controlled its wealth were men of the 'New Interest'. They were not old chieftains or feudal lords. They were merchants and as such had broken their ties with the more traditional society that existed throughout the rest of western Ireland. And as it was the language of trade, they even spoke English.

These men, and the men who depended on them for a livelihood, and their families, had suffered terribly throughout the war. They had all lost most of what they had, and they had lost it to the new Irish administration. The shortages that accompanied the war had resulted in the colonels ordering the warehouses to be opened and the goods to be commandeered on credit. When or if the merchants were paid, they were paid in the new copper coinage. It ruined them. How could they buy goods from France? The French merchants would accept gold or silver, but not one of them was going to part with goods in exchange for copper tokens stamped with King James's head. Their pleas to the colonels and the administrators fell on deaf ears. It was a grim fact that Galway was economically devastated even though the English had not got to within fifty miles of the city's walls.

Quite simply, the men of the 'New Interest', the merchants, the town dwellers and even the farmers, whose prosperity relied on their being able to sell their produce on French or English markets, were longing for peace. And peace under an English Protestant monarch was not such a terrible prospect. They had not only survived under it for the past hundred years, but they had prospered. The only poverty that they had known was under a Catholic king. If peace did not come soon, they would have no better alternative than to join their cousins in the hills to live on a diet of buttermilk and roots.

When King William had been marching towards Limerick, he was met at Goldenbridge by an Irish barrister named John Grady. Grady had been sent on a secret mission by Tyrconnell to ascertain what terms William would offer should the Irish surrender. At that time, before his failure at Limerick, William was not inclined to offer particularly attractive terms. But in early September, when William was leaving Ireland, Grady had travelled to Galway on a second mission and later that month Wurtemburg was able to report:

> He returned yesterday and had sounded out almost all the leading officers, all of whom have declared that, if the amnesty were made more explicit to the effect that they should retain their estates and live in peace as in the time of King Charles, they all wish to submit, particularly the governor of Galway.[6]

Although the English sources are silent as to any plot that there may have been, Sarsfield was convinced that there was treachery afoot. Although the English army's winter activity was a direct consequence of William's fear that the French would land an army in Ireland in the spring, there was also evidence that the English had been invited to march.

'Those who warned me of this plan added that the prince of Orange was urged to this enterprise by the correspondence he kept with some of ours who had promised to deliver up to him our strongest posts,' wrote Sarsfield. 'Here are the principal of those who are accused of having wanted to deliver our positions to the enemy: Lord Riverston, Judge Daly, Colonel John Hamilton and Colonel Alexander MacDonnell, the governor of Galway. As to Riverston, Daly and MacDonnell there are some striking circumstances which persuade me that they plotted something like that. I have seen a letter from the king to the duke of Berwick in which his Majesty informed him that he had received from England the same intelligence concerning the design of those I have just named'.[7] Sarsfield set about removing the 'traitors' from office. His difficulty was that although he was perhaps the most powerful individual in the country, most of the men in senior positions in the civil administration had been appointed by Tyrconnell as had these four suspects. Any attempt by Sarsfield to remove them from their offices was not seen to be a purge of traitors so much as a move to lock up his political opponents.

Thomas Nugent, Baron Riverston, was Tyrconnell's most powerful lieutenant. Before the war he had been the lord chief justice of Ireland and had become, after Tyrconnell, perhaps the man most disliked by the Protestants.* After his arrival in Ireland, James elevated him to the peerage and as the

---

*   As lord chief justice, Nugent had revived an act of Henry VII to prevent Protestants from holding firearms, ruling that it was a treasonable offence to do so without a licence even though the maximum penalty allowed by the laws of the day was a fine of £20. Robbery of the Protestants, he was supposed to have said, was an unfortunate necessity in the furtherance of King James's policies, and before the revolution he had boasted that the Williamites would soon 'be hung up all over England in bunches like a rope of onions'.

leading lawyer in the land he had introduced to the Dublin parliament the successful bill that repealed the Act of Settlement. But he was very much Tyrconnell's man and, like Tyrconnell, when defeat seemed inevitable he was attracted to the idea of salvaging what he could. Both he and Tyrconnell were anxious that the Irish should be able to negotiate the best possible peace treaty with William, and not have penal laws imposed on them after a military defeat. When Tyrconnell had sailed to France, Riverston remained in Ireland as the secretary of state for war, the most senior position after Berwick.

The governor of Galway, Colonel Alexander MacDonnell, was Riverston's brother-in-law and had come to be mistrusted by many. Sarsfield in particular was anxious to have him removed, although he was not typical of Tyrconnell's appointees. He was in fact one of the more experienced officers in the army and had spent many years as a mercenary in Spain. According to O'Kelly, who had a good word to say about anyone with a Gaelic name, MacDonnell was:

> A good commander, raised by merit from a private soldier to the rank of a Colonel, generally deemed an honest man, true to his country, and zealous for the Catholic worship, and for whose removal there was no other motive but that he was allied to Lord Riverston.

But despite this glowing assessment, the Williamite agents had brought back the information that MacDonnell was anxious for peace and was willing to surrender. After the fall of Kinsale he had suggested to a senior French officer that there should be a general capitulation: 'We will all be made slaves,' he said. 'It is better to come to a honourable arrangement'. The Frenchman was so shocked that he made it known that MacDonnell was totally untrustworthy and refused to serve with him. Another Frenchman, Colonel de Santons Boullain described MacDonnell as 'a filthy animal' and noted that he hated the French and neither obeyed nor respected any of his commanding officers.[8]

It is also worth noting the observations of Lord Ronsele, a recent immigrant to Ireland from Flanders, who was in Galway at the time. Ronsele,[9] for reasons that are set out below, particularly disliked Sarsfield. He wrote that MacDonnell 'was very willing to be kind to the Protestants',[10] and that at a time when Ronsele was under arrest for spying, MacDonnell, who knew of Ronsele's Williamite sympathies, had personally warned him to be careful about what he said or did. Notwithstanding this, Ronsele attributed MacDonnell's dismissal to Sarsfield's jealousy and ambition:

> Colonel MacDonnell was suspected himself out of policy because Tyrconnell was his great friend and that he was a great soldier, and Sarsfield not, who had a mind to be general governor himself and to disgrace these two old controllers (as Sarsfield's party called them) knowing very well that he could not compass his foolish and high designs whilst these two gentlemen remained in their employment.[11]

There could have been no satisfactory evidence against John Hamilton as, whatever Sarsfield may have thought, he was certainly no traitor, but he was one of those officers inclined to support Tyrconnell. This in itself was of course not an act of treachery, and was probably brought about as much by personal rather than political motives as Tyrconnell was a close family friend. (They knew each other as 'Jack' and 'Dick'.) Besides, not everyone liked Sarsfield, and not everyone liked those leading members of Sarsfield's party such as Henry Luttrell.

On the other hand, the very able lawyer, Judge Denis Daly was later shown to have been very untrustworthy indeed. He was one of those men whose wealth had been accrued entirely within the years of Tyrconnell's administration. His land had been bought from those Protestants who had received their grants during the interregnum, and if the Dublin Parliament had its way all such land would be confiscated without compensation and returned to the original owners. That in itself did not indicate where his loyalties lay, but he had made himself very unpopular with the Gaelic party by strongly arguing in Parliament against the repeal of the Act of Settlement. His enemies now spared no efforts to bring about his downfall.

Although Sarsfield could not be sure about Hamilton or Daly, he felt that he had enough evidence to insist that both Riverston and MacDonnell be dismissed, if not arrested. Berwick was again placed in a difficult situation. Now that Sarsfield was determined to remove his chief advisor, the secretary of war, there was a direct confrontation between the government set up by Tyrconnell and the faction led by Sarsfield. Despite his well grounded belief that Sarsfield was engaged on an exercise to sweep aside Tyrconnell's men, Berwick was not in a strong enough position to resist. He again gave way. Lord Riverston and MacDonnell were relieved of office.

Berwick's power had evaporated. The news of this was broken to Paris by the French priest, de Gravel, who wrote from Galway;

> Either God's helping hand or Sarsfield's wisdom and penetration made Berwick see what was in the best interests of his father the king. He followed his (Sarsfield's) advice and put him in charge of what remains ours and got rid of those characters on whom there rested more than a little suspicion. He made him sole governor of this town and province, being the most important place in the kingdom.[12]

Sarsfield was now governor of Connaught and governor of Galway. He became, without any doubt, the most powerful Irishman in the country. He was governor of the only province that was in Irish hands and he also commanded the largest corps in the Jacobite army. In fact, it is easier to list those areas under Jacobite rule that did not come under his control; he did not have any direct say in the running of the garrisons of Sligo or Limerick, and he had no say or interest in the command of the ragged Irish troops in Kerry. Berwick and the rump of Tyrconnell's administration were now reduced to waiting in Limerick for news from France.

But news was slow in coming, and Sarsfield now controlled the busiest port in the country. Whereas previously Tyrconnell's appointees had intercepted the mail, the reports leaving Ireland now included those that were full of praise for Tyrconnell's enemies. A spate of letters were dispatched to add weight to what was being proposed by the delegation in France. Tyrconnell's men were shown to be traitors, great emphasis was placed on the sterling work being conducted by Sarsfield and optimism was shown for the forthcoming campaign if only Tyrconnell could be kept in France and a French general could be sent to Ireland with some badly needed equipment and provisions for the enthusiastic and loyal Irish army.

The Abbé de Gravel, who painted with a thick brush, wrote to the French minister of war describing Sarsfield's 'loyalty to his king, gratitude to Louis le Grand, his bravery at Cashel [Ballyneety] which was Ireland's salvation, his incorrigible bravery in the most desperate situations, and the love that he engenders in the people who refer to him as being no less than the father of the homeland'.[13] This was not of course the view of a typical Frenchman. De Santons Boullain sent a dispatch to France accusing de Gravel of spreading rumours injurious to the French and of preaching against them in favour of the Irish.[14]

But although Sarsfield could not be dislodged, he proved to be a bad administrator. Even before he became governor of Galway O'Kelly described his administration thus:

> Sarsfield, who no doubt meant well, gave out so many clashing orders, which related as well to the civil (wherein he had no authority), as to the military government, that it did not a little contribute to increase the confusion . . . for he was so easy that he would not deny signing any paper that was laid before him.

The government of Ireland did not improve under Sarsfield as he was too busy on the Shannon to be able to take any care of the administration of the ports and the regulation of commerce. The only obvious change that he made was in sacking Tyrconnell's men and replacing them with his own. Shortly after his appointment as governor, he nominated a deputy to run Galway in his absence and set off to Athlone to concentrate on the more important task of securing the frontiers.

In Sarsfield's absence, Berwick rode to Galway. For what purpose is no longer important as shortly after his arrival he was struck down with a fever.[15] By the time that the sickness had left him, he was so weak as to be unable to take any active role in the political struggle. It was now clear that Sarsfield was not going to receive any challenge to his authority unless and until fresh orders came from France. He now ruled Jacobite Ireland.

CHAPTER XIV

Lanesborough Bridge

O! Never fear for Ireland, for she has sogers still,
For Rory's boys are in the wood, and Sarsfield's on the hill;
And never had poor Ireland more loyal hearts than these
May God be kind and good to them, the faithful Rapparees!
The fearless Rapparees!
The jewel were you, Sarsfield, with your Irish Rapparees.

D.P. Conyngham, *Sarsfield.*[1]

THE ENGLISH STRATEGY for the winter campaign was highly ambitious. William had ordered Ginckel to launch a series of offensives, and Ginckel in turn had ordered each regional commander to march to the west and place himself in as favourable a position as possible for the spring. In the north, at Cavan, General Douglas commanded the largest of the four Williamite forces. He was given blunt instructions to march on Sligo with the eight thousand men under his command. Preparations for such an expedition could not be concealed from the Irish. Sarsfield noted that much of the baggage and caravans had been sent northwards to be, he suspected, shipped down the Erne to meet an army marching overland. He urgently travelled to Sligo and detached five hundred men from Galway to man the defences. It was sound policy. Galway, despite all its problems, was a long way from the English while Sligo, even in winter, was only a day's march from Ballyshannon.

Further south in Mullingar another six thousand men awaited their orders. They were commanded by General Kirke and by the man who most wanted to destroy Sarsfield, Sir John Lanier. Although Douglas's task appeared to be clear, Kirke was less sure of what was expected of him. His orders were simply to seize a crossing point on the Shannon. He called a council of war in Mullingar on 25 December 1690. The three most senior officers in his army group were present: Sir John Lanier, Brigadier Edward Villiers and Lord Lisburne. Between them they tried to hammer out a common plan, but reaching an agreement proved to be no easy task. In exasperation, Kirke told them each to write down on a piece of paper what they considered the best course of action to be, and he then read out each one for criticism.

Lisburne's plan was the most forcefully put. The English guns and boats were only a few miles from Lanesborough where the Irish held the bridge over the Shannon. They should concentrate their forces there and force a crossing. Lanesborough could then be fortified. It would provide the whole army with a bridgehead to cross the Shannon in the spring. Lanier vetoed the idea. Sarsfield, he was sure, was on this side of the Shannon with a force between Athlone and

Ballymore. If they divided their forces and marched men off to where they could not be reinforced in an attack, they would be taking a great risk. But Lisburne persisted. How did Lanier know where Sarsfield's forces were? It was all guesswork. The argument continued. No plan was formulated save that, to prove his point or otherwise, Lisburne was given permission to lead a patrol as far as Athlone to gather intelligence of the Irish strength on the east side of the river.

Two days later, on Saturday 27 December at eleven o'clock at night, Lisburne rode out at the head of a small force of three hundred infantrymen and two hundred horsemen. Thirteen hours and thirty miles later his men, weary and muddy after having marched through the night, stood on a hill in full view of Athlone. On Monday, Lisburne was back in Mullingar with Kirke. 'In a country entirely possessed by the enemy', he told Kirke, he had only encountered twenty Irish horsemen. Lisburne was allowed to set his plan in motion.

He was anxious to waste no time and on the very next morning, Tuesday, 30 December 1690, accompanied by Lanier, Lisburne marched out at the head of a thousand footsoldiers and three hundred cavalrymen and dragoons. He was determined to push on as quickly as he could and flogged his men along the forty odd miles of soggy road to Lanesborough. The conditions were so bad that much of the march was undertaken in single file, with his riders leading their reluctant mounts behind them. As they neared Lanesborough they found that the Irish had dug deep trenches in the causeways which supported the road. But Lisburne was relentless. Although his men were soaked through, muddy and near exhausted, he forced them on. In mid morning, his advance guard found the causeway barricaded by the enemy. But the Irish were wholly unprepared for him. There was a brief fight and Lisburne's men overran this last obstacle, and the way to Lanesborough was clear. Taking his leading troops with him, Lisburne rode on ahead. At eleven o'clock in the morning on Thursday, 1 January 1691, he appeared on a small hill overlooking the Shannon a hundred yards from Lanesborough Bridge. 'It is impossible', he later wrote, 'for me to express the confusion and surprise the enemy were in at our appearance.' The Irish garrison sprang to life. Lisburne's forced march had allowed them no warning of his approach. They began packing up and driving their cattle away. While Lisburne waited for his troops to catch up with him, they made the most of the time available to them to destroy Lanesborough Fort, and then swarmed across the bridge to the other side of the Shannon leaving the bridge broken behind them. Men were sent off to get reinforcements and warn Sarsfield. Later that day Sir John Lanier and the infantry caught up with Lisburne. Lanier took in the situation and left for Mullingar, promising to hurry the guns and boats on their way.

But having left Lisburne, Lanier had a change of mind. The country on the Longford side of the Shannon was flat and boggy. It had been a great effort to get the men and the horses across it. The countryside was enemy territory and the enemy had already made themselves felt, albeit in a minor way, by breaking down parts of the causeway on the Lanesborough road. To get the cannons and their carriages along the waterlogged and rutted road was going to be no mean task. Even the cannon would be of no use unless the heavy carts with the boats were also wheeled up though the mud. Progress was certain to be slow. If time was the only problem he would not be concerned, but now that their presence was known the chances of an Irish attack increased daily. His artillery was going to be particularly vulnerable as it made its slow and tortuous journey along the open road.

As his natural caution turned him against the plan, the next question Lanier posed was this: what would be achieved by taking Lanesborough Bridge? Even supposing that Lisburne was successful, if the Irish attacked in any force, they would slow down the advance of any reinforcements by breaking down the causeway across the bog and by ambushing the road where it passed through the woods. Lisburne himself had been slowed down in his advance as the causeway had been cut in thirteen places within five miles of Lanesborough. It would be an isolated and vulnerable garrison in the middle of hostile territory.

Any permanent position on that part of the Shannon would be an invitation to Sarsfield to attack. And if the Irish did attack and succeed, the English would not only lose valuable men, but would lose the cannons that they would have needed to defend the place. In any event, there could be no point in going further than Lanesborough. The Irish would be ready for them. For miles on the other side there was nothing but bogs and woods and the remains of what in summer could have been recognised as roads. There was no doubt that the Irish had great numbers of soldiers on the west bank. Lisburne's troops would either have to wait in Lanesborough for an Irish attack or else risk being lured further and further into hostile territory to be surrounded and destroyed.

The more he considered the situation, the more Lanier's mind was made up. He became convinced that Lisburne's expedition was a folly and that the bridge at Lanesborough was of importance to no one except Lisburne himself. To the English army as a whole it would become a costly liability. When he reached the mud splattered men bringing out the artillery and the boats he told them to go back to Mullingar. Cold and wet, they turned the guns around and retraced their steps. Lanier then sent a rider back to Lanesborough with a message to Lisburne to abandon the position and to return to base.

As soon as Lisburne received Lanier's message, he sent the rider back with his refusal. He was a proud man and this was his plan. It had been sanctioned by General Kirke, and Lanier had been against it from the start. He had established that the Irish were not in any position to attack him in the rear, and he had not come this far to march back again empty handed. He set about preparing his position in full view of the Irish. Under the direction of the artilleryman, Lieutenant-Colonel Jacob Richards, his men toiled away on an earthwork where he planned to position the cannon that were to cover his crossing. The days passed. Another order came from Lanier to pull back. Lisburne again refused. Ginckel had ordered them to secure the passes on the Shannon and that is exactly what he was doing. Even by being where he was now, the Irish were prevented from sending raiding parties into Longford.

In the meantime Sarsfield had been busy on the other side of Athlone. At the end of December he had carried out an inspection of the defences at Portumna and had ordered extra work to be carried out on the carefully fortified bridge. Part of it had been broken down, the fort in the middle of it had been strengthened and adapted to allow reinforcements to enter, new walls had been built across the bridge and fortifications had been thrown up along the riverbank to protect the bridgehead against any English troops that might cross the Shannon by boat. Portumna was typical of the crossing points on the Shannon. Throughout the cold and wet of winter, the Irish had been toiling away with pick and shovel on field works and trenches. Also typical was the uneasy relationship between the French and the Irish. In early January, Colonel de Santons Boullain, the senior French officer at Portumna wrote:

> I was discharged from this enterprise four days after Sarsfield left. Prendergast came here with orders to take over even though he is only a cavalry half-colonel and does not have any troops here. I wrote to Sarsfield about this to point out the injustice done to me. He did not answer.[2]

It was not surprising that Sarsfield did not answer. He had been told about Lisburne's activities and had more urgent matters to attend than de Santons Boullain's ruffled feathers. He ordered Robert Clifford to march his brigade to Lanesborough with all speed possible.

That Sunday, 4 January, Brigadier Clifford arrived opposite Lisburne's position with three regiments to oppose an English crossing. Lisburne cursed Lanier. Until now, if only he had the cannons and the boats, a crossing would have been an easy matter. Now the consequence of Lanier's hesitation was going to be a battle.

Sarsfield may not have had many men in the county of Longford at that time. He was unable to attack Lisburne straight away. But he knew where Lisburne was, and he knew what Lisburne was doing. Lisburne was being carefully watched, as were the artillerymen on the road to Mullingar. If anything was seen by a pair of Irish eyes, Sarsfield would get to hear of it. Nothing moved in Longford without him knowing. When he received the news that part of Lanier's force was isolated in Lanesborough, he gleefully rubbed his hands together and began to prepare the very thing that Lanier most feared. As Sarsfield later wrote: 'I formed the design of capturing this party.'

He knew that in the winter months the land which Lisburne now occupied was transformed into a peninsula. It was bounded on two sides by bogs and on the one side by the Shannon. The only ways in and out were across Lanesborough Bridge, which had been broken down and was now defended by Brigadier Clifford, and the narrow causeway, or rather series of causeways, that led across the bog back to Mullingar. Sarsfield's plan was straightforward. He was going to secure the causeway that Lisburne needed to retreat along. He would then march towards Lisburne while Clifford would lead his three regiments across the Shannon at Lanesborough and attack Lisburne in the front. Kirke and Lanier would be unable to intervene as Sarsfield would destroy the causeway behind him. 'I could not fail to succeed in this project', he wrote, 'with the help of God.'[3]

Sarsfield was in Athlone. Thirty miles away General Kirke was in Mullingar. Half way between them was Sarsfield's garrison at Ballymore. Between these places were isolated castles and patrols, but Sarsfield knew that once he was at Ballymore, he could march northwards towards Longford and then trap his quarry in Lanesborough. There was nothing that could stop him. He hurriedly dispatched troops to Ballymore, and that night he prepared to leave Athlone. He was stopped just in time.

A messenger was brought into him: wet, muddy and exhausted. He delivered an urgent despatch from Colonel O'Gara, the commandant of the Jamestown garrison. General Douglas had left Cavan and was expected to attack Jamestown at daybreak. Douglas had with him eight thousand men, and worse still, because of the dry weather the river had dropped and was now fordable in three places. It was a time for rapid decision. Between Jamestown and Sligo there was nothing that could stop Douglas. Lanesborough could wait. Sarsfield cancelled his plans, left orders for his infantry to follow and rode off with what horse he could muster on the road to Roscommon and Jamestown.

In Lanesborough, Lisburne was still waiting. He had finished his gun emplacements and had still heard no more from Lanier. His patrols had scoured the countryside for Irish troops and rapparees, but had found nothing of any consequence. To make sure, they burnt every cabin they came across. On the other side of the water the Irish had dug in and were now also waiting. It certainly was not going to be an easy crossing. The Irish appeared to be confident. They looked upon the English as doomed men. Lisburne had seen Clifford on several occasions as the Irishman had shouted across the Shannon to arrange temporary truces. Clifford appeared to grow more eccentric as the days went by. To the amusement of the men on both sides of the water he took to appearing, glass in hand, to drink the health of the English soldiers. The English, with what little drink they had, returned the compliment, but it became clear that they were not facing an enemy intent on flight.

When Sarsfield next heard from O'Gara, he was glad to hear that the danger had passed. Douglas had not been able to reach the river as the Irish fortifications on the east bank had held off his attack. By the time that he had reached Jamestown his men were in a bad way. Their clothing and equipment had proved inadequate for their long march and the trek across the bogs of Cavan had exhausted them. Besides that, they had been expected to attack the Irish forts with nothing more than the equipment that they were carrying. As

Douglas later wrote to Ginckel: 'The King has writ to me and is very desirous I should besiege Sligo. I am as willing as any mortal but, as I have told Your Excellency before, it is not possible to carry cannon or wagons any way from Ulster to Connaught in the winter.' As Douglas's men had faltered, O'Gara had attacked them with his main force of fifteen hundred troops from the west bank. Douglas was reported to have lost more than a hundred men killed, and as his troops withdrew they were pursued by the Irish who were able to bring in prisoners.

This was Douglas's second failure in Ireland, and although neither of them could fairly be said to have been his fault, William decided to replace him. Even if Douglas had not proved to be a bad general, he had not proved to be a lucky one. But neither William nor Douglas nor any other contemporary observer spotted the main achievement of Douglas's push to the Shannon. He had saved Lisburne.

On Thursday 8 January 1691, Lisburne's eighth day in Lanesborough, Brigadier Villiers arrived with orders from Lanier that were to be obeyed. Lanier clearly felt that Lisburne would ignore anyone of a lower rank. Villiers's message was simply that: 'It was not in the King's service to take a post on the other side of the Shannon' and that the cannon and boats were definitely not coming. Lisburne had to concede defeat. On the next day he ordered the withdrawal. 'Thus', wrote Lisburne later, 'ended this shameful expedition which had every prospect of success'. Furious at Lanier's decision he led his men, slipping and sliding in ankle deep mud as they wearily slogged across the barren countryside past the huts that they had burnt to Castle Forbes. 'This is now a most miserable country'.

Sarsfield in the meantime made all the haste that he could to get back to Athlone. He still planned to make Ballymore where his troops awaited him, and cut across the country to Lanesborough. Presumably to the delight of the weary men who had just accompanied him up and down the Jamestown road, he was met with the news of Lisburne's withdrawal.

The Irish did not know why Lisburne had pulled back. Sarsfield was content to accept what really was an unsatisfactory explanation. 'Colonel Ulick Burke, having beaten, two nights before, the advanced guards of the party which was at Lanesborough, gave the enemy such a fright that four or five hundred of their infantry abandoned their camp and escaped across the bogs to Castle Forbes, and from there hastened in disorder to Mullingar, leaving us part of their baggage and a very great number of tools'.

In fact, the skirmish with Burke's men was unlikely to have concerned either Lisburne or Lanier. Far more disturbing to the English commander in Mullingar was the news that came to him from Mountmellick while Lisburne was still in Lanesborough. A party of three hundred men had been ordered to march from Birr to Mullingar. They were intended to be reinforcements for Lisburne. They got about half way when they were attacked by some fifteen hundred Irish soldiers and rapparees who scattered them after a five-hour engagement, captured all their baggage, and chased them across the countryside to Mountmellick.[4] The importance of this was not lost on Lanier. The fact that the Irish could rove about in groups of over a thousand strong and launch attacks in the 'English' area that lay between Lough Ree, Mullingar, Mountmellick and Birr, was of great concern to a man who had allowed a detachment to march to Lanesborough.

Sarsfield later wrote this of Lisburne's attempt on Lanesborough Bridge: 'In all, this expedition, in which they had put all the soldiers they had, ended only in a disgraceful retreat, the burning of their quarters and the withdrawal of their most advanced garrisons'. He was of course quite right. It had been a wasted effort, but the reasons for the 'disgraceful retreat' were never revealed to him. Lanier perhaps knew more of Sarsfield's mind that Sarsfield knew of Lanier's. Lanier had been cautious, and on this occasion his caution had been the best policy.

On Saturday, 10 January 1691, Lisburne marched into Mullingar. His men, according to Story, were 'much harassed by cold and hunger'. Lisburne did not waste much time in expressing his disappointment with Lanier and Kirke. He rode straight to Dublin and prepared a report on the affair for the Lord Justices. 'I am,' he wrote, 'infinitely concerned that I must give you so melancholy an account of the proceedings of that part of the army under Sir John Lanier's command . . .'. To his dying day, Lisburne never learnt what a lucky escape he had had.*

Military activity in the midlands did not cease that winter with the retreat of Douglas and Lisburne. The eastern side of the Shannon was by no means quiet. By failing to secure the bridges over the river so as to keep the Irish army in Connaught, the English had instead been forced to garrison themselves in towns along the length of the country. As one moved further east, the more the English were in control, but the counties of Longford, Westmeath and Offaly (King's County) were the scenes of sporadic fighting throughout the winter.

The English were garrisoned in the larger towns, 'frontier towns', notably Mullingar, Mountmellick and Roscrea. The countryside was scattered about with small castles and fortified houses, sometimes garrisoned by less than twenty men and sometimes, as at Birr, by several hundred. These small and isolated posts served as an early warning system. They sent out patrols that would be able to report any large scale Irish activity, and would be able to deal with any small groups of rapparees operating in their area. The Irish had also garrisoned various castles on the east of the Shannon, and used them in the same way, and also as forward bases for the raids they carried out into territory ostensibly under English control.

The local population suffered terribly during this time. Irish troops would advance from the west and burn what houses and stores they could to stop the

---

*   Although they may never have met, Lisburne would certainly have heard of Sarsfield well before the war. Lisburne's wife (who had died in the previous year) was the half-sister of the Lady Herbert once carried away by Sarsfield in more peaceful times.

English making any use of them. They would round up any livestock they could capture and make off with it to the west. The English would march to the west and do the same in reverse. In the towns garrisoned by either side, the local population was displaced. Story gave a careful description of the plight of the Irish at Mullingar during the spring. Having been ordered out of the town as a security risk, they had nowhere to go. The buildings in the surrounding area had been destroyed by both the Irish and the English armies, and they were reduced to living in 'huts' in the dry ditches on the approaches to the town. The building of a 'hut' was a simple process:

> It is but bending down two or three sticks with one end on the ground and the other on the top of the ditch, and then a little straw or long grass makes it a cabin in less than half an hour for a family of ten or twelve, young and old, to creep into.

Robert Parker, the son of a Kilkenny farmer, was then serving as a sergeant in the Williamite army. He made the following observation of the displaced Irish in the spring:

> Here the miserable effects of war appeared in a very melancholy manner; for the enemy, to prevent a famine amongst themselves, had drove all useless mouths from among them the last winter, to our side of the Shannon: and we, for the same reason, would not suffer them to come within our frontiers: so between both, they lay in a miserable starving condition. These wretches came flocking in great numbers about our camp, devouring all the filth they could meet with. Our dead horses crawling with vermin, as the sun had parched them, were delicious food to them: while their infants sucked those carcasses with as much eagerness as if they were at their mothers' breasts.[5]

Not that the Irish soldiers were much better off. It was reported to the Danish Secretary of War that:

> We have seen on the march, where the enemy had halted, that their women and children and the sick and wounded ate burned leather of the hides of horses and cows. And prisoners and deserters tell us many of them do this: even the officers do it to encourage the common soldiers.[6]

Even Sarsfield, who always wrote the most confident and optimistic of letters, had little encouraging to say about the situation that would develop if fresh supplies were not sent from France:

> As to the state of our affairs here, it is true that a great many things are wanting, but if they would have the kindness to send them to us we shall have this summer a more numerous army and better soldiers than those who were at the River Boyne. We shall have at least as many cavalry and dragoons as we had then, provided they send us from France enough oats to keep them before the end of spring, for by then our forage will be consumed. In truth, we have not much as the country held by us produces

hardly any grain. That is the greatest difficulty we shall have to overcome. If we can preserve our horses until the grass grows (which could be done with ten thousand barrels of oats) we propose to have seven thousand horse and dragoons and as many infantry as the King wishes, provided they have the necessary equipment. If we are not sent a great deal of corn I fear we shall have a great scarcity here.

The population of mid Ireland dramatically decreased during the winter of 1690/1 as many families, deprived of their homes, their cattle and their belongings and food, made their way to more peaceful areas behind the forward garrisons of the two armies. Those that remained were subject not only to great poverty but also great danger.

There can be little doubt that the sentiments of the local inhabitants were generally behind the Irish army, and they acted as its eyes and ears in the areas in which there was an English presence. Many of the dispossessed went further, and engaged in activities that immediately classed them as rapparees.

'There are a sort of person here called by the name of "raperyes"' wrote Lieutenant James Lonyne, recently back from the fighting, 'which are a very ill sort of people: they come in great numbers to our frontiers, but the least opposition makes them run like a flock of sheep to the mountains or the bogs where there is no following of them.'[7] Story described the situation so:

> When the rapparees have no mind to show themselves upon the bogs, they commonly sink down between two or three little hills, grown over with long grass, so that you may as soon find a hair as one of them. They conceal their arms thus: they take off the lock and put it in their pocket, or hide it in some dried place: they stop the muzzle close with a cork and the touch-hole with a small quill, and then throw the piece itself into a running water or a pond: you may see a hundred of them without arms, who look like the poorest, humblest slaves in the world, and you may search till you are weary before you find one gun: but yet when they have a mind to mischief, they can all be ready in an hour's warning, for everyone knows where to go to and fetch his own arms, though you do not.

The rapparees, and those suspected of being rapparees, could expect little mercy from the English soldiers if they were caught, and could expect no mercy from the Protestant militiamen. The militiamen were generally drawn from the area in which they operated, and since the beginning of the war many of them had endured great suffering. They had lost everything. Their children had died from disease or exposure, their families had been murdered and their possessions had been stolen. Here follow two entries from Story's account:

> 28th February 1691: 'Several rapparees were killed and hanged by the militia near Mountrath, they being usually more severe upon those sort of people than the army was.'

> 7th March 1691: 'The militia kill some rapparees and bring in their heads, a custom in that country, and encouraged by a law which allows so much for every head, according to the quality of the offender'.

'I have seen at Clonmel', wrote one of the Danes in his diary, 'over 40 heads set up over the gates.'[8]

The rapparees were just as merciless in that they generally killed those who fell into their hands and often mutilated the corpses. Story described the end of one of Colonel Gustavus Hamilton's men at Birr. The rapparees killed him, 'drew out his guts and mangled his body after a most barbarous and unusual manner'.

Throughout the winter months there were daily engagements. Story's narrative for the winter campaign contains a whole catalogue of killings, skirmishes and raids by and against the rapparees. The English in the frontier area could only move safely away from their bases in large numbers, and even large numbers were no guarantee against being attacked. The Irish army attacked and burnt Balliboy even though there were six companies of Lord Drogheda's regiment there to protect it. The English burnt down Nenagh, but were forced to leave the castle intact as they had no cannon. Colonel Connor marched to the borders of Kildare, burnt down Edenderry, Daingean and Bally-brittas, 'killed 120 dragoons', and returned 'with a great booty of horses'. Sixty English soldiers from Castle Forbes crossed the Shannon and burnt everything they could on the other side before driving off the cattle. English patrols attacked and were attacked by groups of rapparees throughout the Midlands. Expeditions were mounted to drive out rapparees and Irish troops from the countryside around Birr, Mullingar, Roscrea, Moneygall and Foxhall. There was no peace. No sooner had reports being received of increased rapparee 'mischief' in one area, similar reports would be received from another. Outposts were surprised and overrun. Castles changed hands. Supplies were frequently disrupted. Messengers were ambushed, bridges were broken, causeways were dug up, and trees were felled across roads. Men going out into the woods to collect kindling, or down to the stream for water, had to travel with armed guards and appoint lookouts. Raids and counter-raids were directed from and towards Ballymore, Athlone and Portumna. It was an expensive winter, and not least in lives.

The expense to the English increased because as the winter advanced the Irish army began actively to encourage the rapparees, especially as they were a source of supply for cattle and horses. In March 1691, Sarsfield made the following observation:

> The rapparees take horses from the enemy every day . . . we have already had more than a thousand this winter, and they have brought me thirty-seven from Lanier's quarters of which twenty-two were out of his stable.

The duke of Wurtemberg was another victim. He wrote from Waterford:

> The rapparees are creating a multitude of inconveniences by stealing the horses out on grass; they took 30 horses close to the city a few days ago; most of which belonged to me and the staff.[9]

The Dublin government attempted to improve the situation by issuing proclamations that they could not possibly enforce. On 19 November 1690 the lord justices proclaimed that if a Protestant's house was burnt down it was to be rebuilt and paid for by all the Catholics in the county. If any group of more than ten rapparees was seen, no Catholic priest would be allowed in that county. No protection would be given by the Crown to anyone who had a son in the enemy's quarters unless that son returned to Their Majesties' obedience before 20 December.

As communications became more difficult and interrupted during the winter, the propaganda war was stepped up. The wildest of rumours were quickly spread and believed. The atmosphere in the capital was one of uncertainty and fear. The only contact most Dubliners had with the war in the west was by the second-hand stories spread by those returning, and exaggerated stories they often were. Tales came in of great battles that had never actually taken place and of great victories when in fact there had only been an inconclusive skirmish between an English patrol and some rapparees. Most worrying for the government were the rumours that were put about with great frequency; that Sarsfield had just crossed the Shannon with eight thousand men, with ten thousand men, even with twenty thousand men, and that he was marching straight for Dublin to be welcomed by an Irish uprising in the capital and a general massacre of all the Protestants.[10]

The lord justices proclaimed that all Catholics that had not been noted as housekeepers in Dublin for the last three months were to depart within forty eight hours at least ten miles from the capital, and that not above five Catholics could meet together in Dublin 'upon any pretext whatever'. A week later any Catholic regarded as being suspicious was arrested and secured. The running of Ireland was handed over to a privy council (on which body Lord Lisburne sat) able to make the harshest of proclamations without any outside consultation.

In the frontier areas, the effect was to dispossess more and more people and to force them into starvation or banditry.

CHAPTER XV

Tyrconnell and Saint-Ruth

Saint-Ruth: By us shall Erin be from England freed,
Our fleur de lys and Shamrock we'll display
And drive these foreign heretics away.
         Robert Ashton, *The Battle of Aughrim*, I.i., 1770

THE DUBLIN PRIVY COUNCIL was not alone in imposing increasingly severe restrictions on those under its power. The Irish did the same, not only to prevent the movement of traitors within their borders, but also to seize as much as they could in the way of horses and extra provisions during the lean months. Sarsfield continued to purge the government of Tyrconnell's appointees. Once the immediate danger of Lisburne's raid had receded, he forced Berwick to arrest the third of those four named on his list as being traitors. At last there was firm evidence against Judge Denis Daly, 'one of Tyrconnell's chief confidants', and Sarsfield had him thrown into Galway gaol for corresponding with the enemy.

Tyrconnell's visit to France had been a successful one. He had re-established his position with King James and was again given the king's commission to return to Ireland as viceroy. He had also made a good impression on the French and had been granted audiences with King Louis. The French were greatly impressed by the Irish victory at Limerick and were again willing to invest in the Irish war. They allocated military stores for a fresh convoy and although they could spare no troops they promised the services of a few hundred junior and middle ranking French engineer and artillery officers.

To show his gratitude to his trusted viceroy, James honoured Tyrconnell with the Order of the Garter. 'Now Tyrconnell is as great as the king can make him', remarked one of his supporters.[1] But despite the esteem in which he was held by the king, Tyrconnell could not conceal the vicious faction struggle that he had left behind him in Ireland. The French had already commented on this and were kept guessing as to its outcome by the intermittent news that they received from Limerick and Galway. For the first time in months mail was being received by those members of James's household who were sympathetic to Sarsfield's party. Predictably, once Sarsfield had been made governor of Galway he arranged for the mail from Tyrconnell's correspondents to be seized.

It was inevitable that Tyrconnell would have to give a full explanation to the king. He told him simply that Sarsfield had fallen into bad company. Although a loyal officer, his ambitions were such that he felt that he could topple the viceroy and usurp the king's authority. The problem was easy enough to state,

Sarsfield could not be sacked or excluded from military councils because he held such sway with the army. On the other hand, by keeping him on the council Sarsfield was a divisive influence. He was hostile to the viceroy's authority and threatened to use his supporters outside the council to get his way. Tyrconnell saw this as being no more than a clash of personalities. Although they had once had political differences, now that they were both going to pursue a policy of all out war there was no room for anything other than complete cooperation. And Tyrconnell was confident that he could win Sarsfield round.

King James was disturbed by what he was told. He liked Sarsfield and he had taken him to be a loyal and a very brave man. It was now apparent that Sarsfield's loyalty to the crown did not extend to the crown's representative in Ireland. He decided to take a risk. If Sarsfield was rewarded for his sterling work with a peerage, would that not quieten things down? Would it not bring a rebellious, surly man firmly back to the side of his viceroy? It was an old trick, but it was clear to James that Tyrconnell needed every assistance to re-establish his position. Sarsfield was to be the first earl of Lucan.

In early December 1690, at a farewell audience at Versailles, Louis XIV presented Tyrconnell with the gift of his portrait set in a diamond box. The old viceroy knew, as he set out on the road to Brest to the waiting French fleet, that the best wishes and hopes of two kings rode along with him. But good wishes alone were not enough. The winter journey was too much for the gross old man. He fell ill and spent Christmas convalescing in the Breton town of Vannes, over a hundred miles from the fleet. During the time that he lay there, unable to travel and confined to his bed, he received bad news from Paris.

While he had been travelling to the coast, Sarsfield's delegates from Ireland had sailed to the little Normandy port of St Malo and were now in Paris. Worse still, to Tyrconnell this was no ordinary delegation; it included Nicholas Purcell and the pernicious Henry Luttrell. As soon as he heard the news, he called for a quill and some paper and ordered a horseman to prepare himself for a gruelling ride to Paris. He then scribbled a letter to King James urging him not to receive the delegation. They would only sow doubt in His Majesty's mind where there should be none. They would only tell him falsehoods and half truths. Above all, James must ensure that the delegates be prevented from returning to Ireland. Things would certainly be made more difficult if they were allowed to go back. He referred the king to their conversations about the power struggle within the army.

> Sarsfield's head, now that it was turned to popularity, was quite out of its natural situation. Yet he hoped when he came back to set it right again if his counsellors Henry Luttrell and Colonel Purcell were kept from him.[2]

For Tyrconnell it was a frustrating time. His health prevented him from travelling, and even if he could travel he could not afford to go back to Paris while the French fleet was waiting at Brest for a break in the stormy weather. As soon as he could, he continued on his journey a worried man.

In Brest, the winter storms had prevented any of the ships from leaving the harbour. There the viceroy's men arrested an Irish messenger who was carrying a letter from Randal MacDonnell who Tyrconnell described as being 'the chief of the caballists at Saint-Germain'.[3] The letter was addressed to Sarsfield, Dorrington, Purcell and Henry Luttrell. At the time of writing , MacDonnell did not know that Purcell and Luttrell had left Ireland, but the contents of the letter were not going to help Tyrconnell assert his lawful authority. He seized the messenger and had him locked up in Brest.

There was a break in the weather shortly after his arrival, and Tyrconnell sent a last hopeful message back to Paris. 'On my arrival in Ireland I do not doubt that, by the grace of God, I will restore good order in all affairs and will establish peace and unity amongst the people'.[4] On 6 January 1691, he sailed out of Brest.

At Saint-Germain, King James first heard of the impending arrival of Sarsfield's delegation from Thomas Maxwell who had managed to ride ahead of the others. The king would be ill advised to allow Purcell or Luttrell the opportunity of spreading their poisonous lies. They had been responsible for challenging the authority that had been vested in the king's son and it was now begged of His Majesty to keep them in France. Hot on Maxwell's heels arrived the first of a series of riders bearing messages from Tyrconnell. The king should not grant the mutineers' delegation an audience and should not let them leave France.

As far as James was concerned, Tyrconnell's word was final. Any voice raised against Tyrconnell was a voice raised against the crown. He had complete faith in Tyrconnell's account of the situation and he was now quite satisfied that evil influences had been at work and that the hostility directed against Tyrconnell was motivated not so much by criticism of his policies, but by jealousy of his position.

The king refused to see the delegation, and would have continued to refuse to see them had it not been for the sympathetic clique that Tyrconnell had identified at Saint-Germain. Two of James's senior officers back from the wars were now in France; Mountcashel, who was still lounging about the court, and the newly promoted Major-General Wauchope, who was about to return to Ireland, were anxious that the delegation be heard. But at Saint-Germain the most persuasive voice raised in Sarsfield's favour was that of Sir Randal Mac Donnell,* the Antrim sailor who, now that the English navy did not want Irish captains commanding their men o' war, was employed in King James's household. No longer concerned with the dangers of the deep, he had been appointed a gentleman of the bedchamber. It is hardly surprising that with so much time hanging heavy on his hands he took to court intrigue. MacDonnell had appointed himself as Sarsfield's ambassador and worked tirelessly in his interests, which meant nothing short of mounting a palace war against Tyrconnell.

* Sarsfield and MacDonnell were old friends, and Sarsfield had been a guest at his wedding in London five years earlier. Sir Randal had distinguished himself in King Charles's navy for his actions against the Barbary Coast pirates.[5]

Sarsfield's letters to his allies in France were translated, copied and circulated for the purposes of winning French support for those opposed to Tyrconnell. In one such letter, Sarsfield formally presented his case as follows:*

> I have given the details of the things that we need to those gentlemen who have been deputed by the whole nation to render an account of the state of our affairs. Although they have integrity, judgement and courage they and several others (among whom I am not forgotten) have had the misfortune to be represented at Court as mutineers and as factionaries. However, it is not easy to know of what we are accused unless it is a crime to oppose those who wished to treat with the Prince of Orange and put all Ireland into his hands, and unless it is to be guilty to be determined to die a thousand deaths rather than betray the king's interests or to submit to a usurper. It is true that if that is a crime, there are few who are innocent amongst us since generally speaking the whole army is of this feeling and resolve. I am sure we cannot be charged with any other crime than to have had a disposition so in keeping with our duty.
>
> Nevertheless we so deeply respect the king's commission (which we regard and have always regarded as sacred) that we do not wish to make the same accusation of those who slander us, nor to condemn them for the bad conduct of which they are certainly guilty. We would have resolved to forget it all completely if they had not forced us in spite of ourselves to defend our reputation, and that of the whole country, which they had tarnished by representing us as cowards, as mutineers and as people split between so many different factions. This black and undeserved libel would have brought such scorn on us that it would not be believed that we were worth the trouble of saving, but thank God there is only one party here which perfectly unites all the Irish who are resolved to sacrifice in the king's service themselves and all that they hold most dear, and to give their all to re-establish him on the throne of his ancestors.

Without doubt the question that was posed to James with most force was simply this: why did Tyrconnell not even want these men to be heard? What was he afraid of? More and more of James's court were won over to MacDonnell's view. The pressure mounted on James and he gave in. The bishop of Cork, Colonel Simon Luttrell, Brigadier Henry Luttrell and Colonel Nicholas Purcell were granted an audience with the king.

Their message was straightforward. Tyrconnell must be replaced. If he is sent back to Ireland with the same authority as before, the effect would be to 'utterly dishearten the body of the nation'.[6] The mistakes that Tyrconnell had made in the past were so disastrous that he should have been replaced long ago. He had even persuaded James to flee from Ireland after 'the skirmish at the Boyne', but if the king had stayed in Dublin only a few hours longer he would have seen so many fine troops marching by that he would never have left the country. At Limerick, Tyrconnell had wanted to surrender, and would have done so had not

---

* This letter as well as the others described as being from Sarsfield to Mountcashel are in fact re-translations. The English originals have been lost, and only the French translations remain.

the loyal party, who now sent this delegation, prevented him from doing so. They insinuated that Tyrconnell's rule had been corrupt. Government money had been dissipated to his own private ends. The commissariat in Limerick had been run in the worst possible way. During the siege the soldiers had lived on beans and oats although the city's granary was full of wheat. When Tyrconnell left the country to sail to France he had, despite many protests, appointed wholly unsuitable men to positions of great power. Amongst these were Lord Riverston, Colonel Alexander MacDonnell and General John Hamilton all of who were strongly suspected of conspiring to deliver Limerick and Galway to the enemy, just as Tyrconnell had wanted to do. Further, Tyrconnell was not just untrustworthy, he was now simply unsuited for the high office with which the king had honoured him.

> His age and infirmities made him require more sleep than was consistent with so much business, that his want of experience in military affairs rendered him exceeding slow in his resolves and incapable of laying projects; which no depending officers would do for him, unless first by taking a great deal of pains to him to conceive it.[7]

The enemy had experienced commanders in the field, men who had been soldiers all their lives. The Irish were determined to fight for their king, and now that the remains of the army broken at the Boyne had stopped a victorious army at Limerick, and now that the Irish expected to field an army of thirty thousand in the spring, what was needed was a commander fit to lead them. And most of all, that commander must have sufficient authority to take orders only from the king, and not from Tyrconnell.

James was in an uncomfortable position. Much of what was said had made him doubt his own judgement in sending Tyrconnell back with renewed authority. But the delegation had arrived too late. The French had already made their preparations for supplying a new Irish campaign, and the negotiations between Louvois, the war minister, and Tyrconnell had not been easy. The French had been squeezed to provide their last drop of charity, much of which had been given in the belief that Tyrconnell was the great and heroic leader of the embattled Irish nation, not only the 'Popish Champion', but 'le Vainqueur des Anglais'. If James was now to accept the information brought to him with such eloquence and force by the 'délégation des Mutins' the French would be outraged. They would suspect that they had been duped. If Louvois came to believe that Tyrconnell had lost his grip, he would be unlikely to spend any more money on Ireland.

James now acted for stability. He concentrated his efforts on persuading the French that an experienced French general was needed to direct the forthcoming campaign. He made no decision as to whether such a general would command independently of Tyrconnell, in deference to whose wishes he kept the delegation at Saint-Germain. Whether Tyrconnell was doing a grand job or not, it certainly would not help matters to allow Henry Luttrell and Purcell to return to Ireland.

Tyrconnell sailed into Limerick full of hopes on 14 January 1691. His first enquiries were met with the pleasing information that nothing disasterous had happened since he last heard news. The Irish were still in control in Connaught and Western Munster and several attempts by the Williamites to cross the Shannon had been frustrated. But he was also met with the realisation that the mood in the army was still against him. He discovered that the 'mutineers', and Sarsfield in particular, had not been idle in his absence. Tyrconnell set about exerting his authority. He gave Lord Riverston his position back as secretary of state and ordered that Judge Daly, who had only spent a few days in prison, be released and reinstated. He had brought with him plans to reform the economy and the army. He had also brought orders from King James that Berwick was to return to France. Berwick was not sad to leave.

Sarsfield was still in Lanesborough when Tyrconnell set foot on the quayside in Limerick's Englishtown. His absence gave Tyrconnell time to establish himself. With Purcell and Henry Luttrell still in France, and hopefully to be detained there indefinitely, Tyrconnell was confident that Sarsfield could be won over.

Things did not start well. Sarsfield was at his headquarters in Athlone, and the troops in Limerick were clearly split into factions for and against the viceroy. Tyrconnell sent instructions to Sarsfield to return to Limerick in order to reform the battalions that were stationed there, but without success. The reply came back that Sarsfield was ill and could not travel. After a few days reports to the contrary reached Limerick and the suspicion formed that Sarsfield was actually in good health[8] but was expectantly awaiting fresh news from the delegation. He still had high hopes that their representations at Saint-Germain would bring about a change of government in Ireland. In the meanwhile he was concentrating his efforts on the fortifications of Athlone and Galway. Tyrconnell wrote again and again to order Sarsfield south, but with no better result. However, now that he had regained his authority in the two ports, he re-established his stranglehold on the mail. Sarsfield was consequently starved of information from outside Ireland, and to him no news was bad news. He was eventually forced to accept the fact that Purcell and the Luttrells had failed in their mission. As Tyrconnell was to remain the viceroy, Sarsfield was obliged to swallow his pride and to travel to Limerick.

He decided to be careful when meeting Tyrconnell, but he was met with smiles and cordial greetings. The old viceroy was clearly not going to try and bully him, but wanted to win him over. He greeted him as if he was an old and much missed friend. There was no mention of Sarsfield having kept him waiting a month, and no mention of Sarsfield's mutinous behaviour in forcing young Berwick into sending the unspeakable Luttrell to France to get Tyrconnell sacked. He had asked Sarsfield to come to Limerick firstly to receive the patent of the earldom of Lucan, the viscountcy of Roseberry and the Barony of Tully; secondly to inform him that the king had confirmed his promotion to the rank of major-general; and thirdly, given Sarsfield's experience of these matters and the esteem in which he was held by the troops, to instruct him to reform the Irish army completely so that it would face the summer campaign as an efficient force.

This Sarsfield set about straight away. The initial plan was to increase the number of men in each of the thirty six infantry regiments, but Sarsfield instead raised ten more battalions to bring the total to forty six. He also had one of the dragoon regiments reclassified as cavalry, and had a new regiment of dragoons raised. After his orders were carried out, the Irish army numbered some 36,700 troops, of these 30,000 were infantrymen, 3,000 were dragoons and 3,700 were cavalrymen. Sarsfield's interest in the administration of the new units ended there. The marshalling and training of the recruits could be left to other people, as could the distribution of the eight thousand new muskets and four thousand new pikes that Tyrconnell had bought with him from France.

The French in Limerick were particularly pleased with Sarsfield's conciliatory behaviour. They were generally confused by the factions and wanted nothing more than unity in the Jacobite camp. 'If this conduct is sincere', wrote Fumeron of Sarsfield's show of submission to Tyrconnell's authority, 'it will do much to encourage the troops to follow suit'.[9]

Sarsfield did not stay long in Limerick. Nice though it was to be the earl of Lucan, he had been interrupted in his work. He made haste to return to Athlone and then to Ballymore to prepare the area for the coming campaign. Besides, he clearly had not enjoyed his time with Dick Talbot.

> 'Tyrconnell incessantly compliments me,' he wrote to Mountcashel, 'and professes his friendship, but I have known him far too long not to know that I should place little trust in his false words. If I was not restrained by the profound respect I have always had (and will have for the rest of my life) for the king's commission which he is honoured to hold and which I regard as sacred, I would let him know that he does not deserve the slightest respect from anyone. He is very jealous and he despairs of my reputation and of the influence I have over the army but, thanks be to God, I have not abused this and have worked hard and industriously in the king's service. Not only that, but this perfidious and ungrateful man knows full well that during the siege of Limerick he would have been massacred without me, and he is not ignorant of the fact that I prevented and resisted the pressing entreaties of the whole army who adamantly wanted to remove him and proclaim me general in his place'.

Whereas Tyrconnell had made it clear to King James at Saint-Germain that everything in Ireland would be under control once the Irish were assured of substantial French assistance and the 'mutineers' were silenced, Sarsfield presented the situation very differently. The feeling against Tyrconnell amongst the troops had not changed since the siege of Limerick. 'He is mortally hated by the whole army', and 'I can assure you that he is in danger'. Tyrconnell's only allies were 'three major-generals,* and a few of his nephews who have no more credit than he

* These were John Hamilton, who Sarsfield had suspected of treachery; Dominic Sheldon, who had commanded Tyrconnell's regiment before the war; and Thomas Maxwell:

does'. Sarsfield was so confident in his assessment of the general lack of confidence in Tyrconnell that he wrote that should Tyrconnell try to state otherwise, 'I will give my word that I will send the contrary signed by the entire army from the corporals right up to the generals.'[10]

Sarsfield's views were certainly not confined to the confidential letters that he sent to France. In late March his French surgeon related a tale of Sarsfield boasting to his friends: 'There are two factions here, Lord Tyrconnell's and mine; he can do whatever he wants, I do not care. I will always be stronger than him'.[11] There were clearly stormy waters ahead. The two factions were as far apart as ever, if not more so. When Tyrconnell was in France Sarsfield's supporters had been able to comfort themselves with the hope that Tyrconnell would not return, but now that he was back and triumphant it was doubtful whether or not they could be controlled.

In addition to the worries engendered by Tyrconnell's return, Sarsfield still had great and pressing matters on his mind regarding the war in the midlands. These were not helped by the uneasy relationship that he now had with his once close friend, Robert Clifford. The feelings that they had for one another had greatly changed since the time of Widow Siderfin's kidnapping eight years before. When Sarsfield had eventually left his post to ride to Limerick to meet Tyrconnell, he had left Brigadier Clifford behind to command in his absence. Sarsfield's instructions to him were that Ballymore should be reinforced with another three hundred men and that provisions should be sent there from Athlone so that the fort could withstand a siege. Clifford did neither of these things and, to Sarsfield's mind, worsened the situation by destroying Dysart Castle, a small fort on an island on Lough Ennel. This fort, which had previously been used as something of a storehouse by the English, had been captured by the Irish in a surprise attack during the winter. Amongst other things it housed nine hundred barrels of grain and large quantities of other food stuffs such as corned beef and butter. Also stored there was the confiscated property of many of the local Catholics. The fort was considered to be strongly positioned and Lieutenant-Colonel Burton, the senior engineer responsible for advising on most of the Irish fortifications from Sligo to Limerick, was confident that he could defend it with sixty men against anyone provided that the English did not bring any of those large siege guns that had last been seen at Limerick. Clifford had, according to Sarsfield, ignored Burton's advice and had pannicked when he received some doubtful information that the English were returning to attack Dysart. He set fire to the fort and pulled the defenders back to Ballymore.

It could be that Clifford had acted correctly. After all, Dysart is only some nine miles from Mullingar where the largest single group of the English army was garrisoned. It is in fact nearer to Mullingar than it is to Ballymore, and

together these three—the Irishman, the Englishman and the Scotsman, constituted half the major-generals in the Irish army. The other three—also an Irishman, an Englishman and a Scotsman—were Patrick Sarsfield, William Dorrington and John Wauchope.

even in winter it would not have been impossible for the English to drag some of their artillery across the country for an attack. However, Sarsfield's assessment of his brigadier was now a hostile one. He noted that Clifford clearly found it difficult to work under him. Their personalities clashed to the extent that Clifford was becoming more and more of a Tyrconnellite. He had even written to Sarsfield on two occasions during the winter asking permission to resign his commission. Sarsfield found his attitude hard to accept. He was becoming impossible, Sarsfield wrote, because he had not been made a major-general.

It may well be that the difference between them was not, as Sarsfield diagnosed, just one of character. There were good policy arguments for disagreeing with Sarsfield's strategy of holding on to so many isolated forts scattered around Westmeath and Longford. To Sarsfield, the whole area was kept free of any serious English presence by the physical fact that he had established so many Irish strongpoints. Until the English decided to move into the area in force with their siege artillery, he could control the countryside. Central to this plan was the fortification of Ballymore. From that base, deep on the eastern side of the Shannon, he could supply and reinforce all the other forts in the area. All the Irish raiding parties could use Ballymore as a base and refuge. When the time came for the Irish army to advance, the very presence of a force at Ballymore would ensure that they would have a very favourable forward base from which to march on Mullingar.

The opponents of this policy would argue that it was a folly to keep men garrisoned in small scattered and weakly defended forts so close to the enemy. They provided the English with targets at which to strike. The enemy could just as easily be kept out of the frontier area by frequent patrolling and in any event, there was nothing to show that the English were inclined to move into the vacuum created by an Irish withdrawal. Certainly, if the English did come in force, strong points like Dysart Castle would not stop them.

Notwithstanding this, Sarsfield was confident of his policy, not least because it had worked so far. The English, apart from one insignificant raiding party from Castle Forbes, had failed to cross the Shannon and this was largely due to the wide *cordon sanitaire* that he had established on the east bank. As each successive month had passed, the English had found themselves more confined to their garrison towns.

The English certainly did not want to take any chances. Their small garrison towns were also in danger of being attacked and conscious of that they had concentrated on consolidating their position. Mullingar in particular had the engineers busy throughout the winter in building up its defences. After the débâcle at Lanesborough no major expedition was undertaken until, by coincidence it seems, Sarsfield was out of the way reporting to Tyrconnell in Limerick. In the second week of March 1691 Ginckel, Kirke and Lanier led 'a considerable body both of horse and foot' on a raid towards Athlone. According to Story, the Irish had good warning of this attack and Brigadier Clifford was waiting for them with 2,300 men. Story reported that Clifford withdrew in front of the

English force through Moate all the way back to Athlone and that during the fighting two hundred Irishmen were killed. Sarsfield's account differs in that Ballymore rather than Athlone was Ginckel's target.

> Clifford's folly nearly cost us dearly not long ago, for although he was warned in good time that the enemy intended to take his quarters, he spent the preceeding night seven miles away, and only arrived in the morning to give his orders when the enemy appeared. He then lost his head to the extent that he did not know where he was so that our fellows were forced to retire in disorder, although without danger owing to the weak pursuit by the enemy. However, following this minor success, General Ginckel and Major-Generals Kirke and Lanier appeared next morning before Ballymore believing that we would abandon the fort to their army. But they were mistaken, for having advanced to attack a ruin defended by a hundred musketeers, they were so well received that they retired. If Clifford had been believed the position would have been abandoned, but the governor, who is a brave and honourable man, would not consent, and in fact if we had quitted it we would have lost everything that we have beyond the Shannon.[12]

To the French the fresh appearance of the divisions between Tyrconnell and Sarsfield added to the urgency with which a new general was required. The general would need to be both experienced and French and so above the petty disputes of this petty country and would also need the authority to command the army without interference from either Tyrconnell or Sarsfield. If this new man was going to succeed in Ireland, he would need to have above all else the ability to unite the army, just as the army had been united under King James.

Sarsfield's name was never mentioned as a candidate for such a post. He was clearly a useful man and had proved his ability to lead and control large bodies of men at Sligo and up and down the Shannon, but Ireland needed more than that. Only six years before he had been a captain, and he had never commanded more than a brigade in the field. To the French, who were going to pay for the campaign, there was no man in the Irish army with the necessary experience to be a general. That was the accepted view and it was never challenged by anyone who had any say in the matter.

It certainly was not challenged by Sarsfield who was also looking forward to the arrival of the promised commander-in-chief. He had only one reservation, and that was the same reservation that his delegation had taken to James. 'We are waiting impatiently for our French general and hope that he will be independent of Tyrconnell, otherwise nothing will be achieved as given the minimum amount of authority he is by himself capable of ruining the plans of the greatest captain in Europe.'[13]

James's first choice of a French general was one of the oldest and most experienced men that Louis had, Bernard Gigault de Bellefonds.[14] Bellefonds had been a marshal of France since 1668, and for the fifteen years before that he had been a major-general. He had fought for France for the best part of half a century. Although he was greatly respected and was a one time favourite of Louis, his failure at Gerona had resulted in his temporary disgrace and he was currently unemployed. However, James was impressed with the old man as like him he was deeply religious. They had travelled together to the monastery at La Trappe, and James had learnt that Bellefonds had financed his sister's nunnery at Rouen. He was in every way a good man, and his reputation in England was unsullied by any suggestion of involvement in Louis's suppression of the French Protestants.

But the French considered that they had a better man to send to Ireland, the younger Charles Chalmont, marquis de Saint-Ruth.* Although Saint-Ruth had only been a lieutenant-general for just over two years, he did have a long and distinguished military career behind him and he had more recently directed the French forces in Savoy which included Mountcashel's Irish brigade, so it was felt that he did at least have some experience of Irish soldiery.** He was a big, well built man of a particularly ugly appearance, the effect of which was probably exaggerated by his inability to display the sort of manners that were expected of a man in his position. As Saint Simon politely put it, 'He was a very simple gentleman'. But as a soldier he was well thought of. He was audacious and very brave, but 'he was also most brutal', and his victories were famous for the harshness that accompanied them.15

To King James, Saint-Ruth was not a good choice. He was not just any soldier, his name was already well known in England. He had made a name for himself by his actions in suppressing the Huguenots after the Revocation of the Edict of Nantes in 1685. No man could inspire more horror in the minds of Protestants. He had been responsible for some of the worst excesses of the *dragonnades* which had resulted in the flight from France of a quarter of a million Huguenots. His very name conjured up images of the most terrible acts committed in the name of religion and Louis of France: images of mass hangings, of forced conversions, of whole villages being locked in barns while laughing dragoons set fire to the thatch over their heads. Of 'the famous Monsieur Saint-Ruth', one London journal commented, 'it's the man that has consigned his loathed name to posterity by cruelties, barbarities, rapes, murders, assassinations, burnings, tortures and a thousand other villanies that the ages before him never so much as heard named, and the ages after him will scarce believe one single man could be capable of.'16 The man who had butchered Protestants in France was now to turn his attention to the Protestants in Ireland.

The decision to send Saint-Ruth to command the Irish army was made in January,17 but was not known in Ireland until April. Saint-Ruth was to be given

---

* His correct name was Saint-Ruhe, but English speakers have always referred to him as Saint-Ruth.

** In fact very limited experience. He had conducted the short campaign in September 1690 in which there had been some fleeting contacts with irregulars: the Irish had lost three men killed, and three others (including Mountcashel) wounded.

the temporary rank of general and was to bring with him two assistants, both of whom would hold the rank of lieutenant-general, a rank senior to anyone else in Ireland except Tyrconnell. They were Jean d'Usson de Saint-Martin and Philibert-Emmanuel Froulay, Chevalier de Tessé. The last and the most junior member of the four man French military team was Brigadier Henri de la Tour Monfort, who was to be promoted to the rank of major-general to be as senior as any member of the Irish army.

Sarsfield was delighted with the news that a French commander-in-chief was at last on his way, and the whole army was encouraged by the rumour that Saint-Ruth would command the army independently of Tyrconnell.[18] Even Tyrconnell's supporters were happy at the situation as Tyrconnell had made it clear that he did not want any part in military operations. In fact, almost everyone looked forward to the arrival of the four French generals in the hope that they would bring an end to the faction fighting within the army. 'Never was the arrival of a man more passionately longed for in this world than that of Saint-Ruth by the generality of the Irish', wrote O'Kelly.

Saint Ruth sailed into Limerick on 19 May 1691. His arrival was celebrated by the Irish as if they had won a famous victory.

> At his landing on the quay he was saluted by a discharge of the artillery from the castle. In his proceeding he found the soldiery of the town ranged on each side of the street. The viceroy came to meet him a hundred paces from his palace, and gave him the bien-venu into Ireland, and then brought him to dinner. In the evening he was lodged in a house prepared for his residence.[19]

Saint-Ruth brought with him not only his three assistants: d'Usson, de Tessé and La Tour Monfort; but also, much to Tyrconnell's dismay, Henry Luttrell and Nicholas Purcell. These last two had let King James know that if they did not return certain elements in the army would guess that Tyrconnell had requested their detention and consequently the viceroy would be in great danger. Tyrconnell also noted with sadness that although the French convoy had brought large quantities of arms and equipment, his requests for more money and more French troops had been ignored. The Irish army was to be directed, armed and equipped by the French, but the French would not fight alongside them.

For three weeks Saint-Ruth remained in Limerick. Although he had been advised that the English were preparing to push into Connaught he felt that his first tasks were in training his troops and arranging the distribution of the new supplies. He initially kept in contact with the front not by visiting it but by corresponding with the French officers, especially those engineers who were employed in improving the defences of the Shannon towns. Even before his arrival it was clear that the enemy was gathering in Mullingar, and that was an obvious indication that Ginckel's objective was Athlone. Saint-Ruth knew that time was running out.

CHAPTER XVI

The Bridge of Athlone

There is no certainty yet about the French reinforcements, so it has been decided to make as great haste as possible and all the troops are to be assembled on May 18th in three divisions: Lt-Gen Douglas with his corps at Belturbet, the English at Mullingar, the Danes and French with the Dutch between Clonmel and Cashel. Muskets for ten thousand men are daily awaited from Holland to arm the Protestants and three thousand tents and twenty two pontoons. The two English major-generals, Mackay and Talmash, are also coming here.

Wurtemberg to Christian V of Denmark, 2 May 1691.[1]

THROUGHOUT THE SPRING OF 1691, convoy after convoy of English ships laden with munitions, arms and equipment sailed into Irish ports.[2] William was more anxious than ever to finish the war quickly. Impatient and intolerant of those who had offered him excuses rather than results throughout the winter, he sacked three of his generals. Sir John Lanier, Percy Kirke and James Douglas were relieved of their commands and sent to join the army in the Netherlands. They were replaced by the Englishman Thomas Tollemache, the Scotsman Hugh Mackay and the Huguenot Henri de Massue, marquis de Ruvigny.

The English preparations were such that when Ginckel was ready to march he had assembled together the greatest collection of artillery ever seen in the country. His army, although not as big as that commanded by King William at the Boyne, was nevertheless man for man better equipped and trained. Like Saint-Ruth he was anxious to get under way, and his plan was to strike at the heart of Jacobite Ireland. He had the means to achieve what Douglas had been unable to do in the previous year. Wurtemberg wrote enthusiastically of the coming campaign:

> The plan is to attack Athlone and then to advance on Galway . . . We shall take 32 battering pieces and six large mortars and their teams with us, and in addition 1000 cannonballs for each piece.[3]

Ginckel's main disadvantage was that he did not know what was happening beyond the Shannon. He greatly feared the French would land a whole army in Ireland and march northwards to meet him before he could seize any tactical advantage. Time had again become a scarce commodity, and as Ginckel's generals pored over their maps they knew that Athlone was going to be a difficult town to take. From Mullingar to Athlone was a thirty mile march and almost exactly half way stood Sarsfield's patrol base perched on the peninsula in Lough Sunderlin at Ballymore. The very fact that the Irish held Ballymore

Fort was an irritating reminder to the English of their rapid and disorganised withdrawal after the siege of Limerick eight months earlier. Although Douglas had garrisoned the fort when he withdrew from Athlone, it had been hurriedly abandoned when Sarsfield marched into the area after the attack on Birr. His engineers had in the intervening months made it the Irish army's equivalent to Birr, and although throughout the winter English raiding parties had approached to within sight of the fort, it had proved to be too strong to attack.

But however difficult Berwick may have found Birr, Ginckel had no such fears of Ballymore. On his ill-fated raid, Berwick had taken with him no more than three field guns, and they were manned by decidedly inept crews. Ginckel was going to march through Ballymore with the greatest siege-train ever, a siege-train designed to pulverise the walls of Athlone, Galway and Limerick. Faced with such power, it would not matter whether Ballymore was protected by a stone wall or a privet hedge. There was going to be no cover for the garrison.

Saint-Ruth meanwhile set about his task with a desperate vigour. He 'rested neither night nor day, but galloped between Limerick, Athlone and Lanesborough'. He was staggered by the problems he encountered, especially those of supply. The fleet that had accompanied him had numbered over eighty ships and had brought all manner of equipment including 'arms, clothes for several regiments, powder, ball, a considerable quantity of oats, of meal, of biscuit, of wine and brandy, which caused a plenty in the country'.[4]* But the lack of transport inland was lamentable, and it was no easy task to supply Athlone. All horses not already in the army were commandeered to carry the loads from Limerick. There were only six boats for use on the Shannon, and although these were sent up and down as quickly as they could be loaded, 'what they carried in one load was consumed by the garrison of Athlone and the neighbouring troops before the second load could arrive'.[5] Saint-Ruth was exasperated. He was also running behind time.

Saint-Ruth was determined to hold Athlone, and shortly after his arrival he issued orders for the army to gather itself together in a camp fourteen miles to the west at Ballinasloe. But when Ginckel marched, the Frenchman was still desperately trying to marshal his men. He knew of Ginckel's preparations in Mullingar, and it was quite predictable that the English would march on Athlone and in so doing would attack the one garrison that lay in their path. However, Saint-Ruth never visited Ballymore, it was a detail. But to the Irish army it was a significant detail as it contained almost a thousand soldiers. If the English were capable of making a serious attempt on Athlone, as Saint-Ruth knew they were, they would make short work of Ballymore. Despite this, no effort was made to evacuate the fort even when it was known that the English were coming. The only excuse for this can have been that time was so valuable

---

* Amongst the cargo of clothing, hats, brandy, wine, munitions, pikes, iron and steel bars, scythes, wheat and oats, bridles, harnesses, saddles, fuses and cannons were 15,000 grenades, 5,000 muskets, 500 carbines, 500 pairs of pistols, 5,000 infantry swords, 500 sabres and 20,000 new French army issue grey coats.

that it was hoped that the sacrifice of the Ballymore garrison would buy a few more days, but that excuse was not used.

On Saturday 6 June 1691, Baron Ginckel rode out of Mullingar at the head of his men and led them along the road to Athlone. The third year of the war was now under way. On the next day, his advance guard reached Ballymore and posted itself across the neck of land on which the fort stood. The Irish garrison was cut off, although perhaps not disheartened. Certainly the garrison commander, Colonel Ulick 'Milo' Burke, was not inclined to surrender even when later on in the day the English brought four field guns into position and began to fire random shots across the water into his outworks. The English were not particularly concerned at his attitude as their main artillery was yet to come.

On Monday morning the garrison was roused by the sound of twenty heavy siege guns. Although his position was now hopeless Burke knew where his duty lay. He resolved to use every available ruse to delay Ginckel's march on Athlone, and he was encouraged by the confidence of his chief engineer, the architect of his defences, Lieutenant-Colonel Burton. Ginckel sent Burke a message to the effect that he was either to surrender within two hours or he would be hanged. Burke asked for it in writing. Although irritated by this request, Ginckel sent him a note.* Burke's reply was that he would not consider surrender unless he was to be allowed to march out to Athlone with the full honours of war. The English were amazed. Burke was clearly a brave man, but to them he was not only being foolish, he was being criminally wasteful of his men's lives. His small isolated garrison was facing the greatest siege-train that had ever been seen in Ireland and yet he was making a show of confidence by strutting up and down behind his inadequate walls and threatening to hold out until he was given generous terms. The artillerymen prepared themselves for what amounted to their last practice before Athlone, and the English army sat down on the grass to watch the show.

> Upon which the general ordered all our guns and mortars to fall to work, the bombs tearing up the sandy banks, and the Irish running like conies from one hole to another; whilst the guns were battering the works and making a breach, the Irish in the meantime did what they could with their two guns and small shot: but Lieutenant-Colonel Burton, their engineer, had his hand shot off from one of our batteries, and their works went down apace, which made the Irish very uneasy. This siege however, was very delightful to our whole party, who had a view of it from the adjoining hill.[7]

---

*   Which read: 'Since the Governor desires to see in writing the message which I just now sent him by word of mouth, he may know that if he surrenders the Fort of Ballymore to me within two hours, I will give him and his garrison their lives and make them prisoners of war; if not, neither he nor they shall have any quarter, nor another opportunity of saving themselves: However, if in that time their women and children will go out, they have my leave. Given at the camp this Eighth day of June Sixteen Ninety One at Eight o'clock in the morning. Bar de Ginckel.'[6]

16 Godart van Reede, Baron Ginckel, later to be created earl of Athlone. In the background his army is shown attacking Athlone Castle. (By Sir Godfrey Kneller)

After four hours Burke allowed his men to hoist a white flag. But suspecting another attempt to waste time, Ginckel determined to teach the garrison a lesson and ordered the cannonade to continue. Only when the afternoon had turned to evening, after the defences had been completely breached in two places and Burke had altered his attitude and was 'begging quarter for God's sake', did Ginckel relent and accept the surrender. It was the end of a quixotic gesture, and a gesture that was not even appreciated by those Jacobites who sat behind safer walls. Although Ulick Burke no doubt bitterly reflected on his lot as he and his men were led off to Dublin as prisoners, he would have been far more bitter if he had known that the following was to be written of him in Paris:

> The very next day Ulick Burke the governor, either out of treachery or cowardice, surrendered at discretion without any considerable opposition though he had near eight hundred well armed men in the place.*

Ginckel now had a clear road before him. But he did not move as he thought it unlikely that he would be able to cross the Shannon without the promised pontoon boats that were being shipped from England. His army waited, Ginckel nervously wondering whether a French army had arrived to oppose him and whether he could force a crossing before Athlone was reinforced. He sent out orders for the British troops who were then garrisoned at Belturbet and for Wurtemberg's continental troops who were still in the south to join him. He considered attempting to cut across the Shannon at Banagher or Lanesborough, but these suggestions were rejected as he feared that the reinforced and perhaps adventurous Irish army led by 'one of the most violent of all the persecutors of the Protestants in France' would slip past him and make straight for Dublin. Better to meet Saint-Ruth head on, but with the proper equipment. A week after the pulverising of Ballymore Fort, the pontoons arrived in Dublin. Confident that this necessary equipment was now on the way, Ginckel prepared to move.

Saint-Ruth was fortunate in that Ginckel felt so dependant on his boats, as the Irish army had not even assembled at Limerick, let alone Athlone. He rode about desperately whipping the army together. Units converged on Ballinasloe from all over Connaught and western Munster. Garrisons were left wherever they were needed, but Saint-Ruth's need for men was overriding. Numerically the Irish army was now as great as it had been at the Boyne, but then one fifth of the soldiers had been those continental troops serving in Lauzun's six French regiments. All of those foreigners had been experienced men serving under experienced officers. Although it would be false to describe the French regiments as having been the backbone of the Jacobite army, they certainly included some of the best troops. Now that they had gone, efforts had been made to replace them. The early spring of 1691 had seen Sarsfield and others

---

* The garrison at Ballymore, like that of Charlemont before, would have been hard pressed to survive a long siege as there were so many non-combatants in the fort. After the surrender the English counted 50 officers, 780 private men, 259 rapparees, 645 women and 'about 400' children.[8]

busily recruiting men from the 'militia' and from bands of rapparees, in fact drawing in any men of military age from all those parts of the country under their control.[9] Although Sarsfield had transferred what experienced soldiers and officers he could into his ten new battalions, the men were mostly inexperienced and ill-disciplined. Saint-Ruth needed time not only to get his men to Athlone, but also time to lick his army into shape.

When old Colonel Grace had been governor of Athlone in the previous year, he had held off Douglas by the simple expedient of burning and deserting that part of the town that stood on the east bank, the Leinster town. Then, as now, the Shannon dissected Athlone. The two halves were connected by a five arched mediaeval bridge at the western end of which stood King John's Castle. Although the (eastern) Leinster town and the (western) Irish town were both walled, Colonel Grace had prudently withdrawn to the Irish town and broken down the most westerly arch of the bridge behind him before a shot had been fired. As the river is a hundred or so yards wide and General Douglas had no boats and was even short of powder for the few field guns that he did have, the attack was a wasteful failure.

Since then Sarsfield had directed that the Leinster town be protected by new works to guard the bridge, and throughout the spring its defences were transformed. Ditches and modern earthworks were thrown up around the walls to ensure that the English would not only have a fight to gain control of the bridge, they would also have to fight to get to it. Throughout the month of May, while the Irish army was being collected together by Saint-Ruth, thousands of men were employed in digging trenches and ditches, carrying earth and making fascines with which to stop up breached walls.

As the days went by, the work became more desperate, especially after the fall of Ballymore. Although Sarsfield still held the command in Athlone, the reconstruction of the Leinstertown fell to Major-General Wauchope who had arrived back from France in the spring, and the French engineer Robert, who had been in Ireland since January. It was not a happy partnership. They fell out and Wauchope had Robert arrested, said that he would have him clapped in irons, and then had him sent off to Saint-Ruth.[10] Robert claimed that he had been ill-treated because he was a Frenchman, but even the French were divided in the dispute. Their ordnance officer Fumeron stated that the poor state of the defences was entirely due to Robert's negligence, whereas the engineer Noblesse wrote that he found Robert sensible and hard working. The cause of the friction between them was perhaps no more than frayed tempers and incompatible personalities. Robert later wrote that the argument between them had merely been a matter of whether the measurements for the defensive works should be made in French toises or in yards. 'I immediately complained to Lord Lucan who was commanding there: he appeared to be angry and assured me that he would take some action on it, but it is their custom to make promises and do nothing.'[11]

Saint-Ruth had already had enough of the internal feuding within the Irish army. He was determined that fresh feuds should not break out involving his own engineers. He sent the probably blameless Robert off to Limerick to take the next ship home.

On 19 June 1691, the advance guard of Ginckel's army arrived outside Athlone and on the next day a battery of twelve heavy siege guns started work on the Leinster town wall.[12] The cannonade was highly effective. The walls and the houses came tumbling down and the streets were a hazard of flying splinters of metal and stone. Wauchope, who was commanding the four hundred or so musketeers in the Leinster town, was crushed by falling masonry and carried off over the bridge to safety. Although the English were at first beaten back, on their second assault they stormed the shattered wall and captured the town while those Irishmen who could ran across the bridge to safety. The French were satisfied with Wauchope's 'skillful and gallant'[13] defence which had held the English up for two days and had cost them four hundred dead.

Ginckel was now able to look out over the river to the real fortifications of Athlone that stretched along the western bank on both sides of the old castle. The delay in taking the Leinster town seemed a grave setback to the English as on the next day the entire Irish army formed up in a camp to the west of Athlone. Ginckel was now committed to forcing a river crossing into a strongly defended fortress while opposed by an army of some twenty one thousand men.

> The marquis of Saint-Ruth said the baron of Ginckel deserved to be hanged for attempting to take Athlone while he was at the head of so great an army to defend it, and he himself deserved to be hanged if he should lose it.[14]

Sarsfield was ordered back to the camp to take his command in the army, and d'Usson was sent into Athlone to conduct the defence. As it was to prove an unpleasant task Saint-Ruth insisted that the garrison in the town should be relieved every twenty four hours. Each night, three battalions marched into the town to take their turn in facing the English artillery.

On the first day after the English had taken the Leinster town they began setting up their batteries to fire across the Shannon. Ginckel 'furiously battered the castle and the trench along the riverside, never ceasing night or day till he reduced the Connaught town to ashes, and levelled both castle and trench with the ground'.[15] Within four days the eastern side of the castle had been demolished* as had most of the east facing wall, and the whole town was devastated. The Irish defenders had to break a hole in the back of the castle to be able to get in, and most of them now spent the day behind the town rather than in it.[16] The boats had arrived for the pontoon bridge, but the Irish trenches were so extensive on the far bank that it became immediately clear that they

---

*   Although the present castle at Athlone stands on the same site, it is has been almost entirely re-constructed and most of the buildings are of later date. The modern road bridge stands just over a hundred yards up river from the bridge of 1691.

would be impossible to assemble. Ginckel decided against using them: his delay at Ballymore had been in vain. He decided instead to concentrate on seizing the bridge and, in case that should fail, he sent men off to investigate the possibility of crossing up river at Lanesborough.

When the Irish had withdrawn, they had broken down two of the arches, one at the eastern end and one at the western end of the bridge. They had erected a breastwork behind the last of these from where they could rake the bridge with musket fire. This breastwork became the focus of Ginckel's attention. His men crowded about the bridgehead in the Leinster town to discharge their muskets at the Irish defenders. Their fire was so intense that on the 26th the heads of the Irish defenders were kept down long enough for his men to repair one of the broken arches. All eyes now turned to that last narrow gap over the Shannon.

Despite the dangerous proximity of Ginckel's army, the Irish commanders had other worries on their minds. The viceroy had visited the army. The appearance in Athlone of old Tyrconnell, barking and wheezing, reopened the divisions in the Irish camp. Sarsfield was furious. What business had he with the army now that the king had sent over a French general? The recently returned Henry Luttrell and Nicholas Purcell predictably encouraged Sarsfield to make a move. The three of them set out to ensure that the political victory gained by the viceroy at Saint-Germain was short-lived. Sarsfield was determined to make it clear to both Saint-Ruth and Tyrconnell that the French could command only with his consent, and that his consent would be withheld if Tyrconnell remained in the camp. Charles O'Kelly, whose uncompromising Gaelic faction had become increasingly hostile to the viceroy, left this description of the situation:

> It was greatly wondered by some that Tyrconnell, who was not ignorant how unwelcome his presence must have been to the major part of the army, should presume to appear in the camp: and on the other side it was no less admired by a great many who were not fully acquainted with the transactions in France, how Saint-Ruth could endure it. But the truth is, Saint-Ruth did not imagine that Tyrconnell, who was to content himself solely with the management of civil affairs, would inter-meddle with the military government, James having assured him that he would write to Tyrconnell to that purpose...but either Tyrconnell received no such orders from James, or if he did, he concealed it: for he and his creatures confidently averred that Saint-Ruth was to command the army under the viceroy: and to demonstrate the same to all people, as also to confirm his faction among the soldiers, who otherwise would be altogether disheartened by Sarsfield's more numerous party, it was resolved, in a private consult of his own friends, that he should come and head the army in person.[17]

As Sarsfield had threatened before, if Tyrconnell attempted to assert any military authority he would get the signatures of 'everyone' in the army to deny him. With his two confederates he now set about arranging just that. Their disci-

ples went from regiment to regiment getting the officers to sign a petition that
Tyrconnell be removed. The viceroy, never a man to concede a point easily, was
outraged. But he found himself impotent, especially when it became clear that
Sarsfield's petition had widespread support. To Tyrconnell it was not the
outcome that was important, it was the affront. Although he was willing to
volunteer his services to lead the life guards should there be a pitched battle, he
had already agreed privately with the king not to interfere in military matters
once a French general had been sent over. But Tyrconnell was still the viceroy.
He was not just the king's deputy in Ireland, he *was* the king in Ireland, and as
such any French general must be subject to his authority. Even if there was any
doubt in the matter, which legally there could not be, King James had sent
instructions to that effect. As Tyrconnell later wrote back to France:

> I was shocked to discover that while the enemy was within cannon shot
> of us, these men: Lord Lucan, Purcell and Luttrell: were spending all
> their time and effort taking round a petition calling for my resignation
> from the army to each tent for the officers and people of quality to sign.[18]

Observing that 'such unnatural and irregular conduct was beginning to cause
much division in the army,' he complained to Saint-Ruth who clearly knew
what was going on. Saint-Ruth denied any such knowledge. 'He told me that
he knew nothing of the affair and that he was extremely surprised and would
speak to these people about it'. Tyrconnell was too subtle to be fooled by Saint-
Ruth's protests.

> I wanted to believe that these were his true feelings, but most of the more
> sensible officers in the army cannot believe that Lord Lucan and those
> others who were always with him apparently encouraging him in his
> trouble-making, as well as all their adherents, would choose to risk
> undertaking an affair as serious as this without his knowledge.[19]

Tyrconnell speedily gathered together those men that he could trust and in
turn had them travel around the camp canvassing support. They were too few
and too late. Sarsfield had also made a fresh discovery which he used to
discredit Tyrconnell. The viceroy, in exchange for the equipment sent over by
the French, was to arrange for another battalion of recruits to travel to France
to join Mountcashel's Irish brigade. When he was in Limerick, he had spent a
lot of time attempting to arrange this, but it meant taking men from existing
regiments 'as it is impossible to find any men in the small part of the country
left to us who are not already in the army'. This had not been easy as even the
ill-paid and unarmed Irish troops were very reluctant to go to France. Sarsfield
now eagerly encouraged the growth of the rumour that men were being sent
there in exchange for French gold payable to Tyrconnell personally.

The rumour swept through the camp and was widely accepted, especially by
the most ignorant sections of the army who held O'Kelly's view that
Tyrconnell was hell-bent on carrying out a treacherous plan to secure a

Williamite conquest. Feelings hardened against the viceroy, and a large body of opinion in the army, certainly the majority, who had long been hostile to Tyrconnell now felt that they owed him no allegiance or obedience whatsoever. With the viceroy now more discredited than ever, the army looked solely to Sarsfield. King James heard that:

> A colonel of the army came into my Lord Trimlestown's tent, and discoursing of these dissensions, said he would obey my Lord Lucan independent of the king's authority insomuch that should that Lord command him to kill any man in the army, he would readily do it.

Sarsfield's petition was never given to anyone. It was a device to harden the attitude of his supporters and to intimidate his opponents. Although he was not even among the three most senior officers in the army, he was now undoubtedly the highest ranking Irishman and no one, French or Irish, could expect to command without his say-so. With or without Saint-Ruth's knowledge, Tyrconnell was unceremoniously told to leave Athlone. Sarsfield confidently sent the young and wild Lieutenant-Colonel O'Connor to Tyrconnell. O'Connor told the old viceroy that if he did not leave the camp, he would personally cut his tent ropes. Tyrconnell's supporters were cowed and amazed. 'Here Tyrconnell made a noble conquest of himself', wrote Plunket.[20]

> I cannot but admire how it came to pass that the marquis of Saint-Ruth was induced to connive at this unworthy procedure, the French being so much for venerating authority and quality. But the duke of Tyrconnell, though a man of an elevated spirit, thought it better to smother at present his resentment for the welfare of the king and country, because the time and place were not proper for his vindication without endangering the common cause.*

It is not difficult to accept that Saint-Ruth was quite content to avoid getting embroiled in this controversy. He had sailed from France with Luttrell and Purcell and had been left in no doubt that Tyrconnell could not be trusted to keep away from the councils of war. The old viceroy was all that stood between him and the absolute authority that he wanted. Saddened by the power that Sarsfield now wielded, Tyrconnell left the camp and wearily travelled the road to Limerick.

Ginckel was not an imaginative man, but he could imagine failure and his imagination now led him to the edge of despair. There was only one bridge at Athlone, just wide enough to get a cart across. The Irish had barricaded it and broken down one of the arches. Ginckel and his staff were forced to concen-

---

* Plunket went on: ' . . . though it is believed if he had lived a year longer he would have brought the faction to a condign punishment for the affront offered the king in the person of his lieutenant'. According to Lord Ronsele: 'The duke durst not reply one word for he was disgraced and Sarsfield was now the King of Spades, that signified blood and revenge.'

trate on that one small span on which so much depended. The bridge had to be mended. On 27 July, the English pulled up their cannon to the bridge and fired straight at the Irish breastwork on the other side. By the evening it was shattered and burnt, but the Irish responded with a fanaticism not yet seen in the war and threw up a new wall from the rubble of the old, 'notwithstanding our great and small shot flying like hail'.[21]

On the next day the English, rolling fascines in front of them and under heavy covering fire, managed to get all the way along the bridge to the broken arch and succeeded in carrying out makeshift repairs. Although the Irish were now only twenty feet away, new planks were pushed across the gap and nailed together. A party of grenadiers prepared to dash across and assault the Irish position. At this desperate moment the Irish called for volunteers, and a party of ten men led by Sergeant Custume raced onto the bridge wielding axes and began smashing the English handywork. Within a minute they had all been shot dead. Another twenty men led by a lieutenant replaced them and ran forward to finish the work. With the exception of two of them who 'escaped amongst the fire and smoke',[22] they were also all shot down. But as the smoke cleared the English realised that these heroic men had been successful in their objective. The new planks were now all floating down to Banagher. The bridge was now as impassable as it had ever been.

Ginckel was desperate. He could see no way around the problem. He ordered a new attempt and throughout 28 July the English pushed fresh fascines forward while their gunners smashed the Irish position on the other side. But the Irish musketeers hiding amongst the rubble of west Athlone were too numerous. Although the ruins were ceaselessly swept with cannon fire, the Irish still managed to fire back and force the English off the bridge. The Irish grenadiers even counter-attacked and set the fascines alight. After this second costly and failed assault, Ginckel was no nearer to his objective.

He despairingly cast around for fresh ideas. Athlone had already taken up too much time. In 1690 King William's campaign had been abandoned when the weather had broken at the end of August. If the seasons of 1691 were to follow the same pattern as they had then, Ginckel knew that he had less than two months in which to finish the task, that is, two months in which to take Galway, Limerick and Sligo and to destroy the Irish army. So far, he had only managed to march to the Shannon.

The alternative plans were not inspired. They were simply to attempt a crossing at either Banagher or at Lanesborough. They had already been rejected, but that was before Athlone had proved to be such a tough nut to crack. It was now time to revise the campaign strategy. All possibilities were now to be considered, even the most daring. And soon only the most daring of the alternatives was adopted. The English would wade straight through the river, attack the bridgehead on the Irish side, rebuild the broken arch, and then the army would storm across, seize the town and fight off the entire Irish army. It was known that it was possible to ford the Shannon a few hundred yards downstream of the bridge and, after a dry summer, the river was lower than it had been in living memory.[23] Some of the Irish defenders had been seen escaping that way when the Leinster town fell, and three Danish soldiers dressed in heavy armour had waded across the day before and confirmed the existence of a ford where the water was only waist-high. The plan did not gain the unanimous approval of the council of war. Mackay, for one, was strongly opposed to it. It was, he said, contrary to all the maxims of war. The argument raged and was eventually won by Major-General Thomas Tollemache whose plan it was, and who was anxious to lead the attack through the Shannon himself.[24]

Saint-Ruth's confidence grew in equal proportion to Ginckel's desperation. If the English did get into West Athlone he would drive them back, and at the moment they showed no signs of getting even that far. Some deserters from the English army bought him reports that Ginckel was thinking of marching down to Banagher. Saint-Ruth's strategy was working. He continued his policy of changing the town's garrison each day to give all his men experience of being under fire. Despite the proximity of the English army, on the last day of June the three regiments posted in the rubble were three of the infantry battalions that had been raised during the war; O'Gara's, Cormack O'Neill's and MacMahon's.* Apart from the scratch battalions recently raised by Sarsfield, it would have been difficult to have chosen a trio of ropier regiments. 'Whoever ordered this relief was imprudent or treacherous.'[25] On the afternoon of the same day, Saint-Ruth held a party for his senior officers in the camp.[26] It was not a victory celebration, but he felt that victory was in the air.

At about six o'clock in the early evening, the church bell in the Leinstertown was rung repeatedly. With a great cheer a multitude of grenadiers 'bounced' out of their trenches and ran into the water. It was Ginckel's final assault.

The first sixty Grenadiers into the river wore heavy breast plates and waded through twenty abreast. Pushing them forward were fifteen hundred grenadiers 'holding their fusees and bags of grenades over their heads'. Though the water came up to their chests, their progress was steady. The Irish fired ragged volleys at them, but were themselves subjected to a great cannonade by the English artillery. As the grenadiers stormed up the strand and into the town, the Irish defenders fled. D'Usson, who had rushed into Athlone to direct the defence, was knocked unconscious in the stampede of men trying to get out. While some of Ginckel's troops swarmed over the Irish works, others made for the bridgehead where they attacked the Irish in the flank. As they beat them away, English soldiers raced onto the bridge with fresh planks. Behind them, the first of the infantry regiments doubled over. Within minutes, the English were masters of the whole town.

---

* Colonel Art MacMahon's regiment had been raised as an unarmed labour battalion, although the men had seen action at Limerick when they were responsible for much of the stone throwing during the attack on the breach.

The rubbish and stuff thrown down by our cannon was much more difficult to climb over than a great part of the enemy's works, which occasioned our soldiers to swear and curse even amongst the bullets themselves, upon which Major-General Mackay told them that they had more reason to fall upon their knees and thank God for the victory and that they were brave men and the best of men if they would swear less.[27]

Unknown to the English troops at the time, they had been extraordinarily lucky, and were now to be the beneficiaries of an outstanding and unforgivable mistake by Saint-Ruth. Athlone was a walled town, and the walls that extended all the way around the Irish town were still intact. The approach from the Irish camp was along a causeway across a bog and the entrance into the town was only some thirteen feet wide. Tyrconnell and three successive experts on fortification (Wauchope, Robert, Maxwell)[28] had advised Saint-Ruth to have the whole wall pulled down, so that if Ginckel did manage to launch a successful assault across the river or along the bridge, the entire Irish army could charge straight into the Irish town from the other side and push them straight back into the Shannon. Saint-Ruth was so confident that he delayed doing anything until the day before the assault when he ordered D'Usson to see to it. Nothing was done. Consequently, when the English storming party got into the Irish town and chased the defenders out, they were able to hold it simply by running to the west facing wall which was as sturdy and as intact as it had been at the start of the siege. When Major-General John Hamilton hurriedly marched the Irish reinforcements down to the town, he had to turn back. If he wanted to drive the English out he would have to firstly batter the walls down.

Although the final assault had been an anti-climax, the siege of Athlone had been to Ginckel a most expensive affair. His thirty-two siege guns had used up nearly fifty tons of gunpowder and had loosed off twelve thousand cannonballs and six hundred bombs, and this was in addition to 'a great many ton of stones shot out of our mortars'.[29] Even excluding the mortars, the result was that on average, every minute of the ten-day siege was accompanied by a shot from a siege gun. Athlone was then, and remains, the most bombarded town in the British Isles. Compare these figures with the three thousand cannonballs and just under five and a half tons of powder that had been intercepted by Sarsfield in the artillery train destined for the siege of Limerick the year before. The Connaught town 'had been reduced to ashes'.[30] Bodies were everywhere trapped under the fallen masonry, especially where the fighting had been the most fierce. After the siege, 'one could not set his foot at the end of the bridge, or castle, but on dead bodies; many lay half buried under the rubbish and more under faggots, and many not to be seen under the river whereby the stink is insufferable.'[31]

The feeling of despondency and outrage in the Irish camp was as great as it had been after the Boyne. Once again the English had won an important victory while the majority of the Irish army had not been in a position to oppose them. The suspicion grew in Sarsfield's mind that Saint-Ruth was not all that he had hoped for. The embarrassed Saint-Ruth desperately complained that he should not have left the task of breaking down the western defences to others, but should have supervised it himself. The story was put about that the French engineers were to blame for not following his orders. It was a lame excuse, but people were willing to believe anything that might exonerate their new commander in whom so many hopes lay. The Gaelic faction, as always, attributed defeat to treachery. They were unwilling to blame Saint-Ruth for his inefficiency as he was their champion against Tyrconnell, and so they blamed the man who held the town at the time of the assault, Thomas Maxwell. 'This Colonel Maxwell', wrote O'Kelly bitterly, 'was a Scotchman by birth and, as he pretended, a Catholic; he was of mean extraction and one of Tyrconnell's creatures.'[32] And there you have it. The man was a friend of Tyrconnell and was not a Gael. To O'Kelly's party he was two thirds guilty even before one looked at any evidence and, besides, that evidence was soon produced by Maxwell's accusers. Just before the assault one of his men had been seen swimming across the river to deliver a message to Ginckel. Maxwell had then ordered his men to rest and when the English swarmed into the town this Judas had boldly stepped forward and addressed them with the previously agreed words 'Do you know me?', and so was spared. And if that was not enough, both O'Kelly and Colonel Felix O'Neill reported that when the men from Cormack O'Neill's regiment asked Maxwell for more ammunition, he had sarcastically asked them whether they wanted it to shoot at larks.*[33]

Of course this was all twisted nonsense, as Sarsfield knew full well. But as Maxwell was one of Tyrconnell's party, it would not profit him to say so. He knew that Maxwell was one of those who had insisted that Saint-Ruth level the defences and, in all probability, he also knew that having seen the assault troops collecting on the far bank, Maxwell had demanded speedy reinforcements from Saint-Ruth but had been sent the ridiculous reply that if he was afraid, he could be replaced by an officer who was not.

The fall of Athlone cannot be attributed to treachery, but to a terrible complacency. 'Here the old proverb was verified, that security dwells next door to ruin.'[35] And Sarsfield knew that this cardinal military sin was committed by the vain, strutting and insufferably rude Frenchman from whom he was obliged to take his orders. Now that Tyrconnell had been hounded out, there was no turning back. Saint-Ruth was the generalissimo and Sarsfield was on notice that stormy days lay ahead.

On the same afternoon that Athlone fell, Saint-Ruth ordered the Irish army to march off towards Limerick. As he had not expected to lose the town he had not yet worked out his next move. He rode off ahead of his men to select a place where he could make a stand, and the best place that he could find was at

---

* As his subsequent career proved, Maxwell was certainly no traitor. Ginckel learnt from several conversations with him that he was 'a man of merit and understanding', and had him taken to Dublin with orders that he be strictly guarded.[34]

the bridge over the River Suck at Ballinasloe. But it soon became apparent that the Irish army was in a bad state. The soldiers had begun to desert. Just as had been the case at the Boyne, the majority of them were now ordered to retreat before they had fired a shot. Stevens noted that 'such a panic fear has seized our men that the very noise of ten horsemen would have dispersed as many of our battalions, above half the soldiers scattering by the way without any other thing but their own apprehensions to fright them'. While he was at Ballinasloe, Saint-Ruth took stock of the situation. On the positive side, the English had not followed him; on the negative side, over half of his infantry had disappeared.

Saint-Ruth was a very frustrated man. The enemy had, right under his nose, just achieved one of the most important moves of the war and he had found himself powerless to stop or punish them although if he had taken the correct precautions it all could have been so easily prevented. There grew from his frustration a great determination to confront Ginckel and fight a battle. To say the least, his general officers were unhappy about the plan. Their unease grew when they heard that Saint-Ruth had received a letter from Tyrconnell. Several of them now felt that the old man had been treated rather shabbily, and were now more sympathetic to any advice that he might give. The viceroy instructed Saint-Ruth to return to Limerick, now better fortified than ever, and to defend the town as it had been defended last year. The season was already advanced and the English would be forced to fight through another winter during which time even more French supplies would arrive.

Instructions or no instructions, Saint-Ruth was determined to get the Irish to fight a pitched battle on the ground of his choosing. He was, according to O'Kelly, 'sensible of the affront that he had received at Athlone and was longing for an opportunity to wash away that stain by some notable action'.[36]

Although several officers agreed with Saint-Ruth, especially when they learnt that Tyrconnell disapproved, the majority of the council were against the idea and they were led by a man who could not be accused of being faint-hearted or anxious to avoid bloodshed. He was Patrick Sarsfield, the most successful of the Irish soldiers present. He found himself in what was to him the unique position of agreeing with Tyrconnell. He knew how to keep the English at bay and he knew how to use Irish soldiers to the best effect. He had done so since William had reached Limerick eleven months ago. The way not to do it was to face the might of the freshly equipped English army in a pitched battle. His argument was this:

> Ginckel's army is more numerous and much better disciplined, being composed for the most part of veteran troops whom William drew to his service not only out of Germany, Denmark, Sweden and the Netherlands, but also a considerable party of Protestants out of France, bred up in arms and inured to war. (The Irish army) is inferior in number and discipline, ill-clad and ill-fed, without pay and much discouraged by the loss of Athlone.[37]

The French themselves were not united behind Saint-Ruth. His second in command, Lieutenant General d'Usson, was firmly opposed to the idea of facing Ginckel in battle and noted that Saint-Ruth's plan had greatly dismayed the Irish officers. Saint-Ruth made arrangements to have him packed off to Galway.[38]

Sarsfield's strategy, which was the popular strategy, was to conduct the war as it had been conducted since the Boyne: to garrison and fortify Limerick and Galway, and keep a large mobile force of cavalry and dragoons under his command to threaten any attempt to siege either place. While Ginckel would be engaged in a siege of Galway which 'would keep him long in play',[39] Sarsfield could cross the Shannon into Munster or Leinster and create havoc in those areas under Williamite control. It had been Sarsfield's dream throughout the winter. While Ginckel was occupied in Connaught anything would be possible. 'The Irish might have time enough, after the plundering and taking of Dublin (a rich city without any strength) to return to the relief of Galway'.[40] If Ginckel tried to follow him, he could easily get back into Connaught by way of Limerick. Either way, Ginckel would be forced to withdraw as pitifully as his master had done from Limerick. Ginckel simply did not have the strength to contain the Irish cavalry, and did not have the strength to besiege Limerick and Galway at once. Every day that Ginckel lost, the French supplies were a day nearer. Sarsfield's plan was to ensure one result, that the war would continue into 1692. Saint-Ruth was outvoted. Those more experienced than he in Irish warfare won the day.

The officers began their preparations. D'Usson was sent off to prepare Galway for the coming of the part of the army that he was to command. Wauchope, still badly bruised, was dispatched to join Tyrconnell in Limerick. Sarsfield was sent on ahead to Loughrea to supervise the arrangements being made there to provide for the troops that were to follow. The army prepared to divide itself and march to each of the two garrisons.

There is an amusing account of Sarsfield's visit to Loughrea given in the very hostile memoirs of Lord Ronsele.*[41] Ronsele was a native of Bruges who had married an Englishwoman and settled in Ireland in 1687, eventually settling in Shrule. During the war he took his wife and young children to Galway where he remained until May 1691 when he got Tyrconnell's pass to take his family and household by way of Banagher 'to the enemy's quarter'. Once a Roman Catholic, Ronsele had converted and had, according to his narrative, formed a great dislike for the old religion. During his stay in Galway he had been accused of spying for the English and providing them with a map of the town's defences. He heard that this accusation had been made to Sarsfield who had without making any enquiries ordered that he be placed under house arrest. Despite the fact that by his own admission Ronsele had

---

*   Anthony Adornes (or Adorni or Adorno), Count Ronsele was a scion of what he described as 'one of the most illustrious families in Italy'. He also claimed to be entitled to style himself Baron Corthny as this title had been conferred on his ancestor by James III of Scotland.

helped some Williamite prisoners seize a ship and escape, he was furious: 'They had no reason at all for it: only that they were a malicious, spiteful and unworthy people'. He also heard that when it was suggested to Sarsfield that he had been unfairly treated, Sarsfield had retorted: 'A pox on him!'

By his own account, Ronsele only ever saw Sarsfield twice in his life.

> I remember to have met with Sarsfield accidentally in Galway, three months before the first time I was arrested, and felt such extraordinary emotions in my body that I thought that the fever was coming upon me, and wished the man in the middle of the sea. And as I came home I could not forbear telling my wife that I had seen a man who certainly would do me some mischief though I had only seen him a moment as he was coming out of the church.

The second time was, of course, less happy for Ronsele. Clasping Tyrconnell's pass he had taken his family and servants from Galway and had travelled as far as the outskirts of Loughrea when the axle broke on his coach. Ronsele was forced to stay in Loughrea while repairs were carried out. He could not have been there at a worse time.

In the hope that he would be allowed to continue his journey to the east Ronsele visited Sarsfield's headquarters in the town 'more out of fear than love'. Sarsfield, he wrote, 'standing behind a chair received me very basely, neither moving nor speaking one word to me'. Unfortunately for Ronsele, Lord Clanricarde, who had been the governor of Galway during his stay there, was with Sarsfield and reminded him that Ronsele had been accused of preparing a plan of Galway's defences for the enemy. The adjutant of Galway was called into the room and was able to confirm that there had been trouble with Ronsele before. Sarsfield ordered Ronsele to go with the adjutant, and instead of leaving the room quietly Ronsele went out 'murmuring at this new extravagancy'. Sarsfield called him back 'and made me this following base speech':

> *You are an impudent man to go to the enemy: I'll prove it to your face that you have made the map of Galway, and that you have kept ill company there,* and reproaching me *that I would go away in state with twenty horses.* And when I did offer to speak he would not hear me, but ending his lying discourse, he said (with his accustomed phlegmatic countenance): *Go, go, Master Ronsele, go your ways.**

---

*   Ronsele wrote: 'I know that several people have observed, if one throws a stick at a dog he commonly revenges himself (especially if it be an ill conditioned dog) upon that piece of wood, biting it with great rage because he cannot catch or dares not assault the person who has offended him. I apply this to Sarsfield, who (having made himself, against justice and reason, the great gossip of Connaught) was as mad as a dog because the English had taken Athlone, and not knowing how to appraise his rage and to revenge him on the English who were out of his reach, nor how to excuse himself to King James his master, he vented his furious malice on a stranger who had never offended him nor any of his malicious train.'

Ronsele could have forgiven Sarsfield for anything except addressing him as 'master'. He was descended from 'one of the most illustrious families in Italy' who had been counts of the Empire for seven hundred years. He wrote that Sarsfield knew (although one cannot believe this) that Ronsele had been a Knight of Malta and that to have been such a knight in Bruges one needed proof of sixteen quarters of nobility. To address such a nobleman as 'master' was taken as the most stinging of insults, especially as Ronsele was now reduced to having almost nothing left to him in this world except his social rank. The two men never met again, but Ronsele's narrative is filled with references to the 'barbarous' Sarsfield 'the pretended captain-general of Ireland' and of Sarsfield's 'diabolical malice'. Before leaving this digression, it should be mentioned that of all the documents referred to in the preparation of this volume, this is the most hostile to Sarsfield. There is no evidence of Sarsfield harbouring reciprocal feelings, in fact there is every reason to believe that he forgot both Ronsele's name and face within a day of their meeting.

CHAPTER XVII

Aughrim

Saint-Ruth: Thanks to the saints! Our force the foes o'er power!
Great heaven's just, the victory is ours!
Let shouts of joy re-echo through the air!
Fly, fly, pursue them! Charge them in the rear!
Ruin upon them and their centre waits.
We can now drive them up to Dublin's gates.
Robert Ashton, *The Battle of Aughrim*, IV. i, 1770

WHILE SARSFIELD set about his work in Loughrea, there was every indication that another winter's war approached. It certainly would have done so had it not been for Saint-Ruth. He still commanded the army, and Tyrconnell, technically the only man in Ireland who could overrule him, was a long way away. Saint-Ruth was confident that he was the best general in the country and that he could defeat Ginckel whatever reservations his Irish officers might have about their troops. He also knew what would await him in France should he retire now having achieved nothing except the loss of Athlone. His ambitions would be shattered. The fear of what his master, Louis XIV, would do to him was perhaps greater than his fear of Ginckel and the English army.

While the Irish camped at Ballinasloe, Saint-Ruth's confidence and determination grew. The deserters began to return, and the army's morale strengthened. He busied himself in watching the enemy and exploring the countryside for a suitable place to do battle. Ignoring Sarsfield's warning that he would endanger the whole kingdom, he found the place that he had been searching for. It was a hill five miles away called Kilcommodon. At the base of Kilcommodon Hill lay a small village comprising nothing more than a ruined castle, a church and a few poor cabins. The name of that village was Aughrim.

Kilcommodon Hill stands by the road that leads from Athlone and Ballinasloe to Loughrea and Galway. If Ginckel was to march westwards his route would take him straight through Aughrim. The hill is about a mile long and runs from north to south. While his opponents were out of the way, Saint-Ruth decided to position the army on the eastern slope to face the English advance. At the foot of the hill was a wide band of bog behind which the Irish could establish themselves, and through the bog ran a wide stream. The only approaches over the bog from the east were at the northern and southern ends of the hill, over a paved causeway and through a ford respectively. Better still, the causeway over which the main route to Galway ran was wide enough for no more than two horseman to ride abreast, and lay only some forty yards from the walls of Aughrim Castle. The position was perfect. Saint-Ruth resolved to carry out his plan and ordered the army to march, not to Galway or Limerick as had been expected, but to Aughrim. They arrived on 8 July 1691 and began preparing their positions, while Sarsfield breathlessly galloped in from Loughrea to ask what the devil was going on. He had been completely wrong-footed by Saint-Ruth's change of plan, and was now forced to do as the general commanded.

In the meanwhile, the Williamite army had been in no fit state for a rapid advance. The siege of Athlone had stretched Ginckel's resources to the limit. The massive bombardment had used up most of his powder and ammunition, and a fresh munitions convoy was not due to reach Athlone until 11 July. During the days following Saint-Ruth's departure, Ginckel's mind had been concentrated on consolidating his position rather than pursuing the enemy. His immediate fear was of cavalry raids behind Athlone. He was so short of the necessary materials of war that another Ballyneety would prevent the army from moving at all. Cavalry detachments were sent to guard the Shannon against Sarsfield. Four regiments were marched off to Kilkenny to guard the Dublin road. In Athlone his men set about the task of patching up the town's defences and trying to rebuild what they could from the ruins to give themselves some protection from the elements. There was still a great fear that a French army had landed and in any event Ginckel was uncertain as to what Saint-Ruth was intending to do. Deserters brought in varying accounts of his movements, but the Irish cavalry prevented any English patrols from getting near the main army. Ginckel's intelligence suggested that Irish had marched to Galway. He simply did not know what they were up to.

The English army eventually edged forward to Ballinasloe to find it deserted. Ginckel was satisfied that the Irish had gone, and he prepared his men for the twenty mile march to Portumna so as to secure the Shannon from Athlone to Lough Derg. But they never went, for on 11 July, three days after the Irish had first reached the place, he discovered that they were waiting for him at Aughrim.

Now that he had found the position that he wanted, Saint-Ruth's only reservation about facing the English in a pitched battle was the morale of the Irish troops. Athlone had been a great loss to them. For the first time in the war the main English army was in Connaught, and although rumours circulated about Maxwell's treachery and d'Usson's inefficiency, Saint-Ruth was still the general that had lost them their fortress on the Shannon. Saint-Ruth was satisfied that he had the means to defeat Ginckel, but if despondency was going to prevent the Irish from giving of their best, the outcome could only be disaster. He consequently set about trying to put things right. He went to great lengths to make himself personally popular with the troops, and in this he succeeded in a remarkably short time. The men responded well to his belligerent confidence. His attitude towards the enemy was an inspiration to all. He also appeared to have a pleasing quality that no other Frenchman possessed: he had faith in the Irish. He made a public display of being 'very kind and familiar with the Irish officers whom formerly he had treated with disrespect and contempt'. He made a point 'to caress the soldiers, though a little before he would hang a dozen of them in the morning'. The Irish were flattered and cheered. Arrangements were made to involve the clergy in inspiring the troops with a sense of national and religious fervour. The deserters began returning to the colours. By the time Ginckel's scouts had found the Irish at Aughrim on 11 July, they were ready to give battle.

When he knew that the battle was approaching, Saint-Ruth addressed his troops in a last effort to inspire them to fight. The Irish were fighting for the Church, for their country, their families, their liberty and their property. It was a struggle not only between the native Irish and the invader, but between the forces of the Holy Faith and of heresy, a war that he had been fighting for many years.

> Stand to it therefore my dears, and bear no longer the reproaches of the heretics who brand you with cowardice, and you may be assured that King James will love and reward you, Louis the Great will protect you, all good Catholics will applaud you, I myself will command you, the church will pray for you, your posterity will bless you, God will make you all saints and his holy mother will lay you in her bosom.[1]

At dawn on Sunday 12 July 1691, Ginckle's army moved out of Ballinasloe. Leaving all their tents and baggage behind them, the infantry marched over the bridge onto the Aughrim road while the cavalry waded through the Suck. Ginckle advanced cautiously as he had no information as to what the Irish planned for him, and the landscape was shrouded in a thick morning mist. A mile from Aughrim Castle, Ginckle's scouts led his general staff off the road to the south. They were able to ride quickly across a series of scrubby ridges that together form the hill named Urrachree. When they reached the last ridge, the ground to their front fell away. Before them lay six hundred yards of flat bog beyond which stood the long, low hill of Kilcommodon. With the mist now dispersed, the grey coats of the Irish infantry were clearly visible in the morning sun.

Squinting through his field-glass, Ginckel could see the enemy arrayed before him. They were clearly visible in the village of Aughrim to his right, and in lines stretching southwards for a mile until on his left their formations disintegrated into the trees south of Kilcommodon. Kilcommodon Hill itself was mostly bare of trees. It was covered in coarse grass, bracken and brambles. Along the crest of the hill was the Irish camp. No effort had been made to take down the tents. Saint-Ruth was making an exhibition of his confidence. 'It spoke his resolution to conquer or die'.[2] Ginckel's scouts brought back the news that they had not been able to find a way through the bog. It was clear that the only comfortable crossing points were where the Irish had concentrated their men; in the village of Aughrim and at the southern end of the bog. By the time that Ginckel's infantry had joined him on Urrachree he had seen all that he needed to. It was a daunting sight. Story, who saw it himself, wrote as follows:

> The enemy's camp lay along the ridge of a hill . . . from thence to the bog below was nigh half a mile, and this cut into a great many small enclosures which the enemy had ordered so as to make a communication from one of them to another, and had lined all these very thick with small shot: this showed a great deal of dexterity in M. Saint-Ruth in making choice of such a piece of ground as nature itself could not furnish him with a better, considering all circumstances; for he knew that the Irish naturally loved a breastwork between them and bullets, and here they were fitted to the purpose with hedges and ditches to the very edge of the bog.[3]

Saint-Ruth had arranged his army so as to take full advantage of the terrain. Although his often ill-disciplined infantry was vulnerable to cavalry attacks, Ginckel's cavalry would only be able to approach him across the causeway through Aughrim village or across the ford on the other side of Kilcommodon. With this in mind he placed a division of cavalry at each of these approaches and spread his infantry along the hill in between. His plan was simple. He wanted to commit the English to facing him full on. They would attempt to attack his right over the ford and his centre through the bog. They would fail. They would not attack his left as the causeway was too narrow and was dominated by Aughrim Castle. After the English had failed in their attack, his left wing of cavalry would advance over the causeway and take the English in the flank. It would then be time for a general advance.

The Irish army was divided in four divisions,[4] each commanded by one of the four major-generals present: John Hamilton, William Dorrington, Dominic Sheldon and Patrick Sarsfield. Two of the divisions were made up almost entirely of infantry. They were placed in the centre and formed up in two defensive lines behind a series of ditches and hedges. The Irish had now spent three full days on the hill and had industriously prepared their positions. The ditches that would face an English advance were prepared so that the English would always be exposed as they came forward, while the Irish would remain under cover. These two divisions were commanded by Hamilton and Dorrington, but were to be largely supervised by Saint-Ruth who intended to keep his position in the centre. Behind the centre, hidden beyond the hill, was positioned the only reserve that Saint-Ruth could afford to keep back, a solitary cavalry regiment commanded by Lord Galmoy. Although he did not know it, the troops that Ginckel could see through his field-glass were all the troops that the Irish had.

The other two divisions, made up of the remaining infantry and very nearly all the cavalry and dragoons, were positioned one on each wing. On the right wing was the division commanded by Sarsfield. It was made up of two brigades, each of cavalry and dragoons mixed, and like the infantry was positioned in two defensive lines. Sarsfield's task was to prevent the enemy from crossing the ford. Of all the divisional commanders, he had the most difficult task as on both sides of the stream there was firm open ground. This in effect made the right wing Saint-Ruth's most vulnerable position as his cavalry could well be outflanked, and if that happened the entire centre would be in grave danger. Consequently, Sarsfield had most of the army's horsemen under his command. His task was simply to guard the ford and prevent Ginckel's cavalry from getting near the Irish infantry. If the enemy got through the ford, which was expected, they were to be kept close to the water and prevented from manoeuvring effectively. Initially de Tessé, Saint-Ruth's lieutenant-general and a cavalry commander of more experience than Sarsfield, was also posted to the right wing, but events were to take him elsewhere.

Saint-Ruth considered his left wing to be his strongest position. Securely protected by the walls of Aughrim Castle were Colonel Walter Burke's two hundred musketeers who commanded the approach from the causeway. The castle, although ruined, was a sturdy but small rectangular construction measuring some forty by fifty yards. It was encircled by a stone wall and some new breastworks with which Burke had lined his men. Around the castle, where the narrow causeway reached the Irish side, two of Dorrington's infantry regiments were posted in and close to the village and churchyard to prevent any cavalry from crossing. Behind them, on the open ground, were four regiments of dragoons commanded by Brigadier Henry Luttrell, and some way behind them, so that they had room to charge, were four cavalry regiments. The whole left wing was commanded by Dominic Sheldon whose instructions were simply to hold back his cavalry in preparation for the final charge.

Only at noon, after he had studiously inspected the Irish positions along Kilcommodon Hill, was Ginckel able to start making any sort of plan. He had been occupied in sending out scouts to test the ground to his front and to observe the Irish army from different angles in the hope that Saint-Ruth had left some indication of how he was planning to receive an English attack. He could see the Irish moving down and along the hill to their positions. It was Sunday and they had been celebrating mass at which the priests had urged them to think only of death or glory.

The English were prevented from marching quietly into position at the edge of the bog as Sarsfield had sent out cavalry patrols and dragoons across the ford in front of his division. As Ginckel's horsemen spread out to inspect the land they came under fire. Skirmishing began and the Williamites were forced to try and clear the ground in front of them so that the army could position itself in proper order. The vanguard had to call upon more men to chase off the Irish skirmishers. Orders were sent forward to the English troops to hold back, but the fighting increased in intensity and more squadrons were sucked in the action. From then on the firing did not stop until well after nightfall. 'If the dragoons had obeyed their orders', wrote the Englishman, Major Robert Tempest, 'and had not fired and fallen upon the enemy, which was positively against the general's orders, the battle would not have been. Such small accidents sometimes hazard great bodies'.[5]

This was exactly what Saint-Ruth wanted. The skirmishers were merely bait in the trap. The enemy had engaged his army on his right just as he had hoped, and now they would have to try and dislodge Sarsfield's division. Ginckel's tactics were dictated by the position of the bog. He had no choice but to follow the same deployment as the Irish, with his cavalry positioned on each flank. Facing Sarsfield was the continental cavalry; the Dutch, the Huguenot and the Danish regiments (the latter made up mostly of Germans). Next to them and facing Hamilton were the continental infantry brigades, and beyond them facing Dorrington stood the English infantry. On Ginckel's right wing, facing the causeway and Aughrim Castle, the English cavalry formed up.

The two armies that faced each other were numerically about the same. Each general commanded some twenty thousand men. If there was a slight advantage in numbers it was held by Ginckel, but in his strength lay his weakness as the Irish had proportionally more infantry than him. Ginckel's superiority lay in his cavalry and his artillery, but while the Irish stood behind the bog his cavalry was of limited value. It would be impossible for his cavalry to cross the causeway while the Irish infantry occupied Aughrim village and the castle. Ginckel hurriedly called a council of war. His staff were undecided, but Mackay, the hero of Athlone, had a firm plan. It was clear that Saint-Ruth feared for his right wing. That was where most of his cavalry was. If a major attack were made on Sarsfield's division, Saint-Ruth would have to support him with regiments from the left. If this attack was supported with an infantry attack across the bog, Saint-Ruth would be forced to further weaken his left wing. If the infantry could establish themselves on the far side, even for a short while, other regiments could then move at Saint-Ruth's left, clear the causeway, the village and the castle, and open the way for the English cavalry to cross over and take the Irish infantry in the flank. No one could think of a better plan. Ginckel ordered the twelve squadrons of cavalry that made up Ruvigny's and Sir John Lanier's regiments over to his left wing. The main battle was about to begin. The target was Sarsfield.

At about six o'clock, driving the skirmishers in front of them, the first line of Danish, Dutch and Huguenot cavalry trotted forwards into the ford. Riding kneecap to kneecap they ploughed through the water in a solid phalanx pressed together by the horses on the outside whose riders were trying to avoid the deeper water and mud. The fifteen hundred men of the regiments of La Forest, Donop, Luistadt, Boncour and Monpouillan surged up from the stream onto the western bank. As they did so, Sarsfield's men were on them. It was the most serious cavalry clash of the war. The earth shook from the pounding of thousands of hooves. Hundreds of pistols were discharged at close quarters before the troopers drew their swords and stood up in their stirrups to charge, roaring their lungs out. The air rang with the clash of steel and the screams of the wounded horses. The ground near the waterside was a mess of bodies and threshing beasts. The foreigners could not find the space in which to charge. The exit from the ford was too narrow for them to get by the Irish cavalry and was bordered by the bog.

Irish dragoons, who had long left their mounts, waded into the mud where they were safe from being charged down, and fired and fired again into the enemy caught between the bog and the water and the cavalry.

The Irish were in too strong a position. Portland's regiment of horse came dashing through the water to add weight to the attack and once the full shock of the Irish charge had subsided, the Williamite troops were able to push them back by sheer weight of numbers, but only back as far as Sarsfield's second line of cavalry, and there they stood, hacking at each other. There was no going forward. The two sides separated. The continental troops had gained the ford, but their problem was what to do next. They were exposed to the Irish cannon and under fire from the dismounted dragoons. To the front was Sarsfield's cavalry flanked by his infantry waiting in the tree line. The only way out seemed to be backwards. Standing still in constant danger while Sarsfield marshalled his men, they could only wait for someone else to take the initiative.

Major General Hugh Mackay had sent out scouts in the form of skirmishing parties into the bogs before the cavalry had made a move. The reports came back that it was passable for the infantry. While La Forest crossed the stream to meet Sarsfield, Mackay ordered his men forward. He instructed his officers to do no more than simply cross the bog and establish a foothold on the far side. To his foot soldiers the crossing was a nightmare. The ground 'was all cut up by the bog and by hedges and banks.' As they advanced their line began to get more and more ragged. Slipping and cursing they waded through mud and water up to their waists. As they reached open ground, the Irish, from the cover of ditches and hedges, opened fire. The line deteriorated further.

The Irish had been lying flat on their faces to avoid presenting themselves as targets for the superior fire power of the English artillery. To the advancing troops they were often invisible. Describing the advance of a Huguenot regiment, Story wrote that 'several were doubtful whether they [the Irish] had any men in that place or not, but they were convinced of it at last, for no sooner were the French and the rest got within twenty yards or less of the ditches than the Irish fired most furiously upon them.'

The English ran forward into the smoke, reached the hedges and fired back, but the Irish had gone. Mackay's troops had reached their objective, but before they could organise themselves they realised their positions were untenable. They were still in full view of the Irish who had merely pulled back to the next hedge line. The Irish kept firing. There was no way that the English could crouch where they were while the enemy were still at such close range and behind such good cover. Some officers were shouting for their men to form up and advance in careful order. Other officers were already sprinting ahead

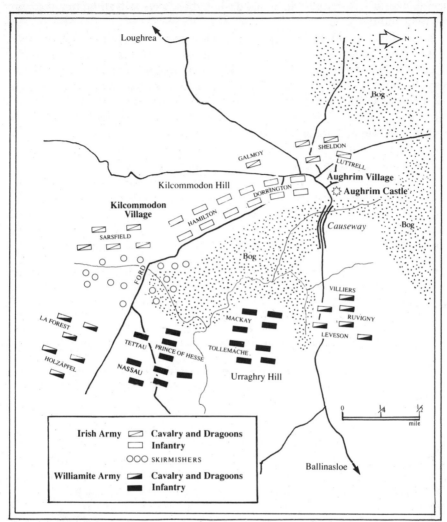

Map V: The Battle of Aughrim, 12 July 1691

urging their troops forward in a mad dash. Others were still struggling through the mud and the water.

One thing was clear to the officers. There was no staying there on the edge of the bog. They must either retreat or go on. Ignoring Mackay's orders, Colonel Erle knew what he had to do. He shouted to his men that there was no way out but to be brave. And brandishing his sword he led them on into the Irish muskets.* His men reached the next hedge to find that the Irish had run off again to a further hedgerow. The English were in the same position as before, exposed and under heavy fire. The officers again took the bait and saw no alternative but to press on. The Irish gave them another volley and fled. Cursing and roaring the English gave chase up the hill.

The English troops were by now exhausted. They were also wet through, caked in mud and, worst of all, they were scattered and disorganised. Nonetheless, they were urged on by the twin frustrating facts that whenever they took an Irish position they found themselves with no cover, and they still had not got to grips with the enemy. One infantry officer described it thus:

> When we, on the right, attacked them, they gave us their fire and away they ran to the next ditches and we, scrambling over the first ditch, made after them to the next from where they gave us another scattering fire and away they ran to other ditches behind them, we still pursuing them from one ditch to another until we had drove them out of four or five rows of these ditches into an open plain where was some of their horse drawn up. Here in climbing these ditches and still following them from one to another, no one can imagine we could possibly keep our order, and here in this hurry there was no less than six battalions so intermingled together that we were at a loss what to do.[6]

The Irish had waited for this minute, and knew exactly what to do. They, who had appeared to have little more fighting spirit than a flock of sheep, were now in perfect order. They charged. The English were in no position to oppose them. Back they went, over those four or five rows of ditches and into the bog, with their reserves pulling back in front of them. The attack had failed and failed very badly.

It was not only the one brigade, as Mackay had intended, that had crossed the bog. He had ordered eight regiments over. He personally led the four regiments on the right of his division and held them back when they got beyond the causeway, but the other four English regiments, those of Colonels Erle, Brewer, Herbert and Creighton had just gone too far. They had been taken in the flank and beaten back. In the meantime the prince of Hesse's brigade of Dutch and Danish regiments had followed Mackay over. Ginckel had mis-read the situation and ordered the continental troops forward in support. They were also forced to withdraw in some disorder. This left Mackay's four Ulster and

---

* Thomas Erle was twice captured by the Irish and was twice freed. He received severe though not fatal wounds for which he was compensated with fourteen days' pay (a total of £16.16s.0d.).

English regiments exposed, and he had no alternative but to order a retreat. The left wing of the advancing infantry, La Mellonière's brigade of Huguenots and Danes, were, as Tyrconnell later heard, 'cut to pieces'. Their losses were the worst suffered by the Williamite troops. John Hamilton unleashed his brigade in a ferocious attack as the foreigners tried to establish themselves on the firm ground. The Irish had charged straight into them, wielding their long muskets like clubs and had chased them not only into the bog but across it.

Back at the ford, the Huguenot Major-General La Forest became painfully aware that his division was doing no good. His position had only improved in that the Irish artillery was now concentrating on La Mellonière's infantry. He could see that he was desperately needed to cut through the Irish cavalry and support the main infantry attack. This had proved to be impossible, but he had noted that the ground to his left was firmer. He decided to attempt to outflank Sarsfield, but this called for reinforcements. The second division of continental cavalry was ordered through the ford behind him to support his next move. Their commander, Major-General Willem van Holzäpfel, moved to the front to lead his men alongside La Forest's. The foreigners charged a second time and there was the same chaos as before. Sarsfield had also been reinforced by some of Sheldon's cavalry from the left wing where there had been no action. Holzäpfel was killed in the melée. La Forest's men simply could not manoeuvre enough in the confined space to be effective. They surged forward, they were halted, and they were beaten back the ford. The two sides parted, and the Irish returned to their original positions. La Forest had failed again even with twice the number of men. He had now taken heavy losses and was back where he started. Worst of all, he was painfully aware that his failure had contributed to the disastrous defeat of the infantry brigade on his right.
In the meanwhile the allied infantry had achieved little. Ginckel responded to each reverse by ordering more reserves forward. There were three attacks across the bog, all of which ended in failure. The Irish not only stopped them, but chased the English back through the bog onto the eastern side, at one time over-running a field battery. Saint-Ruth was jubilant. The battle was going to plan. The enemy had been pushed back across the whole front. 'Le jour est à nous, mes enfants!' he shouted to the men around him. 'The day is ours, my boys!'[7]

As Ginckel sat on his horse inspecting the scene through his field-glass, he was not met with a pleasing sight. Although his continental cavalry had got over the ford, Sarsfield had prevented them from going any further. They were now just standing in the open, praying that each successive cannon ball fired at them would hit someone else. The Irish centre had held and thrown back the allied infantry. On Ginckel's right, beyond Aughrim Castle, the fighting had been less serious, but Mackay's men had still been forced to return. The only part of Ginckel's army that had not yet been tried was his English cavalry who were still awaiting their orders on his right. If they could get over the causeway by the castle, and if the infantry could provide them with sufficient cover while they deployed, then matters well may change. Besides, since Sarsfield had effectively prevented La Forest from moving forwards, the only piece of open ground accessible by horse was now beyond the causeway.

The trouble was this; Mackay's infantry had not done their job. They were meant to push back the Irish infantry facing them and secure the end of the causeway so as to allow Scravenmoer and Ruvigny to lead their cavalry and dragoons over to engage the Irish horse. Although Mackay had personally led four battalions across the bog over to the other side of the causeway, now that he had returned the Irish were back in their original firing positions. The troops on each side of the bog were very much where they had started from. All, that is, except two battalions of Irish infantry. And they made all the difference.

At the start of the battle Saint-Ruth had placed two regiments of foot by the causeway in a position where they could stop any advance by the English along or alongside it. During the great infantry attack these two battalions had been withdrawn at Dorrington's request to support the Irish centre where the infantry battle had been the fiercest. This move had not gone undetected by Ginckel. There was now a real opportunity to get some horse across the causeway.

Mackay was of the same mind. Only one thing could alter the situation now and that was the cavalry. The cavalry officers were less than enthusiastic. They could not advance through a bog and they did not know where the bog ended. Mackay ordered one of the officers to check the ground. He pointed out where he wanted the cavalry to advance. The officer, seeing that he would have to go within easy musket range of Aughrim Castle and village, refused to do any such thing. Mackay was desperate. He galloped off in a rage to do the job himself, made his horse take a wall without seeing the soft ground on the other side, and was thrown off into the bog. When his officers next saw him Mackay was soaked through and covered in mud. Although his strongly held Christian beliefs prevented him from swearing, he was furious. For the honour of the English nation, he told them, for the good of liberty and religion and all that they held dear, get over and turn the Irish flank.[8]

Ginckel's order reached Ruvigny who commanded the cavalry on the right wing. Ruvigny ordered Villiers's brigade to advance, and then joined them himself. It was a great risk, every bit as hazardous and as desperate as the attack on Athlone. Villiers had by then only six squadrons of cavalry and dragoons left as the rest had been detached to help La Forest, but if they could make it along the causeway, the rest of the cavalry could follow.

In Aughrim Castle, Colonel Walter Burke saw the English coming. His men made ready as the path from the causeway passed only forty yards away from their firing positions. By themselves they did not have the fire power to stop any large body of cavalry getting past them, but they certainly intended to thin them out. They started firing. The cavalry sped forward. English dragoons dismounted and returned fire with their carbines to keep the Irish heads below the parapet. Every loophole and window in the castle belched fire and smoke.

Then disaster struck. After the earlier exchange of fire with Mackay's men, the garrison's supplies had been seriously diminished. Behind the walls men began breaking open fresh ammunition boxes and distributing balls to the musketeers. To their horror they found that the new ammunition was for English muskets. It was of too large a bore to be fired from their French flint-locks. They could not even get it into the muzzles. The scene was desperate. As more and more cavalry rode by, the Irish were looking about frantically for something to load their muskets with. They tore brass buttons off their coats, broke up ram rods and even stuffed pebbles into their muzzles. Anything to keep up a ragged fire from the walls. Ruvigny and the English swept past; Lord Oxford's regiment of horse, Villiers's horse and Leveson's dragoons. Their officers sighed with relief when they found that they had crossed the causeway without having had their squadrons decimated by fire from the castle, but when they got beyond the castle, they found that they had even greater reason to be relieved. There was no one to meet them. Dorrington had still not replaced the two battalions that had been left to guard the road.

On the open ground beyond the causeway, the nearest Irish troops were the dragoons of Henry Luttrell's brigade. It had not been intended that Luttrell should guard the causeway as that was a job for the infantry. Charitably it must be assumed that he was not in a position to stop Ruvigny's men from getting over the causeway. His men opened fire at the leading squadrons, but he desperately needed cavalry support. He urgently alerted Sheldon who stood with now perhaps no more than two regiments of horse further up and around the hill. Luttrell pulled his men back to await reinforcements. Ruvigny ordered a charge. Luttrell's men panicked and went further back, and in the meantime fresh squadrons of English cavalry arrived over the causeway and formed up on the Irish side.

Ginckel was delighted with Ruvigny's success. But he could see that the English cavalry had still not secured their position over there. It was now a priority to send reinforcements before the Irish cavalry could beat them back. He issued orders for some of the continental cavalry facing Sarsfield to gallop over to the right wing.

Saint-Ruth was, to say the least, surprised at this development, but to him it was not fatal. He had enough cavalry on the left wing not just to check Ruvigny's men, but to annihilate them. Plunket, who was with Saint-Ruth, described him as being in an elated mood. He dispatched gallopers off to Galmoy and Sheldon. The left wing of his horse was to charge the English squadrons 'which he knew was easily done, and therefore he continued his joy, as being sure of his point'.[9] Saint-Ruth ordered the life guards, who were posted on Sarsfield's wing, to follow him and he rode along the hill to prepare his men for what he intended to be the greatest and most effective cavalry charge of the war. His last words were: 'They are beaten, let us beat them to the purpose'. As he led his men down a small hillock a cannon ball fired from across the bog took his head off.*

The life guards halted in their tracks. To them it was as if the battle had lost its importance. Measures were taken to ensure that news of St Ruth's death did not spread. This was a mistake, as around the ridge of the hill Sheldon's men were nervously shifting in their saddles while they waited for the general and the guards. To their front they could see the English cavalry, now equal to them in numbers, and still with more reinforcements coming over the causeway. The English moved into a position where they were between the Irish cavalry and the infantry. Sheldon still did not move. The exit from the causeway was in Dorrington's sector, not his. He could not move without instructions. He became worried. Where was the general? No one told him. Sheldon awaited his orders.

Without Saint-Ruth the army was paralysed.[10] He had, probably because he had fallen out with his officers in insisting on giving battle, neglected to tell anyone what his plans were. This was Saint-Ruth's greatest crime. 'When the commander was killed the password and order of battle had been committed to none of the leaders, not to Lucan himself.'[11]

Luttrell was still without cavalry support. He was rapidly being outnumbered. If he allowed the English to attack him, his men would be wiped out. Ruvigny threatened to do just that. Luttrell ordered a retreat and his dragoons rode off the field of battle. Sheldon could see all this from his position. He now had insufficient men under his command to beat the enemy back. With Luttrell gone, the English concentrated their efforts on him. While Sheldon was faced by the leading regiments of English cavalry, Ruvigny ordered the rest to charge into the Irish infantry. The Irish were slaughtered. Their defences were designed to protect them against an enemy coming up the hill, but now that the enemy was behind them or charging across the hill, the infantry had no more protection against them than if they had been standing in an open meadow. Ginckel gave his infantry their last order to advance. With Sheldon's division now out of the fighting, and Dorrington's division being attacked in the flank by the English cavalry, the Irish army crumbled.

De Tessé, who took over the generalship of the army on Saint-Ruth's death, was taken by surprise by all this. Since before the first English attack, Saint-Ruth had positioned him to the left of centre with Dorrington's divisions.[12] His concern had been the infantry battle to the front. When he heard of Saint-Ruth's

---

*   Inspiring Robert Ashton to write one of the most moving stanzas of his epic poem, *The Battle of Aughrim*:

> Aughrim is lost, the brave St Ruth is dead,
> And all his guards are from the battle fled,
> As he rode down the hill he met his fall,
> And died the victim of a cannon ball.

This poem was Ashton's greatest literary achievement and ran to over twenty-five editions between 1770 and 1840.

death hc did his best to remedy matters, but by then it was too little and too late. The Irish infantry were already running back up the hill to escape. De Tessé rode towards Sarsfield, ordered the first two squadrons of horse that he could find to follow him, and then dashed back to the centre where the leading English cavalry regiments were already between the two Irish lines. There was no other Irish cavalry around. Sheldon had gone. De Tessé knew that his two squadrons were the only ones in a position to slow down the advancing English cavalry. He formed his men up and led the charge himself down the hill. But the English were by then far too numerous. For his bravery de Tessé was shot three times.[13] He was very lucky to live, especially as one pistol shot hit him in the face and another went straight through his cuirass into his chest. No longer in a fit state to command the army, he was led off the field by his aide-de-camp.

Like de Tessé, Sarsfield did not know of the disaster until it was too late to remedy. Ever since the first shots of the battle were fired before noon he had been concentrating on the ford. He had faced two divisions of continental cavalry and had held them back in check. Throughout the entire battle he had denied them any advantage. In some of the fiercest fighting of the day he had driven them back twice. During the battle, no cavalry regiments had suffered more than these continental squadrons. Although they had outnumbered Sarsfield's division from the beginning, even after Holzäpfel's arrival they had still been unable to do much more than stand, just out of musket range, and face the Irish horse and artillery. When Ruvigny's English cavalry had broken through past Sheldon, Sarsfield had known nothing of it. He was 'still expecting his general's orders'. He had no reason to suspect anything until he saw it with his own eyes, and from his position he could see nothing of Sheldon's division as the hill was in the way. Besides, the light was now failing and visibility was further reduced by a 'thick, misty rain', and the noise of the battle to his left was hidden by the artillery and musket fire directed from and against his men. Like Sheldon he had never been told of Saint-Ruth's death, and he knew nothing of the fate that had befallen de Tessé.

There came a time when a glance to his left told him everything. The infantry were giving way all along the line and the English cavalry were charging into them. Ginckel's foot soldiers had again got across the bog and were advancing up Kilcommodon Hill unchecked. The only regiment of Irish cavalry still involved in the fighting was Galmoy's. Sarsfield was faced with a most terrible prospect. Ginckel's cavalry had outnumbered the Irish at the beginning of the battle. Now the contest was to be between Sarsfield and his eight regiments against them all. He could not change the outcome of the conflict. The battle had been lost. But by charging and threatening each enemy formation in turn he could at least hold back Ginckel's cavalry to allow as many of the infantry as possible to get away. That is what he did. Already outnumbered at the ford, Sarsfield had to slow La Forest's advance and at the same time detach what squadrons he could to divert the English horse away from the broken infantry.

By the time Sarsfield was able to respond it was no longer a matter of covering a retreat. The infantry were in full flight. It was a rout. The English had got behind them so that they were all but surrounded. As they ran across the open the English cavalry cut them down. If they stayed behind, the advancing infantry shot them where they crouched, and neither the English nor the continental troops were very interested in taking prisoners. There was the most horrific slaughter. Those Irish foot soldiers who did get away owed their survival to a combination of the night, the mist, the rain, the bogs and the efforts of Sarsfield.

'Colonel Sarsfield', observed the English, 'who commanded the enemy in their retreat, performed miracles, and if he was not killed or taken it was not from any fault of his'.[14] The Irish also noticed that it was Sarsfield who had been their best man to the end: 'Only the earl of Lucan, with some troops thereof, and the Lord of Galmoy, with his regiment, did good service in covering their retreat as prosperously as so small a body could do'.[15] Sarsfield and his men were the first to begin the fighting at Aughrim, and the last to stop.

It was this final stage of the battle that made Aughrim the bloodiest in Irish history. The horrors were graphically described by a Danish eyewitness, Andreas Claudianus:[16]

> At the very top of the hill cavalry were mixed with infantry. The firing was so intense that the ridges seemed to be ablaze. As dusk fell the cavalry began to move away and take flight, abandoning the infantry who in turn threw down their arms, left their colours and ran. Terrible scenes followed as the English fell on the rear of the fugitives. Stricken with terror we saw them fleeing in all directions across the countryside into the mountains, woods, bogs and wildernesses. Like mad people, the women, children and waggoners filled every road weeping and wailing. Worse still was the sight after the battle of the many men and horses too badly wounded to get away, who when attempting to rise fell back unable to bear their own weight. Some, mutilated and in great pain, begged to be put out of their misery, and others coughed out blood and threats, their bloodied weapons frozen in their hands as if in readiness for some future battle. The blood from the dead so covered the ground that one could hardly take a step without slipping. This grisly scene of slaughter remained untouched and unchanged for several days, the horror of which cannot be imagined except by those who saw it.
>
> When the trumpeters sounded the recall, the English returned in triumph, stripping the tack from the horses and the clothes and arms from the men. They then stretched out their weary bodies on the battlefield under the open sky as the tents had not yet arrived, so that for many the bloodied ground was their bed. Others busied themselves in placing corpses as seats in circles around the fires, the light from which lit up the countryside.

'We killed seven thousand of the Irish upon the spot, as was generally believed', wrote George Story, 'and there could not be many fewer for looking amongst the dead three days after when all our men and some of theirs were buried, I reckoned in some small enclosures a hundred and fifty, in others a hundred and twenty, etc, lying most of them by the ditches where they were shot, and the rest from the top of the hill where their camp had been looked like a great flock of sheep scattered up and down the country for about four miles round. And the Irish themselves though they will not allow so many to be killed yet they own that they lost more which they could never have any account of except they stole home privately or else turned rapparees.'

This perhaps exaggerated estimate of the Irish losses was generally believed by the Williamites and in time was also accepted by successive generations of Irishmen. There had been a great and bloody slaughter, but it had not been a one sided battle. The Irish had maintained the advantage through all the heavy fighting up until the time that Villiers's brigade had forced its way past Aughrim Castle and onto the causeway. Story's honest assertion that the thousands of bodies he saw, after they had been stripped naked, scattered up and around Kilcommodon Hill were Irish is not conclusive. On his side he calculated that less than a thousand men had been killed, but his figures are incomplete. Those of Ginckel's regiments who suffered the heaviest casualties were the continental infantry, the Danes, the Dutch and the Huguenots. They had been 'cut to pieces'.[17] Story has it that they had suffered the least of all, with several regiments having no casualties whatsoever. It is clear that the English did not lose as much as their allies, and the English alone probably did not lose a thousand men dead.

Some of the Irish even believed that the Williamites had lost more men than they had, and certainly none of them at the time put their losses as high as seven thousand dead. Plunket wrote that two thousand Irishmen had been killed while the English and foreigners had lost over five thousand. The compiler of King James's memoirs assessed the losses on each side as being four thousand.* But the truth of the matter is that the Irish had no way of assessing their losses as their army had been so completely scattered. Hundreds, perhaps thousands, of them simply deserted after the battle and were never accounted for. It was generally agreed amongst the Williamites, and only they were in a position to know, that there was somewhere in the region of seven or eight thousand corpses left on and around Kilcommodon Hill after the battle. Robert Parker served under Mackay during the fighting, and his figures are, perhaps, to be preferred: The Irish 'had near four thousand killed and above two thousand taken', he wrote, and Ginckel's army lost 'above three thousand killed and wounded'.

* Only one Williamite eyewitness supports this assessment. Robert Stearne, then a subaltern in the same regiment as Richard Kane and Robert Parker, years later wrote of Aughrim: 'Their [the Irish] loss in this battle was not less than 3,000 men killed and wounded and taken. Our loss was great also, amounting to between three and four thousand men killed and wounded.'

Callous though it is to suggest it, the greatest loss to the Irish was in two things that they could ill afford. They lost heavily in their leadership and in their equipment, and these losses severely affected their ability to continue the war. Of their senior officers the Irish lost, as well as Saint-Ruth, two brigadiers and nine colonels killed. Another nine colonels and a brigadier were among the many officers captured by the English, as were two of the four major-generals, Dorrington and Hamilton. The second of these later died from his wounds. These losses were felt keenly by all and not least by Sarsfield. He had not only lost a great number of friends and comrades but his uncle, Colonel Charles Moore, had been killed and of his brothers-in-law, Lord Galway, had been 'dispatched by foreigners after quarter given',[18] and Lord Bophin had been captured. Also among the dead were eighty priests. 'It was the last effort in which the gasping honour of all the Catholic nobility and gentry of the kingdom struggled to do its utmost.'[19]

The loss of equipment was no less serious. The English had overrun the Irish camp and taken everything. They had also captured all the Irish artillery. The Irish throughout the war had complained of their shortage of muskets and now thousands of them had been lost. Many were simply tossed away as the Irish infantry ran for safety. On the next day, Ginckel offered his men sixpence for each Irish musket handed in, but so many were found that he was forced to reduce the reward to tuppence. The Irish threw aside everything that they could not easily carry. 'Fourteen standards and thirty three flags were taken, as well as a pair of kettledrums', wrote the duke of Wurtemberg to the Danish king, Christian V.[20] 'To all appearances it seems that the conquest of Ireland will no longer be difficult'.[21]

The outcome of the battle had been a shock and a puzzle to the Irish. How was it that they had fought so bravely and beaten back so many attacks and inflicted such terrible losses on the enemy and yet had still ended up in a position where they were forced to run like rabbits? One question was foremost in their minds: who was to blame?

As far as Tyrconnell was concerned it was Charles Charlmont, the marquis de Saint-Ruth. The battle should never had been fought. Sorry though he was that the Frenchman had lost his life, 'his temperament was hardly adapted to our affairs'. Saint-Ruth's decision to fight a pitched battle was very much against Tyrconnell's wishes, and had been taken in his absence, but Saint-Ruth 'got support from those who always oppose my views'. 'If he had taken my advice, neither he nor Athlone nor the army would have come to be lost'.[22] If Saint-Ruth was wrong to attempt to face Ginckel, the most widely repeated criticism of his behaviour on the day is less important: that he did not keep his staff officers informed of his plan of battle, so that the obvious consequence of his sudden death was confusion.

Whether or not one accepts the view that Saint-Ruth should never have fought a pitched battle, Aughrim was without doubt a military disaster for the

Irish. As the outcome of the battle turned on such a small feature of the battlefield, the causeway, what blame there is for the defeat must be laid firstly on those responsible for covering it. The negligent supply of the wrong ammunition to Aughrim Castle is a minor point compared to the removal of the two infantry battalions from the village at the exit from the causeway. They were Major-General William Dorrington's responsibility. He withdrew them, but he never replaced them. There has been a suggestion that he did not request those two particular battalions to move into the centre, and that his orders were misinterpreted. That is not the point. He was responsible for protecting the causeway and this he failed to do.

Following Dorrington's failure to hold the line, Brigadier Henry Luttrell failed to drive Lord Oxford's cavalry back over the causeway, and this has often been attributed to treachery. The road from the causeway became known as 'Luttrell's Pass'. Luttrell was later, and perhaps most unfairly, blamed for losing the battle. It passed into tradition that the English had paid for their passage at Athlone with gold, and had done the same at Aughrim. Although it cannot be suggested that Luttrell remained loyal to the Jacobite cause for the rest of his life, the evidence points to his change of mind not coming until after Aughrim. At the time there were no murmurs against him: the allegations of treachery came much later. It could be argued that the real villain of the piece was Major-General Dominic Sheldon. He commanded the whole left wing and was Luttrell's superior officer. He had enough cavalry to resolve matters but did not do so, even though he knew that it was Saint-Ruth's intention to charge. He instead waited for orders to enter Dorrington's sector, and his inflexible attitude sealed the fate of the Irish army.*

The last two paragraphs contain the only, albeit superficial, observations that can be made of the general officers on the left wing. But these accusations, now set out some three hundred years after the event, are perhaps of little value. It may well be that one or more of these officers conducted himself so deplorably that Mackay's attack would otherwise have been beaten back, but our knowledge of the battle is not enough for us to point with any confidence to the guilty party. No Jacobite account of the battle goes any way in satisfactorily explaining the defeat, and it is now certainly not a useful exercise to suggest that one or other of these officers was a fool or a coward when one is referring to experienced and professional soldiers who were forced to make quick decisions in the heat and confusion of battle. There is no surviving written record of the pressures that Dorrington laboured under as he endeavoured to hold off the Williamite centre. No aide de camp's memoirs related the battle through the

---

* The rest of the army certainly felt badly let down by Sheldon's cavalry: 'The commanding officers of the left wing, by abandoning their station without compulsion, nay, without a stroke, were either traitors to their king and country, or, by exposing their foot to a certain murder, they showed a barbarous indifference to the safety of their friends and countrymen; or, in fine, were notorious cowards. And so let them keep their priding cavalry to stop bottles with.'[23]

eyes of Sheldon's staff as Mackay ordered that last desperate attack, and none of Luttrell's men have left us with an account of the scene behind Aughrim village when Ruvingy's mounted brigade first emerged from the narrow causeway.

To those in the Irish army there was no clear cut explanation at the time. It became accepted that the defeat was brought about by a combination of factors, notably by Saint-Ruth's untimely death and his failure to tell his generals, especially Sarsfield, what was going on. From this grew the myth that Sarsfield had stood quietly by throughout the battle, refusing to help his countrymen in their hour of need because Saint-Ruth had ordered him to stay with the reserves until further notice. Later still, the defeat was to be attributed to Luttrell's treachery, although both he and Sheldon kept their commands after the battle and there is no suggestion that anyone then clamoured for their removal.

It may be that as the Williamite army was better equipped and trained than the Irish, that they would have won anyway. But all that can be hesitantly written now is that it would appear that the seeds of defeat were sown by Dorrington in his failure to replace the two battalions that guarded that one crucial part of the battlefield, and that the effects of this omission were compounded by Sheldon's, or possibly Luttrell's, inactivity. How much Saint-Ruth's secrecy contributed to that inactivity can only be guessed at.

Although happy to attribute to Luttrell the most terrible motive, the Irish were generally fatalistic. They had again been visited by the ill-fortune that had dogged them since the siege of Derry. Commenting on Saint-Ruth's death, Plunket wrote:[24]

> A cursed ball, that carried such a measure of woe! O people of Ireland, you are not, it seems, judged by heaven worthy of those blessings which you expected by undertaking this war, that is, to re-enthrone your king, and in sequel to establish your religion, your property and liberty. Your sins, your sins have been the barrier to that felicity.

So ended the greatest battle and the greatest slaughter in Irish history, and with it passed away the most unsuccessful commander of an Irish army. The fall of Athlone stands out in the annals of the war as being a loss that was unquestionably due to a general's negligence. From Ballymore to Aughrim, Saint-Ruth never put a foot right and it is difficult to think of a time when the Irish people were ever led by a more disastrous general than this coarse, foolhardy French gambler, the marquis de Saint-Ruth.

CHAPTER XVIII

To Galway and Limerick

Sarsfield:	This useless sword shall open every vein, And steep with Sarsfield's blood fair Aughrim's plain.
O'Neill:	Oh! Say not so, Lord Lucan, let us fight, Or push for Galway in the dead of night, Or else to Limerick: for we may stand it there, And all our losses on this field repair. Who knows what articles we may obtain, Which may enable us to fight again?

Robert Ashton, The Battle of Aughrim, v.i., 1770.

BY THE EVENING of the 13th the news of the defeat at Aughrim had reached both Tyrconnell at Limerick and d'Usson at Galway. As the hours went by the full enormity of the defeat became more apparent. The Irish army had been scattered. No one knew how many had been killed or taken prisoner as the entire command structure had broken down. With the exception of some of the mounted units, no body of men had got away other than in small and uncoordinated groups. Two days later the garrisons of Portumna and Banagher surrendered. It was easy to fear the worst, and that is what Galway and Limerick prepared for. The English could be upon them at any time. But General Godard de Ginckel was a cautious man. He knew that the Irish army had taken a bad mauling, but he was not going to take any risks. He decided to press ahead with his original plan and tackle Galway first. He camped on Kilcommodon Hill and waited for his heavy artillery to arrive. There he waited for a week, and in that week the Irish army gathered itself together.

The Irish infantry disintegrated at Aughrim. In their blind panic hundreds of the foot soldiers had thrown away their weapons and run off to the south. As day broke groups of them were still making what haste they could towards Limerick. According to Story, their disorder was such that they were 'robbing and plundering each other' on the way. As the English did not pursue them they began to form up in regular groups and made for the city that had been their refuge in the last campaign. They had fled over the hills towards Portumna and then along the road to Scarriff and Killaloe. At Portumna many of them who were cut off from the main bodies of survivors simply hid. But most of them, as if following their instincts, made for Limerick just as they had done after the Boyne. The roads were now filled with weary men marching south. Amongst them bodies of horsemen, Sarsfield and his men included, were there to direct them and urge them on.* Limerick was again to be the last great Jacobite bastion in Ireland.

In Limerick, Tyrconnell did what he could. He sent envoys off to France to ask for more supplies. He prepared the town's defences and had stocks of food brought in to withstand a siege. Sarsfield was left out of the decision making process. Although his empire was now very much smaller than it had been, Tyrconnell was nearer to being an absolute ruler than ever before. Neither Saint-Ruth's deputy, de Tessé, who was recovering from his wounds, nor his Irish detractors could challenge his decisions. The calamity that had befallen the country had come about because he had not been consulted. He had been vindicated, and those who had opposed him had been proved to be disastrously wrong.

While Ginckel hesitated on Kilcommodon, d'Usson used the time as best he could, but his garrison was made up of less than two thousand 'poor sorry fellows with hardly a rag on their backs.'[2] He wrote to Tyrconnell that he needed fifteen hundred more men if he was to hold Galway. He was told that they could not be spared. He wrote to Sarsfield who he noted 'considers himself to have more authority than the viceroy', but was told that Sarsfield did not even open his letters. 'He does not hold me in high regard', wrote the wretched Frenchman to his masters.[3]

The fact was that Sarsfield knew Galway better than d'Usson did. It was not going to hold out as Athlone had. The people of Galway were dominated by what O'Kelly scathingly called 'the new interest'. They were not going to fight, and any more troops sent there would be as wasted as Ulick Burke's men had been at Ballymore. Sarsfield, and of course Tyrconnell, was more concerned in preparing Limerick for what was to come. It was hoped that Galway would delay Ginckel for no better purpose than to help preserve Limerick.

D'Usson soon found out how difficult his task was going to be. He commanded the garrison and had every intention of holding out for as long as he could, but his subordinate officers had other ideas. Even the clergy were preaching surrender. Some leading citizens sent messages to Ginckel as soon as they heard the news of Aughrim. He was advised by one that he need not even bring his artillery as the town was ready to surrender in any case. D'Usson was forced to arrest the mayor, Arthur French, who had sent the town clerk to Ginckel to negotiate. Not that arresting people really helped, as French was later released without d'Usson's permission. Judge Daly, the man who Sarsfield had arrested in the winter for intriguing with the enemy, rode to Athenry to meet the Dutch

---

* According to Lord Ronsele 'very late in the night' Sarsfield was 'one of the first who came to Loughrea with some few horse . . . ; he was very desperately hungry.' One of the less likely surviving legends concerning Sarsfield attributes to him a ruse not used since Walter Tirel fled after the killing of William Rufus in 1100. 'Ginckel in pursuit of the Jacobites harassed Sarsfield's retreat as far as Woodford [over twenty miles away] and in an attempt to mislead the enemy Sarsfield ordered the shoes on the horses to be reversed. This was quickly done and it did cause confusion to the Williamite cavalry.'[1]

general and cheered him with his descriptions of the factions within the town and his detailed account of the military strengths and preparations.* D'Usson was all but being ignored. There was every reason to believe that Galway would fall in days rather than weeks.

On 19 July Ginckel arrived at Galway. D'Usson managed to get his men to burn down the outlying houses and to retreat behind the walls. Many of the townspeople left the town altogether and asked for Ginckel's protection. Early next morning, the Williamites attacked some outworks, the defence of which had already been weakened by Lord Clanricarde who had withdrawn his men against d'Usson's written orders. The remaining defenders only put up a token show of resistance and then fled. 'No one could get the troops to fire twenty shots at the enemy.'[5] Lord Dillon called a council of war which decided on surrender, and he then told d'Usson what was proposed. The Frenchman was powerless to do anything but go along with them and within two days the articles of surrender had been signed. The citizens of Galway made it clear that they were 'well pleased that the English government was again restored among them'. They held a civic reception for Ginckel, grateful and relieved that their town was undamaged and that they had not been subjected to the terrors of a siege. For them, the war was over and gone with it were the days of uncontrolled and thieving troops and the all-powerful commissaries able to commandeer the merchants' stock without compensation. The town could now get back to its profitable peace time existence.

D'Usson did at least manage to salvage his pride. Ginckel was aware, as William had been when he had marched to Limerick, that time was running out. As William had done before him, he left his artillery train behind his army so that he could reach his objective with all possible speed. If d'Usson had insisted on holding out it could take the best part of a fortnight before the siege artillery would arrive from Athlone. This factor alone was sufficient for Ginckel to grant certain generous terms to d'Usson. So generous in fact that he was criticised for it in England, but Ginckel was willing to give away anything except time.

Ginckel had issued a proclamation in early July promising that those who surrendered would be pardoned and that their liberties would be protected. Although the proclamation was issued before Aughrim, Saint-Ruth's unexpected insistence on fighting a pitched battle had prevented its distribution. Ginckel had later had it sent to Galway so that the garrison would be quite clear as to what terms were being offered. Although the defenders of Galway had shown themselves to be willing to negotiate, they had proved to be hard bargainers. When the negotiations had threatened to drag on, rather than waste any more time, Ginckel agreed to a number of additional terms in order to secure a settlement.

The articles agreed on did not only provide for the garrison, but also for the townspeople and even for certain landowners who were not even in Galway at

---

* In his letter to the Lord Justices describing his success at Galway, Ginckel added in a postscriptum: 'Judge Daly has done good service.'[4]

the time. They were all to be pardoned and given the right to keep their property. Catholic lawyers were to be allowed the same freedom to practise as had been the case in the reign of Charles II. The Galway priests were to be given the freedom to carry out their religious duties without fear of prosecution, and gentlemen were to be allowed to keep firearms for self defence. Most important, as far as d'Usson was concerned, was the term that allowed him to march out of the town with all his arms and men and to go to Limerick. As a result he was able to take to Limerick three thousand men and six guns. Whether these men and guns were of more value to the garrison there than an extra fortnight's grace would have been is a moot point.

Jacobite Ireland was cut in two. There were only two towns left owing allegiance to King James, Sligo and Limerick. Sligo, still governed by Sir Teague O'Regan, had been transformed into a formidable fortress since Sarsfield's success there, but it was isolated and poor and was effectively kept in check by the Ulster troops commanded by Sir Albert Cunningham and John Michelburne. While the status quo remained, neither side at Sligo was capable of doing the other much harm. The only place of any importance to the outcome of the war was Limerick.

It must not be thought that the world stood still while Ginckel attended to Galway. Henry Luttrell, forever active, led a cavalry force northwards from Limerick to hinder the siege,* and may well have done so had d'Usson not capitulated so quickly. Luttrell did not get to within ten miles of the town as the English had detached a strong force of cavalry to block his path at Kilcolgan Bridge on the Dunkellin river.

During this time the Irish army grew day by day. Between the muster on 2 August and that of the 7th, over five hundred stragglers came in. Sarsfield was active in the army's reorganisation. A camp was established at Caherconlish, nine miles from Limerick on the Tipperary road. In that same week he stripped the garrisons of men to build up his force from under fifteen thousand officers and men to just over seventeen thousand. But their lack of equipment was lamentable. He only had firearms for less than two thirds of them, which meant that seven thousand men would have to make do with whatever they could lay their hands on. The garrison troops were in a worse state, only a third of the six thousand men were armed, and they were often scattered far and wide in vulnerable posts.

Despite the losses suffered at Aughrim, there were those who still advocated a pitched battle and Tyrconnell was pressed to meet Ginckel's army before it reached Limerick. But he saw no point in taking any such risks. The city was stronger than it had been when William had besieged it the year before, and time was on his side. The English would come to the city and fire their cannons

---

* The comment must be made that if there had been any serious suspicion that Luttrell had acted treacherously at Aughrim, he certainly would not have been given this command.

until the wet weather arrived. They would then withdraw. The continuation of the war would then be dependent on fresh supplies. There was no more sensible plan than Tyrconnell's, and if Sarsfield's supporters were going to take offence at the undiplomatic way in which Tyrconnell now treated them, it did not matter. He was now strong enough to resist all comers.

Sarsfield, perhaps in the eager but vain hope that d'Usson would delay Ginckel for several weeks, had ideas of again striking a grand blow. He certainly expected the war to last throughout the winter and made plans to prevent the English quartering themselves throughout the counties of Tipperary and Kilkenny as they had done in the winter before. As this area harboured large and organised groups of rapparees, Ginckel had already garrisoned Cashel, Tipperary, Thurles and Clonmel, and it was to these towns that Sarsfield turned his attention.

> 'Sarsfield at the head of all the horse, dragoon and rapparees he could muster together amounting to the number of six or seven thousand men, as was said, adventured over the Shannon, and lay hovering about the country between Limerick and Cashel.'[6]

According to the English he delayed in making his attack on Cashel as he was awaiting the arrival of four cannon that had to be brought up river from Kilrush, over forty miles the other side of Limerick. Apparently, neither Tyrconnell nor de Tessé would release any of Limerick's guns to him while they sent off for the replacements from Kilrush. In the meantime the English were frightened into action. The governor of Cashel sent urgent messages to the lord justices in Dublin demanding an extra two thousand troops. The lord justices sent messages to Ginckel: could they weaken the garrison at Cork and establish a new camp at Goldenbridge to block Sarsfield? The army quitted all the smaller garrisons in the area, as well as the large one at Thurles, and the men were marched to Cashel. Reinforcements were speedily brought across the country from quieter areas such as Wexford, but Ginckel declined to get involved. Having taken note of the situation he sagely commented that if Sarsfield had any plans for Cashel he would certainly have carried them out before any of his men would be able to reach the area.[7]

In the meantime Sarsfield, who had far fewer men under his command than the six or seven thousand that was at first believed, set about destroying the forage and stores in the area, and threatening 'fire and desolation' to the remain-ing garrisons. His plan had been to destroy all the corn and hay in the area between Cashel and Kilkenny 'and thereby render it impracticable to subsist any force for the defence of these parts.' As the days went by the garrison of Cashel grew from strength to strength as reinforcements marched in from the east, and Sarsfield felt obliged to abandon his grand plan. The English reported that he drew his men off from Cashel 'having made only a feeble attempt to surprise the patrols and out-scouts of the place, which he failed to do'. But Sarsfield had by then heard the news of d'Usson's surrender at Galway, and as Ginckel prepared to move south, Cashel again faded into insignificance.

On 28 July 1691, d'Usson led the garrison of Galway out of the town. Two days later, having established his own garrison there, Ginckel led his men back to the Shannon. He was not tempted by the direct route through Gort as it would have presented him with many fresh problems. The Irish had remained in possession of Co. Clare throughout the war and it was to be expected that his passage would be contested. Also, the road passed across several causeways which were certain to be disrupted. If he reached Limerick from the north he would then be in a position where all his supplies would have to come through Portumna as all the crossing points below Lough Derg would be held by the Irish. He would no longer have the relative safety of strong lines of communication to his supply bases at Dublin and Cork. He chose instead to take the uninterrupted route along the east bank of the Shannon to Nenagh and then on to Caherconlish and Limerick as King William had done the year before.

Even without any opposition from the Irish, progress was certainly not fast. On 3 August the army reached Birr and large detachments were sent on ahead to clear the way. The Irish, as they had in the previous year, withdrew in front of them leaving utter devastation in their wake. When it was clear that the English were coming, what little remained of Nenagh was put to the torch by Brigadier 'Tall Anthony' Carroll but he was chased out by Major Wood's Enniskilleners before he could finish the job.[8] On 5 August Ginckel and his army camped amongst the charred ruins of the town. His intelligence was that the Irish army was at Caherconlish, nine miles south east of Limerick, and that they gave every appearance of preparing for a fight. The Irish, he heard, were:

> Forcing all in their jurisdiction to take arms: were arming the foot anew out of the stores of Limerick and threatened to give the English battle before they approached the town.[9]

The news had a sobering effect on Ginckel. Ever cautious, he stopped in his tracks. He wanted to ensure that he was taking no risks. His army meticulously prepared themselves for the next leg of the march to Caherconlish. Squadrons of horse explored and searched that very area where just over a year before Sarsfield had hidden out before attacking the artillery train. Under the protection of these cavalrymen, the English pioneers laboured hard to repair the damaged road through the Silvermine Mountains so that it would take the weight of the heavy siege artillery that had not been used since Athlone.

The progress of d'Usson and his Galway garrison was uneventful. It is over sixty miles from Galway to Limerick, and the Williamites were anxious to satisfy themselves that the garrison went the full distance. They supplied a mounted escort to keep an eye on matters, and messages were sent ahead to Tyrconnell to tell him that they were on their way. Tyrconnell sent out a mounted force to meet them and, happy perhaps to keep him out of Limerick, sent Brigadier Henry Luttrell to command it as he was the only senior officer recently acquainted with the area. Nine miles from Limerick the two groups met. Under a flag of truce Luttrell spoke to the Williamite escort commander and then accompanied d'Usson and his men to Limerick.

The Williamite commander was a Huguenot officer, Lieutenant Colonel Pierre de la Bastide Saint-Sebastien, known to the Irish simply as 'Sebastian'. He had commanded the eager Huguenot cavalry regiment under Lanier when Sarsfield had attacked the artillery at Ballyneety. Indeed, if another Huguenot is to be believed, Sarsfield would have had a rude shock that night if la Bastide had commanded in Lanier's place. He was efficient and brave and dedicated and was well known to Ginckel. In his conversation with Luttrell he asked the question: 'Why would not the Irish come to a treaty rather than continue a war with so much misery?'[10] Luttrell answered that there could well be a treaty if Ginckel had been given enough authority to grant the terms that the Irish would want. Luttrell's reply was, as will be seen, taken very seriously by la Bastide.

Now that he knew that Ginckel intended to advance on Limerick from the east rather than the north, Tyrconnell made his own plans. He intended to defend the city in the same way that it had been defended before. The army was to be pulled back into Limerick and the cavalry units were to cross the river into Clare. The crossing points at Killaloe, O'Briensbridge and Annaghbeg were to be heavily guarded and the Clare bank of the Shannon was to be patrolled. He did not have any expectations of being able to destroy Ginckel as the French had already let him know that he could not expect any reinforcements, but he certainly expected to make life very unpleasant for him. The French had also let him know that he could expect a French convoy laden down with sufficient supplies to equip the whole army. His men would be well armed, clothed and fed inside Limerick throughout the winter. Ginckel's men would find little comfort out in the wet and the cold.

Tyrconnell's fear, as always, was that his authority was waning. He knew that many of the Irish saw that the end was near. The arrival of d'Usson and the Galway garrison at the beginning of August had introduced fresh divisions among the officers and men. The Galway garrison had been granted most generous terms. So generous in fact that it seemed that the army was now to face one of two alternatives: either they returned to civilian life on the same conditions as they had always had as if there had never been a war, or else they fought through the winter in the hope that the French would send them some more men. And a winter's war would mean, as it had for the past two winters, that regardless of any fresh supplies, the army would be at least decimated. And this time they all knew, especially now that Sligo was cut off and out of contact, that they stood completely alone.

Before ordering the army to pull back to Limerick and Co. Clare, Tyrconnell addressed all the officers and soldiers at Caherconlish. It was probably not such a hopeful message as that given out by Sarsfield in the year before, but it was along the same lines. He then made the army take a new oath and made those that could write sign a declaration. Every man was to swear that he would not consider surrendering unless the whole army was going to surrender, and that the army would only surrender if King James gave his consent. The French generals, de Tessé and d'Usson, were unimpressed. It would, they wrote, do nothing to quell the uncertainty and the fears in the minds of the Irish soldiers. Tyrconnell thought otherwise, and to set an example he took the oath himself and then watched as the chaplains administered it to the assembled troops. The simple message was that any unauthorised surrender would carry with it eternal damnation. However uncertain or timid the troops may feel, he reasoned, they will not risk their immortal souls by treating with the enemy even if they are offered such terms as those granted at Galway.

It was all too much for some. Old Colonel Oxburgh rode to Nenagh and gave himself up to the English.[11]

A few days later, on 2 August, a trumpeter came to Limerick from the English army with a query addressed to Sarsfield. The note contained a list of the names of those Williamite officers who had been missing since the battle of Aughrim, and Sarsfield was asked to confirm whether or not they had been taken prisoner. It was a simple request. Sarsfield asked the messenger if he had any more letters on him. The man said that he did not. Sarsfield told him that he was going to be searched and that if he did have any letters concealed about him he would be hanged. The messenger rummaged in his clothing and brought out another letter which was addressed to Brigadier Henry Luttrell. Sarsfield broke the seal and read the contents. It was from la Bastide. Its contents were incriminatory. The essence of the letter was that in answer to Luttrell's query, la Bastide was now able to inform him that General Ginckel had full powers vested in him by King William to negotiate and agree conditions of surrender with the Irish.[12]

To Sarsfield it was a terrible blow. They had known each other all their lives. Luttrell had been his right-hand man throughout the war, ever since the Sligo campaign. They had even fought together at Wincanton, and more than that, he had been his best friend. Now he was corresponding with the enemy on the subject of an Irish surrender. The shock was such that Sarsfield did not do the obvious thing and go to Luttrell to question him. The meaning of the letter was clear. He instead went straight to the man that both he and Luttrell had campaigned against for so long. He took the letter to Tyrconnell.

The French were delighted at this.[13] It was to them a most welcome indication that Sarsfield and Tyrconnell were at last reconciled. All was now going to be well. Tyrconnell was also delighted, and to him it was an opportunity not to be missed. He could now remove a thorn from his side for once and for all. He had the courtmartial arranged straight away, and to be safe he made sure that those who might have some affection for Luttrell were kept off the tribunal. Neither Sarsfield nor Purcell sat to judge their old friend, although they probably attended the trial.

The evidence against Luttrell did not amount to much. He had innocently spoken to la Bastide and had been sent an unsolicited letter which merely stated that Ginckel was empowered to negotiate. Had he received the letter Luttrell may well have passed it on to Tyrconnell, but he was never given the opportunity. Nothing in the letter suggested a conspiracy. (It was of course far less than Tyrconnell had authorised in the previous year when he had sent the lawyer Grady to sound out King William). Half a century later, Lord Westmeath, who had sat through the trial as a young cavalry officer, wrote of the outcome:[14]

> Colonel Luttrell was acquitted, and it was impossible that he could be found guilty by men that had either honesty or honour.

Of the twenty four officers who sat on the tribunal, only five of them voted against the prisoner. Tyrconnell was furious. To him, the evidence was quite clear. He was not going to be thwarted in such a way. Denied the satisfaction of having Luttrell shot by a firing squad, he kept him locked up in King John's Castle. An opportunity would present itself later to have him retried and then dealt with properly.

It was not long before the English heard of Luttrell's arrest and Ginckel sent a messenger to Limerick with the warning that 'if they put any man to death for having a mind to come over to us he would revenge it on the Irish'.[15]

On 10 August, Tyrconnell was entertained to a dinner provided by d'Usson. 'He and the company were very merry, but at night upon his preparing to go to bed, he found himself indisposed'.[16] The viceroy had suffered a stroke. According to Plunket he was conscious enough to prepare himself for the hereafter before, on the 13th, he lost his power of speech. In the early afternoon on 14 August 1691, in his sixty-second year, Dick Talbot breathed his last. Although he had his enemies, and although Sarsfield was not among the mourners, to some it heralded the end of Irish resistance. As Plunket, without intending a pun, wrote: 'it was a fatal stroke to this poor country'. 'Thus this great man fell, who in his fall pulled down a mighty edifice, videlicet, a considerable Catholic nation, for there was no other subject left able to support the national cause.'[17]

The English were hopeful that the viceroy's death had been brought about by the divisions in the Irish high command. They encouraged the rumour that Sarsfield and the French were responsible for Tyrconnell's death:

> Which some say was not without suspicion of foul play in being poisoned with a cup of ratafia (this is nothing but apricot stones bruised and infused in brandy which gives it a pleasant relish) some of which my lord Tyrconnell had given him at an entertainment, and falling ill upon it, he often repeated the word 'ratafia' which made several believe that he had received poison in that liqueur because he would not comply with the prevailing faction then in town.[18]

Inside Limerick it was not generally believed that the viceroy had been poisoned, but there was trouble to come. Before his death, Tyrconnell had issued instructions that a sealed commission from King James be opened. This commission entrusted the government of Ireland to three lord justices. Only one of them, Sir Richard Nagle, was Irish; the others, Alexander Fitton and Francis Plowden, were Englishmen. The control of the army still vested in the hands of the two most senior officers: Lieutenant Generals d'Usson and de Tessé.

Ginckel finally ordered his army out of Nenagh on 14 August, the same day that Tyrconnell died. That evening the English army established itself at Caher-conlish. Ginckel rode half way to Limerick to inspect the land ahead. There were good reasons for him to feel less than confident: it had been raining and the ground was sodden. On the next day he rode to where King William had camped during the siege and was able to study the state of the city's defences: it was immediately apparent that the Irish had greatly improved the fortifications. Ginckel called a council of war to decide on whether to lay siege to Limerick or to merely blockade it. The situation was set out by Wurtemberg:

> 'For the past eight days the weather has been abominable . . . The operation against Limerick appears to be very difficult on account of the numbers in the place . . . The enemy have improved the town with six large bastions, a crownwork and a good counterscarp. Against this we have better artillery than last year. There are 1,000 rounds for each gun. Our artillery consists of 14 twenty four pounders, 10 twelve pounders and 10 mortars for which there are 3,000 bombs and carcasses,* and 4 howitzers.[20]

Wurtemberg was insistent that Ginckel should not waste time in attempting to blockade Limerick. If he did, the French would be given the opportunity of getting supplies through to the Irish and the army would in the meantime suffer heavy losses from sickness. Difficult though it would be, Limerick should be vigorously attacked in order to force an early surrender. The powerful artillery would soon terrify the Irish defenders into surrendering the place 'in which all the women and children of their leading families are shut up'.[21] Ginckel agreed. 'No man', he said 'will take me alive from here till Limerick surrenders.'[22]

On 25 August Ginckel at last marched on Limerick. His men overran the old Cromwellian forts overlooking the town and began to establish themselves in roughly the same positions they had occupied on their last visit. Over the next few days they industriously prepared batteries for the guns and dug trenches closer and closer to the Irish defences. It was soon found that the cannon could not be put as close to the walls as they had been before as the ground was already too marshy. It was dangerous work. In the first five days the Danes alone lost over a hundred men including a colonel of horse to fire from the Irish works.

---

*   'Carcass: is an invention of an oval form made of iron ribs and filled with a composition of meal-powder, saltpetre, sulphur, broken glass, shavings of horn, pitch, turpentine, tallow and linseed oil and then covered with pitched cloth, it is primed with meal-powder and fired out of a mortar; it's design is to set houses on fire' (*Military Dictionary*, 1737).[19]

CHAPTER XIX

Clifford's Bridge and Thomond Bridge

Oh, hurrah! for the men, who, when danger is nigh,
Are found in the front, looking death in the eye,
Hurrah! for the men who keep Limerick's wall,
And hurrah! for bold Sarsfield, the bravest of all.
                    Thomas Davis, 'The Battle of Limerick'

CONDITIONS INSIDE Limerick were grim and the troops were dispirited. Although they were generally paid in advance in bread, meat, brandy and wine, they had received no money for weeks and many were without the necessary clothing to get through the winter. The situation was not improved by the fragmentation of authority since Tyrconnell's death. The army was nominally commanded by the two Frenchmen, but few considered them to have more authority than Sarsfield. The civil government was controlled by the three lord justices, and the same could be said for them. Sarsfield now held his own councils and exerted pressure on the nominal authorities as he had done when Berwick was in command.

On 2 September a council meeting decided that the money should be distributed among the troops to convince them that the French did indeed intend to send them fresh help.[1] Sarsfield's signature was followed by those of the other council members—Lord Kilmallock (his brother-in-law), Lord Galmoy, Lord Riverston, Sheldon, Purcell and Garrett Moore—and was of course approved by the lord justices. The army pay was a matter for the French generals, and the resolution was passed over to them. They had no choice in the matter as their orders were to hold Limerick, and their only way of doing so was by keeping Sarsfield and his friends happy. The Frenchmen knew that they could no longer count on anyone's loyalty.

During the last few days of August the artillery arrived with '800 carts of ball and 800 barrels of powder'.[2] An English naval squadron sailed from Galway and came up the Shannon estuary to within six miles of Limerick where the frigates opened fire on the Irish camp at Cratloe. On 4 September the English busily spent a day taking guns and stores off the ships on the Maigue and transporting them back to the camp.

The bombardment began in earnest on 30 August, the anniversary of the day when King William had abandoned his siege. The batteries were erected to the south west of the Irish town where it was hoped to batter down Thomond Bridge.

We endeavoured to shoot at the great bridge, but the distance was too great to effect any good and it was not thought convenient to approach any nigher so as to engage in a siege, but only to cannonade and ruin the houses. . . .[3] Some of the bombs fell right over the town as it is long in one direction and very narrow: it also has no more than two streets throughout its length.[4]

No serious effort was made to attack the wall between St John's gate and Balls Bridge where the breach had been made in the previous year, in fact little effort was made on the Irish town walls at all. They had been so transformed through-out the year as to make them all but untouchable by cannon shot as they were now masked by massive earthworks. The one weak area was on the western side, but the only position from where the cannons could fire at it had to be abandoned as a spring tide was due.

By 3 September, nothing had been achieved except the ruination of the buildings within the walls. It was decided to concentrate on the English town's walls which, although separated from the English army by a stretch of water, were weaker and less well protected against cannon. If the guns could batter them down, then troops could be transported across the Abbey River to attack the breach. A new battery was to be set up facing the English town. It was no small engineering task:

> 4th September. This night we began our new batteries with about seven hundred workmen. Some little disasters happened this night by a false alarm, the regiments of Verner and Meath not being at their post to cover the pioneers which the general took very ill. This put the whole army under arms and great detachments of both horse and foot were sent towards the right.

> 5th September. One hundred and fifty dragoons were sent to make the ways for our cannon from the camp to their new batteries. Four hundred workmen are also ordered to relieve the seven hundred employed last night, and to continue the same works by day being now under cover.[5]

Things were not getting easier. The heavens opened and the pioneers found themselves knee deep in water filled trenches. The labourers slipped and slid as they worked on the great earthworks that were to protect the guns. It was par-ticularly unpleasant work, not least because they were within easy range of the walls from where the Irish kept up a frequent fire. Although it had been hoped to establish a position on King's Island the plan proved impractical as most of the island would be flooded in the spring tide. But notwithstanding these problems the English cannonade grew more fierce daily as the batteries were enlarged and more guns were brought to bear. On 8 September the English town wall was breached and by the 11th a continuing bombardment had extended the damage to a gap forty yards across. On the 12th, all fire was concentrated on the cathedral as it was believed that it was being used as a storehouse.

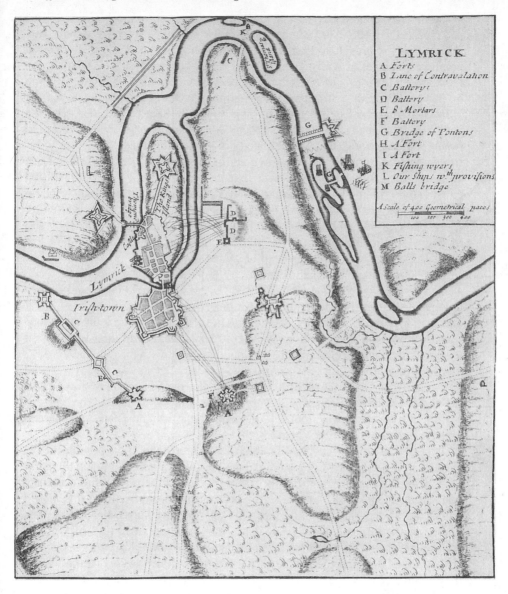

17 A detail from a plan of Limerick and the surrounding area showing the position of the pontoon bridge, from George Story's *Impartial History*, 1693

Inside the city the Irish worked just as hard. The fortifications were repaired and modified. Houses were patched up or pulled down. New retrenchments were built inside the breach so that any storming party would find itself boxed in behind a fresh set of walls. Efforts were made to spread the stores about the town after a magazine of eight casks of brandy and another of biscuit went up in flames. An Irish raiding party crossed the Abbey river and destroyed the woolsacks that the English were hoping to use in their assault, and after the besiegers had desperately hunted around for enough empty barrels to act as floats in the crossing, Ginckel changed his plans altogether. 'The enemy has fifteen thousand infantry in the town and is putting up a desperate defence.' Although the English town wall was in tatters, the new star fort that had been constructed on King's Island and the deep ditch—now waterlogged—that ran along outside the city wall would make a general assault very difficult indeed. It was decided that all efforts should now be devoted to crossing the river and blocking up Limerick from both sides. By this time the bombardment had reduced the English town to 'a heap of stones'.[6]

Fresh dissension broke out inside the city. On 7 September a paper was passed around purporting to be Tyrconnell's will.[7] It was an openly hostile anti-French document that asserted that 'to wait for help from France is a mere chimera' and that Tyrconnell had only insisted on the Irish taking the oath of no surrender without the king's consent 'because I knew that Lord Lucan and Luttrell were looking for an opportunity to ruin my reputation with the deluded masses'. The libel pointed out that Italy, Germany, Spain and Poland were all at war with France and they were all Catholic countries. It also made mention of the ungrateful way in which the French would treat those who served them. The war was not about religion, it was about the French. Catholics and Protestants should unite to fight against French tyranny.

It touched a raw nerve. The Irish had of course discussed the possibilities of surrender. It was to prevent such a debate that Tyrconnell had made the army take the oath. Even then, some of the senior officers, perhaps including Sarsfield, had felt that if they did surrender the best terms would be those that would enable the whole army to go to France to fight for King James. From there they could invade England. They knew that if they were defeated by Ginckel they could expect bad terms: imprisonment for the officers and slavery for the country. If they saved Ginckel the bother of having to wait for the rest of the winter, they could realistically demand what they wanted: a free passage to France.

Sarsfield's military activities throughout the siege are not known in detail. On 1 September, on hearing a rumour that he had made for Killaloe, Colonel Wolseley raced off with five hundred horsemen to prevent a reoccurrence of the Ballyneety raid, but there is no evidence from any Irish source that Sarsfield spent any time with the cavalry at all. He was mostly preoccupied with the condition of the town's defences. The English had now been outside Limerick for nearly three weeks. They had attempted to bombard Thomond Bridge and had failed, and they had set about demolishing the English town wall, but had now given up their efforts. Although they had greatly damaged the city, they had not significantly damaged the defences. They were no nearer to victory than they had been on the first day. It was important to Sarsfield to keep things that way.

On the 15th, Sarsfield's old enemy, Lord Lisburne, 'a man of excellent parts and who had showed himself very diligent and forward upon all occasions since the beginning of this war', was killed by a cannon ball as he came out of his tent. He had taken to sleeping in the trenches so that he could keep a better eye on his men.*[8]

When William had laid siege to Limerick in 1690 he had attacked the city from the southern bank of the Shannon. The river was fordable at Annaghbeg two miles upstream and although he sent Ginckel to force a crossing, no attempt was made to cut off the city from Co. Clare. It had then been impractical as there was still a large Irish force, not to mention Lauzun's French brigade, waiting on the Galway road. Now that the situation had changed Ginckel had fresh ideas as to how Limerick could be reduced. He wanted to surround the city. The problem in relying on a ford to do so, even the lowest ford at Annaghbeg, was simply that once his army was divided on both sides of the Irish garrison, each would individually be smaller than the garrison itself. If the Irish attacked either part of his besieging army, the other half would take perhaps several hours to march round to lend its support by which time it could well be too late. If the city was to be surrounded, a crossing point would have to be established as near as possible so that reinforcements could be sent speed-ily from bank to bank. As there were no fords below Annaghbeg, the crossing would have to be established with pontoons.

The problem was in finding a place to build such a bridge. At first it was hoped to bridge the Abbey River (that narrow part of the Shannon that separates the County of Limerick from King's Island) and then to launch an assault on the English town. This plan was discarded: the Irish were too strong and the open ground of the island was covered not only by the city walls, but by the new star fort outside. Other places were inspected. A Danish swimmer was sent across at one point, but the crossing was so rocky and wide that it was felt that there were not enough pontoons for the job, and that if there were, the anchors would not hold in the current. Ginckel then considered ordering a large force over the river at any point upstream, so that it could march down the Clare bank and guard a bridgehead while the pontoons were prepared. With this in mind, a search was made all the way up the Shannon to O'Briensbridge, but with no success. All the crossings (such as Annaghbeg) were heavily guarded and fortified or else they opened up into thick bog.[9]

* According to Plunket: 'His friends got the bullet that had killed him to be gilded and to be hung over his tomb in the cathedral church of Dublin dedicated to Saint Patrick the apostle of that kingdom, and this to stand a monument of his good affection and fidelity to that usurper. A folly in grain!' This ball still hangs today from a bracket high on the wall on the southern side of the sanctuary.

The breakthrough came on 15 September. As to how it came about when it did remains something of a mystery, but Irish commentators then and since have been quite clear that the crossing would not have been possible had it not been for the treachery, or at least the negligence, of Robert Clifford.

As when King William had approached Limerick, the Irish had taken some trouble to prevent the English crossing into Co. Clare. Before the Shannon reaches King's Island and the city of Limerick there is a bend in its course, and just before the bend is a stretch of water in which sit several small islands. Along this stretch of water was one very good crossing point from the south bank to St Thomas's Island which is situated near the very top of the river's bend. The river has changed much in three hundred years in that the valley is now properly drained, but its course is essentially unaltered. Now when the water is low it is quite easy to walk through the Shannon from the Limerick bank to St Thomas's Island, and easier still to walk from that Island through the water and onto the Clare Bank at Partine. In 1691 the river was deeper but even then there was a ford at that point straight across the river. It was the only one between Annaghbeg and Limerick. Clifford camped his main force at Partine,[10] which sits on a small hill overlooking the island and which afforded him views both up and down the river. From Partine he could also see over St Thomas's Island and keep an eye on the far bank. As an extra precaution he also posted a small garrison of forty dragoons on the island to cover the ford and to give his main force plenty of warning if the English attacked. Immediately downstream from St Thomas's Island was a salmon weir perched upon which was a small fort called Weir Castle (the remains of which are still visible). Clifford posted an ensign and twenty men in this fort. This was the weakest point in his line of defence, and both he and his men knew that much would depend on their vigilance throughout both the days and the nights.

The best part of a mile upstream, before the ford at Annaghbeg, was another group of islands. Between the Clare bank and the nearest island was an easy ford, but that island was separated from the others by a deep, albeit narrow, channel. However, unbeknown to Clifford, the water was fordable to those other islands from the far side. Here the English could get closer to the Clare bank than anywhere else, but to little effect as the penultimate stretch of water was still too deep and fast for them to be able to reach their objective.

On the Clare Bank, just inland from this second set of islands is a small hill that commands the second loop in the river, and here Clifford's command ended. On the hill were posted the remnants of the Irish cavalry still commanded by the most senior cavalryman in the army, Dominic Sheldon. And miserable remnants they were too. Of that great cavalry force that two years before had been compared favourably to anything in Europe, there remained a mere three and a half thousand men, and so conscious were they of their lack of strength that the troopers had been ordered to place sheets over the bushes to give the English the impression that a great many more tents had been erected.

The river banks along Clifford's stretch of water were for the most part overgrown. There were footpaths leading down to the water's edge by the salmon weir and along the bank near St Thomas's Island, but the low land between Partine and Annaghbeg was undrained and uncultivated, and covered by rough bushes, tall rushes and thick wild grass. The bank on which the English were is much flatter and was then completely unused. It provided a flood plain for the Shannon and much of it was a deep and hazardous bog. Clifford had men posted at intervals to watch the river. The sentries were able to conceal themselves along the bank, as the English patrols did on the other side. No one moved along the river bank during daytime as the river is narrow enough to invite men hidden in the bushes on the other side to open fire. But at night troops could move up to the water's edge undetected, and on the bank hidden by the islands, they could even explore the water's depth without being seen.

Hidden from the Irish by the islands, the English pioneers carefully surveyed the riverbed. It was found that the river was fordable to the first island, and then again fordable to a second island. There was then that gap of deeper water to the third island, and then a third ford onto the Clare Bank. The engineers estimated that twenty five pontoon boats would span that stretch of open water.[11] Orders were issued to prepare for a night march, and by one in the morning the English had waded through the two fords and had positioned fifteen field guns on the centre island to guard the bridgehead. Behind them, the engineers with six hundred workmen laboured to bring up the first of the twenty five pontoon boats. A company of grenadiers was rowed across the water ahead of them to occupy the third island.* They sat shivering in the wet bushes, straining their eyes for Irish patrols. Between them and the Clare bank there was just a shallow ford.

Whilst this was going on, Brigadier Clifford was asleep in his camp at Partine. At Annaghbeg, overlooking the islands, Dominic Sheldon's cavalry were camped on the side of a hill. During the night Clifford's patrols rode along the riverbank, but saw nothing. As luck would have it, the river and islands were shrouded in thick mist. The English were working in darkness, and the noise of the Shannon drowned the sound of the bridge builders. But it was a close thing. Just before first light an Irish trooper noticed the grenadiers hiding on the island nearest to him. He galloped off to report to Clifford. Clifford was unimpressed with the news. He 'seemed not to give credit to any such account, as not fearing that the enemy would dare undertake so perilous a passage'.[12] It was just another false alarm. He made the same mistake that Maxwell was alleged to have made at Athlone. By six in the morning, the last pontoon was in place and the way across the Shannon was open.

There was suddenly great consternation on the north bank, but it apparently did not touch Clifford. One of his colonels, Dudley Colclough, got his regiment

* This is the island of Illaunaroan. Silt has long since merged the other two islands to the left bank. This is clear from the 6 inch Ordnance Survey map of 1844, when part of the bank was still referred to as Reboge Island.

to mount up and gallop to Clifford's tent. Such was the urgency of his orders that many of his men had not had time to saddle their horses before riding out. Clifford still would not move. A bridge? 'There was no such thing', he said.[13] There was still nothing to corroborate their excited reports. As Clifford strained his eyes up river from Partine, he could see nothing but dense mist.

Meanwhile the English crossed over. Firstly, twenty horsemen spurred up the bank to ensure that there was no ambush. They were followed by eleven hundred grenadiers and fusiliers. The gravity of the situation dawned on Clifford only when it was too late. He was pushed on by an awareness that he was to blame, but his attempts to save the situation came too late. The English made straight for his camp at Partine. There was no time for the Irish to form up and fight, and in many cases no time to mount up. The only resistance given was a few scattered musket shots and then Clifford was gone, back to Limerick. His men ran along the road behind him: 'some in their shirts, some quite naked'.[14] Rather than give chase, the English were content to loot the tents and round up the grazing horses. They were, to say the least, surprised and relieved at the lack of opposition.

The effect on Irish morale was immediate. 'You see by this act of suffering the enemy to cross the Shannon', wrote Nicholas Plunket, 'that the misfortune of the Irish is continued, who lose ground upon every important occasion, not by the brave prowess of the foe (though brave he is), but rather by the neglect or ignorance or treachery of particular commanders.'[15] Clifford's fighting days were over. His colonels were furious at his conduct and testified against him at a council of war held on the next day. He had been warned time and time again but he had taken no action. He was a traitor. As the senior officers in the army were foreign—French, English and Scots—Clifford could expect little sympathy. The only Irishman that could save him was his one time friend Sarsfield. But Sarsfield had had his fill of Clifford. The council listened to the accusations. 'Clifford protested himself innocent as to any treachery, though he could not deny that he was guilty of unpardonable neglect.'[16] Not for the first time in his life, he was put behind bars. He was locked up in King John's Castle in the English town to await his court-martial.

> It was not prudent of Sarsfield to entrust him with such a post, for he not only knew him to be a creature of Tyrconnell, to be malcontent, and very unfortunate in all his undertakings; but he, Sarsfield, was also earnestly desired, the very morning before that fatal night, by a gentleman named Colonel Charles O'Kelly for whose opinion he always seemed to have a great value, either to come in person from Limerick to command at those passes, or if he could not come himself, to send Major-General Wauchope thither, otherwise that the enemy would come over and besiege the town on both sides. But it looked as if there had been some fatality in the matter.[17]

This new English success was felt as a deadening blow by the Irish, and filled them with fresh despondency. Rumours of Clifford's treachery abounded.

The French felt that the situation was now desperate, not necessarily because of any tactical advantage the English may have gained by crossing the river, but because they felt that Clifford's behaviour was part of a premeditated move by a large group of traitors within the Irish army. 'It is not possible', they wrote to King Louis, 'that Clifford is the only guilty one. Everyone is thinking of surrender. Sarsfield and Wauchope have said that we have already waited too long.'[18]

The successful construction of 'Clifford's bridge', had two immediate and serious consequences for the Irish. The city became more crowded. A camp had been set up a few hundred yards from Thomond Bridge for those not involved in the defence of the city. They were now forced to come inside the walls. Secondly, and more importantly, communication was cut off with Sheldon's cavalry at Annaghbeg. Why Sheldon did not attack was a question raised within the walls. Why indeed; Sheldon had no orders and no knowledge of Ginckel's intentions, but he did have three and a half thousand horsemen and a thousand foot soldiers. The first that he knew of the bridge was the sight of a second English column marching towards him. He took no risks and marched off along the Ennis Road to Sixmilebridge to await developments. O'Kelly put it in stronger terms: Sheldon rode till midnight

> and encamped in a fallow field where there was not a piece of grass to be had: as if he had designed to harass the horses by day and starve them by night. Nor was it doubted if the city of Galway and other towns garrisoned by the enemy had not lain in his way, that he would ever stop till he came to Sligo.[19]

The Irish inside the city were further disheartened by this retreat: 'This was a brave occasion for the Irish cavalry to show themselves, for from the beginning of the war to that day they were not brought to a trial as to the whole body of them'.[20] Limerick was now all but surrounded. For the first time it faced a true state of siege, rather than a one sided bombardment.

That same day, Ginckel sent another of his declarations to the garrison. If they surrendered he could promise them all pardons and ensure that they would keep their property. 'But if they shall still continue obstinate and neglect to lay hold on this favour, which is the last that will be offered them, they must be answerable for the blood and destruction they draw upon themselves, for I hereby acquit myself before God and the world and wash my hands of it.' He gave them eight days in which to answer.[21]

Since Tyrconnell's death the command of the army was held by the two French lieutenant-generals, de Tessé and d'Usson. Serving under them were the four surviving major-generals; their fellow countryman, la Tour Montfort; Sheldon, who was with the cavalry; and Wauchope and Sarsfield. It was no secret that the latter two found this situation difficult to accept. The French had already complained about Wauchope's attitude toward them during the war. It was perhaps an attitude that one would expect in a man that had spent his entire military career fighting against them. Sarsfield's position was more complex. He was the most senior Irish officer in the army, but his authority was given to him by a commission which ranked him below the Frenchmen. His loyalties were to his king and his country, but they could only oppose the Williamites with French help. Both the major-generals knew this, and both of them would knuckle under the two lieutenant-generals while it suited them. But the French were disliked by the Irish, and only Sarsfield could keep the Irish obedient.

Having gained the Clare bank and chased away all opposition the English decided to move their pontoon bridge nearer the city.* They also began digging new trenches nearer to the walls of the Irishtown for a formal siege, or as the engineer, Colonel Jacob Richards, wrote in his diary for 21 September 1691: 'The line of contravallation is traced anew nigher the town.' [22]

On the next day Ginckel led seventeen foot battalions and the greater part of the English cavalry and dragoons over into Clare. The garrison of Limerick had now only a toe hold on the Clare bank, and that was an old fort designed to guard the approach to the city across Thomond Bridge. This fort became the target for the next English attack. After a two hour fight which shrouded the area in thick smoke the Irish left the fort and ran back along Thomond bridge into the city. Up until that time there had been nothing to worry about. The English were bound to take the fort if they tried; the only questions were how many of them the Irish could kill in the process, and how long the fort would hold out. Eventually, with the walls ploughed up by artillery fire and the English grenadiers preparing to rush them, the eight hundred or so Irish troops were ordered back. They jumped over the walls of the fort on the city side and ran for the bridge, and seeing them run the English charged, not just at the fort, but at the bridge as well.

Thomond Bridge was a narrow fifteenth century construction built on fourteen arches and was a little over a hundred and fifty yards long.[23] Despite it being the only entrance into Limerick from Clare it was not even wide enough to carry wheeled traffic. It entered the city through a fortified gatehouse, and half way along its length was another castellated gateway and a drawbridge. At that time the drawbridge was controlled by the town-major,** who was a Frenchman. He panicked. As the Irish ran into the city he saw the English close behind them. He feared that if he did not pull up the bridge the English would break into the city. He issued the order for the bridge to be drawn up while most of the Irish were still outside.

There was a most terrible slaughter. The Irish were trapped on the bridge. Every Englishman within musket shot fired into them. Many of the Irish were forced to fling themselves into the water to escape the massacre. Others entered the water involuntarily, pushed by 'those that were behind, pressing the others

---

* To approximately where the 1830 Athlunkard Bridge now stands.
** Town-major: 'The third officer in order in a garrison, and next to the deputy-governor. He ought to understand the fortification, and has a particular charge of the guards, rounds, patrols and sentinels' (*OED*).

forward and throwing them down over the fall of the drawbridge'. Many men were drowned. The trapped men 'cried out for quarter, holding up their hand-kerchiefs'. No quarter was given. Many of the English troops had just stormed the fort. They still had the blood of their comrades on their cheeks and clothes. They were not going to have any sympathy for an enemy who asks for mercy once he has fired his last shot. In any event, the heavy fire kept up by the guns on the city wall prevented the English from coming close enough to take prisoners. Both sides kept up a steady fire, and those poor devils on Thomond Bridge were caught in the middle. 'Before the killing was over they were laid in heaps upon the bridge higher than the ledges of it.'[24]

The English had also suffered heavy losses in the fighting : 'A great many of our men (were) killed from the walls by their too eager pursuit'.[25]

Although he now had the Irish trapped inside the city, Ginckel was disheart-ened by their fighting spirit. Referring to this action he wrote to his political masters on the next day informing them that he had decided not to proceed with a formal siege, but would instead have to blockade the city. 'He saw yesterday how these people defend themselves and assures their lordships that they do not fear fire and are very steady in the charge.'[26]

But although the ferocity of the fighting had impressed Ginckel, the number of Irishmen who had been slaughtered on the bridge had left the garrison in a state of shock. As many as six hundred soldiers had been shot or drowned or taken prisoner. The Irish knew who was to blame. Their comrades had died because:

> A French town-major, who commanded the gate, pretending a fear that the enemies would pour in with the Irish, shut the said gate against friends and foes. . . . Here again was a ridiculous fear, for had two or three thousand of the enemies entered, they would be soon overcome, though there appeared near the gate not above two or three hundred.[27]

Although the town-major died of his wounds before the Irish could lynch him, they could no longer contain their fury. The disaster on Thomond Bridge had not inspired the garrison with a fresh hatred of the English, it had filled them with a fresh hatred of the French. The position of d'Usson and de Tessé was now untenable. There followed a change of government.

The lieutenant-generals were in effect swept aside. Sarsfield took command of the garrison, and to the great surprise of those outside his circle of confidants, he wanted to sue for peace. His aims had become very different from those of the French, and now that his plans no longer included French aid, the time for obedience had passed.

Sarsfield's position was neither illogical nor defeatist. He knew that the war was not simply about Ireland, at its very least it was about the British Isles as a whole. The war would continue so long as William sat as king in London and the Irish people would suffer as they had for the last two years. He was now willing to bargain with the enemy. He would stop the war in Ireland provided he was to be allowed to ship the Irish army to France. To save his own country, Sarsfield wanted to take the war to England.

Although defeat in Ireland was not inevitable, the Irish position had never been worse. The army was now blockaded inside the walls of Limerick and surrounded by triumphant enemies. Their only hope was that the English would suffer more from the effects of winter outside the walls than the Irish would in the shattered buildings within. The English might well withdraw, but it could not be hoped that they would pull back as they had done in 1690, leaving half the country in Irish hands. This time they would withdraw to strong garrisons at Galway, Athlone, Banagher and Portumna as well as those at Cork and Kinsale. If the promised French supplies did come, it would enable Sarsfield and the Irish to continue the war but not to win it. No one needed reminding that the last civil war in Ireland had lasted a decade. The only way to win the war was to drive William off the English throne. This could be best achieved by marching on London, not by fighting a prolonged war in Ireland.

Sarsfield's change of mind has often been commented on. The man responsible for preventing any negotiation in 1690 insisted on negotiation in 1691. It was a mystery to all the commentators of the time both in the city and in the English camp.

The truth is that Sarsfield feared defeat. That is not to say that he felt defeated, but that he could not be sure that the garrison would hold out until relief came. If the garrison suffered a defeat or was forced to surrender, it would be the end of all their hopes. To allow matters to continue would be to take a terrible risk. There was nowhere else to retreat to in Ireland, and Ireland was the other reason why Sarsfield wanted to negotiate while he still had something to bargain with. The war had crippled the country and the nation's suffering had been as bad as it had been a generation before. He saw his country in ruins and an army that looked to the future with despair.

After the early surrender of Galway, after Luttrell's correspondence with the enemy, and after Clifford's supposed treachery there was reason to fear that the army would not have the will to fight on through a prolonged blockade and all the miseries that it would bring. As d'Usson had put it; 'He who today is ready to die rather than submit to the Prince of Orange will tomorrow talk loudly about the need for a settlement'. And the longer they held out, the more their bargaining power would diminish.

Ever since the disaster at Aughrim there had been a growing number of people who were willing to accept whatever terms the English might offer. Since the beginning of the campaign they had met with setback after setback. Ballymore, Athlone, Aughrim, Galway, 'Clifford's Bridge' and now Thomond Bridge. They were now hemmed in, and all of them knew that Ginckel was willing to treat and to offer attractive terms. There were to be no prosecutions and no confiscations; there was to be no persecution just so long as the Irish agreed to end the war. Since Aughrim thousands of Irish troops had deserted and sought protection from the English. There were no deserters travelling the other way as there had been before Aughrim. Everyone knew that the Irish were all but beaten. The best that they could hope for was to hold out in a blockaded city until the spring. That was going to be several months of misery for an uncertain end, and there was always the fear that the English would manage to storm Limerick. Everyone knew what Cromwell had done at Drogheda and Wexford four decades before. Many now felt that if good terms could be agreed with Ginckel, they should be taken.

When William had attacked Limerick in the previous year, Tyrconnell had shown no particular concern about allowing the English to move troops into Clare. But then the situation had been very different. The Irish held all of Connaught. Sligo, Galway and Athlone were safe, and they held all of Munster including the ports of Cork and Kinsale. The speed of William's campaign had prevented the English from establishing themselves securely in the hinterland of Leinster. But now, after Ginckel's cautious advance, Limerick was all alone. The cavalry was isolated and out of touch. The Irish held a few small garrisons, notably the castles of Clare and Ross, none of which was capable of bringing any relief to Limerick, and Sligo from where there was no news. Although Ginckel had not subdued Kerry, he did not need to. The English navy had made itself felt in the mouth of the Shannon and it was not known whether a French fleet would now be able to get supplies to the city.

The city of Limerick was a mess. It had been heavily bombarded by the English artillery. 'There is not a whole house in the town.'[28] The streets were strewn with rubble and fallen masonry. The buildings were shattered or gutted, and every day and night the English gunners hurled more cannon balls, red hot shot and 'carcasses' over the walls. Part of the defensive wall on King's Island had collapsed. Londonderry, after over three months of siege, had never looked as sorry as Limerick looked now.

But Limerick was not Londonderry. The men of the garrison did not see themselves as the last remnants of a race fighting for their very survival. They all knew that if they surrendered nothing very terrible would happen to them. They would merely be disarmed and sent home which was not an altogether unpleasant prospect. They were drawn from all over the country, few of them had their families with them, and they had no news of what went on outside. They had all lived under the English crown before. They had all been ruled by a Protestant government before. It was not what they had wanted, but life had gone on. They and their families had then all had food and clothes. They had all now seen what the war had done to the country. All of them had seen, if not experienced, starvation. They had all seen the corpses of children who had perished for want of food, shelter or clothing. While the war continued there was going to be no end to this misery. Everyone wanted peace, and peace would still be welcome if it was accompanied by a return to the situation that they had endured in the time of Charles II.

Sarsfield did not make his decision alone. He was encouraged to do so by his circle of confidants. The most senior of them was the only non-Irishman close to him, John Wauchope, whose sole concern as a professional soldier was to save the army.* Lord Galmoy felt the same even though by going to France he would lose all his land, and he was easily the richest man in Sarsfield's group. Another leading figure was Nicholas Purcell who like many other land-owners in the city was anxious that negotiations should be commenced while they were still able to fight. If they did not do so, their fear was that everything they owned would be lost in a confiscation of land every bit as severe as that imposed by the Cromwellians in the 1650s. As well as these leading names there was a group of Irish colonels also now keen to negotiate, either for Sars-field's or Purcell's reasons. There were probably not more than ten men who together brought about this great change.** Outside this close circle, Sarsfield's decision came as a great surprise.

Many of the Irish had not even considered surrender. They had every reason to believe that they could hold out all winter. They had sufficient stores of food and ammunition and the walls between them and their enemies were intact. The fact that the English had crossed into Clare was not fatal to the defence, nor was the fact that they had lost communication with Sheldon. They were shocked when they heard of Sarfield's change of mind, so much so that O'Kelly was of the opinion that no one other than Sarsfield would have been capable of persuading the Irish to give in.

> The authority of Sarsfield and the opinion which all the world conceived of his untainted loyalty and zeal for his country, expressed upon several occasions, made them approve of whatever he proposed, though with a great deal of reluctancy and with equal regret.[30]

Even for Sarsfield, it proved to be no easy task to persuade all the officers. Many of them held him in such esteem simply because he was the man least likely to

*   Wauchope's early career had been as turbulent as Sarsfield's. Although his cousin was a wealthy Midlothian laird, he was the son of a youngest son and had no fortune of his own. A Roman Catholic, he had joined the Dutch brigade in 1672 and served there until his recall in 1688. He distinguished himself as a regimental officer, was wounded at the siege of Maestricht in 1673 and succeeded Mackay and Douglas to the colonelcy of his regiment. He also distinguished himself at the Dutch court by having an affair with Betty Villiers, the prince of Orange's mistress. Before he could return to Britain he needed to be pardoned by King James for killing a fellow officer while serving in Dendermonde some years earlier. He raised a regiment in Scotland in 1688 but fled to France at the revolution. He later served at Derry where for most of the siege he commanded the artillery on the east bank of the river. Through his association with Sarsfield he gained the distinction of being the only foreigner to meet with the approval of O'Kelly who wrote of him as appearing to be zealous both for his religion and 'the Irish interest'.[29]

**   It is not now possible to name these men, but it is most probable that included in their number were those non-lawyers who later signed the treaty; Colonels Nicholas Cusack, Mark Talbot and Garret Dillon. Also included in this group may have been the lawyer Colonel John Browne who has been identified as being a particular friend of Sarsfield's.

treat with the enemy. To their surprise, he was now 'the most active of all the commanders to forward the treaty, and took most pains to persuade the colonels and the captains to a compliance'.[31]

In persuading his officers to accept his plan, Sarsfield deliberately overstated the gravity of their position. O'Kelly wrote of him 'representing that there was but a small quantity of provisions left, and no expectation of any supply out of France until next spring; that if they rejected the conditions now offered, they were to hope for none when their provisions were all spent; and that therefore the necessity to capitulate at present was absolute and unavoidable'. When the time came for an official explanation of the reasoning behind the capitulation, it was Wauchope who set it out.[32] The first reason was the treachery of Clifford who had 'suffered the enemy to build a bridge' and get into Co. Clare. This he stated would mean that the Irish horse and dragoons would have to capitulate or disperse. Secondly, even if the French did send more horse and cavalry, the country was now too desolate to be able to support them. The third official reason is now generally accepted to be false. Wauchope stated that they would run out of bread by 15 October and as they feared that the English had blockaded the Shannon they could expect no relief from the French. Irishmen and Williamites alike later wrote that there were plentiful supplies of food inside the city.

But the majority needed little persuading. It cannot be doubted that there was a certain amount of relief, if not joy, inside Limerick when Sarsfield's intentions first became known. Although the men would have fought on had he commanded them to, without him there was no enthusiasm to continue.

It was of the utmost importance that Sarsfield also persuaded the French to agree to a surrender, as a capitulation without their authority would be an act of mutiny. And to Sarsfield it was important not only that the French agreed to surrender, but that the suggestion should come from them.

One can guess that the four senior Frenchmen in Limerick, Generals d'Usson, de Tessé and la Tour Monfort and the Intendant Fumeron, were quite willing to be pushed into negotiating. They were eager to seek an excuse to authorise such a move as although they, like Tyrconnell, knew that the French had promised a fresh fleet, unlike Tyrconnell, they would be more than glad to get out of Ireland for good. Awkwardly for them, their future positions would largely depend on their behaviour in Ireland. If only they could pin the unhappy outcome of the Irish war on Sarsfield and his party, no one would be able to blame them for coming home.

It is clear from the Frenchmen's reaction that they were not suddenly told by Sarsfield that there was to be a surrender: they were sounded out. Sarsfield was able to discover—or else he knew all along—what their feelings were. They were encouraged to talk of their fears and, although they did not introduce the idea to the Irish, it was the French who first openly voiced the view that an honourable surrender might be the best policy. Sarsfield, who had already decided the same, was careful to make sure that they were the first to say so openly. He would later be able to accuse them publicly, without fear of contradiction, of being the ones who had first suggested surrendering.[33]

Sarsfield's first obstacle to negotiating with the English was the oath that Tyrconnell had made the entire army swear before the siege. No one could surrender without the king's permission. Surprisingly enough, this did not prove to be a difficult problem to dispose of. The weak argument was forcefully put that as the English fleet was blockading the Shannon it was physically impossible for anyone to solicit or receive the king's consent. Consequently, 'the king's permission to treat, considering the extreme want they were in, might reasonably be presumed since it could not be known'. The general mood in Limerick was such that this blatant casuistry went unchallenged.

Outside the walls, by Thomond gate, the English dug in. They were fired at from the walls but were secure in the knowledge that there could be no counter-attack while the bridge was blocked with the dead.

CHAPTER XX

The Treaty of Limerick

The Walls of Limerick is now become the only scene on this side of Europe
where a transaction of the greatest importance is hourly expected.
Mercurius Reformatus or the
New Observator, 10 October 1691

NOW THAT HIS mind was made up, Sarsfield wasted no time in arranging a
truce. The initial approach to the Dutch generals was to be made by John
Wauchope who had spent fourteen years in the Dutch army. Drums were beaten
on both sides of the town to signal a parley. From the Irishtown Brigadier Roth
raised a white flag and called out over the wall for an interview with Ginckel,
but the Williamite commanders were on the Clare side. From the west tower of
the castle, overlooking the river and Thomond Bridge, Wauchope did the same
and was able to speak to Scravenmoer. Scravenmoer invited his one-time com-
rade in arms over the water and the Scotsman was rowed across to the western
bank. Wauchope asked the Dutchman if Sarsfield could join them, and as old
Scravenmoer could barely speak English and Sarsfield spoke no Dutch but was
fluent in French, he also asked that Major-General Ruvigny be present.[1]

Shortly afterwards Sarsfield crossed the river to negotiate the surrender of
Limerick. He came straight to the point. He was only empowered to agree
terms of capitulation if one condition was agreed from the start. 'The first thing
they insisted upon at the time they beat the chamade was a liberty to go and
serve where they would'.[2]

Ruvigny and Scravenmoer were not in a position to comment on the terms
that Sarsfield could expect. Only Ginckel could do that, but they did agree to a
ceasefire until the next day and agreed to arrange a meeting with the general. In
the early evening, after some four hours of talk, Sarsfield and Wauchope returned
to the city. Scravenmoer and Ruvigny were delighted. They had learnt a lot about
the anti-French sentiment inside the city and the intentions of the Jacobite commanders. They knew that Sarsfield was determined to surrender. There could
now be little doubt in their minds that the war was over. Only one thing had
marred their enjoyment of the interviews. Sarsfield had repeatedly stated that he
would only surrender Limerick if he could take the Irish army to France. The
problem was going to be whether the general would agree to such a term.

Ginckel was of course anxious to finish the war as soon as he could. But he
was not going to agree to any terms that the Irish might demand, as he was at
all times confident that victory would in time be his. Only a few hours before
Wauchope had called for a parley Ginckel had finished a letter to the lord

justices in which he expressed his optimism.[3] Had he been in any doubt as to his eventual victory he would have written to them carefully detailing all the obstacles that lay in his path. His only fear was that the city might be relieved by a French fleet but failing that, he wrote, he expected to take Limerick although he had been forced to modify his plans. He no longer intended to try and storm the walls as in his view the ferocity of the Irish rendered such a plan impractical. He was instead going to blockade the city. But that could take months during which time the likelihood of French interference would increase. An early surrender was to Ginckel certainly worth some concessions.

On the next day, Thursday 24 September 1691 at ten o'clock in the morning, Sarsfield and Wauchope were again rowed across the river to the English lines. Sarsfield brought with him some bottles of good claret. They were met by Ruvigny, Scravenmoer and Wauchope's old commanding officer, the devout Hugh Mackay. Sarsfield was anxious to involve Sheldon and so asked for some blank passes to be made out and sent to the cavalry camp some nine miles away at Sixmilebridge. The three Williamite generals—the Frenchman, the Dutchman and the Scot—agreed. Sarsfield asked that the ceasefire be extended for a further three days so that Sheldon could join them. His request was granted. No one wanted anything to go wrong now. The two sides made certain concessions to each other to show their goodwill. The Irish were allowed to send out burial parties to deal with the bodies on and around Thomond bridge, and they released their two hundred and fifty or so prisoners of war.

On Friday, Sheldon, his senior cavalry officers and the archbishop of Armagh arrived in the English camp from Sixmilebridge. Ginckel received them and fed them. In the afternoon they were rowed across to the town. It was a sad voyage. Sheldon had the boatman stop near Thomond bridge where the Irish burial parties were still removing the corpses. The cavalrymen wanted to know what had happened, and who had died. They entered the shattered city and amidst the rubble met Sarsfield. He told them that Ginckel had agreed to allow the army to sail to France. It was quite clear that his mind was made up. Everyone knew that there was now no question of fighting

Next morning Sarsfield, Wauchope and two of their brigadiers crossed the river again and dined with Ginckel. It was a melancholy occasion and Wauchope wept as he recalled his days in the Dutch service.[4] However, they were able to agree on one thing: the Irish army was to be shipped to France. They also agreed to an exchange of hostages while the terms of surrender were finalised.

During the days that negotiations had been taking place between the military commanders, the civil leaders in Limerick had been forming their own plans. To them the articles of surrender offered far more than the removal of the Irish army to France. The leading clergyman in Limerick was now Dominic Maguire, the archbishop of Armagh and primate of all Ireland. To him it was essential that at least the same terms regarding religion were granted as those that had been granted at Galway. At Galway it was agreed that there would be no prosecution of Catholics under any penal laws, and that Catholic lawyers would be permitted to practise. The primate now insisted that Sarsfield should look beyond the details of arranging naval transport; the treaty should also protect the Irish people until King James was re-enthroned.

Archbishop Maguire's proposals were presented under seven heads which it was hoped would form articles in addition to the military ones. The essence of his proposals was that there be a general pardon, that all confiscated estates be restored to their owners, that Catholics be given complete equality under the law, that the Irish army be maintained and that there be an act of Parliament to put the treaty into effect.

These proposals were immediately rejected by Ginckel. According to one source, he 'returned them with disdain'. This may be an exaggeration, but one thing had become very clear to Ginckel and that was that the Irish intended to surrender. The archbishop's draft had not contained the sort of proposals that one would expect from a defeated enemy. They were the best terms possible. They were the sort of proposals that could be expected from a garrison intent on continuing the war. Ginckel felt that he knew better. They were bluffing and he decided to call their bluff. He sent the paper back to Limerick. 'Though (he said) he was in a manner a stranger to the laws of England, yet he understood that those things they insisted upon were so far contradictory to them and dishonourable to himself that he would not grant any such terms.'[5] To underline his point, he immediately ordered the preparation of a new battery outside the town.

This rejection was not of immediate concern to Sarsfield. He had his lawyers fully occupied in preparing a draft of the military articles. If any lawyer had been consulted the archbishop's proposals would have been amended before Ginckel saw them. It was clearly futile for the primate to demand that a general should agree to pre-determine the way in which the members of a future parliament would vote. But in any event Sarsfield was confident that Ginckel would have to grant at least the same terms as he had granted to the garrison of Galway. If he did not do so, he would have created in Galway a class of Roman Catholics that was to enjoy privileges denied to every other Catholic in the country. Sarsfield did not want the demands of the churchmen and the civilians to compromise the military treaty and whereas before he had wanted Colonel Charles O'Kelly, who had held himself out to be something of a spokesman for the Gaels, to contribute to the negotiations, he now excluded him.[6] Although O'Kelly was now seventy, age had not mellowed his robust views on the English and his presence would most certainly be obstructive. Almost casually, and certainly not with the expected degree of bewilderment or anger, Sarsfield sent a message back to Ginckel asking him to let him know what it was that he would agree to. Ginckel's reply was to send him the twelve proposals which were to form the basis of the civil treaty.

Early the next morning, Monday 28 September, a delegation left Limerick and made its way to Ginckel's tent. The delegation was led by Sarsfield and Wauchope and included the archbishops of Armagh and Cashel, Nicholas Purcell and three lawyers—Sir Garret Dillon, Sir Theobald Butler and Colonel John Browne—as well as a number of other officers and leading civilians.

This day decided the treaty. Ginckel was eager to hurry things along and made three main offers to the Irish. He was willing to agree that there would be a general pardon, that those under arms in Limerick who swore allegiance to William and Mary could keep their lands, and that the Roman Catholics of Ireland should enjoy such privileges as they had in the reign of Charles II. The Irish negotiators readily agreed, but there was then some debate as to whether the benefits of these provisions should be extended to those civilians who were still under the protection of the Irish army. Here Sarsfield made his only record-ed contribution to the negotiations for a civil treaty. He insisted that Ginckel's offer should include the civilians and declared that he 'would lay his bones in these old walls rather than not take care of those who stuck by them all along'.[7]

As Sarsfield's efforts were all but entirely concentrated on the military articles, the Irish lawyers were consequently made to do the same. The twenty-nine military articles were carefully worded and comprehensive. They provid-ed that anyone who wanted to go to France could do so, that the soldiers could take their weapons, horses and moveable property with them, that Ginckel would keep the Irish supplied with provisions and would provide them with enough ships to transport them, that all prisoners of war were to be set at liberty and that 'there shall be a cessation of arms at land and also at sea.' The wording of the articles was lengthy and repetitive to avoid any doubt as to what was intended. For Sarsfield it was a triumph. The Irish army was now going to go to France.

Compared with the military articles, the civil articles were a sorry affair. They contained those concessions for the Irish 'as are consistent with the laws of Ireland' and contained certain promises—made with King William's authority—'that Their Majesties will ratify these articles within the space of eight months or sooner, and use their utmost endeavours that the same shall be ratified and confirmed in Parliament'. It was clear from this wording that Parliament, whether it be Irish or English, could not be bound by the treaty. William and Mary would encourage Parliament to ratify the articles, but they could do no more. In the meantime the articles were to be agreed, and would remain in force until a Parliament embodied them in law or else dismissed them. William's powers as king were not the same as James had once enjoyed. William's position was defined. He could neither dispense nor suspend laws, and he was powerless to stop his Parliament passing whatever laws it wished. This was common knowledge. The Irish lawyers knew it and Sarsfield knew it.

To Sarsfield the civil articles were merely a delaying tactic. They were intended to loosely bind the crown of England, a crown that he expected to be on the head of James within the year. The civil articles were to him merely a weak assurance, although the strongest that he could hope for, that in the inter-vening months the Irish would suffer as little as possible. This he achieved. The niceties of what future parliaments may or may not do were irrelevant. To understand this attitude is to understand Sarsfield. He was not a defeatist. He was looking to a better future. He was not going to France to serve the French king. He was going with one purpose only; to prepare for an invasion of England. And once that invasion had taken place Ireland would not be bound by the stifling articles of the treaty.

To the Irish lawyers, the civil treaty was the best that they could do in the short time available. Sarsfield had told them that their priorities lay in drafting a flawless military treaty. The consequence of this was that there were only thirteen civil articles and two of those simply made special provisions for five named individuals.* Only the first article provided for the future liberties of the Irish in Ireland, but it did so in terms so brief and vague as to render the article legally meaningless. The other articles granted a full pardon and certain guarantees to the Irish officers and soldiers, and to those civilians living under their protection. The most important of these guarantees allowed them to keep all their property provided that they swore allegiance to William and Mary. Indeed Sarsfield was so concerned that the military treaty should not be put in jeopardy by demands for civil articles that certain concessions that had been allowed at Galway were not demanded at Limerick. Nothing was done to secure the property of those who had been taken as prisoners of war. This meant that, for instance, Lord Bophin who had been captured at Aughrim was allowed to keep his land because his brother had got him included in the articles at Galway, while Lord Kenmare who was also captured at Aughrim, lost everything.**

It is most important to emphasise the rationale behind the civil treaty as much has been written of it since as if it were a document designed to define for all time the relationship between two equal contracting nations.

On 1 October, at about nine in the evening, the two Williamite lord justices, Charles Porter and Thomas Coningsby, reached Ginckel's camp. They spent the next morning going through the articles with Ginckel and in the mid afternoon Sarsfield and Wauchope led their mixed delegation of lawyers, sol-diers and clergymen over to meet them. Story recorded that the debates then began afresh, and on different subjects such as that of rapparees. But the agreement held. It was midnight when the meeting eventually broke up and the Irish returned to Limerick.

---

* The fourth article did no more than include Simon Luttrell, Rowland White, Maurice Eustace and Lord Mountleinster (who was married to Sarsfield's eldest sister) in the articles provided that they returned to the country within eight months. As Tyrconnell and Sarsfield had commandeered all his wealth during the war 'for public use', the thirteenth article provided that Colonel John Browne's debts 'to several Protestants' were to be paid by those Catholics who were to have their estates returned to them.
** Despite his being Nicholas Purcell's father-in-law.[8]

An anecdote survives of these negotiations which tells us much of Sarsfield's character.

> During the treaty a saying of Sarsfield's deserves to be remembered for it was much talked of all Europe over. He asked some of the English officers if they had not come to a better opinion of the Irish by their behaviour during this war; and whereas they said it was much the same that it had always been; Sarsfield answered, 'As low as we now are, change but kings with us and we will fight it over again with you.'[9]

This quotation has often been seized upon to portray Sarsfield as being somewhat melodramatic in his dealings with the English, but it in fact shows quite the reverse. Far from being a humourless fanatic he was able even at this most difficult time to exchange light-hearted pleasantries with his enemies. Although there can be no doubt that the Irish were disappointed at their king's flight after the Boyne, there can also be no doubt that Sarsfield remained wholly loyal to King James to the last.

On Sunday, 3 October 1691, the Irish delegates dined with the duke of Wurtemberg. It was a nervous affair, as this was the day on which the war was to end. After they had been fed, Sarsfield and Wauchope with, for the first time the three French generals, d'Usson, de Tessé and la Tour Montfort, went to Ginckel's tent. They were accompanied by Lord Galmoy, Sir Toby Butler and Colonels Nicholas Purcell, Mark Talbot, Nicholas Cusack, Garret Dillon and 'Sarsfield's great friend',[10] the barrister and munitions manufacturer John Browne. There the treaties, one military and one civil, had been prepared and laid out in duplicate. They spent several hours going through the articles and checking the drafts, and after dark, on a table in the general's tent, the treaty was signed.*

Sarsfield was anxious that the French signed the military treaty first. They were the senior officers and it was important that there should be no question as to whether he was authorised to sign on behalf of the army or not. Indeed,

---

*   It is quite clear that the tradition that the treaty was 'signed on a large stone near Thomond Bridge within sight of both armies' is of more recent invention. According to Laurence Walsh in *Historic Limerick* this legend of the Treaty Stone cannot be traced back further than 1797. Maurice Lenihan, whose *History of Limerick* was published in 1866, a year after the Treaty Stone was mounted onto the pedestal where it remains, wrote the following: 'The Treaty is said to have been signed at or near the Red Gate within a mile of the city at the Clare side. Tradition does not admit that it was signed on what has been called the 'Treaty Stone' which has occupied a place on the north side of Thomond Bridge for many years, and which was originally a stone used by country-people for getting on horses when leaving town. The Cork *Freeholder* of Monday, 11 July 1814 says "that the late Miss Dobbin of Brown Street had in her possession the TABLE on which the treaty of Limerick was signed; and which was about being auctioned off on decease of the above lady."' However, the Treaty Stone may well have marked the spot where Sarsfield and Wauchope first negotiated a ceasefire with Ruvigny and Scravenmoer.

the preamble to the military treaty read: 'Military articles agreed upon between Lieutenant-General Ginckel, commander-in-chief of the English army, on one side, and the Lieutenant-Generals d'Usson and de Tessé, commanders-in-chief of the Irish army, on the other side, and the general officers hereunto sub-scribing'. Sarsfield forcefully signed himself 'Lucan' after the Frenchmen, splashing ink over the manuscript and all but driving his quill through the paper. His signature was then followed by those of Wauchope, Mark Talbot, Galmoy and Nicholas Purcell. The very number of signatures on the Irish side reflected the state of command in the army. The French generals had signed because they were the senior officers, the next set of signatures represented an assertion of democratic authority to sign. The suggestion was clear: de Tessé and d'Usson did not, despite their rank, command the Irish army, but there was a fear that without their signatures the treaty would be invalid. For the English, Ginckel inscribed his solitary signature.[11] No one disputed *his* leadership.

The civil articles were signed by the two lord justices, Porter and Conningsby, and then by Ginckel. They were witnessed by General Scravenmoer, Mackay and Talmash. The duplicate copy was signed only by the senior Irishmen present, the first signature being that of Sarsfield. It was with a sigh of great relief that he returned to the gaunt walls of the English town that night. He had done his duty, he had saved an army.*

By the twenty-third article of the military treaty, the English were to occupy the Irish town of Limerick on the same day that the treaty was signed. Sarsfield had agreed to this to show his goodwill, and Ginckel had insisted on it to prevent the Irish changing their minds and deciding to continue the war should their circumstances alter. It was his security. However, as the articles were signed so late in the evening General Tollemache, who was to command the operation, was unwilling to do anything more that night except occupy the outworks. It was important at this delicate juncture not to upset anyone, but in the morning five English regiments marched in through St John's Gate and occupied the town. The Irish had already marched out over Ball's Bridge and after fouling the town to make it as uncomfortable as they could, they began to establish themselves on King's Island. There was to be no going back.

* A further indication of how little Sarsfield was concerned with the civil treaty is given by the insufficient time given to proof reading the document. The second of the civil articles provided that the inhabitants of Limerick and the Irish officers and soldiers 'in Limerick, Clare, Kerry, Cork and Mayo, or any of them' should be allowed the benefit of the treaty. The agreed draft had then included the words 'And all such as are under their protection in those counties.' According to George Clarke who had helped to draft the treaty: 'In transcribing the fair copy, which was actually signed, Mr Payzant, my clerk, in whose hand the body of the articles are written left out in the second article these words.' The consequence was that the signed copy of the treaty was sent back to London without this important clause. Sarsfield and the others, even though they had read through the fair copy, did not discover this omission until it was too late. However, the missing words were later inserted when the treaty was ratified by William and Mary, not that this influenced the (all Protestant) Irish Parliament of 1697 who legislated to the contrary.'[12]

Ginckel's intention was to wait with Sarsfield in Limerick until shipping could be arranged to take the Irish away. Although he never attempted to renege on the treaty, he began to question whether he had been too lenient in granting the terms that he had. Most importantly he was concerned that he was allowing several thousand trained men, with all their weapons, to leave the country so that they could join an invasion force that would attack either England or Holland next year. He began to feel not so much that he had cleverly brought a campaign to an end, but that he had assisted his enemies in escaping the jaws of the English army. 'All persons . . . that are willing to leave the kingdom of Ireland shall have free liberty to go to any country beyond the seas' read the first of the military articles. It was important that as few as possible of the Irish troops should choose to leave. It dawned on Ginckel that his success would be measured in the number of his enemies who would travel to France. He prepared a declaration to be made to the Irish soldiers in which he would make them the best possible offers. Without breaking any of the articles of the treaty, he was anxious that an effort should now be made to woo as many of them as he could away from Sarsfield's influence.

The declaration offered the Irish troops immediate quarters and subsistence if they joined King's William's army. If they did enlist they would not, as he was advised the Irish feared, be sent to fight in Hungary 'nor in any other remote place against their wills'. If any Irish soldier wished to quit the military life he would be allowed to do so and would be allowed to sell his arms and horse to the English. But all Irish soldiers should note well that 'if they once go into France they must not expect to return into this kingdom again'.[13]

While the declaration was being drafted, Ginckel received a message from an Irish lieutenant-colonel who claimed to have been locked up by Sarsfield for refusing to go to France. Ginckel exploded. The Irish were going to deny their soldiers any choice in the matter. He roared out orders that four cannon be wheeled onto Ball's Bridge. He was going to teach them to play tricks on him. To the Irish it appeared that the English were going to attack.

Sarsfield made his way to Ginckel immediately he saw what was going on. They had a blazing row. Ginckel accused Sarsfield of breaking the treaty. Sarsfield denied it. 'My Lord Lucan saying at last that he was then in the General's power. Not so (replied the other) but you shall go in and then do the best you can.'[14]

Sarsfield argued that the imprisoned man had not been detained for his unwillingness to go to France. He had been locked up for impertinence. He was a 'prisoner of state' and had been locked up even before the treaty. Sarsfield also pointed out that after the articles had been signed he had released his 'political' prisoners even though he had not be obliged to do so. Some of them had visited the English camp, as this man had, and had then returned to the town to 'rail and speak disrespectfully' of the Irish generals. Ginckel was mollified, especially when Sarsfield agreed to banish the prisoner from the town. But the Dutchman's suspicions continued.[15]

That same day, as the damp afternoon turned to grey evening, the Irish regiments were mustered and harangued by Sarsfield and Wauchope. The message to them was not new but now took on a fresh urgency. These two leaders of the Irish army desperately tried to convey their optimism for the future to the men under them. It was important that they go to France, not to fight for France and not to stay in France but to return to the British Isles to drive out the usurper and avenge the wrongs done in this name. They could do little good in Limerick. The French fleet had failed to supply them in time. The next time that they fought it would be alongside French troops and a mighty army of exiles. Any man that now chose to leave the colours, or worse still, to take the tyrant's pay, would curse the day that he was born when in the spring his erstwhile comrades, invincible and victorious, would strike a mighty blow against tyranny and restore the three crowns to King James. The officers were also told, both privately and publicly, that they would all keep their positions and that they would all be kept on English pay in an English establishment even in France. They were not to be an army of paupers, but for their loyalty they were to be the new elite. So the urging and the coaxing and the speeches went on into the night, and as Story cynically noted, 'a great many other advantages were laid before them which would have seemed improbable to any but an Irishman.'

Having repeatedly been made to listen to these glorious promises in the evening, the Irish troops were woken on the next day for more of the same. The priests blessed and delivered sermons to every regiment. Again the advantages of going to France both for them and their religion were stressed, not forgetting 'the inconveniences, nay, certain damnation, of joining with heretics'. Brandy was liberally distributed among the soldiers, and then, having been filled with as much patriotism and religious fervour as it was possible to cram into them, the fourteen thousand foot soldiers were blessed by the bishops and marched, and often staggered, across Thomond Bridge to line up in County Clare.

There they were subjected to a harangue, far more tedious than the former and to most of them incomprehensible. Adjutant-General Withers had been instructed to ensure that every Irishman was well aware of Ginckel's declaration. Just in case they were not familiar with it in detail, it was read out, and it was stressed to them if they left for France they would never return to Ireland again. They were also made to listen to General Withers's views 'on the advantages of our service above that of France, and how unnatural it was for them to choose to go and serve in a foreign country against the real interest of their own.'[16]

That was the last of the speeches. The drums were beaten and the first of the Irish regiments, the Royal Regiment, marched forward. The two men whose show this was, Withers and Fumeron, had agreed that each Irish regiment was to march past them and return towards Thomond bridge. When they reached a prearranged point they could file off if they so chose. Those that marched on over the bridge were bound to remain in the Irish army and be subject to all its disciplines, and to be transported to France. Those who filed off were then to be given the opportunity of either peacefully returning home, or of joining King William's army. Sarsfield had clearly arranged matters so that the Royal Regiment would be the first to make the decision as they included his best and most loyal troops. They would, he hoped, set the example for the rest to follow. According to Story, 'The Royal Regiment, being then fourteen hundred men, seemed to go all entire except seven men.' Ginckel, he noted, became very concerned.

It was not an example that everyone followed. Some of the foot regiments, notably Dillon's and Lord Iveagh's regiment of the much disliked Ulster Gaels, filed off to the side in each case leaving less than a company of men loyally marching to the front. But Sarsfield had good reason to be satisfied. Overall about seventy per cent of the infantry had elected to stay with him, and of those who decided not to go to France, less than a quarter volunteered their services to the English. Apart from this minority, the Irish remained loyal to King James. Sarsfield's rhetoric had worked. He was now going to France with an army which would be the core of the Jacobite invasion force. The next time they fought, it would be in Kent.

It can have come of no surprise to Sarsfield that some of the leading men in the army chose to desert the cause. The landowners were in the most difficult of positions. If they remained in Ireland they could be called traitors by the Jacobites, but if they went to France all their lands would be forfeited to the crown, a crown that appeared to be firmly on the head of King William. If that were to happen they could only again establish themselves in the world if King James won an outright and crushing victory over this enemy. If there was any compromise they would lose out, just as the hopeful royalists had lost out when King Charles had come to the throne and found it to be bad politics to dispossess the Cromwellians. Most of the Irish lords felt that they owed it to their families, to their sons yet unborn, to stay in Ireland. Of the four lords who had been sent as hostages to Ginckel's camp, three of them (Iveagh, Louth and Westmeath) decided to give up soldiering and to go home quietly, and only the fourth, the teenager Lord Trimlestown, remained with Sarsfield. Even some of those who had been considered hard-liners elected to stay at home. Nicholas Purcell left to retire to his lands in Tipperary. Likewise, the aggressively patriotic septuagenarian Charles O'Kelly decided that it was time to hang up his sword and retire to his estate in Co Galway.[17]

Brigadier Robert Clifford, who since the crossing of the Shannon had reason to fear the welcome that he would receive, also decided to stay behind. He was not a man that Sarsfield would miss. Henry Luttrell went further and made it plain to all that his correspondence with la Bastide may not have been as innocent as he had claimed at his court-martial. He announced that not only was he going to stay in Ireland but that he was going to join King William's army. In fact he cleverly ensured that whatever revolutions were brought about over the next few years, the Luttrells would remain in Luttrellstown, Co Dublin. By playing on Ginckel's fears, he managed to secure a deal whereby if

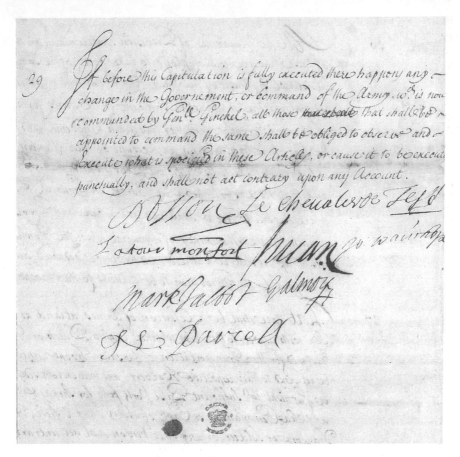

18 The last article of the Military Treaty of Limerick
and the signatures of D'Usson, Le chevalier de Tessé,
Latour Monfort, Lucan, Jo: Wauchope, Mark Talbot, Galmoy, N: Purcell.

he changed sides, which he did, he would take possession of the family estate. As he was the second son, the estate in fact belonged to his brother, Simon, who was at this time approaching Ireland on a French ship. Should the Jacobites ever regain power, Simon would then recover his rightful estate and no doubt thank his brother for preventing the land from being sold off to pay for William's war.

There is no evidence of any animosity between Sarsfield and any of these men, although one suspects that his feelings for Luttrell were no longer friendly. He could not insist on them sailing with him to an uncertain future. The civil treaty had been specifically drafted to make allowances for them, and it was not for him to insist that they gamble their estates. He knew that he and the Jacobite cause already owed many of these men a very great debt. Many of them could be expected to start a rising in Ireland once Sarsfield's invasion of England had established itself. Most of them wished him luck.

In fact, the treaty ensured that very few of the estate owners followed Sarsfield. Lord Galmoy came with him, and lost the most by so doing.

Another who sacrificed great wealth was Sarsfield's cousin and brother-in-law, Dominic Sarsfield, Lord Kilmallock. The senior officers of the Irish army who did elect to go to France were not landed gentry, but professional soldiers such as Sheldon and Wauchope. Although it cannot be doubted that both these men were wholly loyal to King James, their loyalty was never tested by the prospect of losing large estates. The choice to them was either to continue in their positions, or to retire in poverty. In fact, of the senior officers who did not have estates to lose, only Edward Wilson, the inspector-general of the infantry decided to retire and he 'had not one drop of Irish blood in all his veins'.[18]

Over the next two days similar reviews were held for the cavalry and for the garrison troops from Kerry. Two of the cavalry commanders, Henry Luttrell and Colonel John Rice, successfully persuaded their regiments to join the Williamite army with them. Luttrell, it seems, did this by means of a particularly persuasive speech which was a part of the bargain that he had struck with Ginckel whereby he was promised his brother's land, while Rice entered into a bond for £10,000 to guarantee his men's pay if they joined him in serving King William.[19] But despite these losses, Sarsfield still ensured that King James commanded the allegiance of the majority of the horsemen as well as the foot.

Ginckel took most unkindly to this situation. It was to him an end of campaign defeat. Although he had been happy to sign the treaty to end the war, he now began to doubt the wisdom of his action. Many of his high ranking advisors—not to mention the army as a whole—felt that he had given away too much. 'We fight like heroes, but like fools we treat'.[20]

Ginckel had not only agreed to assist the Irish army to sail away to cause unknown mischief elsewhere, but had also given the Irish civil privileges when they ought to have been punished for plunging the country into a destructive civil war. Those Irish leaders who had submitted were even to be pardoned and allowed to keep their property as if the war had never taken place and as if those thousands of dead Protestants had never existed. Although there had been widespread relief when the treaty was first mooted, feelings in the English camp were now running high.

On the day after the review, Sarsfield again quartered his infantry in the English town and on King's Island. The gates were locked to prevent any desertion and the stores of brandy and claret were broken open to encourage the men. When this was reported to Ginckel, he suffered another of his explosions. Despite the fact that Sarsfield had broken none of the articles, the Dutchman claimed that the Irish had 'used indirect means to threaten their men into a French voyage'. Those indirect means extended beyond the breaking open of the stores and intoxicating the men, to giving them firm promises of future victory and spiritual salvation. On reflection, Ginckel could never have seen his methods—promises of decent pay and conditions in a place other than Hungary—as being any less contemptible. He sent Sarsfield an ill humoured note letting him know that if he broke the articles 'he thought himself no longer obliged to observe them'. It is perhaps strange that Ginckel should have allowed himself to write anything of the sort, as the soldiers had already made their decisions and the articles provided that after the muster any deserters from the Irish army were to be handed back to the Irish authorities. But Ginckel still felt duty bound to attempt to lure as many of the Irish troops away as he could, although there was little that he could do. He held a muster for all those Irishmen who had elected not to go to France, and ensured that each of them was given bread, cheese, brandy, tobacco and a fortnight's subsistence.

While the war had focused on Limerick the rest of the country was mostly, though not always, quiet. On 14 September Sir Teague O'Regan had eventually surrendered Sligo on the condition that he could march with his men to Limerick. There had also been several minor clashes in western Munster where Ginckel had sent Brigadier Leveson with his dragoons to keep the Irish troops there occupied and away from Limerick. The fighting in Munster only stopped once the Irish heard of Sarsfield's ceasefire. However one independent although unofficial Irish leader did continue his operations against the English to the end. This was 'Galloping' Hogan who had reputedly guided Sarsfield to Ballyneety. On 24 September, when Sarsfield was already negotiating, he repeated the famous raid, albeit on a smaller scale:

> Galloping Hogan, a fellow that got upwards of one hundred rapparees together, horse and foot, and got much plunder by robbing the sutlers and other people that came into his power; was now so bold as to set upon a party of cars coming towards the camp with little or no guard nigh Cullen and took away with him seventy one small horses.

Later in the month he and his band ambushed a group of eight militiamen and killed seven of them. This was despite the lord justices' proclamation of the 18 September which promised protection and pardon for all the rapparees that surrendered within the month. Even on the very same day that the treaty was signed, it was felt necessary to detach two whole regiments of horse from the English camp to scour the countryside for Hogan's gang. The proclamation offering protection and pardon was repeated on 14 October, and five days later Hogan and his men surrendered at Roscrea.

Alas, there was no happy ending for Hogan. Eager as he had been to seize the opportunities offered by the turmoil of war, he was now eager to seize what opportunities he could from the peace. He was allowed two dozen men to ride about the countryside and hunt down those rapparees who had not surrendered, and so the most famous poacher of the war turned gamekeeper. He was perhaps induced to do so not so much by English gold, but by his desire as a bandit chief to settle old scores with other bandits, 'though this was fatal to him, for some of that sort of people murdered him afterwards'.*[21]

A bitter peace now descended on Ireland. The consequences of the last three years were so terrible that it would be several generations before men's minds again turned to war.

> When the war in Ireland was ended 'tis well known the country was ruined and desolate, the towns and houses for habitation burnt, all the stocks destroyed, hedges fences and all manner of improvements ruined; that a famine was not only feared, but many thousands of poor creatures through the kingdom and great numbers in the streets of Dublin itself lost their lives for want when it was not in the power of the most charitably disposed, without exposing their own families, to relieve them.[22]

---

* There is no contemporary evidence to contradict Story's account, but tradition is more hopeful and has Hogan travelling to France and living happily ever after. See: *The Quest For the Galloping Hogan* by Matthew J Culligan-Hogan, New York, 1979.

CHAPTER XXI

The Flight of the Wild Geese

The Wild Geese come in their thousands with the October moon. They blacken the sky and they cry the coming of autumn. Where there are low marshlands, or sloblands, they settle down, and then the cabins are cooking them with much butter or grease in the bastables all the Winter. About the estuary of the Shannon, and all up the river into Limerick, they must have whizzed and moaned, that Winter of 1691, when Ginckel offered the terms that ended the Jacobite War, and started bitter quarrels among the tired and tattered Irish. The flying Irish, down the Shannon or down the Lee with Sarsfield, looked up at the skies and took the name, The Wild Geese.

Sean O'Faolain, King of the Beggars, p.11

THE FIRST of the military articles of the Treaty of Limerick provided that 'all persons, without any exceptions, of what quality or condition so ever' would be free to leave the country 'with their families, household stuff, plate and jewels'. There were good reasons for this as it was quite natural that his senior officers should take with them their families, servants and moveable possessions, but Sarsfield did not intend that every man in the army should invite his relations along on the voyage. He would not be thanked in France for bringing ten thousand or so useless mouths to Brittany. He made it clear, if only by confining his men to King's Island, that he expected them to embark alone.

Not surprisingly, those 'hospitable' men who had insisted on their womenfolk being with them during the siege of Charlemont were less than enthusiastic about going to France without female company. It soon became clear that if their women and children were not shipped to France, many of the troops would refuse to sail with the army. Those who did have wives and children in or around Limerick could hardly agree to leave them behind to starve. Although the great majority of the soldiers had not had any opportunity to contact their families since the signing of the treaty, it would have been unwise to give those who had done so reason to disobey their orders. There were going to be hard times ahead and Sarsfield needed the loyalty of all his men, even if it did mean suffering their families. Consequently he and Wauchope issued a joint declaration to stress to those concerned fathers and husbands that everyone would be allowed to take their families on board the transports. And it was with this consideration in mind, that they both signed a new shipping agreement on 14 October. This was perhaps performed with some apprehension as to how the French were going to take to feeding not only the troops but their dependants as well.

The English already had a sizeable merchant fleet in Cork and it was there that most of the men were to embark. There were also a few English ships on the Shannon which were to be used to take the troops off, and it was hoped that these would be joined by the expected French fleet which would then serve to collect rather than to deliver. Although it could not yet be clear how many of the men were to be shipped from either port, in the absence of the French fleet most of the troops were going to have to head for Cork. On 16 October, two days after he signed the new shipping agreement, Sarsfield rode out of Limerick for the last time. He set out for Cork to supervise the preparations that were already under way. On the same day the first of the infantry battalions marched out through St John's Gate and on to the road behind him.

Many were now less keen to go to France than they had been. Ever since the end of the siege they had been kept on King's Island where they had been held as if they were prisoners. Sarsfield had even posted guards on both the bridges off the island, but notwithstanding that, there had been a steady trickle of deserters who had either swum or waded through the river. The English were naturally quite happy for them to desert and there are no reported incidents of any of the reluctant soldiers being returned to Sarsfield despite the wording of the third article.* When the order to move out to Cork was given and the Irish troops marched over Ball's Bridge, many of them saw their opportunity. Accordingly to Story, 'as they marched through the Irish town their men ran away by dozens'.

The desertions were both predictable and understandable. These men feared that, as the English had assured them, they would never return to their country again if they set sail for France. They had not been able to travel to visit their families. Even if there was any way of getting a message back to their home areas, only a very small minority of them could write enough to send a letter, and very few of those were married to women who would either be able to read or send a note back. Having been separated for so long from their familiar surroundings and everyone that they knew, their fears increased as the day of their departure drew nearer. With rising panic, many saw that there was a very good chance of their never coming back, and certainly no visible chance of being able to return within a year. To their families, they would simply have disappeared as surely as if their bones had been scattered over Kilcommodon Hill. To the majority of the troops who came from tightly knit rural communities and who had until the war never ventured further than their nearest market town, this was a most fearful prospect to face. If Sarsfield had learnt any skills from his experience of trying to prevent an army from disintegrating at Salisbury three years before, he certainly needed them now.

In the meantime, the great French fleet arrived at last, almost a month after Sarsfield had first sued for peace. The transport ships had been assembling

---

*   The third military article ended as follows: ' . . . the troops that will go into France must remain under the command and discipline of their officers that are to conduct them thither; and deserters of each side shall be given up, and punished accordingly.' The last twelve words of the article were certainly not adhered to by the English. It was the only part of the military treaty which was blatantly broken.

at Brest since August, but had been held back by a series of infuriating administrative delays that prevented them leaving the French coast until 13 October, ten days after Sarsfield had signed the treaty. On 20 October Admiral Chateaurenault's convoy arrived in the mouth of the Shannon where his warships attacked an English frigate and learnt of the treaty. They lay off Scattery Island and sent messages up river to the garrison. With the fleet was Simon Luttrell who had been frustrated at every turn in his attempts to hurry things along. He, and indeed the whole French fleet, felt 'deep resentment at their unexpected disappointment'.

Now that there were fresh supplies and a large part of the English army had left Limerick, the thought clearly crossed some people's minds that there was now an opportunity to storm into the Irish town and to secure the whole city against the English. Chateaurenault's arrival offered no such temptations for Sarsfield, not least because by the time that he heard any news of the fleet he was already in Cork. And, as Plunket bitterly noted; 'men of honesty will rather suffer than break their word, which is a doctrine little regarded by the Protestants of England and Ireland.'

The importance of Chateaurenault's arrival to Sarsfield was that early transport could now be provided for most of the troops still in Limerick. The French had naturally assessed the likely outcomes of the war in Ireland and had been making contingency plans ever since James had first fled across the Channel. Their last great convoy had been that of May 1691 when over eighty ships had brought a wealth of provisions to Ireland as well as their disastrous gift of Saint-Ruth. Even as that convoy sailed, the French began preparing for the next one. It was always clear that the war in Ireland could only be pursued provided they steadily re-equipped and resupplied the Irish army. Willing though the French were to be the paymasters, the success of their investment was always uncertain. As far back as August the new French minister for war was writing of the possibility of a fleet bringing back some eight to ten thousand Irishmen. Accordingly, when the French fleet did sail it did so with extra capacity to take off troops if need be. The result was that when they did arrive, they were able to take off a large part of the Irish army without having to unload their stores.

The French generals were understandably keen to go home as soon as they could, not only because they disliked Ireland but because they wanted to be able to report back to Paris before anyone else could condemn them. They eagerly travelled down to the fleet shortly after its arrival. They also set in motion the first full scale embarkation of troops. A series of smaller ships ferried the men from the quayside in the English town the forty or so miles down to the fleet. Once they had joined the fleet, d'Usson and de Tessé left the organisation of the evacuation from Limerick to John Wauchope.

Wauchope had no doubt in his mind that the English would attempt to lure away as many of his men as they could. Consequently his only concern was to get the troops on board the French ships in the shortest time possible. Once a soldier was afloat, he was trapped. No one would be able to tempt him away. Wauchope's problem was that the total capacity of the ships on the Shannon, both English and French, was not enough to carry off the entire army, and certainly not the whole army as well as all those dependants who had now appeared in Limerick. Having been told how many men the ships on the Shannon would take, he issued orders that those battalions for whom there was no room should march to Cork. His calculations for the number of places on Chateaurenault's ships did not include sufficient consideration for those civilians who were daily joining the army on King's Island and who were now waiting expectantly to be called forward to the boats. Although he continued to assure the men that they would be taking their families with them, Wauchope was still more concerned to use all the capacity available to him for the sole purpose of carrying troops. He had no doubt as to where his duty lay. He issued orders that the civilians were to travel apart from the troops, and that the troops were to board first. The consequences were both tragic and predictable.

> Accordingly a vast rabble of all sorts were brought to the waterside when the major-general, pretending to ship the soldiers in order according to their lists, they first carried the men on board; and many of the women at the second return of the boat for the officers, catching hold to be carried on board were dragged off and through fearfulness, losing their hold, were drowned; but others who held faster had their fingers cut off and so perished in the sight of their husbands or relations.[1]

Although Wauchope callously disregarded these poor people, the extent of the tragedy has been exaggerated. There were probably not more than a few hundred relatives left on the quayside when the last boat pulled away. It was not as if the whole of Ireland had assembled at Limerick to bid the troops farewell. Very few of the common soldiers had their families anywhere near them. Their wives, children and parents were still at home ignorant of their whereabouts. The majority of the civilians hoping to be shipped were the officers' families and their servants who had been camped outside Limerick during the siege, or those who had been brought to Limerick by officers who had been given Sarsfield's pass to go home after the treaty to settle their affairs. Although the scenes of panic described above cannot be doubted, such despair was not widespread. Those who were determined to go to France were told that they could do so by embarking at Cork, and it must be remembered that the Irish soldiers on the ships fully expected to return. At that time they had no intention of living their lives in exile. They were going to France so that they could return to Ireland next year in triumph.

The English were genuinely shocked at the terrible scenes on the quayside. Brigadier Leveson, who during the siege had spent his time burning down every habitation he came across in Kerry, now tried to intercede on behalf of the destitute families left behind. Wauchope would not listen; was he to offload soldiers to take women and children? However, his harsh behaviour had its effects. The English secretary at war reported that 'the ill usage that Wauchope gave those that were to go from the Shannon made at least 3,000 alter their resolution of going to France.'[2] But brutal though he was, Wauchope had managed to get nearly six thousand men on board the fleet, and he did allow a further eight hundred women and children to sail with them.

By 2 November the last Irish soldier had left Limerick. The ships, now full to capacity, made their way down the river and out to sea. It would be many years before ships such as the *Nightingale,* the *Olive Tree* and the *Happy Interest* would again sail in a convoy with the likes of *La Sainte-Croix, L'Alexandre* and *La Marie Daudierne.* With them went Wauchope, d'Usson and de Tessé who together formed that small minority among the passengers who very much hoped that they would never set foot in Ireland again.

In Cork, Sarsfield was also experiencing difficulties. There was already mounting disappointment among the English and European troops that the Irish army was to be allowed to slip away. Count Nassau, William's cousin, had been sent to Cork to supervise the embarkation. Having carefully studied the military articles, he spotted a possible conflict between two of them and insisted that the families of those who had elected to sail to France could not accompany them. He noted that although the first article provided that 'all persons, without any exceptions' should be free to go overseas, the seventh article provided that Ginckel should arrange for shipping 'to facilitate the transporting the said troops . . . for which the persons to be transported shall not be obliged to pay'. Nassau held the opinion that on a strict construction of the words, shipping was to be provided for the troops but that there was no duty to do the same for the civilians. The civilians were of course free to go, but they would have to pay their passage should, of course, they be lucky enough to find any ships willing to take them.

The Irish, and Sarsfield, were furious. This narrow interpretation of the seventh article was quite contrary to the spirit of the treaty and to their understanding of the agreement when it was signed. It was quite clear to Sarsfield, as is implicit in a letter he wrote to Ginckel on 17 October, that Nassau was being deliberately obstructive.[3] Nassau had also demanded that a second examination be made of the troops who had marched to Cork so that he could be fully satisfied that they really wanted to go to France. His only purpose in this was to gain a second opportunity, contrary to the treaty, to persuade as many of them as possible not to embark. Sarsfield, who had already seen many of his men desert, was determined to get the troops on board as soon as he could.

Ginckel, although not happy with Sarsfield's success in persuading his men to leave, was not prepared to allow the treaty to be broken within a fortnight of it having been signed. Nassau perhaps achieved a few days' delay and perhaps a few desertions, but the Irish troops and their dependents were shipped on board the English fleet as planned. First to embark were the remnants of the cavalry led by Dominic Sheldon. They were joined by the first of the Irish infantrymen to embark at Cork, and in late November the fleet set sail.

On 6 December the transport ships arrived back from France. Sarsfield, who had by then ironed out his difficulties with Nassau, was still to have an anxious time. The force that had marched down to Cork had continued to dwindle during the month that they had all had to wait, and the ships now brought back mail from the men already in Brest. That mail brought with it fresh problems. The reception that the Irish had received was as miserable as could be imagined. In winter in Brittany they had been forced to sleep in fields and hedgerows, and several had written to dissuade their comrades from making the grave mistake of following them. There was a fresh spate of desertions. Sarsfield redoubled his efforts to get the men on board as quickly as possible, but it was getting to be increasingly difficult. Colonel Brian O'Neill's regiment and Colonel Brian MacDermot's regiment refused to embark, and Colonel Felix O'Neill's men deserted *en masse,* handing their weapons over to Colonel Tiffin's troops who were supervising the embarkation, and then disappearing.[4]

The full extent of the desertions have perhaps been exaggerated in the English reports. Sarsfield still supervised a fluctuating population of Irishmen and their families. While he was in Cork, more men came to join him, some of them were those who had already returned to their homes to find that everything they had once possessed had since been carried off or destroyed, some were those who had arrived after a long journey across the country, and some were those who had never been at Limerick but who now saw the opportunity of rejoining the colours. The month of December brought with it more delays, but the lord justices in Dublin made sure that the treaty was kept. They ruled that any unnecessary delay would be in itself a breach and at the end of November they hurriedly arranged for additional vessels to speed Sarsfield on his way.[5] On 8 December Sarsfield signed a document releasing Ginckel from any further obligation to provide shipping, and he then waited as long as he reasonably could for those late comers who were still daily making their way down to the quay.

He sailed out of Cork on 22 December 1691. It was just over three years since the prince of Orange had invaded England and had started the war, and just over three years since the apprentice boys of Londonderry had precipitated the northern revolt against Tyrconnell. The war had claimed a hundred thousand victims since then, but Sarsfield could now look to the future with confidence. He had succeeded in supplying James with an experienced army, and with his face to the horizon he looked forward to the invasion of England and the king's reinstatement. He was confident that he had done his duty.

To many of those who sailed with him, the parting was a more terrible experience by far, and with hindsight, the finality of the separation of Irishmen from Ireland became one of the most tragic episodes in the country's history. Colonel Charles O'Kelly concluded his work on the war with these words:

And now, alas! The saddest day is come that ever appeared above the horizon of Ireland; the sun was darkened and covered over with a black cloud, as if unwilling to behold such a woeful spectacle; there needed no rain to bedew the earth; for the tears of the disconsolate Irish did abundantly moisten their native soil, to which they were that day to bid the last farewell. Those who resolved to leave it never hoped to see it again; and those who made the unfortunate choice to continue therein, could at the same time have nothing in prospect but contempt and poverty, chains and imprisonment, and in a word, all the miseries that a conquered nation could naturally expect from the power and malice of implacable enemies. Here might be seen the aged father, whom years and infirmities rendered unfit to travel, giving the last embraces to his only son; brothers parting in tears, and the dearest comrades forcibly divorced by cruel destiny, which they could not avoid.[7]

This was the Flight of the Wild Geese.

CHAPTER XXII

The Last Campaign

Sarsfield: I am Lord Lucan, Sarsfield is my name,
               And where my sword can reach I'll guard my fame,
               Life I despise now, reck'ning death my friend,
               The man's not living who could make me bend
               My neck to bondage . . .
                    Robert Ashton, *The Battle of Aughrim*, v. i.

KING JAMES had mixed feelings about Sarsfield's capitulation. Although he had been ousted from three kingdoms, thanks to Sarsfield he did now have an army of his own in France, and he had the liberty to send it wherever he chose. There was only one place that James wanted his army to go, and that was England.

James had of course pressed Louis for assistance and had been promised that if the circumstances were right, French troops would be released to assist him in an English invasion. With the Irish army in France, the circumstances could not be better. There could never be a cheaper time to invade England. Once his army was re-equipped and supplied James would only need French shipping, the protection of the French fleet and a few battalions of French troops and he would be in a position to regain all that he had lost.

So it was with genuine enthusiasm that James wrote to the first Irish officers to arrive: 'We are extremely satisfied with your conduct, and of the valour of the soldiers during the siege; and most particularly of your and their declaration and resolution to come and serve where we are. And we assure you, and order you to assure both officers and soldiers that are come along with you, that we shall never forget this act of loyalty, nor fail when in a capacity to give them above others a particular mark of our favour.'[1]

It was unfortunate for his Irish troops that however pleased James was with them, there was little that he could do to help them in their present straitened circumstances. They were living in appalling conditions. Their clothing was inadequate to keep out the cold of the Breton winter, their supplies were insufficient, and there were terrible problems in housing this host of soldiers and their dependants. To ensure them shelter from the elements they were over the first few weeks moved inland and billeted on unwelcoming Breton villagers. 'Alas it is a miserable sight to see the condition the poor gentlemen are in, and the women and children invited to go along with their husbands are now begging their bread from door to door, and cannot get it.'[2] 'The soldiers wish they had died in Ireland before they came here, and many of the officers express themselves to the same purpose, and are extremely dejected and melancholy.'

As he had no other source of income, James was entirely dependent on the benevolence of the French government. It was agreed that the French would fund his army, but on their terms. They were understandably not willing to pay the Irish any more than they would their own troops, which was four sous a day for a private soldier. Although this was just enough for a single man to subsist upon, as they had been promised 'English pay' it was certainly below their expectations and it was the cause of much suffering to those who had brought their families with them. 'For when they were reduced in France to four pence a day they were obliged to leave their children to the wide world and only lament with the prophet Jeremiah that their children lay naked in a starving condition in the top of every street.' [3]

Although Sarsfield and Wauchope had issued a proclamation in Limerick stating that every officer who went to France would be able to keep his rank, the French would not hear of it and as they were now the paymasters, their decision could not be challenged. The French felt that many (if not most) of the officers were wholly unsuited to the elevated ranks that they then occupied. After the disaster at Aughrim some of the infantry battalions had been so depleted that it had been necessary to issue hundreds of new commissions to fill the gaps. The consequence of this was that many of the junior officers at Brest had been private soldiers at Aughrim, and the French had no qualms about cancelling their commissions.

The Irish troops in France also needed to be re-organised. There had been over forty regiments at Aughrim and now there was certainly not going to be room for forty lieutenant-colonels. The new organisation was to include not only all the troops that had arrived from Ireland but also all those other troops then in France who were subjects of King James, except those already serving in Mountcashel's brigade. These included the survivors of the Scottish expedition and, more importantly, those troops who had been taken as prisoners of war in Ireland (especially at Cork) and who had been brought to the continent to be exchanged for German, Huguenot and Danish prisoners held in France. A number of these men, including ninety three Irish officers, had escaped from Bruges in late 1691 and were now recruited into the Jacobite establishment.

The prime task of King James's senior officers at that time was to plan, direct and execute this reorganisation. But they were subject to such pressure by the French that this was hurriedly carried out by a committee of officers, and there was the inevitable scramble for positions. Those that were not there to push themselves forward ran the risk of being left off the commission registers altogether.

> My Lord Lucan was by forecast appointed to stay behind and fetch up the rear of those to be transported from Cork, which proved very fatal and the ruin of almost all of the gentlemen that thought themselves happy in being near him and in the possession of many fair promises made them by so brave a man, and so great a patriot, for the regulation [reorganisation] was done at Rennes before he could come thither.[4]

The result was that, with Sarsfield out of the way, the Gaels had no senior officer to champion their cause and when the new commissions were handed out they generally fared badly, 'except Gordon O'Neill and a few drawn in after the regulation almost by the head and shoulders by my Lord Lucan'.[5]

The army which then numbered some fifteen thousand men had by the spring been divided, realigned and at last formed into six new regiments of infantry, two of dismounted dragoons, two of cavalry and two troops of horse guards. James's most favoured senior officers were given the posts of colonels. The colonelcy of the first troop of horse guards was given to his son, the duke of Berwick, and the second was given to the man who he now considered to be his most able and trustworthy general, Patrick Sarsfield. Dominic Sheldon and Lord Galmoy were given the commands of the two cavalry regiments, and Thomas Maxwell (as soon as he was exchanged and released from the Tower) and Francis Carroll the dragoons. The infantry regiments were each made up of two French-style battalions of almost a thousand men and the commands were given to James's teenaged son, Henry Fitzjames, the lord grand prior, and to those general officers of his who had served in the Irish war; Dorrington, Wauchope, Simon Luttrell and Gordon O'Neill; and to the colonel of one of the regiments who had hitherto served in Mountcashel's brigade, Richard Talbot, a natural son of the late great Tyrconnell. The men that were left over, apart from the six hundred who were sent to fill the gaps in Mountcashel's brigade and two hundred others who were formed into independent companies, were offered employment in the French navy.

James was in high spirits when he returned to Paris from Brittany. He had fourteen thousand men in arms and he had received reports from his agents across the Channel that had pleased him greatly; England was ripe for an invasion. He heard that his people disliked William and were clamouring for the return of their lawful monarch. He approached Louis and was promised the necessary naval and military support for an expedition. The French agreed to supply him with an artillery train and an additional seven thousand fully equipped troops from the Normandy garrisons. And to James's delight, Louis also gave him the man that a year before he had wanted to command his troops in Ireland. His commander in chief was to be that pious old soldier, Marshal Bellefonds. His second in command was to be one of the few Frenchmen of senior rank who could claim to have had experience of Irish troops, Lieutenant-General de Tessé. James supplied his two most accomplished Irish soldiers to serve as major generals, Patrick Sarsfield and Richard Hamilton.*

From the end of March 1692 onwards, the re-equipped Irish troops marched eastwards from Brittany in their new red uniforms. Before the end of April they were ready and in position, encamped on the heights above the Channel between

---

* Who had just been released from the Tower in exchange for Lord Mountjoy, the one time spokesman for the Ulster Protestants, who had spent the Irish war gazing through the bars of the Bastille.

Havre de Grâce and Cap la Hague. Their morale was then higher than at any time since William's defeat at Limerick. They had been delivered from their own country and now the most powerful monarch in Europe was lending his assistance to their success. James's army of over twenty thousand men was larger than William's had been when it disembarked at Torbay forty months before. The invasion force was made up of over twelve thousand Irish infantrymen, one thousand Irish cavalrymen, four thousand French infantrymen, three thousand French cavalrymen and a French artillery train.

While all the soldiers gathered, drilled and checked their equipment, there was feverish activity in the harbour at St Vaast-la-Hougue where the transport fleet was gathering. It had been hoped to embark the army at the end of April, but many of the troop ships were damaged in the spring gales and had to be refitted. There were also problems with the French navy itself in that the Atlantic squadron commanded by Admiral Tourville consisted of no more than forty-four ships of the line. Although there was no accurate information as to the whereabouts and disposition of the English and Dutch fleets, it would be too risky for the invasion force to sail with Tourville's escort alone. Even if they were met by only the English navy they would be outnumbered, but the consequences would be disastrous if the English and the Dutch fleets joined together and got in amongst the transports.

Orders were sent to Comte d'Estrées to sail with his Mediterranean squadron from Toulon through the Straits of Gibraltar to join the fleet now waiting in the Bay of La Hogue. It had been hoped that d'Estrées would arrive in early May, but the gales in the Straits ruined his plans. However, although he was delayed his eventual arrival was not doubted and there was every expectation that the three hundred troop carrying ships would be escorted by both his and Tourville's squadrons, which together would consist of over eighty men o'war. The French government was naturally anxious to get the invasion fleet under way as soon as possible. They were also put under pressure from James and his ministers to move sooner rather than later. The Jacobite agents exuded confidence. They had received every indication that the people of southern England, not to mention the rest of the country, would welcome the return of their rightful king. Now that his subjects had experienced the misery of war and taxation into which William had led them, they would flock to James's colours. A complete and bloodless victory was predicted. The English army would not fight, and even those who had genuinely supported the usurper would not be inclined to resist once the king's army had set foot on English soil to the general acclamation of the southern counties.

It was not only James's popularity on land that was stressed to the French government. Confident predictions were made regarding the English fleet. The navy had been built up by James when he was duke of York and it could easily be accepted that the majority of the sailors, admirals and common seamen alike, were still loyal to him. It was asserted that the singular lack of success of the English navy in the battle off Beachy Head twenty months earlier could be attributed to these loyal sentiments. The French were assured that just as the English navy had failed to fight on that occasion when they had been confronted by a French fleet, no opposition would be given to a fleet carrying with it their king. His supporters contrived to get certain assurances from the English admirals to the effect that they would not attack the French even if ordered to do so, and that they would instead set upon the Dutch fleet should it make an appearance. The optimism of the Jacobites was not even shaken when Admiral Russell had asserted that he would attack the French fleet regardless of whether or not James himself was sailing with them. James's prime minister, Lord Melfort, pressed Louis to allow the fleet to sail. Time, he felt, was more impor- tant than any advantage that might be gained by the appearance of Admiral d'Estrées's squadron. The cavalry had already embarked on the transports once, and then had to be brought back on shore. It was feared that morale would suffer if James was not allowed to strike soon.

Reluctantly perhaps, but with the many assurances given him by James and his ministers, Louis issued orders to Admiral Tourville to escort the convoy of troops to England. Tourville was expressly instructed not to avoid an engagement with the enemy. But by the time that Tourville had received his instructions, he was also in possession of fresh information. The English and the Dutch fleets had joined together off St Helen's on the Isle of Wight. The allied fleet was made up of over ninety ships and outnumbered Tourville's squadron by more than two to one. Despite this disadvantage and notwithstanding his knowledge that the orders from Paris had been issued in ignorance of this change of affairs, Tourville resolved to fight. Just as Saint-Ruth had gambled with James's fortunes in Ireland and had them dashed, so Tourville now gambled in the same reckless fashion. Tourville had commanded the French fleet in the inconclusive affair off Beachy Head. He had been accused of cowardice in not pressing his advantage. Now he resolved to fight because he feared such criticism more than he feared the English. He felt that if he held back or questioned his orders, his reputation would be ruined and he would be adjudged too cautious to usefully serve his king. On 18 May 1692, his squadron set sail to seek the enemy.

The Irish troops made their final preparations and began loading their equipment onto the transport ships in St Vaast-La-Hougue. On the next morning Tourville found the Anglo-Dutch fleet and a great naval battle began an hour before noon. For five hours the battle raged. The Jacobites were proved wrong. None of the English ships defected or held off and Tourville did not have the power to scatter them. Only his great skills as an admiral prevented the English and Dutch from bringing their superior numbers to bear. Having punished them as best he could he signalled his squadron to return. At this time, the wind changed, he lost his advantage and his squadron's orderly withdrawal became a flight. The French line was broken by the English ships and close quarter fighting ensued. Tourville's flagship, *Le Soleil Royal*, was itself surrounded and attempts were made to board her. While his men fought with cannon, musket and cutlass to keep the English at bay, Tourville lost control of the battle. He became separated from most of the squadron and his ships raced to the coast by different routes. After sunset, he broke through the encircling English ships, delivered one last cannonade into their battered sides, and made for Cherbourg with the English in pursuit.

With the wind blowing from the northwest, King James and Sarsfield and the troops could hear the battle being fought some twenty miles out to sea. And it was with some joy that they watched the approach of ships flying French colours. The English had been beaten away and the French navy was returning to escort them. Their joy was short lived. As the ships drew nearer the English could be seen giving chase. It became quite clear that the French were racing for the shelter of the shore batteries. Only thirteen French ships sailed into the Bay of La Hogue where they anchored in line as close to the shore as they could, some of them even beaching themselves. Half the French fleet had been driven around Cap la Hague towards St Malo. Tourville's flagship with two smaller ships had limped into the harbour at Cherbourg. Tourville transferred his pennant from *Le Soleil Royal* to the *L'Ambiteux* and made for St Vaast-la-Hougue. Although he had not lost a single ship in the battle, his fleet had been swept from the Channel. As soon as he could , Tourville had himself rowed ashore to Fort Saint-Vaast 'to wait upon the king of England, who lodged near the coast, to receive his orders and consult upon what was proper to be done'.[6]

Sarsfield, Bellefonds, Hamilton and all the general officers were called together to a council of war. Tourville was far from optimistic. As he spoke the greater part of the English fleet was blockading the Bay of La Hogue. Some of his thirteen ships now moored in the shallows under the guns of the forts of Saint-Vaast and Lisset were badly damaged. Although Bellefonds had already made arrangements for his artillery to set up batteries to deter the English from coming in close, the ships were still too far out to be effectively protected by cannon fire from the shore.

> Tourville proposed all the different courses that remained to be taken, but at the same time showed that according to all appearances there was not one by which the ships could be saved, and in case it should be determined to defend them, every soul in them must inevitably perish if the enemy should set fire to them. It was resolved therefore to run them aground after having taken out of them everything we could and to employ the sloops, of which we had a great number destined for this embarkation, to prevent them from being set on fire.[7]

James and his generals were desperate to suggest anything that might save the fleet on which all their hopes lay. But they were powerless to overrule Tourville in naval matters and Tourville, who had proved himself to be as reckless as Saint-Ruth had ever been, now showed himself to be as proud. As Tourville's ships were standing in the shallows, the English would only be able to attack them by boarding them from sloops and setting fire to them. James wanted to cram the ships with Irish soldiers so that a storm of musketry would prevent the English sailors from getting close enough to do any damage. 'But the Admiral thought it a dishonour to commit the care and defence of his ships to any but the seamen themselves.'[8] Tourville had come ashore to explain his plan to James and his officers, not to discuss it with them. The defence of the ships was to be carried out by French sailors who would not only man the ships but also the sloops in order to beat off the English in hand to hand fighting out in the bay.

It was not long before Tourville's plan was put to the test. A flotilla of over two hundred small boats and fireships was led into the bay by Admiral Rooke. The French sloops that had been sent out to meet them were chased out of the way and the French sailors abandoned the ships in the shallows. With no opposition except the generally ineffective cannonade from the shore batteries, the English swarmed on board. All this while James and his officers and indeed the whole Irish army, could only look on in impotent despair as the flames rose up from first one and then another of the French ships. By the end of the day, every ship in the bay of La Hogue had been destroyed and as if to add insult to injury, the English had also managed to attack the transport fleet itself and had burnt eight of the troop ships and towed off several more.

To the English it was a great victory, in every way as important as the defeat of the Spanish Armada a hundred and three years before. It was the greatest victory over the French since Henry V's triumph at Agincourt. But Louis le Grand saw it as being no more than a minor set back and when he received Tourville he told him

> I am very well satisfied with you and with all the fleet. We have been beaten, but you have acquired glory both for yourself and for the nation. It cost us a few ships, a loss which shall be repaired next year and then we shall surely beat the enemy.[9]

Although Louis could afford to take a naval defeat lightly, the disappointment to Sarsfield and all the Jacobites was great. It was not even clear to them who was to blame—Louis for giving the order to give battle, Tourville for carrying out that order even when he knew that the situation was altered, or those Jacobites who had confidently asserted that the English would not fight. Sarsfield was one of those who had looked on in disbelief after the battle as Melfort desperately tried to persuade them that his information about King William's navy had been accurate and that there really had not been any first or second rate ships in the English fleet.[10]

To Sarsfield and his men the battle of La Hogue proved to be the ruination of all their plans. They would have been better employed if they had remained in Limerick and fought on throughout the winter whatever the difficulties. All the work in persuading the Irish troops to sail to France and all the work in arranging their transport and in re-equipping them, now appeared to be wasted. The future, which had been so full of promise when Tourville had set sail from La Hogue, was now very bleak indeed.

The battle of La Hogue marked not only the end of James's invasion plans for England, it also marked the end of his army. Without the fleet there was clearly no purpose to be served by keeping the thirteen thousand Irish troops in Normandy. The French, who had agreed that James could keep his own army, were anxious to use his men themselves. There were battles to be fought along France's eastern borders. All the commissions that James had handed out to his officers were now worthless pieces of paper. James's men, Sarsfield included, were transferred into the French army to serve on the same terms as Lord Mountcashel's soldiers.

The French prudently kept the Irish regiments together in brigades to avoid the inevitable problems that would arise from mixing Irish speaking regiments into French brigades. The administration of the transfer from King James's to King Louis's army was left to the two senior Scottish officers on James's staff, Thomas Buchan, who had recently fled from Scotland, and John Wauchope. Only one officer was singled out and detached from James's army and allowed to keep his rank in the French service—Patrick Sarsfield was made a maréchal de camp, the French equivalent of a major-general.

The French saw Sarsfield as being the most useful officer that James had, and their admiration was not founded on his ability to command the loyalty of his countrymen as Sarsfield was never given the command of any Irish troops again. It has been suggested that Sarsfield's separation from his compatriots followed the sudden fall in his popularity after the disaster at La Hogue. Certainly amongst the Irish officers in France there were those who felt that Sarsfield and Wauchope had 'projected only to build their own fortunes in France upon the ruins of the Irish'[11] It was even suggested that Sarsfield had been 'posted away to appease the said disorders'[12] but the rumour was without foundation. The simple fact was that Sarsfield had impressed the French. Even before La Hogue, he had been told that there was a place for him in the French army. As there was no Irish formation in the French army greater than a brigade if Sarsfield was to be given a rank above that of brigadier he would necessarily have to be put in command of French troops.

It is also clear that only a minority of the Irish officers and men were dissatisfied with Sarsfield. Although they suffered great hardships in France, there was no marked increase in desertion from the Irish regiments, and throughout the next century there was no shortage of Irishmen willing to go to France to 'fight for the Pretender',[13] as Dean Swift put it.

Through the summer of 1692, the Irish troops were marched across France to join the French armies on the eastern border. Some were sent to the south to join Marshal Catinat who was planning a campaign against the Allies in Savoy, but most of the regiments were sent to Flanders to join Marshal Luxembourg's army. It was to Luxembourg that Sarsfield went. Although he had been given the rank of maréchal de camp, there was no command for him and so he was attached to Luxembourg's staff. He was placed in a similar position to that he had occupied when he and Lord Newburgh had served under Oglethorpe in the Monmouth campaign, but he now moved in grander circles. Riding with him in the same capacity was not only Berwick and the Grand Prior, but four members of the French royal family—the prince of Conti and the dukes of Bourbon, Chartres and Vendome. They, together with the flower of the French nobility and the king's household troops were to remain with Luxembourg as his 'Golden Troop'.

The nature of warfare in Flanders had greatly changed since Sarsfield last served there fifteen years before. Then, during the 'Golden Age' of Louis's reign when his foreign policy was at its most aggressive his generals had fought battles deep inside enemy territory. Now that the Allies were better organised and equipped Louis was more concerned to hold on to what he had taken rather than to push his frontiers any further eastward. Every small town in the border area was fortified and garrisoned. Large standing armies remained behind the frontiers, marching and countermarching to prevent the other from seizing any fresh territory. There was consequently less fighting and more preparation. However, before the arrival of the Irish troops, Luxembourg had achieved a singular success in taking the town of Namur from under the very nose of the Allied army. Satisfied with this achievement, he was content to direct a defensive campaign and to prevent the Anglo-Dutch army, commanded by King William in person, from making any inroads into the new French territories.

William on the other hand was determined to achieve something before the campaigning season ended, and frantically looked for a way to punish the French for their success in the only important action fought that year. At the end of July Luxembourg's army was encamped around the village of Steenkirk, half way between Brussels and Mons. A few miles to the north William's army waited outside Hals. Between them were several woods and coppices and the land was undulating and cut across with thick hedgerows and ditches. It was in fact so unsuitable for the control of large bodies of men that Luxembourg felt quite safe from attack.

The result was that, when William did attack on 3 August, the French response was delayed. When the enemy infantry was first seen to be advancing, Luxembourg did nothing. He had received and accepted a false report that William was to send out a large patrol between the armies. when it became clear that William intended to attack, Luxembourg was forced to act quickly. The Bourbonnais brigade that formed the first line of the French defences was attacked and scattered. Luxembourg desperately looked around to see what he could throw at the English vanguard while his army was got into battle order. He ordered his Golden Troop forward to the attack. The slaughter was fearful, but Luxembourg's disregard for the social rank of those whose lives he risked proved successful. The English were halted.

The battle raged all day through the woods, ditches and hedgerows. William lost four of his most senior British officers. Among them was Hugh Mackay who, early in the day, after receiving orders to march into the advancing French cavalry who were sure to envelop him, had said 'The will of the Lord be done'[14] and had spurred his horse forward. Another Scot, the highly educated James Douglas, was also killed. Sarsfield's old opponent, Sir John Lanier, was mortally wounded and died soon afterwards and Lord Mountjoy, who had only recently joined William's army having been exchanged for Richard Hamilton, also met his death. Although the English attack was undertaken with great bravery, it was doomed to failure. Without reinforcements and unsupported by cavalry, William's men were outnumbered and outgunned and beaten off by the French. At the end of the day both the armies were back where they had started having each lost about seven thousand men. As night fell, the field of battle was as deserted as it had been before William's advance except, according to one English report, for two hundred Irishmen who 'had lurked behind after the fight and knocked divers of our wounded men on the head and took away their money and some of their clothes'.[15]

Sarsfield had been in the thick of the fighting. He, along with those other noblemen who had been personally led by the general, had 'been exposed to the hottest fire'.[16] When Luxembourg sent Louis a careful report on the victory, narrow and costly though it had been, he made particular reference to the behaviour of those two senior officers recently transferred to his army. If Louis had been harbouring any doubts about the suitability of Berwick or Sarsfield, Luxembourg dispelled them.

> The duke of Berwick was present from the commencement when we proceeded to reconnoitre the enemy and behaved during the entire combat as bravely as in the last campaign, of which I informed your Majesty at the time.
> With him was the Earl of Lucan in whom we have particularly noticed the valour and the fearlessness of which he has given proofs in Ireland. I can assure your Majesty that he is a very good and a very able officer.[17]

This was praise from the greatest French soldier of them all. There could be no higher recommendation, and following this report, it was resolved to find Sarsfield a command as soon as a vacancy arose.

Even if Sarsfield's contribution to the battle was not immediately discernible to his enemies, his presence afterwards was. He wrote to Count Nassau, who eight months before had attempted to disrupt his embarkation plans in Cork, listing the prisoners in French hands and promising that they would be well looked after until they could be exchanged. He later arranged for passports to be sent to Brussels to be issued to some English surgeons so that they could ride to the French camp and attend to the wounded English prisoners. Of the prisoners, the surgeons reported that 'Sarsfield had taken much care of them;

highly commending their courage, promising they should want for nothing and [promising them that] as soon as recovered they should be exchanged.' Sarsfield also sent 'obliging letters' to Ginckel, the other Dutchman against whom he might have felt some resentment following his treatment after the Treaty of Limerick. Ginckel not only wrote back but, having asked William's permission, sent Sarsfield two horses.[18]

Ginckel's gift, although unquestionably chivalrous, was motivated by a desire to resolve a residual problem that had arisen from the treaty of Limerick. The ninth article stipulated that all the provisions needed by the Irish army on their voyage to France would be paid for on arrival in France. Sarsfield had been given Ginckel's permission to send a few of the transport ships back from France to Ireland with cargoes of French wine and linen. The proceeds from the sale of these goods were to be paid to his agent in Dublin who in turn would discharge those liabilities incurred by him on behalf of the army. Had this agreement not been made, the provisioning of the Irish army would have been funded either by the English taxpayer or by the sale of confiscated Irish land, but it nevertheless was the cause of much trouble. One problem followed another throughout the year when a succession of English ships were seized in either England or Ireland for contravening the Act of Parliament that forbad trade with France. On at least one occasion the queen, who ruled as monarch while William was in the Netherlands, was forced to intervene to order that a cargo be released to Sarsfield's agent. By the time that Ginckel again wrote to Sarsfield, the Irish army's debts had been paid off by these cargoes and the Irish hostages who had been held to ensure payment had been released. But all was not well.

A serious problem had arisen following the seizure of a French ship by the excisemen in Kenmare Harbour. The French merchantman had offloaded its cargo without permission and so was, quite legitimately in a time of war, taken as a prize. The French responded by impounding two English ships which were taking on Sarsfield's cargoes in Saint Malo. On one of the English ships was Captain Daniel Butts, the 'commissary general for the transportation of the troops from Ireland to France', who had been sent to France to supervise the whole operation. The problem was made worse in that before any of this could be sorted out the Battle of La Hogue was fought, and any sympathy that the French may have had for the English position disappeared. Well might Butts lament that the release of the Irish hostages 'and giving my Lord Lucan leave to load goods on the transport ships have brought us into all this trouble' as months later he found himself stranded in an enemy port.

Sarsfield was quick to respond to Ginckel's request for assistance, and promised to sort matters out. He had, he wrote, already taken Butts with him to visit Melfort and Pontchartrain, King Louis's navy minister, to bring their attention to the relevant clauses in the Treaty of Limerick. His letters to Ginckel were characteristically polite, and he asked that Ginckel's next letter to Butts

36.

I am extremly obliged to your Lordship for the care you tooke to gett Leave to send mee a crupell of horses, I desier you willbe plesd to send them by the berer and lett mee know the price, which shall be Retturned the next day to you with a million of thankes, I should be Extreme glade you would charge mee with any comision for any things you may have ocasion of from narise Gutther for your selfe or Ladye or the Ladyes your daghters if for them my wiffe shall have the honour to serve them which is all from your Lordships most Curtive ye 29 of agust

humble servant

Lucan

19 Sarsfield's handwriting. An extract from a letter
written to Ginckel dated 29th August 1692.

be directed via him so that he could ensure its safe delivery. Even when dealing with Ginckel he found it difficult to be anything but polite and courteous. When matters were finally put right he wrote that he was extremely glad of the opportunity of obliging so worthy a man and begged for the continuance of Ginckel's friendship. As to Ginckel's proposed gift of the horses, Sarsfield wrote:

> I am extremely obliged to your Lordship for the care you tooke to gett leave to send mee a cupell of horses, I desier you will be pleased to send them by the berer and lett me know the price, which shall be retturned the next day to you with a million of thankes. I shuld be extreme glade you woulld charge mee with any comision for any things you may have ocasion of from parise either for your selfe or Ladye or the ladyes your daghters if for them my wiffe shall have the honour to serve them which is all from your lordships most humble servant Lucan'.[19]

Once the campaign in Flanders was concluded, Sarsfield retired, as did every other Irish officer not obliged to stay with his troops, to King James's court in exile at Saint-Germain-en-Laye, just outside Paris. His wife, who was now almost nineteen years old, entered Parisian society with great enthusiasm. The fashionable balls and the masquerades of the most sophisticated capital in Europe were a world away from the best entertainment that could be provided in Portumna, especially to a girl who enjoyed dancing as much as she did. She loved Paris, and in turn was herself much admired and was said to have introduced to the French court 'les contredanses anglaises'.[20] Before long she was counted as being among the most fashionable and beautiful women to be seen at either King James's or the French court.*

In April 1693, she presented Sarsfield with a son. They named him after the prince of Wales, James Francis Edward.

Preparations for the 1693 campaigns had been underway since the early spring, but incessant rain had prevented the French from moving until the beginning of May. By that time Marshal Luxembourg had assembled together an army of seventy thousand men outside Mons, and Marshal Boufflers had gathered together another forty thousand men twenty miles away at Tournai. Together they planned to take, one at a time, those fortified towns of Flanders still in Allied hands. Boufflers was to conduct the sieges, and Luxembourg was to cover him by preventing King William from interfering. A position had been found for Sarsfield in Luxembourg's army. He was to serve as maréchal de camp under Lieutenant General Rubantel.

The campaign began badly. Boufflers's success was limited and Luxembourg's advance was blocked by King William on the Senne. The Anglo-Dutch army positioned itself so well that Luxembourg was unable to move for a month.

---

* Saint-Simon wrote of her: 'Elle était à la première fleur de son âge; belle, touchante, faite à peindre; une nymphe.'

Only in July did he manage to outflank William by racing to the east where he laid siege to the fortified town of Huy. William followed him, too late to save the town but in time to prevent Luxembourg marching on Liege. At the end of July the two armies faced each other outside Landen, and prepared to fight the greatest battle of the war.

William, although outnumbered by eighty thousand men to his army of fifty thousand, hoped to be able to confine the French to a narrow stretch of land whereby Luxembourg would be prevented from using his cavalry. The furthest extent of each wing of the Allied army was defined by one of two rivers, the Little Geete and Landen Beck. Between them, on a two mile front which stretched through the villages of Laer, Neerwinden and Neerlanden, William ordered his vanguard to dig in. In a day of frantic activity the hedges, walls and ditches were fortified and strengthened.

The battle of Landen began at half past four in the morning on 29 of July 1693 when William's eighty pieces of artillery opened fire at the densely massed French infantry that was formed up in the open. Taking what cover they could, the French were made to wait until well after sunrise while the gunners on each side kept up a steady fire. Shortly before eight o'clock, Luxembourg ordered his left wing to advance in line across the meadows to attack Neerwinden.

His left wing was made up of eighteen thousand foot and eight thousand cavalry divided between three divisions. The division on the far left of the army was made up of two brigades and was commanded by Lieutenant-General Montchevreuil. The centre division of the left wing consisted of three brigades and was commanded by the duke of Berwick, and the division on the right was commanded by Lieutenant-General Rubantel, with Sarsfield as his maréchal de camp. Berwick described the attack by these three divisions in his memoirs:

> This village extended, like a belly, into the plain, so that as we all three marched abreast of each other and as I was in the centre, I attacked first. I forced the enemy to give way and drove them from hedge to hedge as far as the plain, at the border of which I again formed up in line of battle. The troops which should have attacked to my right and left, instead of doing so judged that they would be less exposed to the enemy's fire by throwing themselves into the village: thus, all of a sudden, they found themselves behind me. The enemy, on perceiving this bad manoeuvre, re-entered the village on the right and the left upon which the firing became terrible. The four brigades under Rubantel and Montchevreuil were thrown into confusion and driven out of the village and in consequence I found myself attacked on all sides. After the loss of a vast number of men, my troops likewise abandoned the front of the village and while I was endeavouring to maintain my ground in the hope that M. de Luxemburg, to whom I had sent for assistance, would advance to relieve me, I found myself at last completely cut off.

Berwick was captured and the three divisions were beaten out of Neerwinden in great confusion. While they formed up for a second attack, Luxembourg ordered reinforcements to support them. They surged forward a second time, but were again beaten back with heavy losses. The French cavalry was ordered across to the left wing to support a third attack, but came under such heavy artillery fire that it had to be pulled back. Nevertheless, Luxembourg persevered and with fresh reinforcements the French attacked a third time and this time succeeded. The fighting had been so fierce that the English and German troops in Neerwinden had by then lost over a third of their strength and were running out of ammunition. When the village fell, Luxembourg concentrated his efforts further along the line and launched an attack on the Allies' centre. Once again French arms prevailed. Luxembourg won a famous though costly victory. In the battle and the subsequent rout the Allies lost at least twelve thousand men and the French lost over eight thousand.

Nevertheless the carnage in Neerwinden was fearful. The artillery barrages and the hand to hand fighting had cost both sides dearly. 'Neerwinden was a spectacle at which the oldest soldiers stood aghast. The streets were piled breast high with corpses.'[21] Despite the confusion of the action, writers on both sides made mention of Sarsfield. He was in the thick of these attacks 'doing actions worthy of himself'. 'It is not apt to be forgotten how gallantly Sarsfield, Earl of Lucan, behaved at Landen.' In Neerwinden he gained, according to a Williamite writer, 'as much honour by his generosity and humanity to the English in that fatal battle, as by his bravery and conduct in the field.'[22]

> His chief Rubantel was already severely wounded, Montchevreuil was killed, Berwick a prisoner, and thus Sarsfield had his chance of coming to the front for the direction of the attack passed into his hands. It was just as the French reinforcements had finally made their way into and through the village, and the supporting cavalry following in their track had reached the plain stretching northwards of it, that Sarsfield was struck by a bullet in the breast.[23]

His wound was serious and, despite the limited surgery of the day, proved to be fatal. He was taken to the recently captured city of Huy, twenty or so miles away, but as so often happened in those days before the discovery of penicillin, the effect of his wound grew worse. He became gripped by fever, and within a few days he died.*

---

* 'He could not have died better. His last thoughts were for his country. As he lay on the field unhelmed and dying, he put his hand to his breast. When he took it away it was full of his best blood. Looking at it sadly with an eye in which victory shone a moment before, he said, faintly, 'Oh! That this were for Ireland'. He said no more; and history records no nobler saying, nor any more becoming death' (Thomas Davis, *Poems*, 1846, p. 133.)

End-Note

O Patrick Sarsfield, Ireland's Wonder
Who fought in the fields like Heaven's thunder,
One of King James's chief commanders,
Now lies the food of crows in Flanders.
Och hone, Och hone.
Traditional dirge.

KING JAMES never left France again. He turned to religion in his old age and died in his palace at Saint-Germain-en-Laye in 1701. King William died in the following year after a fall from his horse. As he had no children, he was succeeded by James's daughter, Queen Anne, and after her the Protestant succession was secured by inviting King James's first cousin once removed, George, the elector of Hanover, to take the throne. James's son, James Francis Edward Stuart ('the Old Pretender') and his grandson, Charles Edward Stuart ('the Young Pretender', 'Bonnie Prince Charlie') devoted their lives to regaining the crowns of their ancestors until their hopes were effectively dashed on Culloden Moor in 1746.

The Treaty of Limerick, Sarsfield's legacy to his country, outlived him and efforts were made by King William's government to ensure that its terms were adhered to. Notwithstanding this, most of it was swept away by the all-Protestant Irish Parliament of 1697 who enacted the first of the Penal Laws against Catholics. However, as most of the land claims under the treaty had by then been settled in favour of the Catholic owners, there was only a limited confiscation of estates. This proved to be the treaty's only lasting achievement.

Sarsfield was survived by both his parents. His mother lived on with the Jacobite court at Saint Germain after his death, and so was able to keep in close contact with two of his sisters, Lady Mountleinster and Lady Kilmallock. The last of these had married Dominic Sarsfield, Lord Kilmallock, and it is his side of the Sarsfield clan that gave rise to the several Sarsfield families that were to flourish in Spain and France.* Lord Kilmallock briefly succeeded his brother-in-law as commander of the second troop of King James's horse guards and thereafter served with the Irish Brigade. He was killed in the Battle of Chiari in Italy in 1701.

Sarsfield's widow, Honora, Countess of Lucan, was nineteen years old when he died leaving her with their three month old child. In March 1695 she married the duke of Berwick who was only four years older than her.[2] Although

---

* Amongst whose members in the 18th century were several senior officers and one queen, Mary Sarsfield, who married the Baron von Neuhoff, King Theodore I of Corsica.[1]

this match did not please King James, who had hoped that his son would marry someone more substantial than a penniless Irish widow, it was a happy marriage and was successful in that it provided Berwick with an heir. But it was not to last as she died before her twenty-fourth birthday 'to the great grief of her husband, who had her heart preserved in a silver box'.[3] Berwick lived to achieve great things as a marshal of France including the great French victory over the Anglo-Portuguese army at Almanza in 1709. He was killed by accident while directing the siege of Philipsbourg in 1734, when one of his own cannon blew his head off.

Sarsfield's son, James Francis Edward Sarsfield, the second earl of Lucan, was adopted by Berwick and was brought up to be a soldier. He spent his twenty-first birthday serving with his step-father and half-brother at the siege of Barcelona where he was wounded in the final assault. In recognition of his bravery, the king of Spain decorated him with the Collar of the Golden Fleece and gave him the command of a company of his guards. He remained in the Spanish service until 1717 when he was given a colonelcy in the Irish brigade in France. This did not last long, mostly because the French pay was so poor, and he returned to Spain where he became involved in the great Spanish-Jacobite design of 1719 which gave him the opportunity of setting foot in Ireland for the first time. The purpose of his visit was to divert attention from Lord Ormonde's invasion of England and the planned uprising in Scotland. With several other Jacobite officers who had been smuggled into the country with him in April, the twenty-seven year old James Sarsfield 'held conferences with divers Papists of distinction, with design to foment a rebellion in favour of the Pretender' and a reward of £1,000 was put on his head. He did not meet with success. Ireland was still haunted by the horrors of the war that had run its course before he had been born, and no one was yet willing to repeat the experience. Although his name ensured him well wishers and sympathetic audiences, it did not gain him any active support and the troops and militiamen that scoured the west of Ireland for the Jacobite agents met with no resistance. The whole scheme was badly misconceived. Ormonde's invasion fleet was destroyed by storms before it reached the British Isles, and the Scottish rebellion was crushed with ease. Young Sarsfield and his companions found it too dangerous to venture outside Connaught and after a few weeks as fugitives they were forced to escape capture by taking a ship from Kilcolgan. It was James Sarsfield's final adventure. On 12 May 1719, a few days after his ship had brought him safely to French soil, he died in St Omers.[4]

The majority of those Irishmen who had left their country after the Treaty of Limerick eventually joined Marshal Catinat's army in the south. Under him they played a crucial part in the victory over the Savoyards at Marsaglia outside Turin in October 1693. Commanded by the two Scots, John Wauchope and Thomas Maxwell, the Irish were said to have 'despatched more than 1,000 of the enemy with sword-thrusts and club muskets' over the distance of a mile and a half. 'The Irish over-ran their orders and Catinat, seeing there was no recalling of them, commanded the whole army to follow'. 'Having fought with an extraordinary valour at the head of the Irish regiments', both Wauchope and Maxwell were shot dead, as were three Irish colonels.[5]

The Irish losses at Marsaglia were very heavy as they were to be in every significant engagement in which the Irish brigade served throughout the next century until its disbandment and integration into the French army in 1791. It is impossible now to calculate how many of Sarsfield's heirs, those generations of Irishmen who left their country to serve in the brigade, died for France, but it has been estimated that over forty thousand of them were killed or wounded in the first twenty-five years.[6] It was generally the case, and most particularly so at Marsaglia and at the great and bloody victory at Fontenoy in 1745, that the French used the Irish as shock troops with the inevitable consequence that they suffered disproportionately high casualties.

Sarsfield's old commander, Justin McCarthy, Lord Mountcashel, died in 1694 in the Pyrenees where he was convalescing from the wounds that he had received while serving with the Irish Brigade.[7] Richard Hamilton retired from active service after La Hogue and died in poverty in Paris in 1717.[8] His brother Anthony also gave up soldiering and lived the rest of his life at St Germain where he took up writing. He is best remembered for his *Mémoires du Comte de Grammont*. He died a much respected man of letters in 1720. William Dorrington and Dominic Sheldon served the Jacobite cause in exile for the rest of their lives. Both of them were promoted to the rank of maréchal de camp in the French army in 1702, both of them were given the rank of lieutenant-general (for what that was worth) in King James's army in exile in 1704 and both died peacefully in France in 1718 and 1721 respectively. The most successful of Sarsfield's Irish contemporaries was Pierce Butler, Lord Galmoy, who was made the earl of Newcastle by James and who after a distinguished military career in the French service, rose to the rank of lieutenant-general in Spain. He died in Paris in 1740 in his ninetieth year.

The one-time commander of King William's forces in Ireland, Count Solms, had a leg shot away at Landen. Like Sarsfield, he died a few days afterwards. His death pleased the English more than Sarsfield's could ever have done, as Solms was generally held to be responsible for the high English casualties at Steenkirk. His successor in the Irish war, Baron Ginckel, was created the earl of Athlone by a grateful king after the treaty of Limerick. He lived to his seventy-third year and died peacefully at home in Utrecht. The Chevalier de Tessé was promoted to the rank of lieutenant-general in the French army in 1697. He died of dysentery in Cremona in 1701. D'Usson, also a lieutenant-general, died of pneumonia in Marseilles in 1705.

Those high ranking Irishmen who had held high positions for King James and who remained behind after the Treaty of Limerick were forced to retire from public life. Although he was determined that it should be otherwise, this was the fate of Henry Luttrell. After the treaty he was rewarded with a pension of £500 a year by King William's government in recognition of his efforts to bring about peace in Ireland, and he was also allowed to enjoy his brother's estate, Luttrellstown outside Dublin. Simon Luttrell, whose estate it was, remained in France with the Irish Brigade and rose to the rank of brigadier before his death in 1698. Although Henry offered his military services to King William and even accompanied him at his own expense during the continental campaigns, he was never given an official position. The nearest he got to employment was when he was at one time chosen to command an Irish brigade in the Venetian service,[9] but this proposal never got beyond the planning stage.

However, unlike those contemporaries of his who had followed Sarsfield to France, Henry Luttrell remained wealthy and his descendants were elevated to the peerage. He led a full life and lived into his sixties when he was killed by an assassin's bullet. He was shot dead in a sedan chair as he was being carried along Stafford Street in Dublin in 1717 not, as might be expected, in retribution for his treachery but for a far more mundane reason. His assassin was thought to be either a jealous husband, a debtor or a poor and distant relation who hoped to inherit the estate as he had heard (incorrectly) that Luttrell had never lawfully married.

> Whether private or public spirit influenced the persons who killed Luttrell, we have no doubt that every rational and religious mind will admit this interposition of divine providence in allowing the chastisement of an infamous man who betrayed his sovereign, his religion and his country.'*[10]

The Lucan land dispute was not resolved until several years after Sarsfield's death. His niece, Charlotte Sarsfield, eventually emerged triumphant from the courts with a full title to all the lands once possessed by her father. She married Agmondesham Vesey, and her daughter Anne Vesey married Sir John Bingham. Patrick Sarsfield's great-great nephew, Sir Charles Bingham, was created earl of Lucan in 1795, a title that is today held by his descendant.

---

*   These words were written in 1809:

> If heav'n be pleas'd, when mortals cease to sin—
> And hell be pleas'd, when villains enter in—
> If earth be pleas'd, when it entombs a knave—
> All must be pleas'd—Now Luttrell's in his grave.

The name of Luttrell, now all but forgotten, was hated for at least a century after his assassination. His tomb was broken into eighty years after his death and his skull was removed and smashed. For illustrations of the loathing with which he was held in the 18th century, see O'Callaghan's *Irish Brigades*, pp. 102–4, Macaulay's note on Junius in his chapter on the Treaty of Limerick in his *History*, and the *Irish Magazine* for July 1809. See also Charles Jenkinson, *The Life History and Remarkable Pedigree of the Rt Hon. Simon Lord Irnham*, London 1769, which states that Luttrell was murdered on the orders of his mistress who then went through a marriage ceremony with his corpse in order to inherit his estate.'[11]

The Sarsfield Portraits

1 KNOW OF FOUR seveenteenth century portraits that purport to be of Patrick Sarsfield. It is easy to accept that two of these are of the same man, and that a third may be, but the fourth portrait is most certainly of someone else. Although it would be a simple matter to merely discount the latter, none of these portraits has any documentary provenance and it is impossible to declare with any degree of confidence that any one of them is genuine.

The waters are further muddied by the eighteenth century engravings of a portrait of Sarsfield painted by Lady Bingham (née Margaret Smith). This portrait is said to have been in the possession of the Binghams at Castlebar, Co. Mayo, but by the beginning of this century it had been lost. Consequently we are left with only the engravings of a lost original, and none of the engravings that I have seen bear any resemblance to any of the four portraits mentioned above. Although Lady Bingham was reputed to be 'a clever copyist' I am inclined to discount her picture as she was born almost fifty years after his death. If we are to accept these engravings as likenesses, there must have been an earlier portrait of Sarsfield, also lost, that Lady Bingham copied from. As it is, no earlier portrait has been identified and we are left no reason to suppose that Lady Bingham's portrait was anything other than the product of her imagination. This aside, the engravings are at best no more than copies of a lost copy of a lost original.

The four seventeenth century portraits are (1) the Franciscan portrait, (2) the Riley portrait, (3) the Kennedy portrait and (4) the Rigaud/Le Brun portrait.

1. *The Franciscan Portrait* (see: *frontispiece*) This portrait provides us with the most striking image of Sarsfield. It hangs in the library of the Franciscan Fathers at Dun Mhuire, Killiney, Co. Dublin. I am indebted to Father Fergal Grannell OFM for the information that this portrait once formed part of the collection of Henry, cardinal duke of York (Henry IX) who died in Italy in 1807. The Irish Franciscans of the Collegio Isidoro in Rome acquired the portrait after his death and it was brought to Ireland in 1869. How the portrait came to be in Rome in the first place is not known, but it is not a surprising destination. The last eighteen months of Sarsfield's life were centered around the Jacobite court in exile at St Germain. He was then one of the most senior military figures there and it is not unlikely that he had his portrait painted. His mother also lived there and she outlived both him and his son. It is not

20(a) The Kennedy Portrait

improbable that his portrait then found its way into the collection of the 'Old Pretender', James III, and finally into the hands of his son, the cardinal duke. (Note also that there is a single fleur-de-lys displayed on the breast plate in the portrait. Although this was then a common enough device in France, the Sarsfield arms were simply a plain shield bearing a single fleur-de-lys.)

2. *The Riley Portrait* (see: plate 2) This impressive painting, the largest study of Sarsfield, is now the property of the National Gallery of Ireland having formerly been part of Lord Talbot's collection at Malahide Castle. I understand from Dr Michael Wynne, the Keeper of the Gallery, that nothing is known of the portrait's origins, although it is now attributed to John Riley. If indeed it was painted by Riley, it would have been completed in London before the Revolution of 1688. It is however remarkable that when the antiquary, R.W. Twigge, made up a list of the Sarsfield portraits in 1903 (see: BL Add MSS 39,267 f.194) he noted that there was a 'head and shoulders' portrait of Sarsfield at Malahide Castle (the Rigaud/Le Brun portrait), but made no mention of this one. My suspicion is that it has only been identified as Sarsfield because of its strong similarity to the Franciscan portrait. Notwithstanding that, it is not improbable that a portrait of Sarsfield would have remained in Ireland as there is no record of Sarsfield taking any of his belongings to France, or indeed of him being able to salvage any of his belongings from Dublin, Lucan or Tully after the Battle of the Boyne.

20(b) The Rigaud/Le Brun Portrait

3. *The Kennedy Portrait.* If the Franciscan and Riley portraits are accepted as genuine, then this portrait is either a poor likeness of Sarsfield or else is of someone else. It was bequeathed by Mrs Ina Kennedy to the National Gallery of Ireland in the 1970s. According to Henry Mangan in an article in the first issue of the *Irish Sword*, this portrait was owned, from at least the middle of the last century, by Mrs Kennedy's grandfather, Edmund Henry Casey of Dublin. How Mr Casey came into possession of the painting is not known, nor how it came to be attributed to Sir Godfrey Kneller, perhaps the most famous portrait painter of Restoration England. One can perhaps be forgiven for suspecting that just as there is a temptation to attribute all late seventeenth century portraits to Kneller, there is a temptation in Ireland to identify all late seventeenth century military portraits as being of Sarsfield.

4. *The Rigaud/Le Brun Portrait.* This painting is also housed in the National Gallery of Ireland and is now attributed to Rigaud. If this portrait is genuine, then none of the others are. Like the Riley portrait it once hung in Malahide Castle, but it is not known how it came to be there. However, Dr Wynne considers it to be more likely to be authentic than the others, although, as he candidly wrote to me: 'I am not at all happy about any of the images of Sarsfield either here in our collection, or indeed the engravings in the National Library of Ireland.' Curiously, this portrait used to hang in a frame that bore the inscription 'C. *Le Brun Pinxt 1680*'. (This is clear from the photograph that appeared on the cover of the 1950s Catholic Truth Society pamphlet *Patrick Sarsfield* by the Reverend William Moran.) Although in my opinion it is very

20(c) An engraving of the long lost Bingham Portrait.

unlikely that this portrait was painted by either Le Brun or Rigaud, one wonders whether the frame was discarded when it was found that the date was unsatisfactory if the portrait was to be held out to be of Sarsfield.

In an article written in 1903 (in the *Journal of the Co. Kildare Archaeological Society*, iv) Lord Walter Fitzgerald published R.W. Twigge's list of the seven Sarsfield portraits thought to exist. Two of these were by Lady Bingham: a miniature in possession of Lord Lucan at Laleham House, Middlesex, and the 'lost' portrait said to be owned by Sir Charles Bingham at Castlebar, Co. Mayo. He also listed the Franciscan portrait and the 'head and shoulders portrait by Le Brun dated 1680' owned by Lord Talbot of Malahide. The three other portraits on the list were said to be in the possession of H.V. Macnamara, Lord Inchquin at Dromoland, Co. Clare, and (a 'head and shoulders' portrait) A.C. Palles. I have not seen any of these last three portraits and know nothing of their whereabouts today.

Notes

The most recent bibliography of this period of Irish history is to be found in *A New History of Ireland*, ed. Moody, Martin and Byrne (Oxford, 1976), iii. Other easily accessible bibliographies are to be found in R. H. Murray, *Revolutionary Ireland and Its Settlement* (London, 1911); C. D. Milligan, *History of the Siege of Londonderry* (Londonderry, 1951); and J. G. Simms, *Jacobite Ireland 1685-91* (London, 1969). As these works are widely available and as this is a biography rather than a general history, no separate bibliography has been prepared. For the same reasons, the sources given for the assertions in the text are not intended to be comprehensive and references have generally not been provided for what may be described as the general historical background, or where the source is clear from the text.

The following abbreviations have been used below:

D'Avaux	*Négociations de M. le Comte D'Avaux en Irlande, 1689-90*, ed. J. Hogan, 1934 (and supplement 1958).
Berwick	*Mémoires de Duc de Berwick* (Paris, 1778).
BL	British Library.
Bodl.	Bodleian Library, Oxford.
Boyer	Abel Boyer, *The History of King William III* (London, 1702).
Burnet	*Bishop Gilbert Burnet, History of His Own Time* (London, 1723-34).
C.S.P.	Calendar of State Papers.
Danish Force	K. Danaher and J. G. Simms (eds) *The Danish Force in Ireland*, 1690-1, (Dublin, 1962).
Davies	*Journal of Rowland Davies, 1688–90*, R. Caulfield (Camden Society, London, 1837).
Dumont	*Mémoires d'Isaac Dumont de Bostaquet, Gentilhomme Normand . . . (Paris, 1968).*
FIC	*Franco-Irish Correspondence, December 1688-February 1692*, ed. Sheila Mulloy (Dublin 1983/4).
Hamilton	Andrew Hamilton, *A True Relation of the Actions of the Inniskilling Men, etc.* (London, 1690).
Harris	Walter Harris, *History of the Life and Reign of William III* (Dublin, 1749).
HMC	Historical Manuscripts Commission
James II	*The Life of James II . . . Collected Out of Memoirs Writ of His Own Hand*, ed. J. S. Clarke (London, 1816).
Kane	Colonel Richard Kane, *Campaigns of King William* (London, 1735).
Leland	Thomas Leland, *History of Ireland* (third edition) (Dublin, 1774).
McCarmick	William McCarmick, *A Farther Impartial Account of the Actions of the Inniskilling Men,* etc (London, 1691).
Mackay	Major-Gen. Hugh Mackay, *Memoirs of the War Carried on in Scotland and Ireland 1689–1691* (Edinburgh, 1833).

O'Kelly	Charles O'Kelly, *The Jacobite War in Ireland 1688–1691*, ed. Plunket and Hogan (Dublin, 1894).
Parker	Robert Parker, *Memoirs of the Military Transactions in Ireland*, etc (Dublin 1746).
Plunket	*A Jacobite Narrative of the War in Ireland, 1688–91*, ed. J. T. Gilbert (Dublin, 1892). [Note: For simplicity's sake, I have referred to this account of the war throughout the text as having been written by Plunket. In fact it is far from certain that Nicholas Plunket—or anyone else of that surname—was the author. See Simms's introduction to the 1971 reprint of this work at pp. vii, viii.]
PRO	Public Records Office, London
Simms	J G Simms, *Jacobite Ireland 1685–91* (London, 1969).
Story	George Story, *A True and Impartial History of the Wars of Ireland* (London, 1691); and *A Continuation of the Impartial History of the Wars of Ireland* (London, 1693).
Todhunter	J. H. Todhunter, *The Life of Patrick Sarsfield* (London, 1895).

CHAPTER I

Generally: see J. T. Gilbert, *History of the Irish Confederation and the War in Ireland* (Dublin 1882–91); Thomas Leland, *History of Ireland* (1774); Charles Dalton, *English Army Lists* (1892); *Irish Army Lists* (1907); John Childs, *The Army of Charles II* (London, 1976); Ruth Clark, *The Life of Anthony Hamilton,* (London, 1921); *The Cambridge Modern History,* v, *The Age of Louis XIV* (1908).

1. For the Sarsfield family generally, see: BL Add. MSS 39,267 ff 90–202, BL Add MSS 39,270PP (published in *Co. Kildare Archaeological Society Journal IV* (2) July 1903).
2. *The Royal Voyage,* 1 (London, 1690).
3. J. C. O'Callaghan, *History of the Irish Brigades* (1886), p.175.
4. *C.S.P. Dom 1673–75,* p. 450; O'Hart, *Irish Pedigrees,* v, p. 323–5.
5. For O'Moore and Ireland during the 1640s and 50s see generally; Thomas Leland, *History of Ireland;* J. T. Gilbert, *History of the Irish Confederation;* and the *Calendars of State Papers* relating to Ireland for the period. For the O'Moore family, see Lord Walter Fitzgerald's article in the *Co. Kildare Archaeological Society Journal,* IX (1918).
6. W. E. H. Lecky, *History of Ireland in the Eighteenth Century* (1892).
7. J. T. Gilbert, *History of the Irish Confederation;* Leland, iii, p. 94.
8. Leland, iii, p. 93.
9. Ibid.
10. Gilbert.
11. Ibid.
12. As quoted by Lord Walter Fitzgerald in *Co. Kildare Archeological Society Journal*, IV (2) July 1903 (see also: BL Add. MSS 39,270PP).
13. HMC, *Ormonde,* ii; Bodl.: Rawlinson A. 14, p. 172.
14. For the Lucan Land Dispute generally see: BL Add MS 39,267 ff 90–202; B L Stowe MSS 200 f 451, 25; HMC, *Ormonde*; HMC, *Eighth Report,* p. 623; Bodl. MSS: Clarendon 80 f300, Rawlinson B 492 p. 154; *Calendar of Clarendon State Papers* (Bodl.) v, p. 520; *Report of Deputy Keeper of Public Records*, Ireland, No. 30, p. 39;

Lady Ann Fanshawe, *Memoirs; C.S.P. Treasury Books*, Vols 6 and 7; and references in *C.S.P Ireland* and *C. S. P. Dom* for relevant years.

15. *C.S.P. Dom.* 1693, p. 483–5; HMC Leeds.
16. BL Stowe MSS 206, f 403.
17. Lord George Scott, *Lucy Walter—Wife or Mistress* (1947), p. 193.
18. BL Add. MSS 39,267, f 201.
19. Berwick, *Memoires*.
20. Todhunter, p. 6.
21. Edward Chamberlayne, *Angliae Notitia or the Present State of England* (London, 1679), part I, p. 191 (as quoted by Childs).
22. D'Avaux later stated that Sarsfield had served in Hamilton's regiment, but Sarsfield in his Chester deposition makes mention only of his service in Monmouth's. It is of course possible that he began his service with Hamilton and later transferred.
23. HMC, *Fourth Report*, p. 238; see also Ruth Clark's *Life of Anthony Hamilton*.
24. Ernest Lavisse, *Histoire de France (*Paris, 1914), p. 236.
25. Bodl. Rawlinson B 492, p. 156; John Childs, *Army of Charles II*; *Letter Book of Charles II*.
26. HMC, *Fourth Report*, p. 242.

CHAPTER II

Generally, see Charles Dalton, *English Army Lists and Commission Registers 1661–1714* (London, 1892), i; John Childs, *The Army of Charles II* (1976); J. P. Kenyon, *The Popish Plot* (1972); Cecil Price, *Cold Caleb—The Scandalous Life of Ford Grey First Earl of Tankerville* (1956).

1. Records of corporation of Chester M/L/4/496–7, extracts of which are printed in HMC Eighth Report.
2. Edmund Calamy D.D., *An Historical Account of My Own Life* (1829).
3. J P Kenyon, *The Popish Plot* (Pelican Edition, p. 52).
4. Records of Corporation of Chester M/L/4/499.
5. John Michelburne, *Ireland Preserv'd, The First Part: The Troubles in the North* (London, 1705).
6. Records of Corporation of Chester M/L/4/498.
7. Op. cit. 496.
8. HMC, *Ormonde* (n.s), v.
9. *C.S.P. Dom. 1681*; *C.S.P. Treasury Books*, vi.
10. See note 14 to chapter I.
11. *True Protestant Mercury*, 10 September 1681; Narcissus Luttrell's Diary
12. P.R.O. P.C. 6/14.
13. P.R.O. P.C. 2/69.
14. *Domestic Intelligence,* 19 September 1681.
15. *C.S.P. Treasury Books*, vii, p. 348.
16. Narcissus Luttrell's Diary.
17. Edmund Calamy D.D., *An Historical Account of My Own Life* (1829).
18. *C.S.P. Dom.*
19. For the Siderfin episode generally, see: HMC, App. *Seventh Report*; *C.S.P Treasury Books*, vii; Narcissus Luttrell's Diary; *London Mercury*, June 1682.
20. *C.S.P. Treasury Books*, vii, p. 1081.

21. *C.S.P. Dom.*
22. *C.S.P. Dom.* 1683 (for the Lady Herbert affair).
23. *Herbert Correspondence*, ed. W. J. Smith (Aberystwyth, 1963) (No. 442).
24. Edmund Calamy D.D., *An Historical Account of My Own Life* (1829).
25. *C.S.P Domestic 1683*.
26. BL Add. MSS 39,267 f 155.
27. Narcissus Luttrell's Diary.

CHAPTER III
Generally: John Childs, *The Army, James II and The Glorious Revolution* (1980); John Carswell, *The Descent on England* (1969); G. M. Trevelyan, *The English Revolution 1688–9* (1938). The Monmouth Campaign is covered in detail by many books, but see especially: Bryan Little, *The Monmouth Episode* (1956).

1. Lord Somers' *Collection of Scarce and Valuable Tracts* (1812).
2. HMC, *Ormonde MSS* (New), vii; HMC, *Stopford-Sackville*; HMC, *Rutland*, ii, p. 89.
3. Hardwicke's *Miscellaneous State Papers,* ii, pp. 324–5.
4. Op. cit., p. 311.
5. HMC, *Stopford-Sackville*, p. 21.
6. Op. cit.
7. Lord Somers, *Collection of Scarce and Valuable Tracts* (1812).
8. Hardwicke's *Miscellaneous State Papers,* ii, p. 311.
9. Charles Dalton, *Army Lists and Commission Registers 1661–1714.*
10. *C.S.P. Dom. 1686.*
11. John Ellis Correspondence.
12. Gregory MacDonald, 'Lime Street Chapel', *Dublin Review,* April and July 1927.
13. Ellis Correspondence, Letter ccxxxv.
14. Luttrell's Diary, i, 375; Ellis Correspondence, i, III, 118–9.
15. BL Add. MSS 34,512, ff 95, 98–99; Letter and Speech by John Beaumont, Pamphlet (BL Ref: 1850 c 6).
16. BL Add. MSS 4194, ff 331.
17. BL Add. MSS 21, 483, f 34; 41805 f 103.
18. BL Add. MSS 34,512, ff 98, 99.
19. Sir John Dalrymple's *Memoirs,* ii, p. 107.
20. HMC, *Dartmouth,* p. 204.
21. *Revolution Politics* (London, 1733), part VII, p. 75.
22. This account of the skirmish at Wincanton is gleaned from the following sources: HMC, App. *Seventh Report,* pp. 408, 417; HMC, *Twelfth Report,* p. 222; Francis Gwyn's 'Journal' *in Fortnightly Review* XL, 1886; John Whittle, *An Exact Diary of the Late Expedition of His Illustrious Highness the Prince of Orange (now King of Great Britain)* (1689; republished Lewes, 1988); Kenney's *Compleat History of England,* p. 530; Oldmixon's *History*; *Revolution Politics*, part VII (London, 1733), p. 78; Richard Burton, *History of the House of Orange* (1813); Edmund Bohun, *History of the Desertion;* Sir John Dalrymple's *Memoirs,* appendix to book V (part I); Ellis Correspondence; *London Gazette,* 23 November 1688; Abel Boyer, *History of William III* (1702); BL Sloane MSS 3929 ff 109, 111; BL Add. MSS 4,194 f 423; 34,517 f 616; 41805 f 245; Roger Morrice's Entring Book, Q 328, in Dr. Williams's Library, Gordon Square, London WC1.

23. BL Add MSS 28,053 f 355.
24. *An Heroick Essay upon the Unequall'd Victory obtained by Major-General Webb over the Count de la Motte at Wynendale* (London, 1709).
25. BL Add. MSS 34,510 f 184.
26. James MacPherson, *Original Papers* (1776), p. 283.
27. *Revolution Politics*, part VII (entry for 21 November).
28. HMC, App. *Seventh Report*, p. 418.
29. Gilbert Burnet, *History of My Own Times* (first edition), p. 794.
30. Op. cit., p. 797.
31. Op. cit., p. 792.
32. BL Add. MSS 28,042 ff 34.
33. Abel Boyer, *History of William III* (1702).
34. Burnet, pp. 807–8.
35. HMC, *Twelfth Report,* App VI, p. 141.
36. *The English Currant*, 24 December 1688.
37. Op. cit., 7 January 1689.
38. Roger Coke, *A Detection of the Court and State of England* (1719).
39. Campana de Cavelli, *Les Derniers Stuarts* (Paris 1871), ii, p. 507 (letter, Rizzini to Duke of Modena, 23 February 1689).
40. Charles Hatton, *Correspondence.*
41. *Orange Gazette*, 8 and 26 February 1689; *London Intelligence*, 2 February 1689; Dangeau's *Memoirs,* London 1825; Campana de Cavelli, Vol II, p. 501 (Letter from Zipoli, 7.2.1689).

CHAPTER IV
1. *The Historical Songs of Ireland*, edited by T. Crofton-Croker (1841).
2. Tyrconnell to James, BL Add. MSS 28,053 ff 432, published in Campana de Cavelli, *Les Derniers Stuarts* (Paris, 1871), ii, pp. 532–3.
3. *Orange Gazette*, 22 February 1689.
4. BL Egerton MSS 917 f 104.
5. *The Montgomery Manuscripts* 1603–1706, ed. Rev G. Hill, Belfast 1869.
6. *Lettres Historiques de Madame de Sévigné*, ed. J. B. Ebeling 1934, p. 207.
7. *A Full and True Account of the Landing of the Late King James II in Ireland* (London, March 1689) [BL Ref: 807 g 21(1)].
8. Berwick.
9. See: HMC, *Finch,* iii; C. D. Boulger, *The Battle of the Boyne* (1911), p. 57.
10. *A Full and True Account of the Landing and Reception of the Late King James* (London, 1689) [BL Ref: 807 f 36]; *A Full and True Account of the Landing of the Late King James II in Ireland* [BL Ref: 807 g 21(1)].
11. HMC, *Charlemont,* ii, and generally: George Bennett, *History of Bandon* (1869).
12. *A Full and True Account.*
13. Ibid.
14. Ibid.
15. HMC, *Ormonde* (n.s.), viii, p. 362.
16. HMC, *Downshire,* i; HMC, *Ormonde* (n.s.), viii; *An Account of the Most Remarkable Occurrences Relating to Londonderry* . . . (1689) [Bl Ref: 816 m 23(60)].
17. See e.g.: *The Royal Voyage or The Expedition. A Tragicomedy* (London, 1690), II. ii; *The Royal Flight, or The Conquest of Ireland. A New Farce* (London, 1690), III. iii.

18. The following references to Birr and Sir Lawrence Parsons are taken from a contemporary chronicle of the war years, a copy of which is preserved in Lord Rosse's collection of manuscripts at Birr Castle (catalogue ref: A/24). Extracts from this manuscript have been published in *The Picture of Parsonstown* by Thomas L. Cooke, 1826.

19. John Michelburne, *Ireland Preserv'd, the Second Part: The Siege of Londonderry* (1705); BL Stowe MSS 977.

20. Ibid.

CHAPTER V

For the Sligo Campaign generally see: Andrew Hamilton, *A True Relation of the Actions of the Inniskilling Men*; Captain William McCarmick, *A Farther Impartial Account of the Actions of the Inniskilling Men*; Story; D'Avaux; HMC Le Fleming, p. 243; and for references to James Caldwell see: William H G. Bagshawe, *The Bagshawes of Ford, A Biographical Pedigree* (London, 1886), pp. 368–370; and John B. Cunningham, *Castle Caldwell and its Families* (Enniskillen, 1980), pp. 28–31. These last two books both draw on the manuscripts in the Bagshawe collection in the John Rylands Library, Manchester.

1. *Reports of the Deputy Keeper of Public Records* (Northern Ireland) 1960–65, p. 85.
2. *An Exact Relation of the Most Remarkable Transactions that Happened Lately in Ireland . . .* 1689 [BL Ref: 816 m 23(52)].
3. J.S., *True and Impartial History of Wars of Ireland* (1692); Hamilton, pp. 10–12.
4. James MacPherson, *Original Papers* (1776).
5. T. O'Rorke, *History of Sligo Town and County* (1889).
6. J.G. Simms, *The Jacobite Parliament of 1689* (Dublin Historical Association pamphlet, 1974).
7. Dalton's *Army Lists*.
8. McCarmick, p. 57.
9. BL Add. MSS 21,427 f 35.
10. Hugh Allingham, *Ballyshannon, Its History and Antiquities* (1879).
11. W. H. G. Bagshawe, *The Bagshawes of Ford*, pp. 368–370.
12. For Belleek see: Hamilton, p. 19; McCarmick, pp. 40–41; Bagshawe, pp. 368–370.
13. *An exact relation of the glorious victory obtained upon the French and Irish Army before Londonderry on Sunday 2nd June 1689* (London, 1689); quoted by Simms, *Jacobite Ireland*, p. 115.
14. HMC, *Eighth Report*, App, p. 494.
15. Bagshawe; the allusion is to St Matthew XXV 32–33.
16. Hamilton, pp. 18–20. McCarmick, p. 44.
17. John Oldmixon, *Memoirs of Ireland* (London, 1716), p. 92.
18. McCarmick.
19. From letters published in W G Wood-Martin, *History of Sligo* (Dublin 1889), book VII, pp. 2–3.
20. N.L.I. MSS 990 (printed in *Irish Sword*, II, and in *The Great Tyrconnell* by Sir Charles Petrie, p. 221).
21. Bodl. Carte MSS 181 f 276.
22. Ibid., f 278.
23. McCarmick, p. 58.

24. For Newtownbutler generally, see especially Story, Hamilton and McCarmick.
25. Bodl. Carte MSS 181 f 281.
26. BL Sloane MSS 1033 (Bonnivert's Journal).
27. Hamilton, p. 45.
28. *A Full and True Account of a Bloody and Dismal Fight* . . . (London, September 1689) [BL Ref: 807 g 21(9)].
29. Letter, James to Richard Hamilton, 1 August 1689 in Ruth Clark, *Anthony Hamilton* (London, 1916).
30. Hamilton.
31. Ibid., p. 49.
32. Ibid., p. 50.
33. Ibid., p. 51.
34. *London Gazette*, 29 August 1689; *A Particular and Full Account of the Burning and Destroying of Several Places* . . . (London, August 1689) [BL Ref: 807 g 21(5)]; *An Account of the Joyning of Maj. Gen. Kirke's Forces with Duke Schombergs* . . . *(*Chester, August 1689) [BL Ref: 807 g 21 (7)]; Hamilton.
35. HMC, *Ormonde* (n.s.), viii.
36. James II, *Memoirs*.

CHAPTER VI

For the attack on Sligo generally see: McCarmick, p. 68; *A Full and True Account of All the Remarkable Actions and Things* . . . *in the North of Ireland (*1689) [BL Ref: 816 m 23(67)]; *Histoire de la Revolution d'Irlande* (1692) [BL Ref: 601 d 13(2)]; Walter Harris, *Life of William III*; Story, p. 33–35; James II; Boyer; D'Avaux, p. 607; and most particularly, *A Relation of What Passed in Connaught between His Magesties' Forces under the Command of Brigadier Sarsfield, and the Rebels led by the Lord Weyer, the Colonels Floyd. Russel, &c upon the army decamping from Allardstown.* (Dublin, 1689) [BL Ref: 807 g 21 (11)]. Note that a different account of Sarsfield's advance is given in Wood-Martin's *History of Sligo*, and some additional material is to be found in Roger Morrice's Entring Book, pp. 669–672, in Dr. Williams's Library, London.

1. James Nihell's Journal for 31 September 1689 (published in James MacPherson's *Original Papers*, 1776).
2. McCarmick, p. 67.
3. *The London Gazette*, 1 October 1689.
4. McCarmick, p. 37.
5. James Nihell's Journal, 28 September 1989; Story, p. 26.
6. *An Exact Account of the Royal Army with Particulars of a Great Defeat* . . . *Near Boyle* (16 October 1689) Dundalk [BL Ref: 807 g 21(13)].
7. McCarmick, p. 68.
8. *An Account of the Most Remarkable Occurrences Relating to Londonderry* . . . (1689) [BL Ref: 816 m 23 (60)]; J S Clarke, *Life of James II* (1816).
9. McCarmick, p. 68.
10. *A Relation of What Passed in Connaught* . . .
11. Story, p. 35.
12. BL Add. MSS 33,589 f 87.
13. McCarmick, p. 68; C Leslie, *An Answer to a Book Intituled The State of the Protestants in Ireland under the Late King James's Government* (London, 1692), p. 161.

14. Story, p. 34.
15. A plan of the work carried out by Burton and Luttrell is reproduced in W G Wood-Martin's *History of Sligo*, ii, p. 134, and also in the *Irish Sword*, vii, p. 125.

CHAPTER VII
1. Burnett, ii, p. 20.
2. HMC, *Rutland,* ii, p. 128; *Memoirs and Letters of Ulick Marquis of Clanricarde* (1757).
3. BL Egerton MSS 917 f 129.
4. PRO W.O. 55/1794 29, 30; Berwick.
5. *Revolution Politics*, part VIII.
6. HMC, *Ormonde* (n.s.) viii.
7. HMC, *Kenyon,* p. 240; PRO W.O. 55/1794 f 54.
8. Birr MS.
9. D'Avaux, p. 519–520.
10. Berwick.
11. D'Avaux.
12. John A. Murphy, *Justin MacCarthy, Lord Mountcashel* (1958), p. 28.
13. *Analecta Hibernica,* iv, p. 128.
14. For Charlemont generally, see Story.
15. PRO W.O. 55/1794 f 114.
16. FIC 654.
17. *Analecta Hibernica* iv, p. 119–120.
18. FIC 844, 846, 867.
19. Letter from Lauzun to Louvois, 1 July 1690 in Von Ranke, vi (Appendix); FIC 867.

CHAPTER VIII
For the Boyne generally see Peter Beresford-Ellis, *The Boyne Water* (1976) which includes a good bibliography to which should be added Sheila Mulloy, 'French Eye Witnesses of the Boyne' in *Irish Sword*, xv, (No. 59, Winter 1982). Other good modern accounts are to be found in Simms and Boulger, and also *Ireland's Fate: The Boyne and After*, by Robert Shepherd, (London, 1990); and W.A. Maguire (ed), *Kings in Conflict*, (Belfast, 1990).

1. BL Add. MSS 38,146 f 94.
2. Story p. 75.
3. Op. cit.
4. BL Add. MSS 38,146 f 94.
5. Colonel Thomas Bellingham, *Diary,* 1908.
6. Bodl: Carte MSS 79 (a letter from Richard Brewer to Thomas Wharton, quoted in Beresford-Ellis, p. 82).
7. HMC, *Leyborne-Popham,* p. 27.
8. BL Add. MSS 38,146 f 96.
9. Plunket at p. 102 (a Williamite account corroborates the assertion that Schomberg was killed by a pistol shot fired by an Irish horseguard; see BL Egerton MSS 917 f 135. Another version states that he was shot by a Huguenot deserter serving with the Irish: BL Add. MSS 41,141).
10. BL Add. MSS 38,146 f 96.
11. Bodl: Carte MSS 79 quoted in Beresford-Ellis, p. 82.

12. Stevens's diary is to be found in the British Library (Add. MSS 36,296). It was published in book form in 1912 having been irritatingly edited by R.H. Murray.
13. BL Add MSS 38,146 f 96.
14. Op. cit.
15. Op. cit; Danish Force; Dumont.
16. Bonnivert's Journal, BL Sloane MSS 1033.
17. BL Add. MSS 38,146 f 98.
18. Burnet, ii, p. 59.

CHAPTER IX
 1. HMC, *le Fleming*.
 2. O'Kelly p. 23.
 3. BL Add. MSS 36,296.
 4. FIC 628.
 5. Plunket, p. 105.
 6. Southwell's Letter Book in HMC, *Finch,* ii; Narcissus Luttrell's Diary, 28 July 1690.
 7. BL Add. MSS 38, 146.
 8. Op. cit., p. 110; *A Letter from an English Officer . . . dated July 29th 1690* [BL Ref: 816 m 23 (76)].
 9. BL Add MSS 38,146, p. 114; Davies.
10. For these conferences and the subsequent plotting, see: Stevens's Journal ff 89–90 (the salient parts are quoted in P.W. Sergeant, *Little Jennings and Fighting Dick Talbot,* London, 1913); FIC 1984; Plunket, pp. 110–113; O'Kelly, pp. 30–33; Berwick.
11. Harris.
12. James II, p. 434.
13. HMC, *Stuart*.
14. 'Reflections of an Irish Brigade Officer', by R.J. Hayes in *Irish Sword*, i, p. 69.
15. See Lauzun's letters from Limerick and Galway in FIC, ii.
16. Harris.
17. Sheffield Grace, *Memoirs of the Family of Grace* (1823).
18. BL Add. MSS 36, 296.
19. *Memoirs of the Family of Grace.*
20. Plunket, p. 259: Harris.
21. Plunket, p. 260.
22. Harris.
23. BL Add. MSS 38,146 f 112.
24. Op. cit.
25. Op. cit., p. 47.
26. Lauzun to Louvois, FIC 1041.
27. *Répertoire Historique de la Gazette de France* (Paris, 1904).

CHAPTER X
For the Ballyneety raid generally, see: Davies; Samuel Mullineaux, *A Journal of the Siege of Limerick*; Story; Parker; Burnet; Robert Southwell in BL Add. MSS 38,146 f 117 and HMC, *Finch* ii, pp. 412–414; D Campbell in *The Rawdon Papers*, ed. E. Berwick, (1819); Dumont p. 245 et seq. The reference to Dean Harrison is to be found in Henry Ellis's Original Letters (1827), iv, pp.209–13.

1. William Rooney, *Poems and Ballads*, (Dublin, 1902).
2. *Poems of David O Bruadair* (Dublin, 1917) (reworked translation).
3. Dumont.
4. Story, p. 114.
5. BL Add MSS 38,146 p. 196.
6. *The approach and signal victory of King William's forces over the Irish army encamped around Limerick* . . . (1690) [BL Ref: 807 f 36 (6)].
7. *The Rawdon Papers*.
8. Burnet.
9. Fouleresse to Christian V, quoted by L. Barbe in *Notes and Queries* (1877), viii, p. 122. See also Wurtemberg in *Danish Force*, p. 67.
10. Harris.
11. PRO W.O. 55/339 f 49.
12. Ferrar, *History of the City of Limerick*, second edition (1767).
13. Dumont.
14. Op. cit.
15. BL Add. MSS 38,146.
16. See for example: Augustus de Morgan, *The Book of Almanacs*, third edition (1907).
17. Maurice Lenihan, *Limerick: its History and Antiquities* (Dublin, 1866).
18. Samuel Lewis, *A History and Topography of Limerick City and County*, (Dublin, 1837; reprint 1980), p. 159.
19. Lenihan gives one version; the other is to be found in Howard Green, *The Battlefields of Great Britain and Ireland*, 1973.
20. Lenihan.
21. Ibid.
22. Dumont.
23. BL Add. MSS 41,141, also published in Richard Kane, *Campaigns of William and Queen Anne*. See also: Robert Parker, *Memoirs of Military Transactions* (1747), p. 26.
24. Dumont.
25. D. Campbell in *The Rawdon Papers*.
26. Harris.
27. *Danish Force*, p. 55.

CHAPTER XI

The two best modern accounts of the siege of Limerick are still those by J.G. Simms (in *Jacobite Ireland*, 1969, and *North Munster Studies*, Limerick 1967, pp. 308–314). Jacobite accounts are given by Stevens, O'Kelly, Plunket (which is published together with a French account) and by several correspondents in FIC. Williamite accounts are given by Davies, Story, Dumont, Fouleresse, Wurtemberg, Southwell and Mullenaux.

1. Harris: Appendix, Item XLlll.
2. Luttrell's Diary, ii, p. 97.
3. *Great News from Limerick giving an Account of the Successful Victory gained over the Irish Rebels* . . . (London, 1690) [BL Ref: 816 m 23 (82)].
4. Davies.
5. Ibid.
6. Ibid.
7. Story, pp. 128–130.

8. *Histoire de la Revolution d'Irlande*, (Paris, 1691) [BL Ref: 601 d 13 (2)]; Fouleresse to Christian V, *Notes and Queries* (1877), viii, p. 122.
9. Ibid, pp. 121–3.
10. Story.
11. Ibid.
12. *Danish Force*, p. 73.
13. Story.
14. BL Add. MSS 38,146 f 126.
15. *Danish Force*, p. 73.
16. Fouleresse to Christian V, *Notes and Queries* (1877), pp. 121–3.
17. *Danish Force*, p. 75.
18. Story.
19. HMC, *Hastings*.
20. BL Add. MSS 38, 146.

CHAPTER XII
1. HMC, *le Fleming*.
2. Berwick.
3. Tyrconnell's deception of Lauzun is taken from O'Kelly's account.
4. FIC 1048 (also in Ranke, vi, pp. 124–5 and translated in R. Barry O'Brien, *Studies in Irish History 1649–1775*, p. 286).
5. Ibid.
6. As quoted by Sir Charles Petrie, *The Duke of Berwick and his Son* (London, 1951).
7. Dangeau; O'Kelly.
8. The account of the attack on Birr Castle is taken mainly from the Birr manuscript which includes a transcription of John Phillips's letter.
9. J.T. Gilbert, *History of the Irish Confederation and the War in Ireland* (Dublin, 1882–91).
10. HMC, *le Fleming*, Newsletter, 30 September 1690.
11. HMC, *le Fleming*.

CHAPTER XIII
1. *The Royal Flight or, The Conquest of Ireland, A New Farce* (London, 1690), III, iii.
2. *A True and Faithful Account of the Present State and Condition of the Kingdom of Ireland* (London, 1690) [BL Ref: 816 m 23 (79)]. For the supposed defeat of Sarsfield in the Mallow area, see also: Story, p. 140; Harris; *Calendar of the Clarendon State Papers in the Bodleian Library,* v, ed. F. J. Routledge, p. 690 (Clarendon State Papers, Vol 90 ff 48–49); *Danish Force*, pp. 78–79; Davies, p. 148.
3. Wurtemberg to Harboe, 17 October 1690, *Danish Force*, p. 90.
4. O'Kelly, pp. 46–48.
5. Ibid. p. 49 et seq; see also Berwick's *Mémoires* on this incident.
6. FIC 1254.
7. *Danish Force*, p. 90; For this whole episode see: J.G. Simms, 'Williamite Peace Tactics' 1690–1, *Irish Historical Studies*, iii, (1953) pp. 308–323.
8. FIC 1254.
9. De Santons Boullain to Louvois, FIC 1236.
10. Ronsele: Bodl. Rawl.C.439 f 432.
11. Ibid; p. 20.

12. Ibid; p. 22.
13. De Gravel to Louvois, FIC 2020.
14. Ibid.
15. De Santons Boullain FIC 2010.
16. De Santons Boullain FIC 1236.

CHAPTER XIV
The account of the attack on Lanesborough is taken from Lord Lisburne's Report in C.S.P.
Dom. 1690; Story's *True and Impartial History,* pp. 155–6 and the French translations of
Sarsfield's letter of 24 February 1691 printed in FIC 1254 (and also retranslated into English
by Henry Mangan in *Irish Sword,* i). The references to the minor incidents throughout the
winter months are taken from Story's *Continuation,* the most detailed day to day account of
the war.

1. D.P. Conyngham, *Sarsfield or The Last Great Struggle for Ireland* (Boston, 1871), p.
   162.
2. De Santons Boullain to Louvois FIC 1236.
3. FIC 1281.
4. Story.
5. Parker, p. 29.
6. *Danish Force*, p. 115.
7. HMC, *Hastings.*
8. Altevelt's journal quoted in *Danish Force*, p. 16, and *Studies* 1954 (vol xliii), p. 431.
9. *Danish Force*, p. 110.
10. See, e.g: JS, *A True and Impartial History and (sic) Wars of the Kingdom of Ireland,*
    London 1692; Story; and newsletters quoted in HMC, *Downshire,* i (12 December
    1690).

CHAPTER XV
1. Plunket, p. 126.
2. James II.
3. FIC 1075.
4. Ibid.
5. Hector MacDonnell, 'A Noble Pretension' *Journal of the Glens of Antrim Historical
   Society,* viii, 1980; see also *The Irish Sword* N. 63 (1985) p. 100.
6. James II.
7. Ibid.
8. Fumeron to Louvois, FIC 1256.
9. Fumeron to Louvois, FIC 1273.
10. Sarsfield to Mountcashel, FIC 1281.
11. Methelet to Louvois, FIC 1295.
12. Sarsfield to Mountcashel, FIC 1281.
13. Ibid.
14. Balteau, *Dictionaire de Biographie Française.*
15. As quoted in FIC, Introduction, p. xxviii; *Règpertoire Historique de la Gazette de
    France* (Paris, 1904).
16. *Mercurius Reformatus or the New Observator,* 5 June 1691.
17. Dangeau, iv, p. 274.

18. Fumeron to Louvois, FIC 1292.
19. Plunket, p. 129.

CHAPTER XVI
1. Danish Force p. 110.
2. See, e.g: PRO WO 55/339 ff 49–62.
3. Wurtemberg to Christian V, *Danish Force*, p. 111.
4. Plunket, p. 129.
5. O'Kelly, p. 73.
6. Story, p. 89.
7. Ibid., p. 90.
8. BL Add. MSS 28,939, f 118.
9. See, e.g. Story, 10 March 1691.
10. Noblesse to Louvois, FIC 1501; Robert to Barbesieux, FIC 1416.
11. Ibid.
12. The best and most detailed modern account of the siege of Athlone is Harman Murtagh's *The Sieges of Athlone* (Athlone 1973; reprinted from the *Journal of the Old Athlone Society*, i, 1970–3) which gives a full bibliography which I have not duplicated here.
13. De Tessé to Louvois, FIC 1498.
14. Plunket, p. 131.
15. O'Kelly, p. 77.
16. Plunket, pp. 133–134.
17. O'Kelly, p. 75.
18. Tyrconnell to Louvois, FIC 1484.
19. Ibid.
20. Plunket, pp. 132–3.
21. *A Diary of the Siege of Athlone by An Engineer of the Army* (1691) [BL Ref: T.1707 (9)].
22. Ibid.
23. Parker, p. 27.
24. See: introduction to *A Diary of the Siege of Limerick* (London, 1692) [BL Ref: 1325 f 11 (3)]; Plunket, p. 134.
25. Plunket, p. 135.
26. Parker; see also the journal of Robert Stearne in the National Army Museum, London, and quoted in G. Le M. Gretton, *Campaigns and History of the Royal Irish Regiment* (1911).
27. Story, p. 108.
28. FIC 1416; MacKay, p. 156; Plunket.
29. Story.
30. O'Kelly, p. 77.
31. *Diary of the Siege of Athlone*.
32. O'Kelly, p. 79.
33. E Berwick (ed.) *The Rawdon Papers*.
34. HMC, *Fourth Report*: Letter, Ginckel to Lord Justices, 5 July 1691.
35. BL Add. MSS 41,141; Kane, p. 10.
36. O'Kelly, p. 84.
37. Ibid.
38. FIC 1499.
39. O'Kelly, p. 85.

40. Ibid.
41. All references to Ronsele are taken from the manuscript entitled 'A Narrative of How Basely The Baron of Corthny has been Abus'd by Ye Irish During Ye Late War and How He Escaped Hanging' in the Bodleian Library (Rawl.C 439 f 232 et seq). Extracts of this document have been published in *Analecta Hibernica*, ii, pp. 22–25.

CHAPTER XVII

O'Kelly's assertion (which must be wrong) that Sarsfield was posted on the left of the line has muddied the waters for those who have since attempted to describe the battle. The only detailed description of the Jacobite battle line is given by Plunket who states that Sarsfield was on the right. Other sources confirm that he was not anywhere else, and certainly not in those crucial positions in the centre or left. Later Williamite assertions that he was in the rear, refusing to stir without St Ruth's orders, can be explained by the fact that when Ginckel's final assault was launched, the English began to roll up the Irish line from the left. Sarsfield at that time was on the far side of Kilcommodon Hill behind the whole of the Irish army.

The only attempt at a full description of the battle from an Irish viewpoint is that given by Plunket. O'Kelly and De Tessé wrote only brief accounts. (Unfortunately, John Stevens's Diary which promised to be the most complete account of all, comes abruptly to an end after describing the opening shots). On the Williamite side, full accounts are given by Kane, Parker, Story, Mackay, Claudianus and Wurtemberg. and other important accounts are given by Ginckel, Tempest (in the *Rawdon Papers*) and Robert Stearne (copies of whose journal are in the National Army Museum, London, and the National Library of Ireland).

The clearest modern account (which includes a good bibliography) is that by G A Hayes-McCoy in *Irish Battles, A Military History of Ireland* (1969; reprinted 1989).

1. Story, pp. 123–5.
2. Parker.
3. Story, p. 122.
4. Plunket, p. 138.
5. *Rawdon Papers.*
6. BL Add MSS 41,141 printed as Richard Kane, 'Campaigns of King William and Queen Anne', p. 12; see also: Parker, p. 35.
7. Plunket, p. 141.
8. Mackay, p. 164.
9. Plunket, p. 142.
10. Noblesse to Barbesieux FIC 1523: De Tessé to Louvois FIC 1506.
11. Latin poem published in Plunket, p. 280 (Simms's translation).
12. Although Plunket states that De Tessé was on the right, De Tessé's own dispatch clearly states that he had been sent to the left. Saint-Ruth himself had remained on the right overlooking Sarsfield's division. See: FIC 1506.
13. Fumeron to Louvois, FIC 1503.
14. Quoted by Todhunter, p. 169.
15. Plunket, p. 147.
16. This is a modification and a précis of John Jordan's translation of Claudianus's account which is to be found in *the Journal of the Galway Archaeological and Historical Society,* xxvi, 1954–5, pp. 1–3. Full reference to the original Latin text is to be found in *Danish Force*, p. 16.
17. FIC 1502.

18. Plunket, p. 147.
19. *An Exact Journal of the Victorious Progress of their Majesties' Forces Under the Command of General Ginckle This Summer in Ireland* (London, 1691), p. 21.
20. *Danish Force*, p. 123.
21. Ibid., p. 120.
22. Tyrconnell to Louvois FIC 1502, Tyrconnell to King James, FIC 1522.
23. Plunket, p. 146.
24. Plunket, p. 143.

CHAPTER XVIII
1. Tadhg MacLochlainn, *The Parish of Aughrim and Kilconnell* (1980).
2. Kane, p. 13.
3. FIC 1518.
4. HMC, *Fourth Report*: Letter from Ginckel to Lord Justices, 10/11 July 1691.
5. *Danish Force*, p. 125.
6. Harris.
7. HMC, *Fourth Report*: Letter from Ginckel to Lord Justices, 25 July 1691.
8. Harris.
9. Ibid.
10. Plunket, p. 149.
11. Harris: A *Diary of Siege of Limerick* (London, 1692), entry for 9 August 1691 [BL Ref: 1325 f 11(3)].
12. Story; James II; Plunket, p. 149.
13. Letters to and from Barbesieux, FIC 416, 421 and 2140.
14. Quoted in Harris.
15. *A Diary of the Siege of Limerick*, entry for 18 August 1691.
16. Plunket, p. 155.
17. Ibid.
18. Story.
19. Military Dictionary published with *The Memoirs of the Late Marquis de Feuquieres* (1737).
20. *Danish Force*, p. 127.
21. Ibid.
22. O'Klopp, *Der Fall der Hauses Stuart*, v, p. 304.

CHAPTER XIX
1. FIC 1703, 1714.
2. *A Diary of the Siege of Limerick* (London, 1692) [BL Ref: 1325 f 11(3)].
3. Richards' diary in Plunket, p. 287.
4. *Danish Force*, p. 130–131.
5. Richard's diary in Plunket, pp. 228–229.
6. *Danish Force*, p. 130.
7. FIC 1702, 1748.
8. Story; Plunket, p. 159; *A Relation of Their Majesties' Forces Passing the Shannon Near Limerick* [BL Ref: 816 m 23(87)]; *Danish Force*, p. 133.
9. Richard's diary in Plunket, p. 291.
10. FIC 1714.

11. Richard's diary in Plunket, p. 292; see also *Danish Force*, p. 132.
12. Plunket, p. 161.
13. O'Kelly, p. 103.
14. Parker.
15. Plunket, p. 163.
16. O'Kelly, p. 103.
17. Ibid., p. 104.
18. FIC 1714.
19. O'Kelly, p. 102.
20. Plunket, p. 162.
21. Story, p. 220.
22. Quoted in Plunket, p. 295.
23. See: *Journal of North Munster Archaeological Society*, i.
24. Story; Letter from Robert Douglas to Sir Arthur Rawdon dated 28 September 1691 in the *Rawdon Papers*.
25. BL Add. MSS 41,141; Kane.
26. HMC, *Fourth Report*, Letter Ginckel to Lord Justices, 23 September 1691.
27. Plunket, p. 166.
28. Richard's diary in Plunket, p. 293.
29. James Ferguson, 'Papers on the History of the Scots Brigade in the United Netherlands', *Scottish History Society*, vols 32, 35, 38 (1899–1901); Coenraet Droste, *Overblyfsels van Gehengchenis* (ed. Fruin) 1879, 1.2790–2797, 4830–4843; Charles Dalton, *The Scots Army 1661–1688;* Berwick's *Mémoires*; O'Kelly, p. 99–100.
30. O'Kelly, p. 106.
31. Ibid.
32. BL Egerton MSS 2618 ff 170–172 and printed in Plunket at pp. 310–11.
33. George Clarke's Autobiography in HMC, *Leyborne-Popham*.

CHAPTER XX
The negotiations and treaty of Limerick are carefully covered in most contemporary accounts, especially those of Story, Boyer and Plunket. See also *A Diary of the Siege of Limerick* (London, 1692) [BL Ref: 1325 f 11(3)] and *An Account of the Surrender and Capitulation of Limerick* (1692) [BL Ref: 816 m 23(88)]. For modern explanations of the treaty see in particular T. D. Ingram, *Two Chapters of Irish History* (London, 1888), J. G. Simms 'Surrender of Limerick 1691' in *Irish Sword*, ii, and J. G. Simms, *The Treaty of Limerick* (Dublin Historical Association pamphlet, 1961).

1. *An Account of the Surrender and Capitulation of Limerick.*
2. George Clarke's Autobiography in HMC, *Leyborne-Popham*, p. 281.
3. HMC, *Fourth Report*, Letter dated 23 September 1691.
4. M. E. Grew, *William Bentinck and William III*.
5. Boyer.
6. O'Kelly, p. 107.
7. HMC, *Leyborne-Popham*.
8. See: article on Purcell in *Journal of North Munster Archaeological Society*, iii.
9. Burnet, ii, p. 81.
10. According to Ronsele (para. 208). See note 41 to chapter 16.

11. The Articles signed by Sarsfield are in the British Library [BL Add MSS 28,939 ff 141]. The full text is reproduced in Plunket.
12. Sec: J G Simms; 'The Original Draft of the Civil Articles', *Irish Historical Studies,* vol 78, 1952.
13. Story.
14. Story; Boyer.
15. Ibid.
16. Ibid.
17. According to J C O'Callaghan in his notes to *Macariae Excidium.*
18. Ronsele.
19. Clarke makes mention of Luttrell's speech in his Autobiography (HMC, *Leyborne-Popham*). See also Luttrell's Petition of 1701: Bodl. MSS Rawl A 253 pp. 79–84; and for Colonel Rice see HMC, *House of Lords* (n.s.), vii.
20. Poem quoted by J. G. Simms in *The Treaty of Limerick* (1961), p. 12.
21. All the references to Hogan are taken from Story.
22. Bodl. MSS: Rawl A 253 f 256.

CHAPTER XXI
1. Story.
2. HMC, *Finch,* iii, Letter from Clarke to Nottingham, 27 November 1691.
3. Plunket, p. 309.
4. Story.
5. HMC, *Finch,* iii (Letter 25 November 1691).
6. BL Egerton MSS 2618 ff 175, published in Plunket, p. 312.
7. O'Kelly, pp. 108–9.

CHAPTER XXII
Most of this Chapter is in the form of a general history and I have avoided giving individual source references. The battles of La Hogue, Steenkirke and Landen are described in detail by Macaulay, O'Callaghan and Boulger. For Landen in particular, see Berwick, *Mémoires*; *The Paris Relation of the Battle of Landen* (London, 1693); General Camon, *Le Marèchal de Luxembourg* (1936); *Journal du Marquis de Dangeau* (Paris, 1855), iv; and the Hon. J.W. Fortescue, *A History of the British Army* (1910), i.

1. Quoted in Plunket, p. 311.
2. 'The Groans of Ireland' in *Irish Sword*, ii, p. 132.
3. Ibid., p. 133.
4. Ibid., p. 132.
5. Ibid.
6. Berwick.
7. Ibid.
8. James II.
9. Dangeau's *Mémoires,* entry for 16 August 1692.
10. HMC, *Stuart,* vi.
11. 'The Groans of Ireland'.
12. Luttrell's Diary, 30 April 1692.
13. *A Modest Proposal.*
14. Burnet, ii, p. 98.

15. Luttrell's Diary, 4 August 1692.
16. Berwick.
17. *Journal de Marquis de Dangeau*, iv, Paris 1855, p. 149.
18. Luttrell's Diary, 4 and 11 August 1692; HMC, *Fourth Report*, Letter from Ginckel to Clanbrasil, 1 September 1692. References to the arrangements for the goods that were shipped from France to Ireland after the treaty are taken from: HMC, *Finch*, iv, pp. 219–221, 413; C.S.P. Dom. 1693, p. 5; *Calendar of Treasury Books 1682–92*, ix, pp. 1446, 1548, 1841, and 1941: BL Add MSS 34,773 f 27 et seq. Dr Simms was quite wrong in describing these as 'private transactions' (*Irish Sword*, ii, p. 27) and suggesting that Sarsfield 'was not adverse from gaining some financial advantage' from them (*Jacobite Ireland*, p. 254).
19. BL Add MSS 34,773 f 33.
20. Sir Charles Petrie, *The Marshal Duke of Berwick* (London, 1953).
21. Macaulay, *History of England*, Chapter 20.
22. Quoted by O'Callaghan, p. 175.
23. Boulger, p. 326.

END NOTE

Unless otherwise specified, material from this Chapter is taken from J C O'Callaghan, *History of the Irish Brigades in the Service of France* (1886), and D. C. Boulger, *The Battle of the Boyne* (1911).

1. Sec: Valerie Pirie, *His Majesty of Corsica* (London, 1939). The Marquis de Ruvigny and Raineval in his *Jacobite Peerage* of 1904 incorrectly identified her as the daughter of Patrick Sarsfield.
2. Micheline Walsh, *Spanish Knights of Irish Origin*, Irish Manuscripts Commission 1965, ii, p. 6.
3. O'Callaghan, p. 148.
4. Ibid.
5. Ibid.
6. See: Richard Hayes in *Irish Sword*, i, pp. 198–201.
7. J.A. Murphy, *Justin MacCarthy, Lord Mountcashel* (Cork, 1959).
8. Lt.-Col. George Hamilton, *A History of the House of Hamilton* (Edinburgh, 1933).
9. BL Add. MSS 35,838 f 323; *C.S.P. Dom. 1693*, pp. 19, 104; see also Luttrell's Petition of 1701 in Bodl. Rawl A. 253, pp. 79–84.
10. *The Irish Magazine or Monthly Asylum for Neglected Biography*, July 1809.
11. For the Luttrells generally, see: *A Genealogical Account of the Family of Luttrell* (1774).

Index